ROHINGYA REPATRIATION

This volume provides a comprehensive analysis of the Rohingya refugee crisis, examining it as a critical 'time bomb' with implications extending far beyond Bangladesh to affect South Asia and the global community. The book explores the core conceptual issues and practical challenges surrounding the repatriation of stateless people, tracing how the seeds of contemporary atrocities were planted through the denationalization of the Rohingya in 1982. Through detailed examination of legal frameworks, diplomatic pressures, and stakeholder responsibilities, the volume argues that safe and dignified repatriation must be fundamental prerequisites for any viable solution. The analysis extends beyond the immediate crisis to consider broader implications for how authoritarian and majoritarian regimes might employ similar tactics in other contexts, making this a crucial study for understanding patterns of state-sponsored displacement and statelessness. The volume will be of great interest to scholars and researchers of Asian studies, international relations, refugee studies, human rights law, and peace and conflict studies. It will also appeal to students and academics working in political science, journalism, history, and philosophy, particularly those focused on statelessness, forced migration, and humanitarian crises.

Mahbubur Rahman is Professor of Political Science and Chair of the Department of History and Philosophy at North South University (NSU). He was Founding Director of the Liberation War Research Center at NSU. Prior to joining NSU, he taught at York College of the City University of New York (CUNY) and Jahangirnagar University, Bangladesh, and worked as a Research Associate at the Bangladesh Institute of International and Strategic Studies (BIISS). Rahman's research and teaching interests focus on Electoral

Governance, Democratization, Refugee Repatriation, Responsibility to Protect (R2P), Islamic Activism, and Countering Violent Extremism (CVE). He has authored/edited many publications, including journal articles, books, book chapters, and encyclopedia entries with reputed international publishers. He serves as a country expert (Bangladesh) for the Varieties of Democracy (V-Dem) Institute, Sweden, and sits on the editorial board of several journals. He received several scholarships/fellowships, including the J. William Fulbright Scholarship.

Abdur Rob Khan is Treasurer of North South University (NSU). Previously, he served as Dean of the School of Humanities and Social Sciences (SHSS) at NSU for seven years. Before joining North South University as a faculty member in 2009, Dr Khan spent 15 years as Research Director at the Bangladesh Institute of International and Strategic Studies (BIISS), a think tank under the Ministry of Foreign Affairs. With a graduation in Economics from the University of Dhaka, Dr Khan earned his Ph.D. in International Relations from the University of Kent at Canterbury in 1994, specializing in Conflict Studies. He did post-doctoral work in South Asian politics at UPenn as a Senior Fulbright Fellow in 2007. His book-length works include *Globalization and South Asian Security*, *Human Security in South Asia*, and the *Human Security Index for South Asia*. Dr Khan has widely participated in seminars and conferences across Asia, Europe, and the Americas.

Md. Rizwanul Islam is Professor of Law and Dean of the School of Humanities and Social Sciences at North South University. He has earned his Bachelor of Laws from the University of Dhaka, Master of Laws from the National University of Singapore, and his Doctoral degree from Macquarie University. He has earned several awards for his research work. Rizwan has worked as a consultant or fellow in projects funded by the International Labour Organization, the United Nations Development Programme, and the World Bank. Rizwan sits on the editorial board of several journals.

Rohingya Repatriation: An Elusive or Achievable Agenda? is a "must read" for scholars and students alike on the plight of the Rohingya. Its authors insightfully address the tragedy of Rohingya refugees, victims of decades of persecution and rendered stateless by the authoritarian government of Myanmar, their life in exile in Bangladesh, and the problems and challenges of repatriation.

—**John L. Esposito,** *Distinguished University Professor and Founding Director of the Alwaleed Center for Muslim-Christian Understanding, Georgetown University, Washington, DC*

The editors and contributors to this indispensable volume comprehensively examine the confounding multi-dimensionality of the Rohingyas' tragedy. Caught between contested sovereignties and identities as well as geopolitical rivalries, those in Bangladesh are in a kind of limbo, neither settled nor repatriated, able to rely on neither international law and institutions nor the cooperation of state actors. Compellingly argued is that any amelioration must lie in the seemingly intractable political and diplomatic realm. To do nothing would be to signal unacceptably that authoritarian policies of displacement can erase minority rights. This volume dispassionately as well as sensitively sets out, rather, the parameters for a reasoned way forward.

—**James Piscatori,** *Emeritus Professor, Australian National University*

In this unique volume, a diverse group of scholars systematically and cogently analyzes the legal difficulties faced by the Rohingya and what it would take to solve the quagmire that has stranded 1.3 million Rohingya in the world's largest refugee camp. The book examines the roles key stakeholders (international institutions, states, and regional organizations) could play in solving the crisis. It also draws broader warning lessons about the dangers of authoritarian or majoritarian states denationalizing minority groups, depriving them of key political and economic rights protections. The book is mandatory reading for any scholar who cares about the plight of the Rohingya, or the problems of statelessness or refugees more broadly.

—**Jennifer Trahan,** *Clinical Professor at the Center for Global Affairs, New York University*

ROHINGYA REPATRIATION

An Elusive or Achievable Agenda?

Edited by Mahbubur Rahman, Abdur Rob Khan, and Md. Rizwanul Islam

Routledge
Taylor & Francis Group
LONDON AND NEW YORK

First published 2027
by Routledge
4 Park Square, Milton Park, Abingdon, Oxon OX14 4RN

and by Routledge
605 Third Avenue, New York, NY 10158

Routledge is an imprint of the Taylor & Francis Group, an informa business

British Library Cataloguing-in-Publication Data
A catalogue record for this book is available from the British Library

ISBN: 978-1-041-29917-2 (hbk)
ISBN: 978-1-041-29913-4 (pbk)
ISBN: 978-1-003-77189-0 (ebk)

DOI: 10.4324/ 9781003771890

Typeset in Sabon
by Deanta Global Publishing Services, Chennai, India

Dedicated to

the cause of the persecuted Rohingya

CONTENTS

LIST OF CONTRIBUTORS

Nafiz Ahmed is a doctoral researcher at the Peter A. Allard School of Law, University of British Columbia, and a senior lecturer (on leave) at North South University, Bangladesh. He reads and writes about legal philosophy and public law theory. His work has been published in reputed academic outlets in the United States of America, the United Kingdom, Germany, and Bangladesh. Nafiz completed his Master of Laws (LL.M.) degree from the University of Cambridge and his Bachelor of Laws (LL.B.) degree from North South University. He also advises national and international organizations on matters relating to access to justice, labor rights, and administrative law. Email: nafiz.ahmed04@northsouth.edu

Emraan Azad is an early career researcher with a special focus on international criminal law/justice. Until March 2025, he taught law at Bangladesh University of Professionals and served as Coordinator for the Liberation War Museum's Center for the Study of Genocide and Justice. As part of the Center, he led research on atrocity crimes prevention and justice for the victims through civic engagement and legal mechanisms. He has over six years of experience working with the Rohingya refugees in Cox's Bazar, mainly collecting their testimonies and analyzing them for policy intervention. In 2022, he co-wrote a synthesis report that explored the challenges and possibilities for education's engagement within the triple nexus of humanitarian-development-peacebuilding interventions, co-published by UNESCO and the Inter-agency Network for Education in Emergencies. He studied law at the University of Dhaka and earned an LLM in International Law at the University of Cambridge with a Commonwealth (Cambridge Trust) Scholarship. Email: emraan.law@gmail.com

Sumaya Halim works as Central Advisor at the Asian University for Women. She specializes in researching inclusive female education and promoting quality education for young women from disadvantaged communities throughout Asia. Email: sumaya.halim@auw.edu.bd

Md Touhid Hossain was the Advisor, Ministry of Foreign Affairs of the Interim Government of Bangladesh led by Professor Muhammad Yunus (2024–2026). A career diplomat by profession, Mr. Hossain previously served as Foreign Secretary of Bangladesh. He was also the High Commissioner of Bangladesh to South Africa with concurrent accreditation to Angola, Namibia, Botswana, Mozambique, Zambia, and Zimbabwe. He also taught as Adjunct Professor at Independent University, Bangladesh (IUB), and Adjunct Faculty at the Bangladesh Institute of Governance and Management, Dhaka University. Email: Hossain_touhid@yahoo.com

Md. Rizwanul Islam is Professor of Law and Dean of the School of Humanities and Social Sciences at North South University. He has earned his Bachelor of Laws from the University of Dhaka, Master of Laws from the National University of Singapore, and his Doctoral degree from Macquarie University. He is the author and editor of many books, book chapters, and journal articles published in top-class outlets across the world, such as Brill, Cambridge University Press, Elsevier, Oxford University Press, Hart, and so on. He has earned several awards for his research work. Professor Islam has worked as a consultant or fellow in projects funded by the International Labour Organization, the United Nations Development Programme, and the World Bank. Rizwan sits on the editorial board of several journals. Email: rizwanul.islam@northsouth.edu

Abdur Rob Khan is Treasurer of North South University (NSU). Previously, he served as Dean of the School of Humanities and Social Sciences (SHSS) at NSU for seven years. He was also acting Pro-Vice Chancellor of North South University for two years (2024–2026). Before joining North South University as a faculty member in 2009, Dr. Khan spent 15 years as Research Director at the Bangladesh Institute of International and Strategic Studies (BIISS), a think tank under the Ministry of Foreign Affairs. With a degree in Economics from the University of Dhaka, Dr. Khan earned his Ph.D. in International Relations from the University of Kent at Canterbury in 1994, specializing in Conflict Studies. He did post-doctoral work in South Asian politics at UPenn as a Senior Fulbright Fellow in 2007. His book-length works include *Globalization and South Asian Security*, *Human Security in South Asia*, and *Human Security Index for South Asia*. Dr. Khan has widely participated in seminars and conferences across Asia, Europe, and the Americas. Email: abdur.khan@northsouth.edu

Shahab Enam Khan is Professor of International Relations at Jahangirnagar University and founding Executive Director of the Bangladesh Center for Indo-Pacific Affairs. He has also served at the Bangladesh University of Professionals (2025–2026) and as a Fulbright Visiting Professor at the University of Delaware during 2022–2023, where he focused on Indo-Pacific geopolitics, governance, and strategic affairs. He regularly advises government bodies, international organizations, and media outlets on issues such as the Rohingya crisis, Indo-Pacific strategy, and security sector reform. Widely published and frequently quoted, Dr. Khan contributes to national and international dialogues on Bangladesh's evolving strategic role in the region. Email: sekhan@juniv.edu

Raymond Kwun-Sun Lau is Assistant Professor of Political Science at North South University, Bangladesh, and was formerly Lecturer in History at Hong Kong Baptist University, Hong Kong. In addition, he is the Book Reviews Editor of *Africa Review*, an interdisciplinary academic journal of the African Studies Association of India (ASA India), and a former Treasurer of the Hong Kong Political Science Association (HKPSA). He holds a PhD in Political Science from the University of Queensland, Australia. His research interests include International Relations, geopolitics in the Indo-Pacific, the Responsibility to Protect (R2P) and humanitarian intervention, Global South (especially Africa and South Asia), Chinese foreign policy, and Hong Kong politics. Dr. Lau is the author of *Responding to Mass Atrocities in Africa: Protection First and Justice Later* (2022) and co-editor of *Hong Kong Politics after the National Security Law: Autocratization and Its Consequences* (2025). Email: Raymond.lau@northsouth.edu

Kawsar Uddin Mahmud is a Lecturer in Internatioanl Relations at Netrokna University. He holds a Bachelor of Social Sciences (BSS) in International Relations (IR) and a Master of Social Sciences (MSS) in International Political Economy (IPE) from the University of Dhaka, Bangladesh. Covering the wide areas of geopolitics, great power rivalry, South Asian politics, and international affairs, his research articles and book chapters have appeared in various journals published by Elsevier, Routledge, Springer, and Emerald. Email: kawsar@neu.ac.bd

Mahbubur Rahman is Professor of Political Science and Chair of the Department of History and Philosophy at North South University (NSU). He was Founding Director of the Liberation War Research Center at NSU. Prior to joining NSU, he taught at York College of the City University of New York (CUNY) and Jahangirnagar University, Bangladesh, and worked as Research Associate at the Bangladesh Institute of International and Strategic Studies (BIISS). Professor Rahman's research and teaching interests focus on Electoral

Governance, Democratization, Refugee Repatriation, Responsibility to Protect (R2P), Islamic Activism, and Countering Violent Extremism (CVE). He has authored/edited many publications, including journal articles, books, and book chapters, and encyclopedia entries with reputed international publishers. He serves as a country expert for Bangladesh for the Varieties of Democracy (V-Dem) Institute, Sweden, and sits on the editorial board of several journals. He received several scholarships/fellowships, including the J. William Fulbright Scholarship. Email: mahbubur.rahman@northsouth.edu

Mohammad Atique Rahman is Associate Professor at the Department of International Relations, University of Dhaka. He is an adjunct faculty member at the Department of History and Philosophy, North South University. He holds a PhD in Political Science from the University of Ghent, Belgium. He participated in two visiting scholar programs in the United States in 2014 and 2023 under the "Study of the United States Institute (SUSI)" and the "International Visitor Leadership Program (IVLP)", respectively. He regularly publishes articles in international and national peer-reviewed journals, namely *Extractive Industries and Society*, *Journal of International Development*, *Development and Change*, *Routledge*, *Springer Nature*, *Mirpur Papers*, *BIISS Journal*, *Journal of International Affairs*, *Journal of Asiatic Society* (humanities), and *Dhaka University-Social Science Review on Extractivism, Governance and Development, Diplomacy*, the 4th industrial revolution, and multilateralism. Email: atique@du.ac.bd

Selim Reza is Associate Professor of Sociology in the Department of Political Science and Sociology and Coordinator of the Center for Migration Studies at North South University. His research specialisms include recruitment practices, precarious work, contingent employment arrangements, and individualized employment relationship issues for migrant workers. He is the author of the book *The Construction Precariat*, published by Taylor & Francis, which critically analyzes systematic exploitation and slavery-like work conditions of migrant construction workers. He has a PhD in sociology of labor migration, work, and employment from Flinders University, Australia. Before his PhD, he was a researcher at the Refugee and Migratory Movements Research Unit (RMMRU) of the University of Dhaka and worked for the UK aid-funded multidisciplinary, multi-country *Migrating Out of Poverty* Research Programme Consortium based in the University of Sussex, UK. Email: reza.selim@northsouth.edu

Ali Riaz is Distinguished Professor of Political Science at Illinois State University, USA, and President of the American Institute of Bangladesh Studies (AIBS). He has served as a Nonresident Senior Fellow of the Atlantic Council, as a Visiting Researcher at the Varieties of Democracy (V-Dem) Institute in

Sweden, and as a Public Policy Scholar at the Woodrow Wilson Center for International Scholars. Professor Riaz served as special assistant to Chief Advisor Professor Muhammad Yunus during the interim government (2024–2026) with the rank and status of an adviser. He was also the Vice-Chair of the National Consensus Commission and the Head of the Constitution Reform Commission. His research interests include Democratization, Violent Extremism, Political Islam, South Asian politics, and Bangladeshi politics. His recent publications include *A Fractured Path: Challenges of Democratic Transition in Bangladesh* (2025), *Pathways of Autocratization: The Tumultuous Journey of Bangladeshi Politics* (2024), and *More than Meets the Eyes* (2022). He has several books in Bengali, including *Ami'i Rashtro* (I am the State, 2025). Email: ariaz@ilstu.edu

Sayere Nazabi Sayem is a legal researcher with an interest in international human rights laws. She graduated from the Department of Law at North South University with the highest distinction (Summa Cum Laude) in 2023. She is a Research Assistant at the Department of Law, North South University. Prior to that, she served as a Legal Practitioner at the Centre for Peace and Justice at BRAC University, as a Research Associate at Tanjib Alam and Associates, and as a Legal Intern at the National Legal Aid Services Organization of the Government of the People's Republic of Bangladesh. She is also the Assistant Editor of *Progress* Magazine and a Drafter of Case Summaries for *Transnational Dispute Management Journal*, in collaboration with *International Arbitration Case Law* (Netherlands). Apart from her research endeavors and stints in mooting, Sayere is a pro bono legal educator, theater enthusiast, and an environmental and animal rights activist. Email: sayerenazabisayem@gmail.com

Mohammad Jalal Uddin Sikder is Associate Professor in the Department of Political Science and Sociology and Member of the Center for Migration Studies (CMS) at North South University. He is also Adjunct Senior Research Fellow at the Refugee and Migratory Movements Research Unit (RMMRU), a research center that studies Rohingya refugees, internally displaced persons, stateless people, labor migrants, and diaspora communities. He has published several books and articles on refugees and migration studies with reputed international publishers. He serves on the editorial board of various top-ranked journals on refugees and migration. He regularly appears on television talk shows and writes for national newspapers, offering insights on migration, refugee affairs, and political issues. He has a PhD in Sociology from Monash University, Australia. Email: jalal.sikder@northsouth.edu

Ishrat Zakia Sultana is Associate Professor at North South University. She teaches Sociology. Her research includes refugees, children, policy, and RMG workers in Bangladesh, etc. She has published books, book chapters, and in peer-reviewed journals on her research findings. She studied at the University of Dhaka, Bangladesh, Brock University, Canada, and later earned her PhD in Sociology from York University, Canada. She has been researching the Rohingya issue in Bangladesh since 2013 and has conducted her research in Malaysia, Thailand, Nepal, and Pakistan on the Rohingya issue apart from Bangladesh. She has been a columnist in national and international dailies on the Rohingya issue. Email: ishrat.sultana@northsouth.edu

Norman K. Swazo is Professor of Philosophy in the Department of History and Philosophy, North South University, Dhaka, Bangladesh. He specializes in recent European philosophy, ethics in international affairs, and applied ethics. He is the author of *Levinas, Ethics, and the Israeli-Palestinian Conflict* (2025), *Heidegger's Entscheidung: "Decision" between "Fate" and "Destiny"* (2020), *Destroying Idols: Revisioning the Meaning of "God"* (2019), and *Crisis Theory and World Order: Heideggerian Reflections* (2002). He is the editor and co-author of *Contemporary Moral Philosophy and Applied Ethics: An Anthology* (2018) and co-author of *The Rohingya Crisis: A Moral, Ethnographic, and Policy Assessment* (2020). Email: Norman.swazo@northsouth.edu

ACKNOWLEDGEMENTS

This book has come out of considerably long preparation and time. We are deeply grateful to everyone who contributed to making this possible. Our heartfelt thanks go to our contributing authors for their outstanding contribution to this edited volume. We are extremely thankful to the publishing team of Routledge for their guidance, patience, feedback, and exemplary support at every stage of this journey. We are particularly thankful to Dr Shashank Sinha, Publishing Director of Routledge, who has been a great support from the beginning to the end. We also owe special thanks to Routledge editorial assistants Ms. Anvita Bajaj and Ms. Ishita Mahato for their excellent editorial guidance and assistance. Their sincerity and generosity were beyond description. We also appreciate the feedback of the anonymous reviewers for their valuable and constructive comments. Their guidance sharpened our ideas and made this project far stronger than it was in its preparatory stage.

We are truly fortunate to have three illustrious mentors—Professor John Esposito, Distinguished University Professor and Founding Director of the Alwaleed Center for Muslim-Christian Understanding of Georgetown University, Professor James Piscatori, Professor Emeritus of Australian National University, and Professor Jennifer Trahan of NYU, who have so kindly responded to our request for reviewing the manuscript at short notice and provided their generous endorsement comments. We are deeply indebted to their encouragement and unwavering support.

Finally, we owe more than we can express to our family members for their constant encouragement, understanding, and practical help—especially during the long hours of research, communicating, compiling, reviewing, editing, and publishing the manuscript. We are indebted to the authority of North South University for their all-out support and facilitation. Any errors or shortcomings that remain in the book are, however, our own.

1
INTRODUCTION

*Mahbubur Rahman, Abdur Rob Khan,
and Md Rizwanul Islam*

Repatriation of Rohingya refugees is a complex phenomenon as it deals with stateless refugees forcibly displaced and rendered "stateless" in their own country. It is important to mention that while often used interchangeably, refugees and stateless people are two distinct categories – each with their own UN convention outlining their respective rights and protections. The nature of repatriation also has a bearing upon it. For example, UNHCR promotes three durable solutions for refugees as part of its core mandate: voluntary repatriation, local integration, and resettlement. As stateless people have no country de jure and often lack "effective" or "functional" citizenship, they cannot truly be repatriated (Bradley, 2013). However, if they do return, either voluntarily or involuntarily, their status as stateless may be all but a guarantee of continued insecurity, not only for the stateless population, but also for the state of origin and even the region, as their repatriation is unlikely to be a durable solution.

Despite all the above negative or challenging factors, there do exist successful cases of repatriation, however. The voluntary repatriation of Angolan refugees, for example, ended in September 2015, with approximately 4,600 persons returning that year. It is also reported that some 18,000 Angolan refugees have returned home since 2014. The Angola case suggests that the absence of statelessness can improve prospects for successful repatriation. Though each factor contributed to the success of the refugee repatriation in Angola, citizenship rights available to returning refugees significantly improved the prospects for stability and longevity. It is also important to mention that unlike the Rohingya, Angolan refugees were not stateless prior to conflict and arguably never were designated as such. Instead, status as "traditional" refugees increased the likelihood of adherence to guaranteed

DOI: 10.4324/9781003771890-1

refugee protections within countries of asylum as established under international law that can be blurred for stateless refugees. In Zambia, for instance, Angolans fleeing conflict had been granted asylum since 1966 and the Zambian government even went as far as committing to the integration of 10,000 Angolan refugees who chose to remain (Bakewell, 2008; Rohwerder, 2015; Kambela, 2016). Further, a vast majority of Angolans desired to return and did so spontaneously without UN assistance, even in the face of uncertainty. This is perhaps one of the strongest indications that citizenship rights (a lack of statelessness) are paramount in ensuring the sustainability of repatriation efforts. These rights can both encourage return and increase the opportunities for stability post-return.

Another recent case of successful repatriation took place in Bhutan. What happened is that in Bhutan, a restrictive citizenship law in 1985 saw the Lhotshampas, ethnic Nepalese residing in Bhutan as early as the nineteenth century, stripped of their citizenship. This was followed by the group's exile to Nepal where they lived as refugees for roughly two decades before the US, Norway, Denmark, Canada, Australia, and New Zealand agreed to participate as part of a third-country resettlement option (Dhungana, 2024). In Côte d'Ivoire, repatriation was suspended in 2014 due to the outbreak of Ebola in West Africa. The process resumed in December 2015. By June 2016, UNHCR had helped repatriate 16,030 Ivorian refugees from Liberia to their communities of origin. UNHCR helps the returnees reintegrate in their homeland, with income-generation programs, training and start-up aid. The Côte d'Ivoire government has put in place a number of programs to help the returnees regain access to their lands and for children to get access to education.

A quasi-successful repatriation did take place in the case of Rohingyas in Bangladesh. In the 1990s, Myanmar agreed to the repatriation terms with Bangladesh, and later with the UNHCR. It occurred due to the pressure from regional players (Malaysia and Pakistan), international pressure from the US and UN, and diplomatic attempts to improve relations with Bangladesh to avoid a looming border war – each contributed to Myanmar's willingness to move forward with repatriation. However, a closer examination of the 1992–1997 repatriation of Rohingya refugees also reveals that the condition of statelessness can undermine safeguards often granted to refugee status, decrease incentives for refugees to return, and impair opportunities for long-term solutions, while exacerbating state and human security issues.

Since 1978, Bangladesh has provided refuge to Rohingyas on several occasions and, as already mentioned, the country was also able to send a portion of them back to Myanmar. This was possible due to Bangladesh's diplomatic initiatives as well as UN assistance and interventions. But the current scenario is completely different and extremely delicate. Since August 25, 2017, more than 750,000 Rohingya refugees, mostly women and children, have fled Myanmar and have taken refuge again in Bangladesh. In total, Bangladesh is currently hosting over 1.3 million Rohingya refugees, making Cox's Bazar the largest refugee camp in the world. What is more worrisome is that there is neither progress nor a possibility of these displaced Rohingyas' returning to Myanmar in the near future.

Pertinent questions, in this context, are, therefore: Is repatriation of Rohingya refugees an elusive or achievable agenda? More specifically, why is Myanmar so defiant and why is China condescending to Myanmar's brutal policies and deliberate delays? Why does the international community seem to be reticent here? Is it because of geopolitical complexities or legal inadequacies? Is it also due to any conceptual ambiguity among the stakeholders with regard to determining what repatriation itself means and entails when it comes to dealing with the "stateless" people? Or is it because of geopolitical complexities or legal inadequacies? Indeed, there are reasons to believe that the Myanmar government is unwilling to take the Rohingyas back and it is also evidently clear that China, a key regional player despite showing some diplomatic gestures – is not doing enough, albeit due to its preferred national (or parochial?) interests. Following the military takeover of Myanmar in February 2021, the situation seems to have become more precarious. There is a question of whether the so-called National Unitary Government (NUG) would stick to its current humane position to the Rohingya or renege on its promises. Today, there exists almost a stalemate situation and with the emergence of new refugee situations in other parts of the world, the attention of the international community to the Rohingya crisis has been further dissipated. What options and strategies can Bangladesh adopt to get itself out of this quagmire and what can it expect from the international community?

It is worth noting, as the Bangladesh government rightfully asserts, that the Rohingya crisis is not and should not be viewed exclusively as "Bangladesh's problem"; rather, it's a regional and global challenge. No one knows what may happen if the Rohingya refugees are left without a future. By now, it is evident that the long-term dispossession of the Rohingya could create several security threats for the whole region, and the international community cannot afford to be indifferent to this crisis for too long. While the military coup and renewed interest and stakes of China in Myanmar have made the case more problematic than before, the international community can still facilitate the repatriation of Rohingyas. The question is how, and if not now, then when? It is therefore critical to examine the Rohingya repatriation issues thoroughly, and this book is an attempt in that direction. It especially examines the role of all the key stakeholders, including the United Nations (UN), International Court of Justice, International Criminal Court, and regional organizations, particularly the Association of Southeast Asian Nations (ASEAN). Other key players include China and India, and also the USA. The book would address both theoretical and practical issues and attempt to provide some policy inputs as well.

The book examines the core conceptual issues regarding the repatriation of "stateless" people from various perspectives and chronicles how the seed of the latest wave of the atrocities was laid in the denationalization of the Rohingya and how the existing international legal framework is adequate or inadequate to deal with the capricious denationalization of a minority group. This is not just a question relevant to the Rohingya but could increasingly be relevant for authoritarian or majoritarian regimes willing to chart a similar route in other countries in the future.

This edited volume brings together the rich and diverse expertise of scholars and practitioners from various backgrounds and disciplines. It seeks to revive and advance the Rohingya repatriation dialogue by focusing on the role, perceptions, and responsibilities of the stakeholders concerned. The book argues that while legal avenues need to be pursued to make the Myanmar regime accountable for its genocidal actions, the judgment of international courts, lacking any direct coercive force, would not suffice to elicit an adequate response from the Myanmar regime. It is precisely where diplomatic pressure on Myanmar from the UN and geopolitically powerful states would be required. In exerting such pressure, the role of Bangladesh, which is shouldering the heavy responsibility of providing refuge to nearly a million Rohingya, is critical and hence, a dispassionate analysis of its options is warranted. While the judgment and diplomatic pressure on Myanmar would be important, the assurance of safe and dignified repatriation and a conviction of enduring security would be essential prerequisites for any viable solution to this problem. This book analyzes these questions and seeks to answer them to offer some practical solutions to a perennial problem of the contemporary era.

According to Myanmar's government, the Rohingya do not belong to Myanmar. The group was officially stripped of their recognition as an ethnic national group when Ne Win's regime came to power, placing Myanmar (then Burma) under military rule (Nemoto, 1991). After enacting the 1974 Emergency Immigration Act, the Rohingya were considered illegal immigrants (Nemoto, 1991). Their status as stateless was made official by the 1982 Burmese Citizenship Law that distinguished three categories of citizenship, excluding the Rohingya from each (Razzaq & Haque, 1995). The crux of the problem, therefore, lies in the deliberate attempt by the Burmese authority to disenfranchise the Rohingya population living there for centuries by refusing to acknowledge their legitimate right to be fully recognized as citizens of Myanmar. They are still seen as illegal Muslim immigrants who arrived in Burma during the British colonial period.

Against this backdrop, in Chapter 2 of the book, Norman Swazo brings out the historical narratives juxtaposed with "moral-legal" principles and argues that the Rohingya in Bangladesh and in the diaspora of temporary resettlement are rightly denominated *refugees* first and foremost.

Therefore, they should be accorded all the rights and privileges of refugees under international humanitarian law, a responsibility the government of Bangladesh should adopt forthwith despite not being a signatory to the Refugee Convention. In doing so, the Bangladesh government can overcome the implicit assumption motivating Western government refugee assistance policies and "source control measures," viz., that the strategy of voluntary repatriation requires keeping forcibly displaced persons close to the nation-state from which they have been displaced, rather than working earnestly for an alternative durable solution of third-country resettlement when the host country does not permit integration. The Rohingya are, indeed, *Myanmar nationals* and *not stateless* persons. One need not be agnostic about the Rohingya claim of indigeneity in Arakan/Rakhine State, especially if (a) one sets aside the arbitrary and discriminatory Citizenship Law of 1982 relative to international human rights law, and (b) one concedes that the Bamar majority itself cannot claim exclusive Burmese indigeneity without admitting to this group likely having resulted from migration into Arakan from Tibet and Yunnan, China ("Tibeto-Chinese" forebears). On the contrary, then, while recognizing that there are competing historical narratives on the Rohingya claim, the available evidence adduced in support of that claim makes it an inductively warranted true belief, i.e., the claim is *more likely to be true than false* that the Rohingya are an indigenous group in Arakan/Rakhine State.

In Chapter 3, Shahab Enam Khan deals with the complexity in repatriation decision-making for the Rohingyas. Following the mass influx of Rohingya refugees of Myanmar origin in Bangladesh on August 25, 2017, it has become essential to understand the linkages between complex Rohingya identity and the idea of "repatriation" that dominates the core of the Rohingya discourse in Bangladesh. A compound intermingling of identity, fear of persecution and deprivation, and multifaceted spectrums of failures in governance have led to collective confusion and psycho-social resistance toward the idea of "repatriation." While the host country has national security and national interest to protect, the process of repatriation primarily lies with Myanmar and the Rohingyas. The interplay of "national security" perceived by Myanmar and Bangladesh and the identity crisis accentuated by the Tatmadaw-backed socio-political structure in Myanmar has further complicated the repatriation process. Therefore, it is crucial for the multi-layered repatriation process pursued by different actors, i.e., the government, civil society, political, regional, and international actors, and multilateral institutions, to be receptive to the causes of the repatriation dilemma among the Rohingyas living in Bangladesh.

Md Rizwanul Islam in Chapter 4 takes a legalist perspective to scrutinize the malevolent stripping of nationality of the Rohingya. This chapter argues that the seed of this atrocity has been sown in the capricious denationalization of the Rohingya by the Citizenship Law of 1982. This is because nationality or citizenship is intrinsically interlinked with many civil, political, economic, social, and entitlements. Denationalization deprives people of these rights. This chapter critically evaluates the Citizenship Law of 1982 of Myanmar and its legality or otherwise in the contemporary international legal framework. It also argues that had the international community reacted duly, the recent wave of atrocities could have been averted. While nationality would still be in the realm of municipal law, the community of states cannot be oblivious to the whimsical denationalization of a group of people based on their ethnicity, race, or religion. The chapter argues that international law needs to evolve to respond.

In Chapter 5, Mohammad Atique Rahman and Kawsar Uddin Mahmud argue that Myanmar's systematic denial of sustainable repatriation is one of the deeper structural impediments rooted in decades of institutionalized exclusion. The prevalence of contested sovereignty in Myanmar's borderland, especially in the Arakan region, by non-state actors as well as state-sponsored systemic denial of Rohingya citizenship instrumentalized ethnic hatred against them. They reveal how the "illusion of readiness" helps deflect international pressure while maintaining systemic exclusion. The 2021 coup has further deteriorated prospects by eliminating even nominal civilian oversight. This chapter suggests that international approaches must move beyond technocratic solutions toward comprehensive accountability mechanisms and alternative protection frameworks that will address the root causes of displacement and arrange the safe and voluntary repatriation involving all stakeholders and actors, including non-state ones.

Touhid Hossain in Chapter 6 stresses the fact that the Chinese role in Rohingya repatriation is highly complex, marred by regional geopolitical and domestic constraints. Drawing on the realist perspective, this chapter provides a historical analysis to assess how Beijing acted in international forums on Rohingya issues, which reflects its long-term strategic and diplomatic engagements with Myanmar. Meanwhile, Bangladesh, being overburdened with overreliance on Chinese finances, is constrained to pursue hedging strategies that combine legal recourse at the International Court of Justice (ICJ) with normative appeals to the West. This chapter offers that reforming domestic governance, diversifying economic and military partnerships, and engaging informally with non-state actors emerge as critical pathways for enhancing Bangladesh's leverage. Given the dynamics, this analysis underlines that resolving the Rohingya impasse depends not only on multilateral diplomacy but also on Dhaka's ability to recalibrate its foreign policy toolkit amid intensifying great-power competition.

In a related note, Chapter 7 by Raymond Kwun-Sun Lau deals with India's approach to the Rohingya crisis. Given that Bangladesh is historically and geographically close to India, any lasting solution to the voluntary, safe, and sustained repatriation for the Rohingya, which is Bangladesh's lead priority, will require India's active involvement. Yet, instead of playing a constructive role in realizing the Rohingya resettlement and repatriation, the Border Security Force (BSF) in India has adopted a refugee pushback policy by actively "pushing back" Rohingya refugees into Bangladesh. By examining the driving force behind New Delhi's approach, the chapter pays particular attention to the role India can and should play in resolving this crisis.

Mohammad Jalal Uddin Sikder, Selim Reza, and Sumaya Halim in Chapter 8 expand further the diplomatic discourse to cover mainly the role of the USA. While the humanitarian assistance from the US and international organizations has immensely supported the Rohingyas in Bangladesh's refugee camps, the absence of strong political pressure from the US on Myanmar has turned the Rohingya crisis into merely a humanitarian issue, rather than a political issue. This has eventually made the international community skeptical about potential opportunities for managing the Rohingya crisis politically. Myanmar, as a result, has become negligent and adamant about political solutions for the Rohingya crisis. The chapter explores many facets of the Rohingya crisis, illuminating the complex web of issues that have prevented the US from taking sustainable political interventions to end the crisis. By reviewing the success of diplomatic efforts, sanctions, and international forum in pressing Myanmar to alter its position, the chapter reveals the difficulties and limitations of international efforts to handle the issue by looking at the role of global actors, such as the US, and international and regional organizations.

Mahbubur Rahman, in Chapter 9, takes an international humanitarian perspective and explores whether the R2P doctrine could help remove the barriers to Rohingya repatriation. He seeks to find out if R2P suffers from any conceptual ambiguity or if there is a gap between its principle and practice, which is indicative of the ineffective and withering status of this doctrine. Rahman notes that the support for R2P still exists, even though there are some cracks in the intensity of this support. In the case of Rohingyas in Myanmar, he observes that the UN has been unable, if not unwilling, to stop atrocities primarily because of non-cooperation and the threat of veto by two Permanent Members of the UNSC – China and Russia. To overcome this predicament, Rahman suggests that the P5 of the UNSC have to agree to find at least a common R2P ground: the idea of a responsibility not to veto R2P-related resolutions within the Council. He concludes that to remove roadblocks to Rohingya repatriation, R2P can be a useful tool provided that the international community finds ways of expanding the support base for its effective implementation.

Going beyond bilateral diplomacy, Sayere Nazabi Sayem, in Chapter 10, looks at the missed opportunity of doing something through the Uniting for Peace Resolution. One of the largest humanitarian crises in the world, the forced exodus of the Rohingya population, has sought several remedies, including the attention of the Security Council to restore peace and security. But the resolutions of the organ get vetoed by permanent members, i.e., mostly Russia and China, causing a deadlock. This chapter focuses on how the Uniting for Peace Resolution or Resolution 377 (V) is an option yet to be explored. It has seen the light of day several times in the past when used in the General Assembly to fulfill the primary function of the Security Council – help maintain peace and security. Notwithstanding a few flaws, the Uniting for Peace Resolution can be invoked as a resort to welcome collective recommendations and measures by member states of the UN to protect the Rohingya refugees and finally help culminate their successful reparation after multiple and consecutive failed attempts.

Going one step ahead, Emran Azad, in Chapter 11 explores the limits of international courts in the Rohingya repatriation process. The chapter argues that a safe and dignified Rohingya repatriation is essentially subject to global politics played by three elite States, i.e., the USA, Russia and China, in and beyond the UN Security Council. In so doing, the chapter first makes a theoretical position on the issue relying on the theory of "Genocide as Social Practice" propounded by Argentinean sociologist Daniel Feierstein. With reference to this, the chapter builds on the claim that as the very act of genocide (which leads to destruction of group – wholly or partially, displacement of population, refugee crisis, etc.) takes place as a social phenomenon, the possibilities of refugee repatriation in a post-genocide scenario depend on the overall political atmosphere, not on the legal accountability mechanisms and their pronouncements supplied afterwards. This becomes more evident when the perpetrator State is itself an elite State or is on good terms with either of the elite States as well as geo-strategically is in a better position than the State which hosts the refugees.

Chapter 12 by Nafiz Ahmed takes the Rohingya discourse to a newer plane and focuses on the rigid citizenship laws of Bangladesh and its potential role in the Rohingya crisis. Nafiz Ahmed argues that if the Rohingya refugees were to fully integrate into the locality of Bangladesh and live a dignified life, they need to be citizens of Bangladesh. Under the existing laws, the Rohingya, however, are not entitled to be citizens by birth or descent. Their only way of acquiring citizenship of Bangladesh may be through naturalization. However, the government's actions at the time of writing this chapter indicate that an application for citizenship by naturalization by a Rohingya citizen is unlikely to be successful. If the government of Bangladesh decides to integrate the Rohingya refugees into its locality, it must radically change its legal framework governing matters of citizenship substantially. Otherwise, repatriation would remain the only option.

In Chapter 13, Ishrat Zakia Sultana examines how repatriation includes Rohingya women's rights, safety, and dignity once the repatriation takes place. Women – regardless of their status as human rights defenders, or indigenous community members, or from war-torn regions or in a refugee situation – experience marginalization and violence differently than men. When it comes to repatriation, Rohingya women are under a double-edged sword because they were already victimized during their stay in Myanmar.

Ali Riaz, in the concluding chapter titled "The Quest for Rohingya Repatriation," suggests that the most preferred solution to the Rohingya crisis – safe, voluntary and dignified return of the refugees – is contingent upon creating an inclusive system of governance in Myanmar, which would ensure citizenship to Rohingyas with equal rights, but there is no political will within the Myanmar elites – civilian and military – to tread the path; neither is there an incentive for them to dismantle the apartheid system. The absence of both points to a continuation of the status quo. According to Riaz, there are four ways forward regarding the current refugee situation. The first is maintaining the status quo, or in other words, muddling through. This is increasingly becoming untenable, thanks to donor fatigue, a deteriorating security situation within the refugee camps, continued environmental degradation due to overcrowded camps to name but a few. The second option, as Riaz notes, is to accept that Rohingyas will not be able to return to their homeland; therefore, they have to be integrated into Bangladeshi society as citizens. This option has several downsides including the challenge of their acceptance to Bangladeshi society and its resultant political, social and economic impacts. This may also act as a pull factor for more Rohingyas to cross the border and enter into Bangladesh. The third option is resettlement of the refugees to third countries. As Bangladesh is not a signatory to the 1951 Refugee Convention and the 1967 protocol, it cannot ask for such help from the international community. However, the country did allow third-country resettlement until 2010 for refugees who came during the previous two large-scale exoduses. The fourth and final option is to bring about a significant change in Bangladesh's Myanmar policy and work with the insurgent groups, especially the Arakan Army (AA), as the latter is making significant progress in its operation against the junta since October 2023. Although what that will yield is uncertain.

This edited volume reveals the most unpleasant truth that the Rohingya repatriation cannot be addressed through the conventional repatriation framework or be implemented overnight. The crisis is deeply rooted in Myanmar's deliberate act of ethnic hatred and statelessness of Rohingya. Traditionally, voluntary repatriation can be a durable solution; however, the Rohingya presence in Bangladesh demonstrates that return without citizenship, security, and political inclusion will create a vulnerable situation for them. Therefore, legal citizenship, access to rights and properties, and state support are fundamental to a sustainable and voluntary repatriation process. Bangladesh should adopt creative diplomacy, including wider public diplomacy, engagement with civil society in Myanmar, and establishing people-to-people contact to sensitize Myanmar's people about this crisis. Bangladesh should also engage with regional organizations like ASEAN and (though now moribund) South Asian Assocation for Regional Cooperation (SAARC) to stress that the restoration of Rohingya citizenship and inclusive governance in Rakhine state are necessary for sustainable repatriation. Finally, it is only achievable if Bangladesh, Myanmar, regional, and international communities move beyond a rhetorical approach to adopt more practically oriented diplomacy and political actions at the national, regional, and international levels, which ensure rights and dignity for Rohingyas to live well in their motherland.

References

Bakewell, O. (2008). 'Keeping them in their place': The ambivalent relationship between development and migration in Africa. *Third World Quarterly*, *29*(7), 1341–1358. https://doi.org/10.1080/01436590802386492

Bradley, M. (2013). *Justice, responsibility and redress*. Cambridge University Press. https://doi.org/10.1017/9781107699557

Dhungana, S. K. (2024, January). Third country resettlement and the Bhutanese refugee crisis: A critical reflection. *Journal of Peacebuilding & Development*, *3*(2), 14–36.

Kambela, L. (2016), Angolan refugees in Zambia: Reflecting on local integration as a sustainable solution. https://archive.ids.ac.uk/eldis/document/A100112.html

Nemoto, K. (1991). The Rohingya issue: A Thorny obstacle between Burma (Myanmar) and Bangladesh. http://www.mcrg.ac.in/WC_2015/Reading/D_Rohingya_Issue.pdf

Razzaq, A., & Haque, M. (1995). *A tale of refugees: Rohingyas in Bangladesh*. The Centre for Human Rights.

Rohwerder, B. (2015). *Refugee return in protracted refugee situations* (GSDRC Helpdesk Research Report 1282). Governance and Social Development Resource Centre (GSDRC), University of Birmingham.

2

CONTESTED IDENTITY AND HISTORICAL TRUTH

The Rohingya as an "Indigenous" yet "Stateless" People

Norman K. Swazo

The Epistemological and Ethical Challenge of Historical Narrative

Methodological disputations have epistemological implications concerning the validation of knowledge claims. They also have ethical implications for the writing of history in a way that assures academic integrity in the quest for "historical truth," assuming there is such a thing. Yoav J. Tenenbaum (2020), e.g., writes:

> Historical truth is objective by its very nature. It is there, so to speak, to be discovered and unearthed. Certainly, there may be occasions in which the truth cannot be discovered. However, the inability to discover the truth does not negate its objective existence. In this context, a distinction ought to be drawn between Historical truth and interpretation. The first is objective and the latter is subjective. The first refers to a fact, which can be determined as true, at least in principle, by empirical study, whereas the latter entails an explanation of the fact in question... Thus, "narratives," a commonly-used catch-phrase, to afford legitimacy to historical interpretations are, at best, an attempt at explaining historical events from a subjective perspective. Their importance resides in the influence they wield in shaping the perception of reality by groups or nations. Narratives may determine historical truth insofar as they describe the perception of groups or nations as they exist objectively, but the historical veracity of the facts which those narratives depict do not derive necessarily from them. They may be objectively true or false.

DOI: 10.4324/9781003771890-2

Thus, historical narratives are subject to contestation in recounting matters of fact and eliciting explanation, interpretation, and historical understanding. The latter are presumed to contribute to identity formation, e.g., by ethnic groups within nation-states. Controversially, philosopher of science Alex Rosenberg (2018) has challenged the legitimacy of "narrative history." Narrative history is conceived as "explanation of what happened in terms of motives and the perspectives of the human agents whose choices, decisions, and actions made those events happen." At issue is the philosophy of mind that such historians tacitly adopt as they claim to discern such motives in human agents. Accordingly, Rosenberg (2018) claims, history (historiography) "is almost always wrong." The supposed causal connections between internal (mental) motives and external (historically evident) events are by no means to be taken as historical "truth."

What is wrong with narrative history? Rosenberg answers: "What narrative history gets wrong are its explanations of what happened," in which case, "It's crucial to disabuse ourselves of the myth that history confers real understanding that can shape or otherwise help us cope with the future." Rosenberg is concerned with the hegemony of historical narrative, inasmuch as such narratives are "responsible for the trail of tears, pain, suffering, carnage, and sometimes extermination that make up most of human history." Granted, there is a benevolent motive to Rosenberg's critique: he is concerned with the use and abuse of history that informs present action with a view to the future. However, the reality of human affairs is such that we cannot dispense with historical narrative entirely. More importantly, as anthropologist Stanley Diamond (1974) cautioned, one must not resign before the tyranny of "official definitions of reality." Indeed, as Diamond (1974, 3) might put it, "the complexities of experience" that indigenous peoples can recount cannot be reduced to the written word, all the more so if "writing provides the ruling classes with an ideological instrument of incalculable power."

Instead, academic historians have to work both *inductively* (acknowledging the *probability* of adduced evidence) and *abductively* (argument to the *best explanation* available). Both modes of argument combine to support claims of historical fact to an reliable[1] degree of probability for justification of true belief. Even so, historical understanding is not merely a function of empirically validated scientific explanation. As philosopher Alexandre Leskanich (2020) observes, "The presupposition on display in Rosenberg's book is that scientific explanation is the most valuable sort of explanation, and that because historical explanation is not scientific, it cannot produce explanations with real value. But not everything can (or should need to be) explained in terms of mechanistic processes that can be empirically shown to exist."

Rosenberg's focus on the possibility of narrative history as "true" history privileges the methodological task of scientific explanation of historical events over the task of historical understanding. He even goes so far as to dismiss the latter, consistent with his critique of a particular theory of mind and epistemological concerns about human cognition. This contra-positioning of explanation and understanding is well known in the philosophy of the social sciences, the philosophy of history, and philosophical hermeneutics. Thus, there is ample reason *not* to dispense with historical narrative. Rather, the task is to sustain a *critical* engagement of narratives, consistent with a practical rationality. This is especially so when historical narratives contend with each other from extra-cultural or intra-cultural bases of historical facticity, and when ideological commitments shape the rhetoric of political interests.

Consider insights of philosopher Hans-Georg Gadamer (1977, 2004) in his reputed *Truth and Method* and *Philosophical Hermeneutics*. Gadamer (1977, xxi) reminded that, "the experience of truth ... transcends the domain of scientific method," such that, in the case of history one finds a mode of experience "in which a truth is communicated that cannot be verified by the methodological means proper to science." Moreover, Gadamer (1977, xxix) clarifies that historiography proper will invariably be read and understood differently over time, inasmuch as people "read the sources differently... moved by different questions, prejudices, and interests." Gadamer's choice of words is salient here. Historians who write narrative history are moved by any number of questions, have their prejudices in understanding (in a "forestructure" of understanding including prejudices in understanding), and manifest their interests in the resulting exposition of fact, explanation, and interpretation. The task of historical understanding, then, is not to dispense entirely with prejudice (in the Cartesian and Enlightenment sense), but to recognize prejudice for its positive character, to make prejudices explicit rather than to keep them hidden.

As Gadamer (1977, 278, italics added) reminds: "If we want to do justice to man's finite, historical mode of being, it is necessary to fundamentally rehabilitate the concept of prejudice and acknowledge the fact that *there are legitimate prejudices*," and thus it is "the undeniable task of critical reason to overcome" those that lack legitimation. This may involve an appeal to authority (to the historiography of learned historians), but this is a matter of acknowledgment and deference to their authoritative engagement of the facts, their *bona fide* effort at reasonable explanation, and their attention to the task of interpretation that discloses the contextualized significance of the facts. As Gadamer (1977, 281) put it, "Thus, acknowledging authority is always connected with the idea that what the authority says is not irrational and arbitrary but can, in principle, be discovered to be true."

The Question of Indigeneity

Bearing the foregoing orienting remarks in mind, we may therefore turn to the substantive problems of concern, including the problem of contested historical narratives pertinent to contested identities in present-day Myanmar (formerly Burma). One begins with the decidedly ambiguous question of *indigeneity* as it is engaged in contemporary international political and anthropological discourse. Thereafter, the question is how this concept applies to the Rohingya people, who have long resided in the Arakan (northern Rakhine State) region of Burma/Myanmar,[2] but who have long suffered from persecution within Myanmar for being Muslim and declared "Bengalis." Since around 2012 and more recently in 2017, the Rohingya have been forced to endure territorial displacement, mostly into Bangladesh. Their forced migration is consequent to a multiplicity of factors, including Buddhist/Muslim religious conflict and violent military/police actions tolerated by the Myanmar military (coup) government and the Tatmadaw (Myanmar's military force).

These actions led to over one million Rohingya—denominated "forcibly displaced Myanmar nationals (FDMN)" by the Bangladesh government—rendered effectively stateless persons. They are not recognized legally within Bangladesh as refugees while they are nevertheless sheltered in settlement camps[3] in the southeast region of Bangladesh as they await prospective secure repatriation. The latter depends on Myanmar's recognition of their ethnicity and right to citizenship. The Burma-born political scientist Ardeth Thawnghmung (2016) reminds that there remains "an unresolved and ongoing dispute over the legitimacy of the Rohingya claim as an ethnic nationality (*taing-yin-thar*) of Myanmar." Michael R. Dunford (2019, 64) explains, the Burmese government considers the Buddhist Bamar as "exclusively indigenous…according to the *taingyinthar* rubric." Citing Micah Morton (2017), Dunford clarifies, "Indigenous Peoples' networks have instead chosen to use the term '*htanay taingyinthar*'…in order to differentiate Indigenous Peoples' status from that of Myanmar's 'national races', which include the Bamar majority and groups who do not self-identify as indigenous peoples" (Tucker, 2001).[4] The dispute was magnified in 1982 when Myanmar's Citizenship Law denied the Rohingya recognition as a lawful ethnic group, thereby automatically denying them claims to Myanmar citizenship.[5] Fundamentally at issue here is a Rohingya claim to indigeneity, hence how that relates to the ostensible truth of the historical narratives in contention.

Dominic O'Sullivan (2017) remarks that, "Indigeneity is a theory of justice and political strategy that indigenous peoples use to develop their own terms of belonging to the nation-state. In particular, it is distinct from theories of minority rights because its claims are grounded in extant rights of prior occupancy." Anthropologist Mathias Guenther (2006) opines,

"'Indigenous' is a term applied to people—and by the people to themselves—who are engaged in an often desperate struggle for political rights, for land, for a place and space within a modern nation's economy and society." Risa J. Toha and Thomas B. Pepinsky (2022) argue that, "Indigenous identity describes a social relationship between the state and a community whose terms are defined by practice rather than history or genealogy," that "indigeneity is not an inherent feature of individuals or communities, but rather a political status that may be achieved through the practice of state-sanctioned collective behaviors."

Each of the above conceptualizations of indigeneity is a *constructivist* assessment of who may count as indigenous peoples. One says "constructivist" because at issue is a relation of these people to "the State," rather than having the legitimation of an appeal to some "primordial"[6] "geocultural" status (as intended, e.g., in the term "aboriginal" and the notion of "prior occupancy" or "land tenure") in relation to a given territory *qua* "homeland" of sociocultural origin and residence. That is, the relation to the modern nation-state is *structurally determinative* of their political and legal recognition (even though the "State" is a form of political association having its historically contingent provenance and political authority derivative of European political modernity). The fact is that intensively protracted processes of colonial rule, often involving dispossession of indigenous peoples and expropriation of their territory, have entailed what J. Marshall Beier (2005, 3) calls "violences of erasure."

The logic of statecraft, including commitment to the principle of state sovereignty, has been transferred to peoples in "the Global South" as part of a dominant Western conception of international relations. The latter includes a discourse of domination, what Beier calls "the 'hegemonologue' of the dominating society: a knowing hegemonic Western voice that, owing to its universalist pretensions, speaks its knowledge to the exclusion of all others." Furthermore, it remains problematic for all indigenous people that, "there is no universally accepted legal definition of 'indigenous peoples' in international law" (Fodella, 2006). Hence, adjudication of contested historical narratives lacks a legal remedy at that level of appeal. Thus, since the onset of Western modernity and European colonial rule, indigenous peoples have been marginalized and/or erased relative to any and all claims to political, social, cultural, and economic rights, despite efforts to articulate such rights and assure compliance.[7]

Francesca Merlan (2009) remarks, "The term indigenous, long used to distinguish between those who are 'native' and their 'others' in specific locales, has also become a term for a geocultural category, presupposing a world collectivity of 'indigenous peoples' in contrast to their various others." Ironically, Myanmar is one among a number of countries that insist the internationalized concept of indigeneity does not apply to it, in which case any ethnic group's claim to indigeneity in Myanmar is rejected in the absence of "State-sanctioned" determination of lawfully recognized ethnicity and, consequently, lawfully recognized citizenship (Merlan, 2009, 303). Once there was a supposedly legitimate claim to a "first peoples" status, to a geocultural/primordial (if not genealogically defined) presence and identity. This was so for the Rohingya prior to British colonial rule. However, British colonial governance and subsequent post-colonial independence movements in the Indian subcontinent installed new forms of the nation-state. These have led to what—to use her words in present context—Chandra Mohanty (1991) calls "cartographies of struggle" involving erasure.[8]

Rejection of a local geocultural warrant for claims to primordial indigeneity amounts to what some—reflecting on the impact of colonial domination and alteration of the geocultural map of the Global South in particular—call either ethnic cleansing[9] or ethnocide.[10] Imposition of colonially framed practices of domination, in contrast to traditional practices, also includes rejection and displacement of indigenous languages, contributing to the loss of a significant element of cultural identity and the manner in which indigenous peoples self-identify. So it is with the Rohingya, who speak neither the dominant Burmese language of Myanmar nor the Bengali of Bangladesh. The fact is that the colonial "metropole" superintends the indigenous homeland with intentional dispossession. As anthropologist Audra Simpson (2007) put it,

> "Culture" described the difference that was found in these places and marked the ontological end-game of each exchange: a difference that had been contained into neat, ethnically-defined territorial spaces that now needed to be made sense of, to be ordered, ranked, to be governed, to be possessed. This is a form of politics that is more than representational, as this was a governmental and disciplinary possession of bodies *and* territories.

Whatever anthropologists and colonial or post-colonial apologists of nation-state authority may say, efforts to internationalize the concept of indigeneity were successful (even if only symbolically) with the adoption of the UN Declaration of the Rights of Indigenous Peoples on 13 September 2007 by a majority of 147 member states in favor [four against (Australia, Canada, New Zealand, and the USA—all of which reversed their positions later), and eleven abstentions (UN, 2006)].[11] Yet, there is an irony here in the case of South Asia; for, as geographer Ian G. Baird (2016) reminds, "many governments of Asia signed onto the United Nations Declaration on the Rights of Indigenous Peoples (UNDRIP) in 2007, but with the understanding that UNDRIP does not apply to them"—because, so the claim goes, of "a relative lack of European settler colonization in the continent."

Both Bangladesh and Myanmar reject the claim that their countries have indigenous peoples. But there are indigenous groups in the Chittagong Hill

Tracts (CHT) in eastern Bangladesh[12] (western border of Myanmar) and, of course, the Rohingya of northern Rakhine State in Myanmar and other composite groups such as "Karen" and "Chin" who make a claim of indigeneity there. Bangladeshi social scientist Salahuddin M. Aminuzzaman (2022), e.g., reports that, "Bangladesh is essentially a homogenous society with a little over 2 percent of its population belong[ing] to different indigenous groups." Aminuzzaman has reviewed the "peace accord" between the government of Bangladesh and the indigenous Jumma people of the CHT region; the accord follows "armed struggle for autonomy of the CHT since the mid-1970s," even as "communal attacks by Bengali settlers" continue.

In encounters between indigenous peoples and the modernizing elite of nation-states, constitutional governance is hardly sympathetic to the interests of the former. As Aminuzzaman (2022, 5) adds, "The process of alienation and identity formation for the Hill people of Bangladesh is rooted in the political and economic policies adopted by the state," after the British colonial administration affiliated the CHT area with then Pakistan rather than Burma. Thus, he reminds, "Especially the constitutional political measures taken in the name of Bengali/Bangladeshi nationalism threatened their cultural and ethnic identity." It is not surprising, then, that the Jumma people of CHT "sought constitutional safeguards for their protection and recognition as a separate community within the new state [of Bangladesh, formerly East Pakistan]" (Aminuzzaman, 2022, 5). Here, too, it is clear how the modern "State" privileges homogeneity, despite the artificiality or "imaginary geography"[13] of nation-state borders.

At the time of Bangladesh's independence, Sheikh Mujibur Rahman insisted these indigenous people "assimilate the new, nationalist Bengali identity." Subsequent Bangladesh governments continued to tolerate territorial displacement of the Jumma people and settlement of Bengalis in the CHT. This presumes to assure control over the CHT and to eliminate any indigenous people's movement, thus blocking the establishment of an autonomous political region that would be effectively "indigenous" and manifestly not "Bengali/Bangladeshi." In subsequent negotiations with the government of Bangladesh during the Ershad administration, Aminuzzaman reports, the Jumma demanded autonomy for the CHT, to be named "Jummaland" in recognition of the Jumma people's ancestral presence there, with a right to self-determination as an indigenous people and not as Bengalis/Bangladeshis. All of these demands were, of course, rejected in preference to the dominant national narrative legally sanctioned by the Bangladesh Constitution.

Similarly, Myanmar does not recognize any Rohingya claim of indigeneity, thwarting any movement seeking autonomy of the Rakhine State (as pursued by some Muslims denominated *mujahids*, "freedom fighters." In fact, Thawnghmung (2016, 539) reminds, historian Jacques Leider and former British senior diplomat Derek Tonkin concluded, to the satisfaction of the Myanmar authorities, that Rohingya identity is itself a construct: "Neither could find any evidence to support Rakhine Muslims' claim that their roots lay with 8th-century Arab settlers, rather than with large-scale migration from Bengal during British rule." Even so, in one instance of writing, Tonkin (n.d.) does refer to the Rohingya as indigenous, "Rohingya" and "Ruhingya" being "one of several variations of 'Rwangya', the word for *indigenous 'Arakaner' Muslim* communities in circulation." These terms refer to this people's *ethnicity* even if not to their citizenship status at the time under review (circa 1954), even though Tonkin opined that it is problematic to correct "the original Burmese" spelling for this ethnicity ("Ruhingya" or "Ruhinja") by replacing that word with "Rohingya" or of "replacing the term 'Arakan Muslims' with 'Rohingya' wherever it appears. Neither practice is conducive to historical accuracy or compatible with academic integrity" (Tonkin, n.d., 3). Accordingly, Tonkin (n.d., 4) concluded, "By any standards, the majority of Muslims in Maundaw and Buthidaung in 1954 were not descendants of indigenous communities, but of British-era migrants from Bengal, *though entitled to full citizenship by birth and by statutory right.*"

Elsewhere, Tonkin (2018) opines that, "the extent of illegal immigration from Bangladesh [i.e., former East Pakistan] into Rakhine State since independence in 1948 is difficult if not impossible to assess," hence the inductive status of such a claim is not obviously settled so as to determine the question one way or the other. Leider opines, "Since the 1950s, Rohingya writers have strenuously minimized and largely denied the Bengali roots of their origins, insisting on the cultural differences between Muslims in the Chittagong district and themselves" (Thawnghmung, 2016, 541). It is further important to understand that the two propositions—"Rohingya in Arakan/Rakhine State are Muslims" and "Some Arakan Muslims are Rohingya"—are subject to critical assessment. As Thawnghmung (2016) observes, some Arakan Muslims do not identify themselves as Rohingya, while nonetheless rejecting any assertion they are "Bengali." The foregoing observations disclose the local politics of communalist struggle within the larger national frame of contending historical narratives. Hence, for some Burmese Rakhines, it is one thing for Rohingya to claim indigeneity (which these Rakhines reject) and another to seek either associate or naturalized citizenship (which they may accept consistent with provisions of the Citizenship Law of 1982).

A View from India

Reporting in the *Mail Online India* in October 2017, at the time of the mass exodus of Rohingya from Myanmar's Rakhine State into Bangladesh, Brahma Chellany (2017) asserted, "The current international narrative on the plight of Myanmar's persecuted Rohingya minority has failed to recognize the roots of the present crisis or the growing transnational jihadist links of Rohingya militants…" This asserted association of the Rohingya with *militant/jihadist* Islam contributes to regional political and religious group recalcitrance to engage Rohingya with more than superficial hospitality. The asserted association leads to concerns about inter-religious conflict (Hindu vs. Muslim; Buddhist vs. Muslim) and regional and local security against separatist movements. It contributes to ill-treatment of Rohingya who fled to India over decades of persecution in Myanmar (Shwe et al., 2021). Chellany (2017) links the present crisis to the time of Partition of the Indian subcontinent, remarking that "Rohingya militants have actually been in the vanguard of the global rise of Islamic radicalism since the early 1940s, when they joined the campaign to press the British to establish Pakistan by partitioning India." The claim that Rohingya are actually Bengali from the former East Pakistan adds to the characterization of Rohingya as militant/jihadist.

Chellany's statement is problematically framed, since the press for partition of Hindu India and Muslim Pakistan at the time is not itself equivalent to support for militant Islamism. Nonetheless, this asserted historical fact, at least for the Hindu majority in India supportive of the current Hindutva ideology, is sufficient reason to depreciate the Rohingya as they seek protection from persecution and refugee support while being forcibly displaced. Furthermore problematic is the appropriation of the concept of "militant Islamists" along with the word "*jihad*," which has negative meaning in the post-9/11 terrorist context. Granted, the Rohingya "rebelled" or "struggled" against the intolerant policies of the Myanmar government—thus they were called "*mujahid*"—while seeking citizenship and an autonomous (not separatist) region (a "Muslim National Area") as promised by the British colonial rulers.[14] But, this does not mean that they are "terrorists" in the post-9/11 sense of militant Islam. Any such discourse is equivocal and misleading.

Chellany (2017) takes up the refrain of many that the Rohingya are actually "Bengali" and, therefore, belong to present-day Bangladesh, reminding that, "It was the British who earlier moved large numbers of Rohingyas from East Bengal to work on rubber and tea plantations in Burma, now Myanmar, which was administered as a province of India until 1937 before it became a separate self-governing colony." Consequent to this British administrative action, we are informed, the Rohingya thereafter settled in Burma's Arakan region (Rakhine State). Hence, Chellany's (2017) argument goes, there were ethnic tensions ongoing between the Rohingya Muslims and the Burmese Buddhists (Buddhist Bamar and Buddhist Rakhines) until "civil war" erupted and World War II led to British-Japanese armed conflict, "with the local Buddhists largely siding with the Japanese and Rohingyas with the British."[15] Problematic for writers such as Chellany is the historical fact that, "When the British eventually regained control of Arakan in 1945, they rewarded Rohingya Muslims for their loyalty by appointing them to the main posts in the local government." A year later, some emboldened "Rohingya militants" formed the North Arakan Muslim League seeking secession from Myanmar, preferring that northern Arakan (i.e., the areas of Maungdaw and Buthidaung) become "part of East Pakistan" (what became present-day Bangladesh).

The foregoing historical account manifests a persistent undercurrent of trepidation and lack of trust in the Rohingya, despite the mass forced displacement that occurred in late 2017. The automatic assumption is that s/he who takes up the cause of Muslim *jihad* cannot be a legitimate refugee. Burmese Buddhists in particular and Myanmar's military government assert that Rohingya agitate communal conflict and separatism.

The View from Human Rights Watch

The fact is that ethnic and religious conflict links to political conflict in northern Arakan (Rakhine State). Human Rights Watch (HRW) reminds of a "long history of refugee flows in the area." While using the word "refugee" here, HRW (2000) also asserts unequivocally that its "historic overview of the region…traces the attachment of the Rohingya to northern Arakan and thus *their firmly established link* to what is modern Burma," despite sustained discrimination in Myanmar, including denial of citizenship, restrictions on their freedom of movement, arbitrary confiscation of their property, forced labor, and other loss of civil rights. HRW presents the singularly salient notice that, "The Rohingya were once counted as a part of the Mrauk-U (Mrohaung) kingdom in Arakan which stood independent of both the Burman kingdoms in the Irrawaddy delta and central Burma as well as Bengal and the Moguls to the west." This statement of historical fact thereby supports the Rohingya claim to *indigenous presence* in northern Rakhine State, irrespective of subsequent political factors (Partition, independence of Pakistan, independence of Myanmar, then independence of Bangladesh, all altering the governing structures of the region despite the diversity of peoples, their cultural practices, and languages).

The Rohingya claim to indigeneity was not by any means terminated when, "In 1784, the Burman King Bodawpaya conquered and incorporated the Arakan region into his kingdom of Ava in central Burma." And, all the more pertinent to the notice that the Rohingya are "merely Bengalis transplanted by the British," HRW reports that, "As a consequence of the invasion [by King Bodawpaya], [Rohingya] refugees began to pour into what is today the Cox's Bazar area of [British controlled] southern Chittagong." Hence, the forced migration was *from the territory of Arakan* into the territory that eventually became East Pakistan and then Bangladesh. After ongoing armed conflict into the early 1800s, "Many of the Rohingya that fled during this period never returned to Burma, but instead settled in the area of Cox's Bazar and became integrated with the local community." Thus, according to the foregoing narrative, despite this local integration, the Rohingya are not "Bengali" as a matter of ethnicity. They became residents in that area only consequent to the altered political geography of the region, including the British colonial rule of Burma after 1824. HRW concludes categorically: "The reality is that the Rohingya have had a well established presence in the country [Burma/Myanmar] since the twelfth century." They are victims of political upheavals that have altered the "human geography" of *their homeland.*

The View from "Buddhist" Myanmar

"Bengalis," "illegal Pakistani immigrants," "militant Muslims," etc., are terms in use that characterize the Rohingya as illegally present in Myanmar over decades and even centuries. Thus, while considering the idea of Rohingya indigeneity, Muhammad Busyairi and Bui Thi Kim Siem (2021) begin their remarks in a published article from 2021 with the statement in their abstract: "Rohingya first came to Arakan State, Burma (Myanmar) between the eighth and ninth centuries...Their arrival correlated with the British colonialism and Japanese colonialism (1942–1945) which played a crucial role in initiating the conflicts between Muslims and Buddhists." They clarify that "some historians" claim the foregoing historical account to be accurate. But, the motivations are mixed: Thus, "it is also important to recognize that it is most often a combination of factors rather than a straightforward 'religious' motive that has led to violence. Myanmar's long history of exclusion and violence against the Rohingyas has been framed as much by the question of who counts as a legitimate ethnic minority and who is a foreigner as by questions of 'religious' identity" (Asian Global Affairs, 2020).

One notes immediately the historical reference to inter-religious conflict between Muslims and Buddhists, the former (it is asserted) residing in Burma/Myanmar only as a consequence of migration from former East Pakistan territory under British colonial rule. Burmese Buddhists, by contrast, are considered a local "national race." Such is the discursive conflict between many Rakhine State Buddhists (supported by the Myanmar government's military and police forces) and the Rohingya Muslims who have resided there, but also for Rohingya forcibly displaced into neighboring countries. At issue here, however, is the fact of contested Buddhist historical narratives.

Consider the analysis of Matthew J. Walton and Susan Hayward (2014). Some Buddhists within Myanmar, viz., those associated with the "969 Movement" (emerging in 2012) and "MaBaTha" (the Organization for the Protection of Race and Religion, formed in 2014), are decidedly nationalist in their *political* (not religious or doctrinal) orientation.[16] They believe their existence as Buddhists is "threatened by foreign elements within and outside the country." They have accused Muslims—particularly those from the Rohingya ethnic community—of seeking to displace Buddhism, and they have articulated through sermons and publications anti-Muslim sentiments that are often based on rumor or mischaracterizations of Islamic teachings and objectives" (Walton and Hayward, 2014). According to the World Population Review (2022), the ethnic Rohingya are denominated a "foreign" element within Burma/Myanmar, in contrast to the nationalist Bamar ethnic group (representing ~68% of the total population) in Myanmar. The claim of existential threat is by no means supported by the demographic data, since the projected annual change between 2020 and 2050 is estimated to drop from 0.65% to 0.11%, with net change in migrants estimated to manifest a loss of around 163,000 in 2020 with continued losses of around 20,000 each year up to 2045 (Worldometer, n.d.).

Despite the fact that Muslims comprise only around 4% of the Myanmar populace (World Population Review, 2022), the Buddhist monk Oo Wi Ma La laments the situation with Buddhism, commenting: "In Indonesia, Bangladesh, Pakistan, Malaysia, and so on there used to be so many Buddhists, but the Muslims came and kicked them out, and now they are Muslim countries. So based on history we worry Burma could become like that" (Wade, 2013). Clearly, while the emotional element of "worry" is present, logically the probability of such a massive demographic and religious change is not supported by the data. U Wirathu similarly argues illogically that, "'If Buddhists don't do anything to stop it, the whole country will be like the Mayu region in Arakan state by 2100,' referring to an area of the [Rakhine] state that is populated primarily by Rohingya Muslims" (Walton and Hayward, 2014, 17). Again, the claims are manifestly fallacious; they serve rhetorical aims only.

According to reports such as from Walton and Hayward (2014), such historical narratives have popular appeal among many Buddhist Burmese, thus influencing their ethnic and nationalist loyalties. Among Buddhist monastic authorities is U Wirathu (BBC News 2015, Oppenheim 2017), a vocal monk from Mandalay who is strident and noted for his vitriol favoring "Buddhist terrorism" or "militant Buddhism" (Fuller, 2017),[17] referring to the Rohingya as "Bengalis." Nevertheless, Walton and Hayward (2014, xi) report that (given the multiplicity of ethnic groups) Buddhists within Myanmar are not uniformly nationalist and do provide counterarguments that appeal to Theravadan Buddhist ethics. Ashin Issariya, one of the leaders of the "Saffron Revolution" of 2007, has taken issue with Wirathu (Khaing, 2018). Decrying the latter's rhetoric, Issariya remarks, "As a Buddhist monk, and as a citizen, he [Wirathu] has a responsibility to speak the truth…When U Wirathu says he is working to protect race and religion, he is misleading the people. If you want to protect Buddhism, you must abide by the rules of conduct set by the Lord Buddha" (Khaing, 2018).[18]

Similarly, those associated with the Buddhist Humanitarian Project (n.d.) (including representatives of Theravada, Mahayana, and Vajrayana traditions) do not mince words and are clear that, "The Myanmar (Burma) government and military is engaged in an ethnic cleansing of the Rohingya people…We call on Buddhist friends around the world to take a stand against this violence, and to support Rohingya refugees." Indeed, they write, "Mean-spirited words and direct provocation led by Ma Ba Tha monks (the Buddha Dhamma Parahita Foundation, formerly known as the Organization for the Protection of Race and Religion) stand in stark contrast to monastic precepts and Buddha's teachings on universal morality, peace, and tolerance." They thereby call on the government of Myanmar and the international community "to see that the survival and safety of the Rohingya is ensured; and to take steps to provide them with full rights as citizens of Myanmar."

The foregoing differences of opinion are important as a matter of critical identification of the truth to be found in these historical narratives. Thus, Walton and Hayward (2014, 18) comment, "Quasi-historical claims…are commonly shared on social media sites. Their questionable historical veracity is beside the point because the monks who make these claims enjoy a respected status among Burmese Buddhists, and it is assumed that they have correct information about the history of Buddhism." Such appeals to the authority of Buddhist monks are displaced when the rhetoric is distinguished from the truth as historically validated.

Given the sizable Rohingya population ("over 90 percent Rohingya [Bengali]") in Maungdaw and Buthidaung townships in Rakhine State, Burmese Buddhists in Rakhine State believe themselves to be "guarding Myanmar's western door" against further Muslim encroachment from Bengal (Walton and Hayward, 2014, 20). Therefore, they are by no means willing to see the Rohingya population grow as a result of Rohingya repatriation from the settlement camps in southeast Bangladesh. Sectarian Muslim presence in Myanmar also contributes to the unease of the Buddhist Burmese, since, as Walton and Hayward (2014, 20) report further, "there has been an increasing presence of more conservative forms of Islam throughout the country, spread by missionaries who travel from village to village, often recruiting young men. This form of Islam derives from the Deobandi school, preaches a message that is perceived to be less tolerant of other religions and cultures…" Such "messaging" is deemed by many within Rakhine State to be a menace to local Buddhist security interests and, by extension, to those Burmese who insist that Burma/Myanmar must remain decidedly Buddhist and by no means permit a separatist movement in Rakhine State. Notwithstanding variation in local Burmese Buddhist doctrinal beliefs and practices, "Over the centuries in Theravada Buddhist-influenced kingdoms, political and religious elites cultivated a worldview in which the health of the religion and the strength of the polity were seen as interdependent." Thus, Walton and Hayward (2014, 21) conclude, "in this frame, protecting the Burmese nation requires solidifying Buddhism as its primary moral touchstone and, to a certain degree, as the ideological infrastructure for the state." That means curbing Muslim demographic growth, hence restricting Rohingya presence.

The View from Bangladesh

Before the 2014 and 2017 exodus of Rohingya from Myanmar into Bangladesh, it was argued, "the Rohingya refugee problem was created in the course of several historical trajectories. It has been demonstrated that the Rohingyas are both stateless and refugees. First, they became stateless in their homeland and then eventually they had to embrace the status of refugeehood under conditions of persecution, discrimination and torture" (Ahmed, 2010). Yet, the discourse remains entirely problematic, insofar as the Rohingya within Bangladesh are said to be FDMN, refugees, or stateless persons, and the government of Bangladesh is bound to provide humanitarian care whatever the designations.

The Bangladesh government had little option but to provide the Rohingya people local accommodation in "temporary" settlement camps, especially since the 2017 mass exodus of Rohingya from Rakhine State. Bangladesh is not a signatory to the UN Convention on the Status of Refugees; hence, the government does not consider itself obligated to provide the Rohingya all rights and privileges *de jure* associated with refugees. Bangladesh and Myanmar have engaged in bilateral negotiations that might permit repatriation, although the barriers are multiple and unlikely to generate voluntary return of Rohingya in the absence of security of person, reclamation of properties of which they have been dispossessed, and guarantee of their recognized ethnicity and right of citizenship. Attempts to return Rohingya to Myanmar in 2018 and 2019 failed (Banerjee, 2020).

On 26 February 2021, then Bangladesh Foreign Minister A.K. Abdul Momen spoke before the Council on Foreign Relations in a virtual meeting to provide "a view from Bangladesh" (Council on Foreign Relations, 2021). As he observed, despite three signed agreements and multiple proposals with the government of Myanmar, the Rohingya lack of trust in a "safe and dignified return" and the Myanmar government's lack of response has resulted in none being returned. "We have been trying bilaterally to resolve the issue because the problem was created by Myanmar. The solution also lies with Myanmar," Momen remarked. Recognizing the need for "accountability and justice," Momen expressed his gratitude to the Gambia for taking up the matter in the Organization of Islamic Cooperation (OIC) and for the engagement of the International Court of Justice. Whatever the process and proposals, the government of Bangladesh insists that repatriation is the only credible solution. Moreover, in the absence of repatriation, Momen was concerned there could be an increased chance of "pockets of radicalism," i.e., terrorist activities, that would further destabilize the region.[19] There is also a developing problem of local host community-Rohingya conflict. Momen added, "the local community is very frustrated. They are very unhappy because the Rohingya are taking away their jobs, low-paid jobs. The Rohingya are destroying their farms, their trees...and the inflation in the area has tripled" (Council on Foreign Relations, 2021).[20]

In response to a further question, Momen cautioned that, "the future of Rohingya is very bleak, unless the global leadership comes forward to solve that problem." Thus, given the failure of bilateral efforts between Bangladesh and Myanmar, the task falls to the international community to work to resolve the problem. In response to a question of whether the Rohingya might be settled ("be absorbed") in Bangladesh, Momen insisted the Rohingya are "citizens of Burma" despite their being "disenfranchised" in 1982. Rather than settlement in Bangladesh, the alternative is third-country resettlement—"there are so many countries that can do the burden sharing...We have R2P facility...If the coalition of the willing agrees to provide them a shelter in their own land, I'm sure this can be done." However, then Bangladesh Prime Minister Sheikh Hasina informed the UN High Commissioner for Human Rights that the Rohingya must return to Myanmar (Aljazeera News, 2022).

Even so, as So-June Rhee, UNHCR Interim Country Representative in Bangladesh reminded, "The solution lies in Myanmar. But in the meantime, we have to bridge the gap. We are in a protracted situation...we have to look at this strategically. Going into sixth year, funding [from donor agencies] is dwindling" (BRAC, 2022). Accordingly, Asif Saleh, Executive Director of BRAC (a Bangladesh non-governmental organization) suggested, "We should now look for a mid-term strategy for the refugees as we continuously advocate for their safe and dignified return to their homeland. There is a growing consensus within the sector that the current work needs to shift towards a development-like approach from a very short-term humanitarian crisis-focused approach." He added, "The only solution for the Rohingya refugees is their sustainable and voluntary repatriation to Myanmar."

"Ethnohistory" *qua* "Historical Truth" and the Question of "Repatriation"

The sequential alteration of the structures of governance in the Indian subcontinent in the late modern period has wholly disturbed local indigeneity and thus claims by indigenous ethnic groups to traditional land tenure.

Anthropologist Mark Woodward (2020) reminds, e.g., that as "colonialism and nationalism disrupted a traditional political-social order in which Muslims were systematically incorporated into precolonial Arakanese and Burmese Buddhist kingdoms," the fact is, "These [modern era] disruptions began with the First Anglo-Burmese War (1824–1826) and continued with the incorporation of all of Burma into the British Indian Empire at the conclusion of the Third Anglo-Burmese War in 1885. These disruptions culminated with the establishment of Burma as a *de facto* Burmese Buddhist ethno-religious nationalist state when it gained independence from Britain in 1948."

Bangladeshi anthropologist Nasir Uddin (2019, italics added) rightly remarks that the concept of indigeneity is "*nationally installed* and *locally translated* within the context of the ethnohistory of an Indigenous movement that stemmed from local-societal relations with the state. The idea of indigeneity is seen as both local and global because it is *globally circulated* but *locally articulated* as well as *globally charged* but *locally framed*." Accordingly, he argues, "the local translation of global indigeneity is necessary for ensuring the rights and entitlements of Indigenous Peoples." What matters in the case of the Rohingya is that they present us with a locally articulated and locally framed claim of indigeneity as a matter of *self-identity*, whatever the external critiques of the historical narrative they voice in various forums.

Analysis of concepts can proceed in various ways, of course, consistent with diverse methods. Thawnghmung (2016, 533), e.g., in her approach to the issues of Rohingya/Buddhist disputations, uses discourse analysis, which she takes to be "a method of inquiry that helps us understand how specific actors construct an argument, and how this argument fits into wider social practices." That said, however, insofar as the concern is to engage historical narratives critically, to determine where "the truth" is likely to be found, she concedes, "this form of analysis assesses neither the truthfulness of communications nor the authenticity of historical facts put forth by people and organizations that are disseminating the information." Hence, discourse analysis presents us with a limitation on settlement of the central question at issue, viz., the factuality of Rohingya self-identity and their claim to a rightful homeland in Arakan.

It is, therefore, important to understand, as reported by Dunford (2019), that there are both Burmese and Rohingya appeals to indigeneity within Myanmar. Notably, the Rohingya-led National Democratic Party for Development (NDPD) in Myanmar issued its attestation of Rohingya indigeneity in April 2012 (National Democratic Party, 2012). It is asserted that Rohingya are historically "natives [of Burma, and Arakan in particular] by race," and in that sense therefore they are "citizens" of contemporary Myanmar, despite the Citizenship Law of 1982 perpetrating the injustice of denying them citizenship. In October 2012, the Arakan Rohingya National Organization (ARNO) similarly asserted that, "Myanmar's Rohingya Muslim population is indigenous to the land despite being classified as illegal migrants," even as ARNO (2012) grants that some Rohingya are "Muslim descendants of Persian, Turkish, Bengali, and Pathan origins, who migrated to Myanmar as early as the 8th century." Thus, on this view, the fact of trans-border migrations is not a barrier to acknowledging the Rohingya right to citizenship. Those who are "native" (*taingyinthar*) are contrasted to those of "mixed blood" (*thwehnaw*), the latter considered "foreign settlers" (Tea Circle Oxford, 2020). It is entirely problematic, therefore, from the perspective of expected repatriation of the Rohingya from Bangladesh, that this repatriation is "conditional on the participation in the NVC [national verification cards, issued since 2014] scheme, which treats them as foreigners," hence with no lawful claim to Myanmar citizenship (Tea Circle Oxford, 2020).

Writing in the *Washington Post* in December 2018, political scientist Mollie Gerver (2018) asked: "Would it be ethical for the U.N. refugee agency [United Nations High Commission for Refugees—UNHCR] to send Rohingya back to Myanmar?"[21] Gerver engaged the ethical dilemma she characterizes as one of consent: "On the one hand, if UNHCR helps refugees repatriate, many will return who have no reasonable alternative, and so perhaps their choices are involuntary. If UNHCR has failed to obtain refugees' voluntary consent, it may be acting unethically in helping them return. On the other hand, if UNHCR is fairly certain refugees will remain detained and destitute in Bangladesh, helping with return may seem the best option." Such is the "consent dilemma" operative for international agencies and the government of Bangladesh. Even so, whereas the government of Bangladesh has characterized the Rohingya as FDMN while working bilaterally with the military government of Myanmar to facilitate voluntary repatriation, then Prime Minister Sheikh Hasina was clear, in speaking of the Rohingya at the UN General Assembly in 2022, that she considers Myanmar "their ancestral home" (Bangladesh Sangbad Sangstha, 2022).

The dilemma of repatriation is operative for all who are engaged in providing humanitarian assistance to the Rohingya or who undertake a "responsibility to protect" consistent with "R2P" (United Nations, n.d.)[22] criteria of a warranted international legal response to this crisis. It is assumed that the Rohingya have a *right* of return, a right of *repatriation*, insofar as they are "Myanmar nationals" and indigenous to Arakan. Yet, that very choice of terms is indicative of the ambiguity various governmental and international intergovernmental organization authorities face when working to resolve the forced displacement of the Rohingya. To say the Rohingya are "Myanmar *nationals*" is not to say unequivocally that they are "Myanmar *citizens*." Not saying explicitly that the Rohingya are *citizens* of Myanmar implicitly concedes to the Burmese government its narrative that the Rohingya are "Bengalis" with no legal right of repatriation.

At issue here is the legitimacy and truth of the historical narratives in protracted contention and contestation of identity: (1) a self-identity the Rohingya articulate as they insist on their right to their homeland in Arakan/Rakhine State; (2) the historical narrative issued by the Burmese (both governmental and Buddhist religious groups) characterizing the Rohingya as "Bengali," thus as an illegal migrant population; (3) the historical narrative issued by the Bangladesh government as it denominates the Rohingya as FDMN, without explicitly positive assertion that the Rohingya are *bona fide* "citizens" of Myanmar; and (4) the historical narrative of other affected parties, such as in nearby India, where there is a negative discourse of Rohingya Muslim involvement in militant *jihad* threatening both Hindu (Hindutva) and Buddhist sociopolitical interests in the region.

Whatever the perspective, despite the epistemological issues, historian Jacques P. Leider (2018) is entirely correct that historical research is "a prerequisite both for understanding the nature of the conflict and for keeping opportunities for competing historical interpretations alive." Thawnghmung (2016, 532, italics added) states the central question of historical fact that is essential to the legal determination of right to citizenship: "whether Rohingyas established roots in Myanmar *before Britain's annexation of the country in 1823*." The question of fact here is essential because, as Thawnghmung observes, "Under current laws, Rohingya who settled in Burma prior to British annexation would qualify to be one of Myanmar's ethnic nationalities, entitled to full citizen rights under the 1982 citizenship law." In the absence of that validation, and as long as the Myanmar government's Citizenship Law of 1982 is not challenged on human rights grounds for its manifest injustice, the Rohingya remain effectively a stateless people.[23]

If the Rohingya remain categorized as stateless rather than as *de jure* Myanmar nationals with the right of citizenship,[24] then their prospect of repatriation is bleak indeed, because "Statelessness has long been largely absent from considerations related to global migration governance," even as there is "relative ignorance of statelessness among global actors" (Bloom, 2018). As a matter of international law, the international community does not consider the Rohingya to be stateless, even as it is acknowledged that their forced displacement can nevertheless lead to long-term *de facto* statelessness (Medicines sans Frontieres, n.d.).[25] Journalist Rebecca L. Root (2022) reports that, "Aung Kyaw Moe, human rights advisor to Myanmar's National Unity Government—the civilian government-in-exile formed in the wake of the February 2021 military coup...[has called for] aid organizations to stop using the nomenclature [of 'stateless' or 'statelessness' in reference to the Rohingya] and for all Rohingya to admonish its use." She adds,

> By saying "stateless," we are neutralising...Rohingya, those who are in Bangladesh, fall comprehensively under the definition of the refugee, so calling them refugees is the best term. Those who remain in Myanmar are Myanmar citizens ... First and foremost...calling someone stateless [impacts their morale]. Instead, if you tell them, "you belong to a state and the state belongs to you, and your citizenship was taken away and you still belong to a state, you live there, or you escaped because you were going to be killed," that gives hope, motivation, and moral support to those who survived this horrible genocide.

This is perhaps the most salient recommendation after five years of Rohingya external displacement in Bangladesh. Hence, accounting for the contention of historical narratives there is ample warrant to assert several propositions as "historical truth" and applicable "moral-legal" principle:

1. Those Rohingya in Bangladesh and in the diaspora of temporary resettlement are rightly denominated *refugees*. Therefore, they should be accorded all the rights and privileges of refugees under international humanitarian law. This is a responsibility the government of Bangladesh should adopt forthwith, despite not being a signatory to the Refugee Convention.[26] Thereby, the Bangladesh government overcomes the implicit assumption motivating Western government refugee assistance policies and "source control measures," viz., that the strategy of voluntary repatriation requires keeping forcibly displaced persons close to the nation-state from which they have been displaced,[27] rather than working earnestly for an alternative durable solution of third-country resettlement when the host country does not permit integration.
2. The Rohingya are *de jure Myanmar nationals, not stateless* persons. One need not be agnostic about the Rohingya claim of indigeneity in Arakan/Rakhine State, especially if (a) one sets aside the arbitrary and discriminatory Citizenship Law of 1982 relative to international human rights law, and (b) one concedes that the Bamar majority itself cannot claim exclusive Burmese indigeneity without admitting to this group likely having resulted from migration into Arakan from Tibet and Yunnan, China ("Tibeto-Chinese" forebears). On the contrary, then, while recognizing that there are competing historical narratives on the Rohingya claim, the available evidence supports that claim as an inductively warranted true belief: the claim is *more likely to be true than false* that the Rohingya are, generally speaking, an indigenous group in Arakan/Rakhine State.[28]
3. Having been Myanmar nationals consistent with the facts of constitutional and statutory recognition prior to 1982, the Rohingya are *de jure citizens* of Myanmar, despite their disenfranchisement and dispossession

of land tenure by the Citizenship Law of 1982 that deliberately excluded them from legally recognized ethnicity, consequent to a Bamar and Buddhist campaign of ethnic cleansing and erasure.

4. Accordingly, the Rohingya have every legal right to a voluntary and dignified *repatriation to their homeland in northern Rakhine State/Arakan*, with the understanding that they ought not agitate for a separation of Rakhine State (i.e., "the creation of a Muslim autonomous zone") from Myanmar's current territorial borders.
5. That said, however, the reality is that the government of Myanmar is wholly recalcitrant to facilitate repatriation. Therefore, Bangladesh and the international community are obligated to do more on behalf of the Rohingya consistent with the "R2P" principle.
6. As has been proposed by various observers cited hitherto, the recalcitrance of the Myanmar government entails continued efforts to facilitate *third-country resettlement* and, in the interim, to take a *proactive development* approach (rather than a crisis management approach) to improving the livelihoods of the Rohingya in the settlement camps in Bangladesh. This may include allowance for permanent residency (rather than full citizenship) in Bangladesh, with rights and privileges that follow from this designation.
7. A proactive development strategy cannot but include formally approved opportunities for *gainful employment* within Bangladesh (this may be limited geographically, given the demographics of employment opportunity) and *planned resettlement*, as well as *structured and robustly supported K-12 education* for the Rohingya youth, so as to avoid a "lost generation" (UNICEF, 2018; Amnesty International, 2020; Al-Haddad et al., 2022) and to diminish prospects of Islamic radicalization and drug trafficking both within and beyond the extant settlement camps in Bangladesh.
8. UN agencies such as UNHCR must continue to take the lead to assure sustained humanitarian assistance to Bangladesh, even as the international community works to facilitate third-country resettlement so as to reduce the economic and social burdens imposed upon the government of Bangladesh.

The foregoing set of commitments does not mean that investigative and/or judicial processes underway in the International Court of Justice or the International Criminal Court should in any way be diminished. On the contrary, international justice requires that the allegations of crimes against humanity and genocide be properly investigated and due judgment rendered on behalf of the Rohingya people, whether sooner or later.

Notes

1 For further discussion, see "Reliability Epistemology," *Stanford Encyclopedia of Philosophy*, 21 May 2021, https://plato.stanford.edu/entries/reliabilism/, accessed 26 December 2022.
2 For some Rohingya, from at least 1799, thus prior to the cut-off date of 1825 being used by the Myanmar government to validate claims to citizenship, Rohingya had legitimate residence in the land. See "Myanmar's Rohingya Question, Part 3 of 3," Institute of Security and International Studies, Chulalongkorn University, 07 March 2014, https://youtu.be/qh/9rT_TQkoM, accessed 25 December 2022.
3 For a discussion on the morality of "encampment" see Parekh (2017).
4 Tucker (2001), pp. 9 & 11, speaks of "successive waves of immigration" into the territory of Burma, with even the majority Bamar and "Rakhines (Arakanese)" being "Tibeto-Burmans," and even asserting unequivocally that, "All came from China." Further, "The Burmans arrived between AD850 and 1050. T'ai pressure, it is surmised, forced them to leave Yunnan."
5 Thawnghmung (p. 531) notes: "The citizenship law of 1982 (enforced from 1987 on) stripped Rohingyas of the NRCs [National Registration Cards] and categorized them as Bangladeshi." For further discussion, see Parashar and Alam (2018).
6 For example, M.S. Kuropjatnik (2019) writes: "In its contemporary meaning, the concept of indigeneity expresses the desire of indigenous peoples and various social and cultural communities, formerly marginalized within the borders of national states, to independently determine their development."
7 See, e.g., Al Faruque and Begum (2004).
8 See Mohanty, Russo, and Torres (1991). Burmese-born political scientist Ardeth Thawnghmung clarifies that, "The Myanmar government has thus far shunned the use of the term 'indigenous peoples', and relied instead on the term *taing-yin-thar* (translated from Burmese as 'sons/offspring of the geographical division') which pertains to 135 officially recognized groups." That said, however, see Transnational Institute (2014).
9 See the related Human Rights Watch report, " 'All You Can Do is Pray': Crimes Against Humanity and Ethnic Cleansing of Rohingya Muslims," 22 April 2013, https://www.hrw.org/report/2013/04/22/all-you-can-do-pray/crimes-against-humanity-and-ethnic-cleansing-rohingya-muslims, accessed 20 December 2022.
10 See Agoos (2020).
11 United Nations, Human Rights Council, Resolution 1/2, 29 June 2006, Official Record of the General Assembly, Sixty-first Session, Supplement No. 53 (A/61/53), part one, chap. II, sect. A. Also see, United Nations, Department of Economic and Social Affairs, United Nations Declaration on the Rights of Indigenous Peoples, https://www.un.org/development/desa/indigenouspeoples/declaration-on-the-rights-of-indigenous-peoples.html, accessed 11 December 2022.
12 As cited by Nasir Uddin, Sarajjoti Chakma, Bangladesh Adivasi (Indigenous) Peoples Forum, Chittagong Division, says: "We are still fighting for our identity as we are no-one in Bangladesh because its Constitution doesn't have any space for Indigenous People. How could we demand the rights of Indigenous People unless our identity is constitutionally settled in the structure of the state?"
13 This is a term used by reputed international law scholar Richard A. Falk.
14 See here Abdelkader (2017).
15 Writing in an op-ed, "How WWII Shaped the Crisis in Myanmar," *Washington Post*, 10 March 2019, Jayita Sarkar refers to declassified records from British

archives, reporting that, "the origins of the current plight of the Rohingya people can be traced to their participation in World War II, notably the communal violence that broke out between the Muslim Rohingya and the Buddhist Rakhine communities during and after the war."

16 See Lal (2021): "Buddhist nationalism in Burma is the transformation of religion into an ethnic, cultural identity. The philosophical teachings of the Buddha are fundamentally peripheral to the group. Moreover, Buddhist philosophy is disturbingly reinterpreted to follow a fascist ideology, and then relabeled as Buddhist nationalism."

17 Fuller (2017). See also, Artinger and Rowand (2021).

18 Khaing, "As preaching ban on U Wirathu ends, split in the Sangha widens..." By contrast, see Kleine (2006).

19 On this point see Rahman and Sakib (2021) and Rana (2022).

20 See also, Siddiqi (2022).

21 Gerver (2018). Gerver is author of *The Ethics and Practice of Refugee Repatriation* (Edinburgh: Edinburgh University Press, 2018).

22 United Nations, Office on Genocide Prevention and the Responsibility to Protect, "Responsibility to Protect": "The responsibility to protect embodies a political commitment to end the worst forms of violence and persecution. It seeks to narrow the gap between Member States' pre-existing obligations under international humanitarian and human rights law and the reality faced by populations at risk of genocide, war crimes, ethnic cleansing and crimes against humanity."

23 Notably, the International Commission of Jurists has asserted that, "Myanmar's legal framework for citizenship is incompatible with bedrock rule of law and democratic principles. In particular, the 1982 Citizenship Law is highly discriminatory and arbitrary, and manifestly fails to satisfy the State's obligations under international human rights law." See International Commission of Jurists (2019).

24 Article 1 of the Convention Relating to the Status of Stateless Persons (1954) defines a stateless person as "a person who is not considered as a national by any State under the operation of its law." See https://www.unhcr.org/ibelong/wp-content/uploads/1954-Convention-relating-to-the-Status-of-Stateless-Persons_ENG.pdf, accessed 28 December 2022.

25 Medecins sans Frontieres (n.d.). Likewise, see deChickera (2021) and Habib (2021).

26 As Parekh (2017, 18) has commented, the current "refugee regime," with "encampment or containment" being the "de facto" solution for displaced persons, is wholly problematic inasmuch as this strategy "systematically undermines the rights of the displaced for the sake of protecting our [i.e., a given host state's] sovereignty..."

27 On this point Parekh (p. 26) cites Aleinikoff (1992, 130). Encampment becomes a morally problematic option for care of displaced persons when "protection of borders" is privileged over "protection of persons" and when the implicit utilitarian calculation is that an eventual good (viz., repatriation) justifies an ostensibly short-term (but what, in fact, turns out to be a protracted) harm (viz., encampment).

28 The two competing historical narratives with contending hypotheses explaining the Rohingya presence in Myanmar—H1: "The Rohingya are an indigenous ethnic group of Arakan/Rakhine State" and H2: "The Rohingya are illegal 'Bengalis'"—are not mutually exclusive, since H1 is more likely to be true *prior* to the Anglo-Burmese wars (1824–1826; 1852; 1885) and H2 likely true *after* Burma was incorporated into British India (1824–1937), when the British both permitted and encouraged migration without there being any "cross-border migration" in the usual sense of that term. The truth of H2 does not undermine the claim to indigeneity of H1.

References

Abdelkader, Engy. (2017). "The history of the persecution of Myanmar's Rohingya," *The Conversation*, https://theconversation.com/the-history-of-the-persecution-of-myanmars-rohingya-84040, accessed 11 December 2022.

Agoos, Ella. (2020). "Linguistic essentialism and indigenous authenticity: The role of indigenous languages in defining indigeneity," *Inquiries: Social Sciences, Arts, & Humanities*, 12(9), http://www.inquiriesjournal.com/articles/1790/linguistic-essentialism-and-indigenous-authenticity-the-role-of-indigenous-languages-in-defining-indigeneity, accessed 12 December 2022.

Aleinikoff, Alexander T. (1992). "State-centered refugee law: From resettlement to containment," *Michigan Journal of International Law*, 14(120): 120–138.

Ahmed, Imtiaz. ed. (2010). *The Plight of the Stateless Rohingyas: Responses of the State, Society & the International Community*, Dhaka: University Press Limited.

Al Faruque, Abdullah and Najnin Begum. (2004). "Conceptualizing indigenous rights: An emerging new category of third-generation rights," *Asia-Pacific Journal on Human Rights and the Law*, 2: 1–29.

Al-Haddad, Robin E., Kendra L. Duran, and Saleh Ahmed. (2022). "A lost generation: Perpetual education insecurity among the Rohingya," *Race, Ethnicity and Education*, 25(6): 874–900, https://doi.org/10.1080/13613324.2022.2069738, accessed 29 December 2022.

AlJazeera News. (2022). "Bangladesh tells UN that Rohingya refugees must return to Myanmar," 17 August, https://www.aljazeera.com/news/2022/8/17/rohingya-refugees-have-to-be-taken-back-bangladesh-pm-says, accessed 27 December 2022.

Aminuzzaman, Salahuddin M. (2022). *A Review of the Chittagong Hill Tracts (CHT) Peace Accord*, Dhaka: South Asian Institute of Policy and Governance.

Amnesty International. (2020). "A 'lost generation' of Rohingya children will have nowhere to go," 24 January, https://www.amnesty.org/en/latest/news/2020/01/a-lost-generation-of-rohingya-children-will-have-nowhere-to-go/, accessed 29 December 2022.

ARNO. (2012). 'Rohingya not foreign population in Myanmar,' 27 October, https://www.rohingya.org/rohingya-not-foreign-population-in-myanmar/, accessed 20 December 2022.

Artinger, Brenna and Michael Rowand. (2021). "When Buddhists Back the Army," *Foreign Policy*, 16 February, https://foreignpolicy.com/2021/02/16/myanmar-rohingya-coup-buddhists-protest/, accessed 26 December 2022.

Asian Global Affairs. (2020). "The militant Buddhist perspective in Sri Lanka and Myanmar," 6 January, https://www.asiainglobalaffairs.in/reflections/the-militant-buddhist-perspective-in-sri-lanka-and-myanmar/, accessed 19 December 2022.

Baird, Ian G. (2016). "Indigeneity in Asia: an emerging but contested concept," *Asian Ethnicity*, 17(4): 501–505, https://doi.org/10.1080/14631369.2016.1193804, accessed 12 December 2022.

Banerjee, Sreeparna. (2020). "The Rohingya crisis and its impact on Bangladesh-Myanmar relations," Observer Research Foundation, *ORF Issue Briefs*, No. 396, August, https://www.orfonline.org/research/the-rohingya-crisis-and-its-impact-on-bangladesh-myanmar-relations/, accessed 27 December 2022.

Bangladesh Sangbad Sangstha, National News Agency of Bangladesh. (2022). "Full text of PM Sheikh Hasina's speech at UNGA," 24 September, https://www.bssnews.net/news/84222, accessed 27 December 2022.

BBC News. (2015). "Ashin Wirathu: Myanmar and its vitriolic monk," 23 January, https://www.bbc.com/news/world-asia-30930997, accessed 19 December 2022.

Beier, J. Marshall. (2005). *International Relations in Uncommon Places: Indigeneity, Cosmology, and the Limits of International Theory*, New York: Palgrave Macmillan.
Bloom, Tendayi. (2018). "Statelessness and the global compact for safe, orderly, and regular migration," Policy Brief, Leverhulme Trust/European Network on Statelessness, 4 December, https://www.statelessness.eu/sites/default/files/2020-09/ENS_Statelessness_Global_Compact_Migration_policy-brief.pdf, accessed 28 December 2022.
BRAC. (2022). "Policy dialogue held on Rohingya crisis response," 1 December, http://www.brac.net/latest-news/item/1368-policy-dialogue-held-on-rohingya-crisis-response, accessed 27 December 2022.
Buddhist Humanitarian Project. (n.d.). "Buddhist response to Rohingya crisis: A call to action from the global Buddhist community," https://www.buddhisthumanitarianproject.org/, accessed 26 December 2022.
Busyairi, Muhammad and Bui Thi Kim Siem. (2021). "Rohingya, A struggle for recognition as 'indigenous'," *Jurnal Ilmiah Kagian Keimigrasian*, 4(1): 117–124.
Chellany, Brahma. (2017). "'Long history of Rohingya jihad starts with Partition'," *Mail Online India*, 3 October, https://www.dailymail.co.uk/indiahome/indianews/article-4945700/Long-history-Rohingya-jihad-starts-Partition.html, accessed 11 December 2022.
Council on Foreign Relations. (2021). "Meeting—understanding the Rohingya crisis: A view from Bangladesh," 26 February, https://www.cfr.org/event/understanding-rohingya-crisis-view-bangladesh, accessed 27 December 2022.
deChickera, Amal. (2021). "Stateless and persecuted: What next for the Rohingya?" Migration Policy Institute, 18 March, https://www.migrationpolicy.org/article/stateless-persecuted-rohingya, accessed 28 December 2022.
Diamond, Stanley. (1974). *In Search of the Primitive: A Critique of Civilization*, New York: Routledge.
Dunford, Michael R. (2019). "Indigeneity, ethnopolitics, and *tangyinthar*: Myanmar and the global Indigenous peoples' movement," *Journal of Southeast Asia Studies*, 50(1): 51–67, https://doi.org/10.1017/S0022463419000043, accessed 24 December 2022.
Fodella, Alessandro. (2006). "International law and the diversity of indigenous peoples," *Vermont Law Review*, 30: 565–594.
Fuller, Paul. (2017). "Myanmar and Buddhist extremism," *The Conversation*, 14 November, https://theconversation.com/myanmar-and-buddhist-extremism-86125, accessed 26 December 2022.
Gadamer, Hans-Georg. (2004). *Truth and Method*, 2nd edition Revised, trans. revised by Joel Weinsheimer and Donald G. Marshall, New York: Continuum.
Gadamer, Hans-Georg. (1977). *Philosophical Hermeneutics*, trans. David E. Linge, Berkeley: University of California Press.
Gerver, Mollie, (2018). "Would it be ethical for the U.N. refugee agency to send Rohingya back to Myanmar?" *Washington Post*, 17 December, https://www.washingtonpost.com/news/monkey-cage/wp/2018/12/17/would-it-be-ethical-for-the-u-n-refugee-agency-to-send-rohingyas-back-to-myanmar/?noredirect=on&utm_term=.16a641c1f071, accessed 08 December 2022.
Guenther, Mathias. (2006). "The concept of indigeneity," *Social Anthropology*, 14(1): 17–32.
Habib, Md. Reza. (2021). "The 'stateless' Rohingya in Bangladesh: Crisis management and policy responses," *Asian Politics & Policy*, 13(4): 577–596, https://onlinelibrary.wiley.com/doi/10.1111/aspp.12611?af=R, accessed 28 December 2022.

Human Rights Watch. (2000). "Historical background," *Burma/Bangladesh Refugees in Bangladesh: Still no Durable Solution*, 12(3): (C), https://www.hrw.org/reports/2000/burma/burm005-01.htm, accessed 11 December 2022.
Human Rights Watch. (2013a). "Burma: End 'ethnic cleansing' of Rohingya muslims: Unpunished crimes against humanity, humanitarian crisis in Arakan State," 22 April, https://www.hrw.org/news/2013/04/22/burma-end-ethnic-cleansing-rohingya-muslims, accessed 20 December 2022.
Human Rights Watch. (2013b). "'All you can do is pray': Crimes against humanity and ethnic cleansing of Rohingya Muslims," 22 April, https://www.hrw.org/report/2013/04/22/all-you-can-do-pray/crimes-against-humanity-and-ethnic-cleansing-rohingya-muslims, accessed 20 December 2022.
International Commission of Jurists. (2019). *Citizenship and Human Rights in Myanmar: Why Law Reform Is Urgent and Possible: A Legal Briefing*, https://www.icj.org/wp-content/uploads/2019/06/Myanmar-Citizenship-law-reform-Advocacy-Analysis-Brief-2019-ENG.pdf, accessed 2 January 2023.
Khaing, Htun. (2018). "As preaching ban on U Wirathu ends, split in the Sangha widens," *Frontier Myanmar*, https://www.frontiermyanmar.net/en/as-preaching-ban-on-u-wirathu-ends-split-in-the-sangha-widens/, accessed 19 December 2022.
Kleine, C. (2006). "Evil monks with good intentions? Remarks on Buddhist monastic violence and its doctrinal background," in *Buddhism and Violence*, edited by M. Zimmerman, Lumbini: Lumbini International Research Institute, 65–98.
Kuropjatnik, M. S. (2019). "Indigeneity in the context of globalization: Epistemological and sociocultural aspects," *Rudn Journal of Sociology*, 19(3): 387–396, https://journals.rudn.ru/sociology/article/view/21674, accessed 12 December 2022).
Lal, Rollie. (2021). "Buddhist Nationalism in Myanmar," GARNET (Global Affairs and Religion Network), 12 November, https://garnet.elliott.gwu.edu/2021/11/12/november-12-2021-buddhist-nationalism-in-myanmar-with-prof-rollie-lal/, accessed 26 December 2022.
Leider, Jacques P. (2018). "History and Victimhood: Engaging with Rohingya issues," *Insight Turkey*, 20(1): 99–118, https://www.jstor.org/stable/26301070, accessed 11 December 2022.
Leskanich, Alexandre. (2020). "Haunting history: For a deconstructive approach to the past, by Ethan Kleinberg; How history gets things wrong: The neuroscience of our addiction to stories, by Alex Rosenberg," *The English Historical Review*, 135(573): 435–438, https://doi.org/10.1093/her/ceaa009, accessed 18 December 2022.
Medicins sans Frontieres (Doctors without Borders). (n.d.). "The Rohingya: The world's largest stateless population," https://msf.org.au/rohingya-worlds-largest-stateless-population, accessed 28 December 2022.
Merlan, Francesca. (2009). "Indigeneity global and local," *Current Anthropology*, 50(3): 303–333, https://doi.org/10.1086/597667, accessed 11 December 2022.
Mohanty, Chandra, Ann Russo, and Lourdes Torres, eds. (1991). *Third World Women and the Politics of Feminism*, Bloomington: Indiana University Press.
Morton, Micah. (2017). *Indigenous Peoples Work to Raise Their Status in Reforming Myanmar*, Perspective, No. 33, Singapore: Institute of Southeast Asian Studies.
National Democratic Party for Development. (2012). *In Respect of the Fact That the Muslim Inhabitants of Rakhine State are Natives by Race and Citizens of the Republic of the Union of Myanmar Under Law or By Natural Birth*, Yangon: NDPD.
Oppenheim, Marella. (2017). "'It only takes one terrorist': The Buddhist monk who reviles Myanmar's Muslims," *The Guardian*, 12 May, https://www.theguardian

.com/global-development/2017/may/12/only-takes-one-terrorist-buddhist-monk-reviles-myanmar-muslims-rohingya-refugees-ashin-wirathu, accessed 19 December 2022.

O'Sullivan, Dominic. (2017). "Chapter two: The politics of indigeneity," in *Indigeneity: A Politics of Potential: Australia, Fiji and New Zealand*, edited by Dominic O'Sullivan, online edition, Policy Press Scholarship, Bristol, Online, 18 January 2018), https://doi.org/10.1332/policypress/9781447339427.003.0003, accessed 11 December 2022.

Parashar, Archana and Jobair Alam. (2018). "The national laws of Myanmar: Making of statelessness for the Rohingya," *International Migration*, 57(2): 94–108, https://doi.org/10.1111/imig.12532, accessed 20 December 2022.

Parekh, Serena. (2017). *Refugees and the Ethics of Forced Displacement*, New York: Routledge.

Rahman, Mohammad Sajedur and Nurul Huda Sakib. (2021). "Statelessness, forced migration and the security dilemma along borders: An investigation of the foreign policy stance of Bangladesh on the Rohingya influx," *Springer Nature Social Sciences*, Online 30 June, https://doi.org/10.1007/s43545-021-00173-y, accessed 27 December 2022.

Rana, Sohel. (2022). "Securitization of the Rohingya refugees in Bangladesh," *Journal of Asian and African Studies*, https://doi.org/10.1177/00219096221082265, accessed 27 December 2022.

Root, Rebecca L. (2022). "Interview: Why aid groups, and Rohingya themselves, should stop using the term 'stateless'," *The New Humanitarian*, 10 November, https://www.thenewhumanitarian.org/interview/2022/11/10/Rohingya-Coxs-Bazar-Myanmar-citizenship-stateless, accessed 28 December 2022.

Rosenberg, Alex. (2018). *How History Gets Things Wrong: The Neuroscience of Our Addiction to Stories*, Cambridge: The MIT Press.

Sarkar, Jayita. (2019). "How WWII shaped the crisis in Myanmar," *Washington Post*, 10 March.

Shwe, Maung, Jessica Field and Natalie Brinham. (2021). "Failure to protect: The Denial of status, detention and refoulement of Rohingya refugees in India," Briefing Paper, Institute on Statelessness and Inclusion, August, https://files.institutesi.org/Rohingya_Refugees_in_India_Brieifing_Paper.pdf, accessed 28 December 2022.

Siddiqi, Bulbul. (2022)."Challenges and dilemmas of social cohesion between the Rohingya and host communities in Bangladesh," *Frontiers in Human Dynamics*, 1–10, 31 August, https://doi.org/10.3389/fhumd.2022.944601, accessed 10 January 2023.

Simpson, Audra. (2007). "On ethnographic refusal: Indigeneity, 'voice' and colonial citizenship," *Junctures*, 9: 67–80, https://pages.ucsd.edu/~rfrank/class_web/ES-270/SimpsonJunctures9.pdf, accessed 12 December 2022.

Tea Circle Oxford (2020). A forum for new perspectives on Burma/Myanmar, "Race in Myanmar: Rigid hierarchies, blurred boundaries and the human cost of racism," 12 November, https://teacircleoxford.com/opinion/race-in-myanmar-rigid-hierarchies-blurred-boundaries-and-the-human-cost-of-racism/, accessed 20 December 2022.

Tenenbaum, Yoav J. (2020). "Truth and history: Historical truth and historical narrative," *History News Network*, https://historynewsnetwork.org/article/174493, accessed 17 January 2023.

Thawnghmung, A. M. (2016). "The politics of indigeneity in Myanmar: Competing narratives in Rakhine state," *Asian Ethnicity*, 17(4): 527–547, https://dx.doi.org/10.1080/14631369.2016.1179096, accessed 20 December 2022.

Toha, Risa J. and Thomas B. Pepinsky. (2022). "The political construction of indigeneity: Theory and evidence from Indonesia," Draft 13 June, Posted 17 June, https://papers.ssrn.com/sol3/papers.cfm?abstract_id=4135406, accessed 11 December 2022.

Tonkin, Derek. (n.d.). "The Labyrinth of the Rohingya conundrum: 'The Burmese path to Genocide': Further thoughts on the special exhibition in the US holocaust memorial museum," https://www.networkmyanmar.org/ESW/Files/Labyrinth.pdf, accessed 22 December 2022.

Tonkin, Derek. (2018). "Chapter 8: Exploring the issue of citizenship in Rakhine state," In: *Citizenship in Myanmar: Ways of Being in and from Burma*, edited by Ashley South and Marie Lall, Cambridge: Cambridge University Press, online 28 June, https://www.cambridge.org/core/books/abs/citizenship-in-myanmar/exploring-the-issue-of-citizenship-in-rakhine-state/D944031688A081D285D388A746CA7255, accessed 22 December 2022.

Transnational Institute. (2014). *Ethnicity without Meaning: Data without Context: The 2014 Census, Identity and Citizenship in Burma/Myanmar*, Amsterdam: TNI.

Tucker, Shelby. (2001). *Burma: The Curse of Independence*, London: Pluto Press.

Uddin, Nasir. (2019). "The local translation of global indigeneity: A case of the Chittagong Hill Tracts," *Journal of Southeast Asian Studies*, 50(1): 68–85, https://doi.org/10.1017/S0022463419000067, accessed 12 December 2022.

UNICEF. (2018). "Futures in the balance: Building hope for a generation of Rohingya children," UNICEF Report, August, https://www.unicef.org/child-alert/rohingya-refugee-children-futures-in-balance?utm_campaign=rohingya-child-alert&utm_medium=referral&utm_source=media, accessed 29 December 2022.

United Nations. (n.d.). Office on genocide prevention and the responsibility to protect, "Responsibility to protect," https://www.un.org/en/genocideprevention/about-responsibility-to-protect.shtml, accessed 20 December 2022.

Wade, Francis. (2013). "The Monks who hate muslims," *Foreign Policy*, 22 April, https://foreignpolicy.com/2013/04/22/the-monks-who-hate-muslims/, accessed 19 December 2022.

Walton, Matthew J. and Susan Hayward. (2014). *Contesting Buddhist Narratives: Democratization, Nationalism, and Communal Violence in Myanmar*, Policy Studies No. 71, Honolulu: East-West Center.

Woodward, Mark. (2020). "Islam, ethnicity, nationalism, and the Burmese Rohingya crisis," *Epistemé*, 15(2): 287–314.

Worldometer. (n.d.). Myanmar population, https://www.worldometers.info/world-population/myanmar-population/, accessed 20 December 2022.

World Population Review. (2022). "Myanmar population 2022," https://worldpopulationreview.com/countries/myanmar-population, accessed 20 December 2022.

3

THE ROHINGYA REPATRIATION DISCOURSE

What Repatriation Means for the Rohingyas Living in the Refugee Camps in Bangladesh

Shahab Enam Khan

The Repatriation Complexity: Traumas and Memories

Repatriation has become a critical issue in the Rohingya discourse in Bangladesh. Rohingya refugees of Myanmar origin in Bangladesh, formally referred to as Forcibly Displaced Myanmar Nationals (FDMNs) by the Governments of Bangladesh and Myanmar [henceforth referred to as Rohingya Refugee(s)], have emerged as a critical case for understanding the changing patterns in the repatriation discourse in social science. Repatriation discourse combines the political elements with socio-economic and national security parameters and is a critical factor perpetually contributing to the making and unmaking of new political narratives in the host countries and beyond. Throughout the history of the Rohingya crisis across the border between Bangladesh and Myanmar, explaining and reviewing the deconstruction or reconstruction, or perhaps the organization or reorganization of relationships between the Rohingyas and society remains the focus for the epistemic community. The approaches to understanding the Rohingyas as refugees are primarily based on the relational intersections between state and society, security, politics, economy, and geopolitics. While the conventional geopolitical thoughts engage with political geography and regional security dilemmas, the reconfiguration of geopolitics constantly allows space to interrogate and challenge the normative understanding of negotiation among society, identity, and geopolitical existence of different actors. Hence, the state becomes a more orthodox entity that constantly has to resort to its legitimate political obligations, be it a host country or the country that persecutes, within the prism of national security or security of the state.

DOI: 10.4324/9781003771890-3

Given the competing national security conundrums, the question is how the refugees perceive and define the idea of repatriation as a solution to their crisis linked with their identity, socio-political existence, and security. Hence, the repatriation discourse includes a wide spectrum of approaches and narratives spanning from social science to human sciences. Repatriation evolves around the fundamentals of the "personal right" of the refugees to determine "return" to the country of "nationality" under "specific conditions laid down in various international instruments and human rights instruments as well as in customary international law" (International Organization for Migration 2011). International refugee law lacks any provision designed to protect any individual within their national or sovereign territory; hence, one must cross an international border to become a refugee. While the threats to life, structured persecution, and prevailing hostile political, economic, or security conditions force an individual to flee, the return or repatriation to the country of nationality becomes subject to the individual's right. Therefore, repatriation has the component of "voluntary" in it (Office of the United Nations High Commissioner for Human Rights 1950). As a result, Medecins Sans Frontieres (2022) argues, "the only protection guarantee for individuals is the fact that repatriation to their country of origin must be voluntary" (Medecins Sans Frontieres 2022).

The Convention Relating to the Status of Refugees, also known as the 1951 Refugee Convention, defines refugees as "As a result of events occurring before January 01, 1951, and owing to a well-founded fear of being persecuted for reasons of race, religion, nationality, membership of a particular social group or political opinion, is outside the country of his nationality and is unable or, owing to such fear, is unwilling to avail himself of the protection of that country; or who, not having a nationality and being outside the country of his former habitual residence as a result of such events, is unable or, owing to such fear, is unwilling to return to it" (United Nations High Commissioner for Refugees 2010). Bangladesh is not a signatory to the 1951 Refugee Convention nor its 1967 Protocol (United Nations High Commissioner for Refugees 2013). However, the UNHCR Executive Committee revisited and examined the issue of repatriation in detail under the changing global political scenarios in 1980. As a result, session XXXI obliged the United Nations High Commissioner for Refugees to ensure "the voluntary character of repatriation is respected," obtain formal guarantees for the safety of returning refugees, and monitor the situation of returning refugees to their countries of origin (United Nations High Commissioner for Refugees 1980).

However, the repatriation debate in Bangladesh becomes complicated as Bangladesh has not ratified the 1951 Refugee Convention. Nonetheless, Bangladesh continues to adhere to the principles of the 1951 Refugee Convention. Therefore, the Supreme Court of Bangladesh has potentially become a key actor in upholding the rights of the refugees. In May 2017, the High Court Division of the Supreme Court of Bangladesh delivered a judgment in favor of a Rohingya individual to return to the refugee camp under Section 14 of the Foreigners Act, 1946 (Hossain 2020, Refugee and Migratory Movements Research Unit (RMMRU) v. Government of Bangladesh 2017). The Supreme Court acknowledged that the individual might potentially "suffer persecution or torture." The honorable Court justified its decision in the RMMRU v. Government of Bangladesh case further by referring to the fact that "Bangladesh is a signatory to the 1987 Convention Against Torture," which provides that States Parties shall not "expel, return ("refouler") or extradite a person to another State where there are substantial grounds for believing that he would be in danger of being subjected to torture" (Hossain 2020). The honorable Court further noted, "Though Bangladesh has not formally ratified the Convention relation to the Status of Refugees, yet all the refugees and asylum-seekers from scores of countries of the world to other countries have been regulated by and under this Convention for more than 60 (sixty) years. This Convention by now has become a part of customary international law which is binding upon all the countries of the world irrespective of whether a particular country has formally signed, acceded to, or ratified the Convention or not" (Refugee and Migratory Movements Research Unit (RMMRU) v. Government of Bangladesh 2017). This coincides with the Constitution of Bangladesh's Article 25 that stands in support of the "rights" of the "oppressed peoples throughout the world" and Article 31 that guarantees the right to protection of the law (Ministry of Law, Justice and Parliamentary Affairs 2022).

The rights of the Rohingya as refugees are delivered by the Government of Bangladesh in the designated refugee camps through international agencies. However, the '"insecurity" syndromes and the obligations under "voluntariness" in the host country and the country of origin continue to dominate the discourse. This is mainly where the security concept diverges between the state and the refugees. That means the discourse of repatriation must be seen in a combination of what refugees think about "returning home," the host country endorses as penetration under its national and international obligations, and the international community that has its definitions and frameworks to adhere to. In most cases, repatriation is considered a process of the right to return to one's place of origin, often referred to as "migration of ethnic affinity," and an endorsement of legal, political, religious, and ethnic rights to identity (Zeveleva 2014). The "right to return," as endorsed by the international conventions on human rights and refugee laws, is determined by legal provisions and frameworks dealing with freedom of movement, the right granted to every person to relocate to the country they deem to be their home country under the principles of the Universal Declaration of Human Rights and the International Covenant on Civil and Political Rights (OHCHR 1966).

The Identity and the Passage for Return to Myanmar

The universal endorsement of the concept of "right" perpetuates the idea of shared responsibility, as codified under the 1951 Refugee Convention, recognizing that the political economy of refugee-related security and socio-economic financial burdens may become problematic for some countries in both the developed and the developing worlds. One of the critical challenges for the international community is finding a way to facilitate transformative changes in refugee discursive policies and practices in countries like Bangladesh, where "national security" is becoming blended with regional and extra-regional stability. Although Bangladesh rightfully argues that the international community should continue to be forthcoming in addressing the prolonged refugee crisis in Bangladesh, creating a conducive environment in Myanmar for voluntary repatriation of the Rohingya refugees remains subject to international political and geopolitical interests.

Such a mismatch between priorities has posed a challenge in safeguarding the human rights of refugees in camps, leading to threats to human security, human rights, and humanitarianism with implications for national and international refugee laws and policies (Otieno 2017). Moreover, the priorities accentuate the necessity to see the refugee repatriation process, or the refugee security framework, as a collective phenomenon rather than an obligation based on generosity and compliance. Rohingyas abroad, often known as the Rohingya diaspora, have been vigilantly observing the changes in Myanmar and the host countries where Rohingya refugees live. Although in the case of Bangladesh, there is an international recognition that the country has been forthcoming in accommodating the Rohingyas to find refuge and protect life from state-led persecutions, no meaningful change has taken place in Myanmar to stifle the process of expulsion of its population. This has caused the refugee situation to be protracted and prolonged.

Systemic persecution has led to the gradual expulsion of the significant Rohingyas from the state of Rakhine over the past six decades to secure a Burman majority in Myanmar. Such a process is designed to serve the political ideology of the ethnoreligious military junta backed by state-sponsored Buddhist nationalism. The Myanmar political establishment's ethnoreligious and political ideology project, a classic example of a military-ruled government with occasional interregnum power-sharing with so-called democratic entities, has converted the Rohingyas into one of the longest-suffering persecuted minority groups in international history. Such persecution has repeatedly forced the Rohingya population to flee to Bangladesh for many years, with significant spikes following political oppression and violent attacks in 1978, 1991–1992, and 2016.

However, in August 2017, the largest and fastest refugee influx into Bangladesh occurred. The August 2017 episode, identified as a "textbook example of ethnic cleansing," forced an estimated 854,704 individual Rohingyas to leave Rakhine to live in various camps in Cox's Bazar, Bangladesh (UN News 2017) (UNHCR and Government of Bangladesh 2019). Despite repeated expulsions and hostilities staged by the Myanmar government, neither of these neighboring countries, Bangladesh and Myanmar, have resorted to any cross-border confrontation nor hostility, which many scholars often feared or expected. While the fundamental national security concern around cross-border possibilities of war has largely been absent, the problem lies in the long lineage of hostile political thought that the Myanmar government continues to pursue. The inability to return to the homeland and the generation to generation transcended the "plight of refugees time and again exposed the impossibility of a political form of life outside of citizenship" (Erensu 2016). The absence of cross-border hostility automatically does not guarantee the rise of political thoughts beyond the thoughts pursued by the mainstream political actors and agencies in Bangladesh and Myanmar. However, this is precisely where insecurity converges for the state of Bangladesh, the refugees, and the international community, which is an essential part of regional geopolitics.

The lack of Rohingya identity further complicates the refugee situation, making the refugees a living testimony of the impracticality of enforcing human rights outside the camps and legal citizenship. The 1982 Burma citizenship law, enacted after the mass exodus of the Rohingyas in 1978 to Bangladesh, identified them as "resident foreigners," denying them full citizenship rights. The citizenship law paved the way for solidifying majoritarian-minoritarian racial asymmetry further to encapsulate hierarchical power for the interest of the Burman ethnic group. In addition to the lack of social recognition of the Rohingya as an ethnic identity, denial of full citizenship rights gradually emerged as a legal instrument to restrict fundamental rights for the Rohingya population over the following decades. The denial by the Myanmar state came in the forms of human rights abuses, restrictions on the freedom of movement, discriminatory limitations on access to education, and arbitrary confiscation of property (Human Rights Watch 2000). At the same time, Myanmar embarked on an "ethnocracy" that "acts as the agency of the dominant ethnic community" and needs multiple ethnic groups for "assimilation into the dominant ethnic culture" (Brown 1994).

Ethnocracy and Social Structure Dynamics in a Majoritarian Political System

Given the nature of ethnocracy, the identity of the Burmans, the largest ethnic, cultural, and linguistic group in Myanmar, covering almost two-thirds of the population, continued to retain primacy in the state machinery (Harvard Divinity School 2022). The non-Burmans retained minority presence with conditional citizenship yet remained subject to "suspicion of disloyalty."

"The Burman identity and dominance continued to be enforced through educational, political, and military systems where non-Burmans are marginalized and often demonized." (Walton 2012). The Burmanization, a term coined by James Lee Lewis in 1924 (Lewis 1924), became embedded in the socio-political structure of old Burma that transformed into a new Myanmar in the 1980s. The new Myanmar adopted its new name as the Union of Myanmar in 1989, later as the Republic of the Union of Myanmar, to create a more inclusive state system. Houtman referred to this process as "Myanmafication" with Burman characteristics (Houtman 1999).

The Burmese socio-political transformations continued to exhibit elitist attempts to construct an inclusive Myanmar based on "national culture" and "nationalism" since 1989, which essentially nationalized Burman's ideological, racial, and cultural foundations across the Myanmar territory. The ideas of "nation," "national," and "nationalism" became synonymous with the Burman identity, relegating "others" to second-string entities. International Commission of Jurists (2019) identified, "The intentionally discriminatory character of the 1982 Law, and its equally discriminatory implementation in practice, partly explains why many residents lack a legal identity (more than 25 percent, according to the 2014 Census)" (ICJ 2019). The Burman argument in favor of assimilation is that non-Burman ethnic groups can adapt and assimilate with different dimensions of the "national" ideologies and culture to create an inclusive Myanmar and "cultural nation." Furthermore, the ICJ report (2019) notes, the law effectively introduced a corresponding hierarchy of citizenship categories that effectively prescribes first-class and second-class citizens based on this framework. Members of "national races" are considered as (full) "citizens," while others, including individuals with mixed ancestry, may be eligible for "associate citizenship" or "naturalized citizenship" (ICJ 2019).

The Burman project and the hierarchical citizenry made several ethnic groups (Rohingya, Gurkha, Tamil, and Hindu speakers of Bengali dialects), many non-Burmans, life-long residents of Myanmar, and children of mixed ancestry practically stateless. The Rohingyas constitute the largest population of groups excluded in the law. The UN General Assembly in December 2019 noted: "in spite of the fact that Rohingya Muslims lived in Myanmar for generations prior to the independence of Myanmar, they were made stateless by the enactment of the 1982 Citizenship Law and were eventually disfranchised, in 2015, from the electoral process" (UN Watch Database 2020). While the Burman project continued, the military junta embarked on an ethnic cleansing process designed to protect national "security," "culture," "religion," "identity," and most importantly "unity." In addition, the project has created socio-political narratives, not limited to the Rohingyas but including the non-Burmans too, that impose the minority groups to learn the history of the Burmans more than their own. As a result, in terms of social psychology and cultural fabric, the newer generations of dominant Burmans have a lesser sense of empathy for the minoritarian ethnic groups. Inevitably, engineering history and identity under the "national interest" terms has created fragmented social psychology in which majoritarian supremacy persists as a culturally embedded phenomenon.

The complex cultural attitude toward the Rohingya is not limited to the majoritarian Burman society. It has its spillover effect on the other ethnic groups that seek to either coexist or put up armed resistance against the government of Myanmar. The term "Rohingya Muslim," interchangeably used with "Rohingya" in Myanmar's social and political discourses, exhibits a compound identity construct in which the Burmese societies do not recognize the term "Rohingya," and the term "Muslim" has politically emerged as synonymous with Islamophobia. While the government recognizes Muslims as members of the Rohingya ethnic group, under the 1982 citizenship act, around 20,000 Muslims are recognized as a race part of the Kaman – a national race category from Rakhine state (Crouch 2016, Lynn 2017). One Kaman Muslim who rose to political prominence post-1947 independence in Myanmar was Justice U Si Bu. Justice Bu sat on the trial of the assassination of General Aung San, founder of the Myanmar Armed Forces and father of the NLD leader Aung San Suu Kyi (Crouch 2016). The identity as a Muslim has been a crucial driver of the Rohingya genocide in 2017. A Justice for All Analysis for OHCHR (2020) noted, "the 2015 Race and Religion laws restricting intermarriage with Muslims were enacted because of widespread promotion of a public narrative warning of the threat of 'Islamization,' i.e., that Muslims would take over the nation, despite Muslims comprising less than five percent of the population" (Justice for All 2020). The regime propaganda targeted the systematic promotion of Islamophobia through social media and information communication tools, apart from social tools, in connivance with Buddhist nationalist groups to ensure widespread popular rejection of the Muslims associated with Rohingya identity (Justice for All 2020). Therein lies another pivotal problem – the government promotes fear of a Rohingya Muslim dominant autonomous area in Rakhine along the border of Bangladesh with or without the support of transnational non-state actors.

The perception of the Myanmar government and polity that the Rohingya Muslims are a decisive threat has further complicated the status of the Rohingya in Myanmar. The status of the Rohingya, due to such a long history of discrimination and arbitrary legal frameworks, law enforcement practices and policies, and socio-economic deprivation, most certainly alienated and marginalized this large chunk of the population from the mainstream Myanmar societies. Factors such as alienation and marginalization are deeply rooted in the Rohingya psychology and social capital, particularly in Rakhine. This has complicated their access to the social capital that modern society has to offer in Myanmar. On top of that, the inability to perform as a practical legal human resource has also complicated their access to cross-border economic resources, entitlements, and even access to asylum abroad. Moreover, they remain subject to a broad spectrum of rights-based violations and legal persecution. Due to the structural repression, one can perhaps understand that, until recently, Burmans merely displayed concern regarding the astronomical levels of violence in the Rakhine state carried out by Tatmadaw.

Tatmadaw's offensives, *viz* ultra-ethnoreligious nationalism infused military responses to the ongoing civil conflicts in Myanmar, are backed by regime propaganda that portrays ethnic resistance and armed groups as "illegitimate uncivilized terrorists seeking to jeopardize national security and development and drag the country into anarchy" (Fink 2008). Mar (2018) argued that the minority victims are

> targeted not because of their political views or activities but because they are perceived as bearers of unwelcomed attributes, such as poverty, criminality, and ill-health. It shows that many of the perpetrators of "ethnic cleansing" are state agents, often members of the National Police or paramilitary groups operating with official license and backing. Members of the business sector are also deeply mixed up in the violence.
>
> *(Mar 2018)*

That means the armed resistance of non-Burman ethnic groups has become convenient scapegoats for Myanmar's perennial underdevelopment and continuous militarization.

Socio-politically Embedded Structure of Alienation and Marginalization

The militarization of Myanmar manifests apparent differences between Burmans' socio-economic and political position and non-Burmans across the country. The international community exhaustively documented the effects of militarization and marginalization in Rakhine. The Report of the Advisory Commission on Rakhine State, known as the Kofi Annan Report, noted:

> *In general, the government should ensure freedom of movement for all people in Rakhine State, irrespective of religion, ethnicity, or citizenship status. The freedom of movement and access to services are deeply interlinked and, therefore, should be addressed in parallel. All communities should have access to education, health, livelihood opportunities, and basic services.*
>
> *(Advisory Commission on Rakhine State 2017)*

The Report further noted, "*Although Rakhine is rich in natural resources, the development of extractive industries – such as oil and gas-related investments in Kyaukpyu – have not generated a significant number of new jobs nor other benefits for local residents. Both Rakhine and Muslim communities feel marginalised and disempowered by decisions taken in Naypyitaw"* (Advisory Commission on Rakhine State 2017).

The independent international fact-finding mission report on Myanmar identified that *'Since reforms began in 2011, Myanmar has seen an increase in Buddhist nationalism, virulent anti-Muslim rhetoric and violence between Buddhists and Muslims'* (United Nations Human Rights Council 2018). The Report further noted that

> *A campaign of hate and dehumanisation of the Rohingya had been underway for months, and escalated after June 08 2012, led by the Rakhine Nationalities Development Party (RNDP), various Rakhine organisations, radical Buddhist monk organisations, and several officials and influential figures. In November 2012, the RNDP, in Toe Thet Yay, an official publication, cited Hitler, arguing that "inhuman acts" were sometimes necessary to "maintain a race."*
>
> *(United Nations Human Rights Council 2018)*

The International Court of Justice (ICJ) gave a ruling in favor of the Gambia v. Myanmar case, filed under Article 9 of the Convention on the Prevention and Punishment of the Crime of Genocide, in November 2019, backed by the Organisation for Islamic Cooperation (OIC). Article 9 empowers a country to file a case "relating to the responsibility of a State for genocide" and related acts (UNOGPRP 1951). The case alleged that atrocities against the Rohingya ethnic community in Rakhine, Myanmar, carried out by the Myanmar government and Tatmadaw, have gravely violated various provisions of the genocide convention. In December 2019, ICJ unanimously agreed to Gambia's request for provisional measures against Myanmar to protect the Rohingya living in Myanmar (Human Rights Watch 2022).

On November 17, 2021, the UN General Assembly Third Committee adopted a Resolution on the "*Situation of human rights of Rohingya Muslims and other minorities in Myanmar*," jointly placed by the European Union (EU) and OIC (Europa.eu 2021). The consensual adoption of this resolution is a strong endorsement of evidence of violence and abuse by Tatmadaw and a strong condemnation of the socio-political silence regarding the persecution of the non-Burman population. On February 1, 2021, Tatmadaw staged a coup to overthrow the democratically elected Aung San Suu Kyi's National League for Democracy (NLD)-led government. Once again, the military formally took over the power in Myanmar and reinstated itself as the absolute authority. In a twist of political cavalry, Suu Kyi, who once led Myanmar in ICJ to defend its government's acts against the Rohingya, came under arrest by the military. In April 2021, the government defectors and the ousted elected representatives, representatives from various ethnic minority groups, and several civil society activists formed the National Unity Government (NUG) as a parallel administration. Though reluctant during its formation phase, NUG has issued "a plan to end discrimination against the Rohingya and replace the 1982 Citizenship Law" (Frontier Myanmar 2021). However, the plan received cold responses as NUG failed to include any Rohingya representative in its administration, and the Rohingya leaders were not consulted before the plan's release. Moreover, the fluid relations between the dominant Rakhine armed groups, such as the Arakan Army, and the parallel government NUG, continue to pressure the Rohingya community regarding choosing a political side for security guarantees.

Structural Dilemmas in the Repatriation Decision-Making among the Rohingyas

The competing issues ranging from identity to security guarantees have complex implications for refugees' decision-making about whether to repatriate or remain in exile (Omata 2013). The refugee policies and narratives often argue that for refugees or, in that matter, forced migrants and displaced people, violence, genocide, ethnic cleansing, or political persecution were the elemental causes for fleeing. However, a simple reversal of the threats to physical safety is not a sufficient reason to go back to the country of origin (Monsutti 2008). The existing literature on repatriation aptly indicates that the nature of return and perception of "home" and "homeland" are contingent upon structural conditions in which physical safety and rights are two aspects (Omata 2013, Stefansson 2004, Hammond 2004, Black and Koser 1999). That means the repatriation process has to be seen beyond the prism of physical safety or, in that matter, voluntariness. A stringent refugee policy by national and international regimes will undoubtedly add to the complexity of making repatriation and return decisions. Based on the prejudiced cultural structure and the Burman projects, the question of information about the future has more tremendous implications in the repatriation decisions for Rohingya in Bangladesh. This creates a precarious Prisoner's Dilemma trap in choosing options for repatriation. Hence, the decision to return or stay is primarily linked to practical considerations, future chances of survival, and dignified existence in Bangladesh and Myanmar.

During exile, one must note that the Rohingyas living in the camps in Bangladesh continue to struggle to meet their needs, be it mental or physical, to create a meaningful life based on two critical factors such as the social contract with the host community and kinship-based society within the camps. Such social contract and formation processes make the Rohingya community a homogeneous political entity negotiating with the states on both sides of the border. This homogeneity is considered a prime threat by Tatmadaw. At the same time, the demonization of the Rohingya can always be counterproductive for the host community. The crux of the problem lies in the absence of Rohingya leadership that can politically negotiate with Tatmadaw and continue to keep the homogeneity preserved in the interest of repatriation. The assassination of Mohibullah, a Rohingya human rights activist and leader, on September 29, 2021, in his office at the world's largest refugee camp in Kutupalong, Cox's Bazar, Bangladesh, attests to the fact that the elimination of a unifying voice serves the purpose of creating fear among the Rohingyas willing to raise their voice in favor of repatriation.

In the case of bilateral efforts for repatriation, Myanmar repeatedly delays the talks and joint verification process. Hassan (2021) noted, "the repatriation of Rohingyas had been put on the back burner partly because of Myanmar's unwillingness to take back the Rohingya refugees" (Hassan 2021). The international community has supported running the camps and beyond. However, the colossal cost of maintaining the camps in a densely populated country like Bangladesh has to be calculated in line with environmental, social, and political costs. So far, approximately 34% of the $1 billion required to sustain the refugee camps in Bangladesh has been disbursed to the government and humanitarian aid agencies (Hassan 2021). Here again, the notion of "shared responsibility," as laid under international covenants, becomes a challenging factor for the Government of Bangladesh and the Rohingya community. The possibilities of third-country resettlement or even regular migration appear to be a non-practical and non-attainable solution for all the agencies creating a framework for repatriation. Of course, to minimize the "pressures" on public health and environmental risks, the government undertook a project to relocate 100,000 to an island called Bhashan Char (Islam and Siddika 2021). The fact is that 854,704 Rohingyas from 187,530 families, each with an average of 4.6 family members, most of whom live in a single room per family, can be seen as a looming public health concern and hotspots for the crisis of access to entitlement. One should note that camps present a staggeringly high population density of 40,000 people per square kilometer (Khan 2021).

As a result, the complexity embedded in a refugee's cognitive and social decision-making processes favoring repatriation or migration denotes the urgency of revisiting the generalized and simplistic perceptions of repatriation. A decision to return can only be influenced by taking the refugee's current state of identity and existence in the host country and the perception of the country of origin. This will require creating a conducive environment within the camps for the Rohingya community to identify and nominate a unifying leadership to address the Prisoner's Dilemma syndrome regarding repatriation. In addition, repatriation is better understood as an offshoot of social and community decisions, not as a result of individual decisions based on economic, social, cultural, or political indicators (Omata 2013). Perhaps it is an interplay of all these indicators shaping the day-to-day narratives in the refugee camps. However, in the context of statist narratives, the critical interaction between the process of return migration and the motivations that would inspire a refugee to return is often missing. Hear (2003) observed, "refugees' motivations and expectations often become transmuted into betterment during the period of exile" (Hear 2003). Moreover, it is natural that new priorities and aspirations for a better future will gain cognitive momentum among the refugees. Henceforth, skills building and equipping them with new knowledge are the practical solutions to address the natural necessities, both cognitive and biological. In that case, one must also note that Bangladesh's growth trajectories and political economy will have profound implications for decision-making.

Conclusion: Rethinking the Idea That Is Rohingya

As explained above, the term "Rohingya" has become complicated when one sees this particular group from multiple spectra – politically stateless, socially marginalized, economically uncertain, and at an individual level deprived. At the bilateral level between Bangladesh and Myanmar, Rohingya are subject to one typical objectivity – national security. In the regional context, the Rohingya is a geopolitical entity that sits between the great power rivalries between the Chinese and the US blocs. In the global context, this identity is subject to international aid and humanitarian assistance; sustainability of that remains effectively uncertain. Henceforth, a decision to repatriate or not is contingent upon circumstantial livelihood, the political future, sustainability in the refugee camps, the memories and traumas, and of course, the ability to assimilate with the Burman majoritarian republic. Security, as well as the aspiration to live dignifiedly, would require de-securitization of the idea that is Rohingya. It reminds a classic note from Considine (2017), "While the Israeli occupation continues to stir up feelings of anger and powerlessness, another ethnic group – the Rohingya – is now emerging as the symbol of global injustice for Muslims," and Lall noted, "the Rohingya are acquiring a status so far only given to the Palestinians" (Considine 2017, Lall 2017).

While a number of the literature suggests that reforming the citizenship law may create an enabling environment for repatriation, it does not guarantee greater inclusion of non-Burman representation, precisely the Muslims and the Rohingya, in the political decision-making process in Myanmar. As seen earlier in this article, the repatriation process is a complex idea that links socio-psychological phenomena with political realities. For example, a child who was five years old during the exodus in 2017 is now a ten-year-old kid in 2022. By 2027, he will be fifteen, with a high possibility of becoming a youth with an uncertain future. For that child, the political realities will be more challenging than those of his/her ancestors. The point here is the rise of a new generation of Rohingyas with a less faint memory of Rakhine. This is what the state would perceive as a new challenge to deal with and, for Myanmar, an advantage to the extent that identity verification of these children will become problematic. That means the Government of Bangladesh will eventually have to think about a newer approach to ensure the rights of the older and the newer Rohingya population in Bangladesh. What is critical for the government is to ensure four pathways for the Rohingyas:

1. A Rohingya Civil Society: A Rohingya civil society is a crucial option for the government to consider. This is primarily to build the capacity of the Rohingyas to negotiate peacefully and politically with various actors, including Tatmadaw and NUG. In addition, it is a conflict of identity between the Burman majority and the Rohingyas.
2. Strengthening of a Civil Society in Rakhine State: Indeed, this will be a challenging task for the government, but the global community recognizes the absence of a meaningful Rakhine civil society to promote peace and stability between the ethnoreligious nationalist groups and the conflicting armed rebels struggling to gain a political foothold in Rakhine. A Buddhist-Muslim civil society can reshape the identity narratives required for the Rohingyas to reconsider repatriation to Rakhine.
3. Capacity Building of the Rohingya and Rakhine Diasporas: Diaspora plays a critical role in reshaping the repatriation narratives. This is a critical area to consider by the political and diplomatic stakeholders. The capacity building of various diasporas from Rakhine is necessary to deal with the changing geopolitical and geostrategic changes in and around Rakhine.
4. Rohingya Archive of History and Identity: Documentation and the archival platform are required to let people access the history of Rakhine and the Rohingya narratives. The archives will remind the international community about the memory and identity of the Rohingyas and provide future directions to the coming generations to reshape, reinterpret, and reinvent the modalities of their engagement with the state of Myanmar.

As an alternative to the mainstream political structure, armed groups such as the Arakan Army or the parallel government, i.e., NUG, provide meaningful solutions to the Rohingya problem if they acquire legitimacy. This is a diplomatic and political capital that the Rohingyas may need to realize. The purpose of this article by no means has been to identify the Burmans as a prejudiced entity or chauvinist state actors (that would be a generalized assumption) or to actively vilify any particular racial group; instead, it is to highlight the perils of ethnonationalism and ultra-rightist nationalism dominating the Burmese power relations. As a subset, the Tatmadaw-led national security and national unity projects encounter insidious impediments. That means the racial privilege theory is not necessarily applicable to all the individuals in a majoritarian race; instead, it means that the historical construction of racial identities and their institutionalization in contemporary power structures have detrimental effects on national, regional, and international regimes (Walton 2012).

Finally, in the context of Rohingya refugees, the repatriation discourse must be seen as a struggle of the minorities living in the socio-political periphery of Myanmar. Of course, the Rohingya have been involved in armed struggle against the regime since before independence, compelled by the Second World War politics and the military's ambition for a post-independence ultra-right republic, which has created a nationwide perception of disloyalty. As a result, unless there is a change in Burman perception of the Rohingya, the repatriation process may continue to remain protracted. Hence the solution lies within the Rohingya and the state of Myanmar, while the international community must embrace the realities of the transnationalization of the refugee status. The regimental ethnoreligious ideology and the repeated attempts to create a uniform identity by the Myanmar government have a deep presence in Myanmar's socio-political ecosystem. The complex ethnic and religious configurations of the Rohingya and the other ethnic and racial groups in Myanmar have failed to demonstrate an overarching Burmese or Myanmar identity, which in turn has perpetuated civil conflicts between this state of Myanmar and the armed groups, e.g., Arakan Army, Chin National Defense Force, Kachin Independence Army, Karen National Defense Organization, Shan State Army, United Wa State Army to name.

That means social scientists must take new standto make sense of the emerging patterns and perceptions regarding repatriation in which strengthening the capacity to negotiate with the state and state identities both in world politics and on the level of society need to be factored in. How the Rohingya will march it themselves or respond to narratives of nationalizing identity will determine the repatriation process in the coming decades. The new repatriation discourse should be seen as an interplay between repatriation, negotiation skills to deal with the state and agencies, and perceptions regarding refugee identity. In the case of the Rohingya, creating identity, given the perennial deprivation and oppression, has become a situated process rather than solely a narrative process based on the securitization of identity and entitlement. However, Bangladeshi or international institutions have profound effects and implications on how refugees are identified, how their access to protection is governed, and how they see their lives in Myanmar that continue to thrive despite the competing geopolitical pressures.

References

Advisory Commission on Rakhine State. 2017. *Report of the Advisory Commission on Rakhine State*. Yangon and Geneva: Advisory Commission on Rakhine State. Accessed December 12, 2019. http://www.rakhinecommission.org/app/uploads/2017/08/FinalReport_Eng.pdf.

Black, R., and K. Koser. 1999. "The End of the Refugee Cycle?" In *The End of the Refugee Cycle?*, edited by R. Black and K. Kosher, 2–17. Berghahn: Oxford University Press.

Brown, D. 1994. *The State and Ethnic Politics in Southeast Asia*. London: Routledge.

Considine, Craig. 2017. "The Rohingya Are the New Palestinians." *Foreign Policy*, September 26: Online.

Crouch, Melissa. 2016. "Myanmar's Muslim Mosaic and the Politics of Belonging." In *Islam and the State in Myanmar: Muslim-Buddhist Relations and the Politics of Belonging*, edited by Melissa Crouch, 9–39. New Delhi: Oxford University Press.

Erensu, Asli Ikizoglu. 2016. "Notes from a Refugee Protest: Ambivalences of Resisting and Desiring Citizenship." *Citizenship Studies* 20 (5): 664–677.

Europa.eu. 2021. UN General Assembly: EU and OIC join forces to denounce the human rights situation in Myanmar, with a focus on Rohingya. November 17. Accessed March 5, 2022. https://eeas.europa.eu/delegations/un-new-york/107440/un-general-assembly-eu-and-oic-join-forces-denounce-human-rights-situation-myanmar-focus_en.

Fink, C. 2008. "Militarization in Burma's Ethnic States: Causes and Consequences." *Contemporary Politics* 14 (4): 447–462.

Frontier Myanmar. 2021. *The NUG's Rohingya Policy: 'Campaign Statement' or Genuine Reform?* July 15. Accessed February 12, 2022. https://www.frontiermyanmar.net/en/the-nugs-rohingya-policy-campaign-statement-or-genuine-reform/.

Hammond, L. 2004. *This Place Will Become Home*. Ithaca: Cornell University Press.

Harvard Divinity School. 2022. "Burmans." *Religion and Public Life*. March 01. Accessed March 01, 2022. https://rpl.hds.harvard.edu/faq/burmans#:~:text=Burmans%20(also%20known%20as%20Bamar,Irrawady%20Basin%20and%20speak%20Burmese.

Hassan, Asif Muztaba. 2021. *Why Is the World Ignoring Repatriation of Rohingya Refugees?* October 25. Accessed October 26, 2021. https://thediplomat.com/2021/10/why-is-the-world-ignoring-repatriation-of-rohingya-refugees/.

Hear, N. Van. 2003. *From Durable Solutions to Transnational Relations: Home and Exile among Refugee Diasporas*. New Issues in Refugee Research, Geneva: UNHCR.

Hossain, M Sanjeeb. 2020. "Bangladesh's Judicial Encounter with the 1951 Refugee Convention." *Forced Migration Review* Online. Accessed March 9, 2022. https://www.fmreview.org/issue67/hossain.

Houtman, G. 1999. *Mental Culture in Burmese Crisis Politics: Aung San Suu Kyi and the National League for Democracy*. Tokyo: Institute for the Study of Languages and Cultures of Asia and Africa, Tokyo University of Foreign Studies.

Human Rights Watch. 2000. "Burma/Bangladesh: Burmese Refugees in Bangladesh: Still No Durable Solution." *HRW* (Human Rights Watch) 12 (3C): Online. Accessed March 1, 2022. https://www.hrw.org/reports/2000/burma/index.htm.

Human Rights Watch. 2022. "Developments in Gambia's Case Against Myanmar at the International Court of Justice." *Questions and Answers*. February 14. Accessed February 15, 2022. https://www.hrw.org/news/2022/02/14/developments-gambias-case-against-myanmar-international-court-justice.

ICJ. 2019. *Citizenship and Human Rights in Myanmar: Why Law Reform Is Urgent and Possible: A Legal Briefing*. Geneva: International Commission of Jurists.

International Organization for Migration. 2011. *Glossary on Migration*. Geneva: International Organization for Migration (IOM). Accessed March 1, 2022. https://publications.iom.int/system/files/pdf/iml25_1.pdf.

Islam, Didarul, and Ayesha Siddika. 2021. "Implications of the Rohingya Relocation from Cox's Bazar to Bhasan Char, Bangladesh." *International Migration Review* Open Access. Accessed March 9, 2022. https://journals.sagepub.com/doi/full/10.1177/01979183211064829#:~:text=In%20the%20face%20of%20these,Baldwin%2C%20and%20Marshall%202018.

Justice for All. 2020. *Islamophobia in Three Asian Contexts: India, Myanmar and China: Justice for All Analysis for OHCHR*. Chicago: Justice for All. Accessed March 7, 2022. https://www.ohchr.org/Documents/Issues/Religion/Islamophobia-AntiMuslim/Civil%20Society%20or%20Individuals/JusticeForAll.pdf.

Khan, Shahab Enam. 2021. "Is Bhashan Char Really the Answer to the Rohingya Crisis?" *The Daily Star*. October 14. Accessed October 14, 2021. https://www.thedailystar.net/daily-star-books/news/bhashan-char-really-the-answer-the-rohingya-crisis-2198106.

Lall, Rashmee Roshan. 2017. *Are the Rohingyas the New Palestinians?* September 17. Accessed August 30, 2022. https://www.thearabweekly.com/are-rohingyas-new-palestinians.

Lewis, James Lee. 1924. "The Burmanization of the Karen People: A Study in Racial Adaptability." Doctoral Dissertation. University of Chicago, Illinois, USA.

Lynn, Kyaw Ye. 2017. *Myanmar's Kaman Muslims Face No Option But Relocation*. April 28. Accessed June 11, 2019. https://www.aa.com.tr/en/asia-pacific/myanmars-kaman-muslims-face-no-option-but-relocation/807343#:~:text=There%20are%20believed%20to%20be,and%20Kyauk%20Phyu%20before%202012.

Mar, Tin Cho. 2018. "Applying Social Psychology: From Problem to Solution on Myanmar Community Conflicts." *International Journal of Innovative Research in Engineering & Multidisciplinary Physical Sciences* 6 (5): Online. Accessed February 12, 2022. https://www.ijirmps.org/research-paper.php?id=285.

Medecins Sans Frontieres. 2022. *The Practical Guide to Humanitarian Law*. Online. https://guide-humanitarian-law.org/content/article/3/repatriation/.

Ministry of Law, Justice and Parliamentary Affairs. 2022. "The Constitution of the People's Republic of Bangladesh." *The Constitution of 1972 to P. O. No. 76 of 1972*. March 9. Accessed March 9, 2022. http://bdlaws.minlaw.gov.bd/act-367.html.

Monsutti, A. 2008. "Afghan Migratory Strategies and the Three Solutions to the Refugee Problem." *Refugee Survey Quarterly* 27 (1): 58–73.

Office of the United Nations High Commissioner for Human Rights. 1950. *Convention Relating to the Status of Refugees*. December 14. Accessed February 11, 2022. https://www.ohchr.org/Documents/ProfessionalInterest/refugees.pdf.

OHCHR. 1966. "The International Covenant on Civil and Political Rights." *OHCHR*. December 16. Accessed March 1, 2022. https://2covenants.ohchr.org/About-ICCPR.html.

Omata, Naohiko. 2013. "The Complexity of Refugees' Return Decision-Making in a Protracted Exile: Beyond the Home-Coming Model and Durable Solutions." *Journal of Ethnic and Migration Studies* 39 (8): 1281–1297.

Otieno, Alex. 2017. "Transforming Refugee Discursive Practices." *Peace Review* 29 (1): 76–84.

Refugee and Migratory Movements Research Unit (RMMRU) v. Government of Bangladesh. 2017. Writ petition no. 10504 of 2016 (High Court Division, The

Supreme Court of Bangladesh, May 31). Accessed March 9, 2022. https://www.refworld.org/cases,BAN_SC,5d7f623e4.html.

Stefansson, A. 2004. "Returns to Sarajevo and Contemporary Narratives of Mobility." In *Coming Home?*, edited by D. L. Oxfeld and E. Long, 170–186. Philadelphia: University of Pennsylvania Press.

UNHCR and Government of Bangladesh. 2019. *Joint Government of Bangladesh – UNHCR Population Factsheet. As of December 31, 2019*. Government of Bangladesh and UNHCR.

United Nations High Commissioner for Refugees. 1980. "Voluntary Repatriation." *Voluntary Repatriation, No. 18 (XXXI) – 1980*. Geneva: UNHCR. Online. Accessed March 2, 2022. https://www.unhcr.org/excom/exconc/3ae68c6e8/voluntary-repatriation.html.

United Nations High Commissioner for Refugees. 2010. *Text of the 1951 Convention Relating to the Status of Refugees*. Geneva: UNHCR. Accessed January 2, 2022. https://www.unhcr.org/3b66c2aa10.

United Nations High Commissioner for Refugees. 2013. *Bangladesh*. Accessed January 11, 2022. https://www.unhcr.org/4ec231060.pdf.

United Nations Human Rights Council. 2018. *Report of the Independent International Fact-Finding Mission*. Geneva: United Nations Human Rights Council, 11 02. Accessed September 11, 2019. https://www.ohchr.org/Documents/HRBodies/HRCouncil/FFM-Myanmar/A_HRC_39_64.pdf.

UN News. 2017. "UN Human Rights Chief Points to 'Textbook Example of Ethnic Cleansing' in Myanmar." *UN News: Global Perspective Human stories*. September 11. Accessed March 2, 2022. https://news.un.org/en/story/2017/09/564622-un-human-rights-chief-points-textbook-example-ethnic-cleansing-myanmar.

UNOGPRP. 1951. "Convention on the Prevention and Punishment of the Crime of Genocide 1951." *United NationsOffice on Genocide Prevention and the Responsibility to Protect*. January 12. Accessed March 2, 2022. https://www.un.org/en/genocideprevention/documents/atrocity-crimes/Doc.1_Convention%20on%20the%20Prevention%20and%20Punishment%20of%20the%20Crime%20of%20Genocide.pdf.

UN Watch Database. 2020. *Situation of human rights of Rohingya Muslims and other minorities in Myanmar*. Session 75 (UN General Assembly, New York 2020). Accessed March 1, 2022. https://unwatch.org/database/resoltions/a-res-75-238/.

Walton, Matthew J. 2012. "The "Wages of Burman-ness:" Ethnicity and Burman Privilege in Contemporary Myanmar." *Journal of Contemporary Asia* 43 (1): 1–27.

Zeveleva, Olga. 2014. "Political Aspects of Repatriation: Germany, Russia, Kazakhstan. A Comparative Analysis." *Nationalities Papers: The Journal of Nationalism and Ethnicity* 42 (5): 808–827.

4

THE WANTON STRIPPING OF NATIONALITY AND INTERNATIONAL LAW

Exploring the Genesis of Atrocities Against the Rohingyas

Md. Rizwanul Islam

Introduction

The atrocities perpetrated on the Rohingya were neither coincidental nor the result of a sudden spike in propaganda spread against them across both social and mainstream media. While the latter may reflect a symptom of the problem, the real cause has a longer root in the past, specifically in the Citizenship Law of 1982. This chapter argues that to render justice for the atrocities committed against the Rohingyas in Myanmar, one must go back in history and examine the capricious stripping of the Myanmar nationality of the Rohingyas by the Citizenship Law of 1982. Additionally, it argues that the dogmatic insistence on treating nationality exclusively within the realm of national law is incompatible with the ethos of modern international law, where the *domaine réservé* of states is shrinking.

While the chapter is intrinsically linked to the main theme of the book, as the issue of citizenship[1] of the Rohingya may be connected to the question of their safe and dignified repatriation, its findings should also appeal to a broader audience. This is because the analysis of the legal issues in this chapter is not exclusive to the condition of Rohingyas. Their plight is but one example of authoritarian or majoritarian regimes toying with the identity of the minority. If such mala fide stripping of nationality of a minority group cannot be regulated by international law, then this could not only set a bad example for minority communities in various parts of the world, but the displacement of minorities would also destabilise regional peace and international security. This is evident from the fact that a very high proportion of people who are rendered stateless by the wanton antics of states happen to be ethnic minorities. Unlike refugees, who at least fall under international

DOI: 10.4324/9781003771890-4

refugee law and may receive some protection, stateless people, however, "belong nowhere" and are denied basic human rights. Furthermore, refugees may have hope of one day returning to their homeland when the reason for their persecution dissipates due to, say, a regime change or any other political alterations. But for the "stateless" there is no homeland to return to, and that therefore can cause much greater desperation and hopelessness. Also, a person may, for various reasons such as by taking up the nationality of another state, by marriage, lack of birth registration etc. lose the nationality of a state (Sahni, 2021), that phenomenon is nonetheless beyond the scope of the chapter.

The Evolution of International Legal Obligations

In the early 20th century, nationality was almost exclusively within the realm of municipal law. The perception of municipal law's exclusive authority to deal with questions of nationality was manifest in the Permanent Court of International Justice's holding in *Nationality Decrees in Tunis and Morocco (French Zone)* that "in the present state of international law, questions of nationality are, in the opinion of the Court, in principle within this reserved domain" (para. 40). However, the ICJ in *Nottebohm* implied that states might not enjoy unbridled freedom in regulating the nationality of persons (Nottebohm, 1955). The reliance on *Nottebohm* has to be taken with a caveat, as in that case, more than one state wanted to invoke their right over their national. *Nottebohm* was not dealing with the situation of stripping off or the loss of nationality.

There are some international legal instruments that (to varying degrees) deal with statelessness. However, a review of the international legal instruments and the judicial precedents demonstrates that it is a law of patchwork. The first question that arises is how international law defines statelessness. Under Article 1 of the *Convention relating to the Status of Stateless Persons, 1954*, "a person who is not considered as a national by any State under the operation of its law" is a stateless person. On the other hand, a person is not treated as a refugee unless that person is outside the country of the person's nationality or habitual residence (Refugee Convention, Article 1A). Thus, under international law, within her/his usual place of residence, a person may be stateless, but a person is not a refugee unless she/he moves beyond borders. At the outset, such a distinction appears somewhat problematic, since individuals rendered stateless within the border of a state where they have habitually resided may receive disproportionately less attention from the international community than those living as refugees in another state, thereby creating a direct concern for the latter.

The origin of international law on the question of statelessness also indicates a complex and reluctant origin. It was the mass deprivation of their nationals branded as enemies by the Bolshevik regime of the USSR that gave impetus to the question of dealing with statelessness (Siegelberg, 2020, at 45–46). For several years, many of the Westerners did not recognise the communist government of the USSR, and thus, the response to many Russians losing USSR nationality and becoming stateless was not apparently based on any legal or humane motivation to address the problem of statelessness. Hence, even the advent of the Nansen passport, issued mainly for stateless Russians, was a mere aberration rather than the norm.[2] And it did not in any way deal with the root cause of the problem, which is Russians losing their nationality by the operation of the new Russian regime's laws.

However, the two legal instruments that followed: the 1930 Hague Conference for the Codification of International Law, which adopted a Convention on Certain Questions Relating to the Conflict of Nationality Laws and a Protocol Relating to a Certain Case of Statelessness, did not go far enough (Hudson, 1930). Their emphasis was on the loss of citizenship at birth, and there was hardly anything about subsequent loss by the deliberate act of states (Weis, 1962). The limited approach of the state parties to the Hague Diplomatic Conference would be evident from what was proposed but did not find a place in the Convention. They did not accept a proposal by Harvard Research in International Law that the nationality of one country should not be lost without acquiring the nationality of another (Kuhn, 1936). A narrower proposal that stateless persons should be admitted to the territory of the state to which they previously belonged upon request of the state of current residence also failed to sway the state parties (Kuhn, 1936). Thus, it was abundantly clear that the interest in the stability of international relations had primacy (Bauer, 2014). The Preamble to the *Hague Convention on Nationality*, 1930, made it aptly evident by stating that, "it is in the general interest of the international community to secure that all its members should recognize that *every person should have a nationality* and should have *one nationality*" (emphasis added). The interest is clearly that of states, *not* of individuals, and it is precisely in state interests that some limitations began to emerge on the sovereign competence of the state to determine who should be recognised as its nationals.

Article 15(1) of the *Universal Declaration of Human Rights* (UDHR), 1948 provides that every person has the right to possess a nationality. However, the unequivocal pronouncement does not appear to impose any direct legal obligation on states, as it merely proclaims a right without imposing any direct obligation on anyone. Article 15(2) in a bit more direct terms states that "[n]o one shall be arbitrarily deprived of his nationality nor denied the right to change his nationality". It, of course, does not even go far enough to say anything about whose nationality a person is entitled to or how one would be entitled to such nationality and what the remedies of arbitrary deprivation of statelessness would be. While the pronouncement of the aspiration of the international community in the founding years of the

United Nations (UN)[3] and the very frequent reference to the UDHR carry significant weight, there is no direct authority to say that every provision of the UDHR embodies customary international law. It was the understanding of the UN members that the UDHR was merely declaring human rights and operationalising them would take place through later covenants (Moyn, 2012). Indeed, if the broad aspirations were self-enforcing, the substantive provisions of the *International Covenant on Civil and Political Rights*, 1966, and the *International Covenant on Economic, Social and Cultural Rights*, 1966, as well as other human rights treaties, could have been mere duplications. And the United Nations High Commissioner for Refugees (UNHCR) further clarifies that there has been a subsequent treaty which has given effect to Article 15 of the UDHR (UNHCR's Introductory Note), which further fortifies the assumption that Article 15 only manifested an aspiration of the international community and did not create an enforceable legal obligation. In addition to the UDHR, there are also some resolutions of the United Nations General Assembly and United Nations Human Rights Council proscribing the arbitrary deprivation of nationality and thereby rendering people stateless . While they may be commendable aspirations of the international community and may form part of the corpus of state practice, they alone cannot create legal obligations unless they are backed up by *opinio juris* or legal necessity (The Lotus Case, 1927).

Perhaps the most direct pronouncement of the international treaty obligation on statelessness is the *Convention on the Reduction of Statelessness*, 1961 (Statelessness Convention). As the title denotes, it only seeks to reduce (*not eliminate*) statelessness. It is essential to note that the idea of a Convention on the Elimination of Future Statelessness failed to gain sufficient traction among states and was ultimately abandoned. Of particular relevance for this chapter is Article 9 of the Statelessness Convention that categorically states "[a] Contracting State may not deprive any person or group of persons of their nationality on racial, ethnic, religious or political grounds." It is important to note that, unlike the strong assertion in UDHR, the comparable provision in ICCPR is narrow in its scope as it is limited to a pronouncement in Article 24(3) that "[e]very child has the right to acquire a nationality".

Forced denationalisation of citizens that renders people stateless violates the Rohingya's right to nationality (or, for that matter, any minority group) and may arguably, in some circumstances, be contrary to norms under customary international law. It is only in the context of the regional Courts that have dealt with the wanton stripping of nationality. For instance, in *Anudo v. Tanzania*, the African Court on Human and Peoples' Rights issued a decision that the right to nationality as set forth by the *UDHR* was a part of customary international law. The Court observed that "the power to deprive a person of his or her nationality has to be exercised in accordance with international standards, to avoid the risk of statelessness" (para. 78). It accepted that in very exceptional circumstances, a state may denationalise a *person* provided certain strict conditions are met. Basing its holding on a report of the Secretary-General of the Human Rights Council, it observed that in extremely rare cases, subject to fulfilling certain conditions, the decision is based on a clear legal basis, serves a legitimate purpose that conforms with international law, is proportionate to the interest protected, and has set up some procedural safeguards allowing the concerned individual to legally question it before an independent body (para. 79).

The African Commission on Human and Peoples' Rights, in turn, has found that Article 5 of the 1981 Charter, which deals with dignity and recognition as a person before the law, includes the right to nationality, even though nationality is not formally mentioned in the Charter. This observation was based on a complaint that the Nubian community of Kenya, who were mainly conscripted by the British during the colonial era, whose ancestors had lived there since the early part of the 20th century, were denied identity papers or faced procedural challenges not faced by other Kenyans. The Commission accepted that in matters of nationality, the state has discretionary powers, but it observed that such "discretion is limited by its obligations to prevent statelessness and the prohibition of discrimination" (para. 145). Reiterating the provision of the Statelessness Convention that a state "shall not deprive a person of his nationality if such deprivation would mean that the concerned person has become stateless", the Commission accepted that Kenya is not a party to the Convention but observed that it has been a part of the corpus of customary international law (para. 146). It concluded that Kenya has failed to respect its obligation to prevent statelessness because its arbitrary administrative practices affect the ability of Nubians to obtain ID cards, meaning that many of them do not enjoy the protection of the Kenyan legal system and become stateless (para. 148).

In Europe, in *Kurić v Slovenia* the Grand Chamber of the European Court of Human Rights (ECHR) held that Slovenia is legally obliged to pay many people "erased" from the list of permanent residents after the country's separation from Yugoslavia (Kurić v Slovenia, paras. 259–70, 339–62). It is considered evidence submitted by UNHCR that this disproportionately affected vulnerable groups and particularly minorities, and interfered with their family lives. Arguably, the Court could do it because it had in its armour Article 8 of the European Convention on Human Rights, providing that:

1. Everyone has the right to respect for his private and family life, his home and his correspondence.
2. There shall be no interference by a public authority with the exercise of this right except such as is in accordance with the law and is necessary in a democratic society.

Thus, clearly, the above provision, though resorted to by the Court in giving remedy to prevent statelessness, arguably, if statelessness occurs on such a massive scale that a full group of people are rendered stateless, that may remain beyond the scope of the provision. More importantly, the applicability of the provision is only to those states that are parties to the ECHR. And a similar broad pronouncement is absent in general international law. In *Yean and Bosico Children v The Dominican Republic*, the Inter-American Court of Human Rights has ruled that the Dominican Republic's attempt to deny citizenship to Dominicans of Haitian ancestry was in breach of several rights guaranteed by the *American Convention on Human Rights*.

However, the above cases are quite fact-specific and depend to a substantial degree on the national and regional laws in force, and thus, treating them as amounting to customary international law is somewhat challenging (Jain, 2022). Even a customary law violation in and of itself may not be amenable to challenge in an international court unless the jurisdiction of the relevant court can be triggered by an international treaty. Given that many states are not subject to the jurisdiction of any supra-national human rights treaties, there would be an additional hurdle in ensuring accountability. Unless an *erga omnes* violation of international law (Barcelona Traction, 1970, para 33) may be proven, the challenge may be insurmountable. And there would be an additional challenge, for no state is likely to contest another state's antics of myopic revocation of nationality unless those deprived of citizenship eventually become a burden to it.

One may argue that the right to nationality has not yet matured into customary international law; Myanmar accepted it when it voted in favour of the UDHR, which includes the right to a nationality and provides for the prohibition of arbitrary deprivation of nationality (Global New Light of Myanmar, 2016; Immanuel, 2022). The limitation with that line of argument is that states' voting practices on a broad proposition do not automatically lead to a definitive legal stance on the subject matter of the vote. Thus, reasonable minds can differ on whether rendering a group of people stateless, due to discriminatory considerations, constitutes a violation of customary international law. And without an authoritative pronouncement from the World Court or at least a body such as the International Law Commission making a clear and definitive conclusion, it is somewhat difficult.

At best, it would be a violation of some of the provisions (in particular Article 9) of the *Convention on the Reduction of Statelessness*. However, a problem with the existing international law is that it is based on treaties and may not apply to non-state parties unless it can be demonstrated that existing treaty law is a mere codification of customary law (Vienna Convention on the Law of Treaties, Articles 34–37). However, as of 20 December 2025, only 82 states are so far parties to this treaty, and that list includes a few Asian countries.[4] Indeed, the international law on statelessness is so haphazard that if Myanmar authorities had not resorted to atrocities on the Rohingya, arguably, they could not possibly be held liable for any violation of international law. This, of course, is not to imply that their Citizenship Law of 1982 could not amount to a violation of the laws against racial discrimination. This is only to imply that Gambia could only trigger the jurisdiction of the ICJ by resorting to the *Genocide Convention* to which Myanmar is a ratifying party. Myanmar, not being a party to the *International Convention on the Elimination of All Forms of Racial Discrimination*, 1965, its jurisdictional clause could not be of any use to Gambia or any other state. Therefore, the law on statelessness, on its own, is unlikely to yield much for the victims of statelessness. One may be excused for summing up the position of international law that as long as a state renders people stateless and does not force them to leave the borders, the community of states may be willing to concede to that state's antics. States that want to abuse the latitude offered by international law can deploy on the face, objective race-neutral criteria such as time, territory, and administrative practice as the factors determining citizenship, with a subjective design to target it against the minority to deprive them of citizenship (Jain, 2022).

For state parties to the Convention, a violation of the *Statelessness Convention* may be brought before the ICJ pursuant to Article 14 of the Convention.[5] But the response to the statelessness manufactured by states has been muted or muttered by other states. Muttered and weak responses may be due to economic self-interest, but they may also be partially owed to the ambivalent state of international law. In addition, an even bigger challenge is that, assuming *arguendo* that there is a customary legal obligation not to render people wantonly stateless, it would not be enforceable by law until there is a judicial or quasi-judicial international body to enforce this legal obligation. The cases discussed in this chapter could only be brought to the regional juridical bodies because respective states accepted treaty obligations that conferred jurisdiction on those bodies. There is no such regional juridical body beyond Africa, Europe, and the Americas. As already indicated, it is also problematic that few states are parties to the *Statelessness Convention*, meaning that even if there is a customary international law prohibition of wantonly depriving persons of nationality, there will often be no recourse to an international legal body, as the wanton stripping of nationality may not be amenable to the jurisdiction of an international court or tribunal. Thus, Rohingyas in Myanmar, Romas in Europe, and Kurds in Iran, Iraq, Syria, and Turkey and many other minority groups in various corners of the world would often be the victims of discriminatory laws and policies of states.

Is There a Customary International Law on Preventing Statelessness in South Asia?

A recent scholarly work has argued that there is an emerging customary international law norm to prevent statelessness (Immanuel, 2022). By referring to state practice in South Asia (going beyond the region covered by the South Asian Association for Regional Cooperation, including Myanmar), it argues that there is ample evidence of state practice from South Asia in support of this customary norm. It is open to question whether the state practice of South Asia leads to such a conclusion. It needs to be remembered that the ICJ in *Nicaragua* has put the threshold of uniform practice quite high for it to amount to customary international law. It observed that:

> The Court does not consider that, *for a rule to be established as customary, the corresponding practice must be in absolutely rigorous conformity with the rule.* In order to deduce the existence of customary rules, the Court deems it sufficient that the conduct of States should, *in general, be consistent with such rules, and that instances of State conduct inconsistent with a given rule should generally have been treated as breaches of that rule, not as indications of the recognition of a new rule.*
>
> *(Nicaragua, para. 186, emphasis added)*

The uncertainty over the regional state practice in South Asia becomes even more prominent when one considers that, even if there is uniform practice across states, there may not be the *opinio juris* required for the practice to constitute customary international law as one of the cases cited in the article, *Fakku v Bangladesh,* is read closely. The Court observed that:

> Question of citizenship of the Urdu speaking has got another aspect, which is very important from the constitutional perspective. Miseries and sufferings of such people due to statelessness were [from] time to time reported in the national media, electronic and print ... By keeping the question of citizenship unresolved on wrong assumptions over the decades, this nation has not gained anything rather was deprived of the contribution they could have made in the nation building.
>
> *(para 38)*

The apparent tenor of empathy in the above words might imply that the Court did not feel that there was any *opinio juris* to prevent statelessness which was obligatory in Bangladesh. In another case, *Bangladesh v Azam and Others* (1994) decided by the Appellate Division of Bangladesh, it has merely stated "Bangladesh has not yet signed the Convention on Reduction of Statelessness, but thanks to judicial pronouncements, several salutary features of the growing international norms in this regard have stood embodied in our national jurisprudence" (para 48). However, despite stating this, the Court did not make any mention of any other explicit reference to international law or the *Statelessness Convention,* rather than simply noting "According to the Convention on the Reduction of Statelessness, 1961, a contracting State shall grant its nationality to a person born in its territory who otherwise will be stateless and shall not deprive a person of his nationality if such deprivation would render him stateless" (*Azam*, para 48). Such a wholesome allusion to the Statelessness Convention, without any pronouncement as to which provision/s of the Convention have assumed the character of customary international law, is hardly an acknowledgement of the customary nature of international law obligation to prevent statelessness. Rather, the AD's substantial reliance on the provisions of the Constitution of Bangladesh and other statutory provisions would imply, on the contrary, that any consideration of international legal obligation did not influence the AD's determination.

Myanmar's Citizenship Law and the Rohingya

Scholarly work has argued that part of the blame for atrocities perpetrated on the Rohingya may go to the continuation of artificially constructed colonial borders created by the British in post-independence Myanmar (Shahabuddin, 2019). While that may partially explain the predicament of the Rohingya, the post-independence Myanmar ruler's policies played a decisive role. The recognition of self-determination of the people of the Rakhine state or some form of autonomy of Rakhine (which was not apparently based on any religious line) during the independence of Myanmar could have averted the ensuing atrocities on the Rohingya (Shahabuddin, 2019). However, that lack of attention from the British colonial regime or the founding leaders of Myanmar could not in any way subvert the subsequent repression of the Rohingya. And laying too much emphasis on the colonial baggage may arguably not only lessen the immutable responsibility of the Myanmar regime but may also pander to what their propaganda machine wants to propagate.

It is widely accepted that, for at least centuries, the Rohingyas have been living in Myanmar (Mohajan, 2018). When Myanmar gained independence from the British in 1948, the Rohingyas were not treated as foreigners or illegal Bengali immigrants as they have been branded in recent decades. Of particular importance is the Citizenship Law of 1982, which states that for being eligible for citizenship, a person must belong to one of the 135 recognised national ethnic groups or that their ancestors must have settled within the territories of the country before 1823 (Section 3 of the Burma Citizenship Law; Jain, 2022). What exactly is the reason for emphasising 1823 as the starting point is not explicitly mentioned in the law, but this is a year before the first Anglo-Burmese War, and there may be an implicit idea on the part of the authorities in Myanmar that Rohingyas started to enter Rakhine. However, as already pointed out, most analysts do not accept this as a fact. Members of the Rohingya minority and other Muslim groups did not find a place in these newly recognised ethnic groups. However, before this enactment, the civil government had recognised 144 ethnic groups, and the Rohingya were included in them (Ullah, 2016). Now, persons enjoying citizenship were relegated to the status of associate or naturalised citizens or non-citizens, rendering them stateless (Arraiza and Vonk, 2017). Apparently, this sort of racial discrimination is not only incompatible with Article 9 of the Statelessness Convention but may arguably be a violation of the *jus cogens* norms of racial discrimination (Foster and Baker, 2021).

The denationalisation of the Rohingya seems to stem from a pathological hatred towards the race, as is apparent from the lamenting of Myanmar's Leader of the National League for Democracy, that she had not been informed earlier that Mishal Hussain, a Muslim presenter of the British Broadcasting Corporation, would interview her (Ibrahim, 2018). It is improbable that the astute politician Ms. Suu Kyi would have been so patent about her disdain for the Rohingya unless she was convinced that her words would resonate with most of her electorate. Thus, while the majority of Burmese may not be in favour of the atrocities perpetrated on the Rohingya, they appear to believe that by clinging to live in Rakhine, they themselves are to be blamed for what they endure (Ibrahim, 2018). The Myanmar Citizenship Law is clearly discriminatory and arbitrary, as it deprives groups of their nationality and violates Article 15(1) of the UDHR (Mohajan, 2018).

As our nexus to many of the rights conferred by states depends on nationality, the deprivation of nationality means that we lose many of the political and economic rights, rendering us vulnerable. Even during the recent COVID-19 pandemic, the various health restrictions and measures could serve as a case in point of how many states differentiated between nationals and non-nationals as if the pathogens could identify and respond to passports differently. Stateless persons living in Myanmar, or in any other country, may fare worse than foreigners living within that respective territory. This is because if a foreigner is wrongfully treated, the state of nationality of the foreigner may seek to defend her/his interests by invoking international legal provisions on the treatment of aliens.

One potentially legitimate ground for denationalisation could be grave disloyalty of the concerned individual. Considering that nationality is a bond involving mutual rights and obligations, such a nexus in rare cases may be acceptable. This is recognised in international human rights courts and local courts, which seem to have endorsed this idea in several cases. As the Court observed in *Pham v Secretary of State for the Home Department* that states "should not have to provide protection to a person who has in the past so fundamentally repudiated the obligations which he owes as a citizen" ([2018] EWCA Civ 2064, paras. 53, 57). But if liberally used, even this narrow exception may pose challenges.

Assuming *arguendo* that in the ongoing case filed by The Gambia against Myanmar, the ICJ eventually pronounces a judgement that the Rohingyas have a right to repatriation, it does not solve the problems of statelessness of the Rohingyas. And the judicial pronouncement notwithstanding, it is likely to create challenges for many living in Bangladesh and others to prove that they belong to Myanmar's Rohingya community. It is not even improbable that the Court may be approached by either party seeking an interpretation of its judgement.[6] Inevitably, such a course of action would further delay any dignified repatriation process of the Rohingya.

What May Be Done?

To eliminate or at least abate statelessness, two fundamental re-orientations appear to be in order. The first is that the deference to state sovereignty in rendering people stateless needs to be significantly reduced, if not eliminated. Secondly, international law needs to unequivocally pivot to an individual's right to citizenship (from the state's nearly exclusive control over the membership within its borders). That is to say, there should be some sort of new international law of citizenship (Spiro, 2011). Unless international law and policymaking take these two fundamental points into account, statelessness would persist.

Considering the origin of the law on statelessness and refugees, a scholar has commented that while their origins lay in the same period, the former has been "[i]n a litter of two of spring, statelessness was the metaphorical runt. It was overlooked and unloved while the refugee mandate received all of the attention" (Manly, 2014). Hersch Lauterpacht mooted the idea of an international refugee organisation to combat denationalisation by an international organisation (Lauterpacht, 1948). However, critics such as Chamberlain accused this modest proposal of bestowing too much power on an international organisation (Siegelberg, 2020). The contemporary international law provides at least some latitude for states to use the patchwork to wantonly "manufacture statelessness" (Jain, 2022). It is time to adopt a perspective that centres on the plight of individuals (Anghie, 2005). International law cannot remain indifferent to individuals as victims of international law or pave the way for victims being created due to its absence (Anghie, 2005).

Even from the state-centric vantage point, the wanton stripping of nationality (either de jure or de facto) would appear to be problematic. As across the border movement of stateless people to neighbouring states and beyond may create challenges for the states facing the movement. Thus, wanton stripping of nationality needs to be a core concern of international law. One may contend that states being sovereign cannot be obligated by the dictates of international law, as using the exclusive power of law-making within their national borders, it would regulate the loss of nationality. As a 17th century religious thinker stated, that submission of states to the domain of international law may mean the lessening of their powers, "only because the great fish can no longer eat up the little ones, and each sovereignty is equally defended from injuries and disabled from committing them" (Quoted in Postema, 2022).

Excluding the highly unusual case of people being born in *terra nullius* or *res communis*, every individual would be born in the territory of a state. And thus, stripping the nationality of an individual is arguably an anomaly. When states argue that nationality is the principal link between individuals in international law, it is for them to create a situation where people become stateless by the willful act of the state (Transactions of the Grotius Society, 1942). For that reason, international law and the international community must act to prevent statelessness in the first place. Addressing the antecedent consequences of statelessness, that is, dealing with the status of stateless people, would only respond to the problem, not address its *root*.

There has to be a two-pronged approach: strategically pursuing litigation to respond to arbitrary deprivation of the minority of citizenship and curbing the state's freedom to render people stateless. In particular, the UNHCR's Statelessness Unit requires increased access to resources and needs to tackle statelessness more assertively, just as the UNHCR takes a more direct role in addressing the travails of asylum seekers and refugees. By closely observing the state's practices and policies, the UN human rights treaty bodies may also play a more assertive role in holding states at least politically accountable for wantonly depriving minorities of citizenship. The argument here is not that rogue regimes would always abide by the dictates of international law, but rather that international law can be a potent tool in making them accountable and curbing their antics.

Conclusion

Anyone advocating a restrained role for international law on the stripping of nationality may point to the latter's traditional location within the domain of national law for centuries. Due to the horizontal origin of contemporary international law as manifested through the Peace Treaties of Westphalia, such deference to the state's sovereignty may have been justifiable. However, increasingly international law is considering individuals not just on the fringe of its attention, rather as a core subject of international law and an object of protection. Indeed, the very notion of human rights is premised on the conviction of the rights of *individuals*, not as members of any political unit called states.

Indeed, "at the time of the San Francisco conference, 'peace-loving' was not to be defined by reference to the internal level of democracy, because this would constitute unlawful interference in internal affairs" (Baillie, 2019, at 12). So, the domain of internal affairs was presumed to be impenetrable. However, since World War II, international law has gone through a seismic shift, and individuals in some parts of the world can sue their states for violation of human rights. States as political units are created for human beings, and blissful indifference to the sufferings caused by the capricious acts of the very institutions created by human beings is indefensible. In any case, a practice's continuity cannot be a justification for its validity. As Moyn aptly quotes:

> In these words you are defining the only point of view (one now much shaken) from which the past used to regard all social evils – i.e., the point of view of resignation – as one looks at what is inevitable...But if ever, at the sight of a great evil, the doubtful question has forced itself on one's heart, "Must this be so?" then the heart can no longer remain cold; and besides pity, a kind of repentance springs up. Not a personal repentance indeed – but how shall I express it? – a *protest from the conscience of the age.*
>
> *(Quoting Suttner, 1894, 98–99)*

Just as the once-accepted notion that states could wage brutal and unrestricted war is no longer the law, a paradigm shift appears to be in order in the domain of capricious denationalisation of a group of people. The misery that a state can unleash on a vulnerable minority group cannot be inevitable within the dominance of national law. If the international legal regime on wantonly rendering a group of people stateless is not regulated more strictly, the antics of authoritarian or majoritarian regimes would continue. Following the post-October 1917 revolution, it was the USSR; in 1982, it was Myanmar that caused mass denationalisation (though for different reasons); and in decades to come, it could be another state. The recipe for a brutal regime to systemically persecute a group of minority populations could be relatively straightforward: denationalise the group on one pretext or another, render them second-class individuals, and then gradually encourage them to move beyond borders.

For preventing systemic discrimination against minority groups in authoritarian or majoritarian countries, the international community has to deal with the wanton stripping of nationality of a group of the population. The grounds of sovereignty should not justify the antics of states. It is the state whose action creates the grave problems of statelessness, and remedying them should also be an obligation for the state. The current state of international law may, in many ways, entice an authoritarian regime to strip the nationality of a minority group. For the Rohingyas, nationality rights can be a sort of conviction that upon their eventual repatriation, they would belong to Myanmar as *equals*.

Acknowledgements

The author gratefully acknowledges the able research assistance of Ahamed Musa, Fateha Tun Noor, Nayeem Ahmod, Rabeya Akter Nayna, and Suhi Samannaz Ilma.

Notes

1 Throughout this chapter, the two terms have been used interchangeably. However, Bryan A Garner (ed) Black's Law Dictionary (Thomson Reuters, 10th ed, 2014) at 1186 defines nationality as "The relationship between a citizen of a country and the country itself". However, the same source recognises that the two are commonly used in a synonymous way.
2 The Nansen passport was a refugee travel document, an internationally recognised identity card issued by the League of Nations to stateless refugees. The system was designed in 1922 by Fridtjof Nansen, a Norwegian. It was designed after the October Revolution, when more than a million Russians became refugees.
3 Importantly, although 10 UN member states abstained from voting on the adoption of the UDHR, no state voted against it, which would arguably imply that it embodied the consensus of the community of states existing at that time.
4 A similar trend applies to the Convention relating to the Status of Stateless Persons, which includes only 99 states and few Asian parties; <https://treaties.un.org/pages/ViewDetailsII.aspx?src=TREATY&mtdsg_no=V-3&chapter=5&Temp=mtdsg2&clang=_en> accessed 20 December 2025.
5 Although even in that case, the other state party may take the plea that the party filing the case is not in any way affected by its action and thus, is not a proper party. Only if an *erga omnes* violation of international law can be proven, may this challenge be countered.
6 For an example of this happening in the past, see *Request for Interpretation of the Judgment of 20 November 1950 in the Asylum Case* (Colombia v Peru), Judgement of 27 November 1950.

References

Anghie, Antony. *Imperialism, Sovereignty and the Making of International Law.* Cambridge: Cambridge University Press, 2005.

Anudo v. Tanzania, No. 012/2015, Decision, African Court on Human and Peoples' Rights [Afr. Ct. H.P.R.], para. 76 (22 March 2018). https://www.african-court.org/cpmt/storage/app/uploads/public/5f5/646/bfc/5f5646bfc496d510939321.pdf

Arraiza, José María, and Olivier Vonk. *Report on Citizenship Law: Myanmar.* [Global Governance Programme], GLOBALCIT, Country Reports, 2017/14. http://hdl.handle.net/1814/48284

Baillie, Cecilia M., ed. *Researching International Law and Peace.* Cheltenham: Edward Elgar, 2019, 12.

Bangladesh v. Professor Golam Azam and Others, (1994) 46 DLR(AD) 192.
Barcelona Traction, Light and Power Company Limited (New Application: 1962), Belgium v. Spain, Judgment, merits, (1970) ICJ Reports 3.
Bauer, Jon. "Multiple Nationality and Refugees." *Vanderbilt Journal of Transnational Law* 47, no. 4 (2014): 905–1005.
Case Concerning Military and Paramilitary Activities in and against Nicaragua (Nicaragua v. United States of America) (Merits), ICJ Reports (1986) 14.
Convention on Certain Questions Relating to the Conflict of Nationality Law, LoNP, Treaty Series, vol. 179, p. 89, No. 4137, 13 April 1930. https://www.refworld.org/docid/3ae6b3b00.html
Foster, Michelle, and T. R. Baker. "Racial Discrimination in Nationality Laws: A Doctrinal Blind Spot of International Law?" *Columbia Journal of Race and Law* 11, no. 1 (2021): 83–146. https://doi.org/10.7916/cjrl.v11i1.8018
Hudson, Manley O. "The First Conference for the Codification of International Law." *American Journal of International Law* 24 (1930): 447, 450.
Ibrahim, Azeem. *The Rohingyas: Inside Myanmar's Hidden Genocide.* London: Hurst Publishers, 2018.
Immanuel, Andrea Marilyn Pragashini. "The Customary Obligation to Avoid, Reduce, or Prevent Statelessness in South Asia." *Asian Journal of International Law* 13, no. 2 (2022): 1–29. https://doi.org/10.1017/s204425132200056x
Jain, Neha. "Manufacturing Statelessness." *American Journal of International Law* 116, no. 2 (2022): 237–88.
Kuhn, Arthur K. "International Measures for the Relief of Stateless Persons." *The American Journal of International Law* 30, no. 3 (1936): 495–99. https://doi.org/10.2307/2191021
Kurić v. Slovenia, App. No. 26828/06, Judgment (Merits and Just Satisfaction), Grand Chamber (26 June 2012).
Lauterpacht, Hersch. "The Nationality of Denationalized Persons." *Jewish Yearbook of International Law* 1, no. 1 (1948): 165–85.
Manly, Mark. "UNHCR's Mandate and Activities to Address Statelessness." In *Nationality and Statelessness under International Law*, edited by Alice Edwards and Laura van Waas, 88–92. Cambridge: Cambridge University Press, 2014.
Md. Sadaqat Khan (Fakku) And 10 Others v The Chief Election Commissioner, Bangladesh Election Commission and Others (2008) 28 BLD (HCD) 261
Mohajan, Haradhan. "History of Rakhine State and the Origin of the Rohingya Muslims." *IKAT: The Indonesian Journal of Southeast Asian Studies* 2, no. 1 (2018): 19–46. https://doi.org/10.22146/ikat.v2i1.37391
Moyn, Samuel. *The Last Utopia: Human Rights in History.* Cambridge: Harvard University Press, 2012.
Nationality Decrees Issued in Tunis and Morocco (French Zone), Advisory Opinion (1923) PCIJ Series B no. 4.
Nationality in International Law, Transactions of the Grotius Society, vol. 28, 1942, pp. 151–68.
Nottebohm Case (Second Phase), (Liechtenstein v. Guatemala) (Judgment of 6 April 1955), ICJ Reports 4 (1955).
Postema, Gerald J. *Law's Empire: The Nature, Value, and Viability of the Rule of Law.* Oxford: Oxford University Press, 2022.
Protocol Relating to a Certain Case of Statelessness, signed on 12 April 1930, entered into force on 1 July 1937.
Sahni, Binda Preet. "The Myopic Loss of Nationality Rights Leading to Statelessness." *Gonzaga Journal of International Law* 24, no. 2 (2021): 111–45.
Shahabuddin, Mohammad. "Post-Colonial Boundaries, International Law, and the Making of the Rohingya Crisis in Myanmar." *Asian Journal of International Law* 9, no. 2 (2019): 334–58. https://doi.org/10.1017/S2044251319000055

Siegelberg, Mira. *Statelessness: A Modern History.* Cambridge: Harvard University Press, 2020.
Spiro, Peter J. "A New International Law of Citizenship." *American Journal of International Law* 105, no. 4 (2011): 694–746. https://doi.org/10.5305/amerjintelaw.105.4.0694
Suttner, Bertha Von. *Lay Down Your Arms: The Autobiography of Martha von Tilling.* Translated by T. Holmes. Ulan Press, 1894.
The Lotus Case (1927) PCIJ, Series A, No. 10, 18.
The Nubian Community in Kenya v. The Republic of Kenya, African Commission on Human and Peoples' Rights, Communication 317/06 (28 February 2015). https://www.justiceinitiative.org/uploads/66fcd2c5-e02a-4485-963b-ef5b71c23b52/ali-communication-20100517.pdf
Ullah, A. K. M. Ahsan. "Rohingya Crisis in Myanmar: Seeking Justice for the 'Stateless'." *Journal of Contemporary Criminal Justice* 32, no. 3 (2016): 285–301.
UNHCR. *Convention Relating to the Status of Stateless Persons*, 360 UNTS 117, 28 September 1954.
UNHCR. *Text of the 1961 Convention on the Reduction of Statelessness*, 11 January 2023. https://www.unhcr.org/ibelong/wp-content/uploads/1961-Convention-on-the-reduction-of-Statelessness_ENG.pdf
Universal Declaration of Human Rights, adopted 10 Dec. 1948, G.A. Res. 217A (III), U.N. GAOR, 3d Sess, art. 15, U.N. Doc. A/RES/3/217A (1948).
. *Global New Light of Myanmar: Opinion*, 10 May 2016. http://www.globalnewlightofmyanmar.com/universal-declaration-of-human-rights-udhr/
Weis, Paul. "The United Nations Convention on the Reduction of Statelessness, 1961." *International & Comparative Law Quarterly* 11 (1962): 1073–74.
Yean and Bosico Children v. The Dominican Republic, Ser. C, No. 130 (8 September 2005).

5

FROM STATELESSNESS TO SYSTEMATIC DENIAL

A Critical Assessment of Myanmar's Multi-layered Predicaments to Sustainable Rohingya Repatriation Process

Mohammad Atique Rahman and Kawsar Uddin Mahmud

Introduction

Refugee repatriation to their home countries is often regarded as the most durable solution to the displacement context, enabling individuals to rebuild their lives in a familiar environment. In this context, the country of origin plays a crucial role in the refugee repatriation process. It is central to the principle of safe, voluntary, and sustainable repatriation to determine whether refugees and displaced people can safely return home and reintegrate with the local communities. However, returning to the home country is daunting due to the fact that certain push factors in the past forced people to flee from their country of origin. If such push factors remain persistent, then safe repatriation is somewhat of a challenging task. For example, the Afghan refugees living in Pakistan and Iran have faced a repeated cycle of displacement due to instability and violence in Afghanistan, which made return unsafe (UNHCR 2025a). In contrast the repatriation of refugees from Liberia and Sierra Leone in the early 2000s was marked as a successful, safe, and voluntary repatriation process. These repatriations were possible after the transition to democratic governance in these two countries and the signing of peace agreements among the parties in conflict. Both countries (Liberia, 1989–2003, and Sierra Leone, 1991–2002) have experienced prolonged civil wars and violence, which forced millions of people to flee to neighboring countries such as Guinea, Côte d'Ivoire, and Ghana. With the assistance of the international community and peacekeeping operations, namely UNAMSIL in Sierra Leone and UNMIL in Liberia, the protracted civil wars have come to an end. Moreover, the signing of peace accords such as the Lome Peace Accord (1999) in Sierra Leone and the Comprehensive

DOI: 10.4324/9781003771890-5

Peace Agreement (2003) in Liberia helped these countries improve political and security conditions . Following these two peace agreements, these two neighboring countries of West Africa have made great strides toward achieving political stability with legitimate authority via elections and strengthening democratic institutions. Refugees were assured local reintegration, dignity, identity, and safety to return to their home countries. Black and Gent (2006) argue that political and security conditions are two fundamental requirements necessary for the country of origin for voluntary return, which may require democratic governance, cessation of violence, disarmament of armed groups, and development assistance. It is natural that, at the beginning, the country of origin may face a lack of resources to provide shelter, healthcare, community reconciliation initiatives, and livelihoods for the returnees. This is not possible to achieve overnight. However, there should be coordinated efforts and commitment from the state to attain these objectives for safe and voluntary repatriation.

Bangladesh has been currently hosting approximately 1.2 million Rohingya since August 2017. According to UNICEF, more than 52 percent of them are children, which is approximately 683,000 living in the congested and squalid camps in Cox's Bazar, Bangladesh (UNHCR 2019a). Also, each year since 2017, nearly 35,000 new births are registered in the Rohingya camps. In this context, an additional 150,000 new members have been added to the Rohingya community by 2022 since 2017 (UNHCR 2025c). Rohingyas have experienced one of the direst forms of violation, loss, and lack of resources by the Myanmar authorities, and they now confront various obstacles that undermine their physiological, psychological, and socio-behavioral well-being as well as their futures. The poor conditions of the shelters, lack of access to educational and recreational facilities, skill development facilities, as well as access to toilets and hygiene create extremely vulnerable conditions for them. In 2017, the local people (or host community) of Cox's Bazar set an example of humanity and solidarity toward the Rohingya displaced people by hosting more than one million of them.

The long-term Rohingya presence has put tremendous demographic and socio-economic pressures on the host community. Moreover, since there is no progress on the Rohingya repatriation issue, it further aggravates the situation. In this context, several factors like environmental degradation, economic instability, unequal access to relief and humanitarian assistance, and uncertainty about the recovery of their lands, which are now being used as campsites for the Rohingyas, are some of the factors that may lead to social tension between the host community and Rohingyas (Rahman and Mahmud, 2024). The return of Rohingya is now at the forefront of Rohingya discourse in Bangladesh. In recent times there have been extensive research and publications on Rohingya repatriation focusing on strategic and diplomatic options from the Bangladesh and international perspective. However, there is a gap in understanding factors and dynamics in the country of origin—Myanmar—determining the identity and status of Rohingyas. In addition, the socio-economic contexts of the country of origin are crucial in many contexts influencing refugees' decisions to return. It is evident that security issues are one of the preconditions for safe return. Beyond security, factors such as economic stability, property rights, and access to health and basic services are also essential. In the Rohingya case, the question of citizenship rights and identity is paramount. In this backdrop, this chapter intends to gaze on Myanmar—a country of origin of the Rohingyas—to explore its political, economic, and security contexts in order to assess Myanmar's role in the safe Rohingya return process.

This chapter is divided into five sections along with an introduction and conclusion. Section one presents the theoretical framework to assess how the sovereign and legitimate authorities in Myanmar have been contested since the military takeover in this country gave birth to the rise of non-state armed and non-armed actors. Section two briefly presents the resource competition in Rakhine State leading to the perpetual resource conflict dynamics in the region. Section three explores the contemporary political situation in Myanmar after the 2021 coup. Section four discusses the emergence of the non-state armed actors and how they contest the sovereign authority of Myanmar. Finally, section five discusses the current state of international response, especially the US-Burma Act provisions, to analyze the prospect of international engagement in Myanmar to stabilize Rakhine State.

Theoretical Discussions: "Sovereignty Contests" as Obstacles to Rohingya Repatriation

This chapter addresses Myanmar's strategic and varying role in the dual process of facilitating and resisting exclusion and instability, through a discursive focus on the ideas of "sovereignty contest" and "sovereign mimicry". The term "sovereignty contest" was first used by James Read (2020) in his book, "Power versus Liberty". Later, "contested sovereignty" was used by van Schendel (2005) in his studies of "The Bengal Borderland" (Schendel 2005). By using the concept, these scholars refer to the conflicts over authority and legitimacy both within the territory and on its peripheries where state power meets subnational actors that define their identity distinct from the state. In addition to this, borrowing Taussig's (1993) concept of mimetic opposition in colonial contexts, and further elaborated by Hansen and Stepputat (2006) to include postcolonial spaces, "sovereign mimicry" defines how non-state actors emulate state functions like taxation, justice, and administration to establish de facto sovereignty and subvert the state's juridical monopoly (Hansen and Stepputat 2006; Taussig 1993). These lenses delineate that the Myanmar government's continued blocking of Rohingya return is not simply an administrative delay, but a deliberate deepening of one of the dimensions of the overarching games of power in which the power of the military junta in the center is both feeding and being fed by insurgencies and revolts against that power in the periphery (see Figure 5.1). Situating these notions within both Myanmar's past and present realities, we can understand that such contestations only deepen statelessness and inhibit returns, reproducing displacement and cementing fracturing along ethnic lines.

The historical bond between the center of Burma and its many borderlands and ethnic-nationalist groups has long been a patchwork system of uneasy alliances and lingering tensions—one that long predates colonial rule. However, that experienced a new stage of fragmentary social development during the British colonial era, an epoch in which seeds of lasting conflict were sown. Burmese kingdoms based in the Irrawaddy Valley had variable hegemony over upland peripheries before British annexation in the 19th century, where different ethnic groups traded, intermingled, and paid tribute, traversing borders of historical fluidity without tight control (Sadan 2013). The Naga and Chin Hills in the west, the Shan Plateau in the east, and the Arakan Mountains to the south formed important frontier zones that acted as buffers and pathways connecting Burma to broader regional circuits while

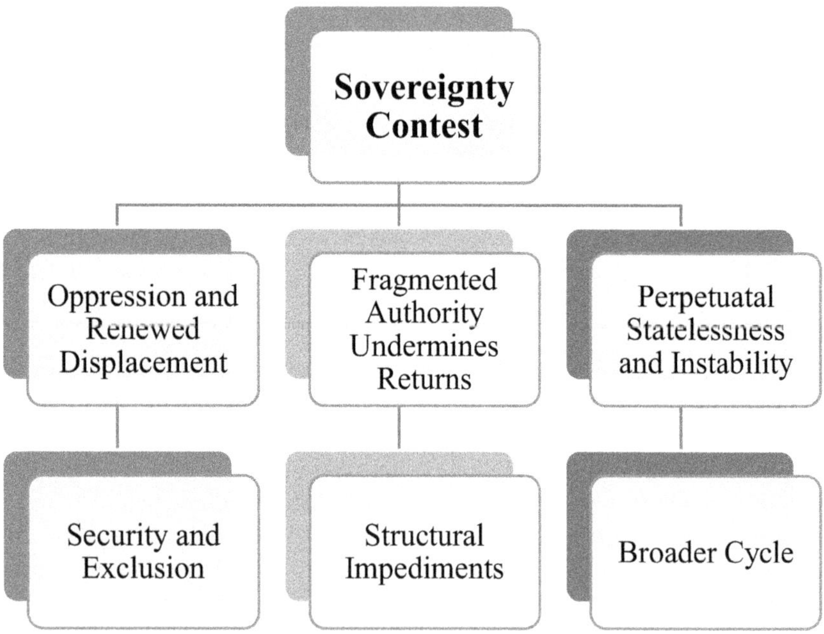

FIGURE 5.1 "Sovereignty Contest" Hindering Rohingya Repatriation.

Source: Prepared by the authors.

they were not fully incorporated into the expanding lowland Burman core. British colonialism codified this division, drawing international borders and splitting internal governance; "Burma Proper" fell under direct rule, allowing for administrative centralization, while the "Frontier Areas" faced indirect rule through local chiefs, solidifying ethnic separateness and low state penetration (Smith 1999). This legacy would come back to haunt the fledgling Union of Burma post-independence in 1948 when the 1947 Panglong Agreement quickly pulled these divided areas together under a tenuous federal promise, before breaking apart amid charges of Burman domination. In this line of thinking, contested sovereignty acts as a legacy from the past in which the center's efforts to solidify insurgency on the periphery illustrate van Schendel (2005) vision of borderlands as "privileged sites of rebellion" (see Figure 5.2 for details).

This dispersed basis gave birth to a multitude of armed and non-armed resistance groups, each one posing serious threats to the state integrity and compounding the Rohingya plight. The 1949 Kuomintang invasion of the northern borderlands revealed the weaknesses of the newly independent state, precipitating Tatmadaw transformations that solidified military supremacy and legitimized dictatorship in the name of national unity (Tun 2009). Ethnic grievances had candid into armed insurgencies by the coup of 1962 under General Ne Win, with groups such as the Karen National Union (KNU) and Kachin Independence Organization (KIO) demanding territorial autonomy and enjoying popular legitimacy in their enclaves. These

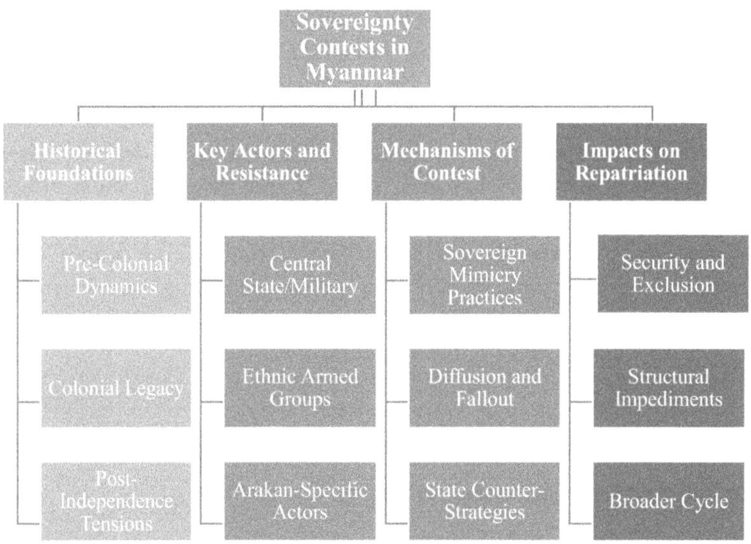

FIGURE 5.2 Factors Regarding Sovereignty Contest in Myanmar.

Source: Prepared by the authors.

assertions were then advanced by non-armed actors through advocacy and informal governance by civil society networks and ethnic political parties, further undermining Naypyidaw's authority. In Karen State, the KNU's tactics of military offensives, ceasefires, and development projects infiltrated these semi-autonomous zones, meaning alternative sovereignty was imposed through resource extraction and local governance. As outlined in The Asia Foundation's report on contested areas, this mosaic of resistance highlights how Myanmar's subnational conflicts carve up the country into "spheres of overlapping authority" and how the military's characterization of "unruly" borderlands provides legitimacy for violence against minorities like the Rohingya, whose situation intersects with these larger cleavages (Burke et al. 2017).

The phenomenon of armed groups adopting sovereign mimicry has been especially pronounced in Shan and Kachin States, where the likes of the United Wa State Army (UWSA) and KIO have created parallel administrative systems. In Shan, the UWSA outweighs the Tatmadaw in taxation, education, and even foreign relations, mimicking the trappings of statehood and carving out de facto autonomy (Burke et al. 2017; Hansen and Stepputat 2006). Likewise, the KIO in Kachin replicates the state by not only wielding state-like power, including courts, schools, and revenues to continue rebellion amid jade-endowed economies of war, but by parading its organizational structures in the media to position the KIO as the legitimate governing authority. Not only does this imitation weaken central authority, it also promotes diffusion; having developed in Kachin alliances within the 2010s, the method of the Arakan Army (AA) was transplanted to Rakhine State in the aftermath of the 2021 coup. After perfecting them in the fighting in Kachin, the AA stormed Arakan riding on the weakness of the junta to take territory and has created the self-governance framework called "Way of Rakhita", comprised of "administrative councils", policing, and aid delivery (Brenner 2025). As (Oh 2013) notes in her study of Karen parallels, such dynamics turn borderlands into zones of interstitial hybrid sovereignty, characterized by permanent inconsistency and armed mimicry. The AA wages an anti-junta struggle in the name of Rakhine independence and autonomy, but it executes this sovereignty simulation by taxing fisheries, detaining civilians in labor camps, and imposing ethnic hierarchies.

Resource Conflicts among the Ethnic Groups in Rakhine Region

Natural Resource Wealth and Geostrategic Competition

Paradoxically, although Rakhine State suffers from extreme poverty, it is simultaneously one of Myanmar's most resource-rich regions, endowed with substantial deposits of oil, natural gas, coal, and other valuable minerals

(Bhattacharjee 2024). The exploitation of these natural resources became intricately linked to the persecution of the Rohingya population and gave rise to notable hurdles to their safe return from Bangladesh. Myanmar initiated exploration of approximately 37 new offshore oil and gas fields along the Rakhine coast in January 2017, with companies from France, Indonesia, China, India, Russia, Singapore, Thailand, Malaysia, and Hong Kong investing in onshore projects, while firms from South Korea, France, Malaysia, China, India, Thailand, and Vietnam engaged in offshore exploration. The Shwe Gas Project, which began commercial production in August 2013, was expected to produce 500 million cubic feet of gas per day, with the vast majority (379 million cubic feet) exported to China (Dhaka Tribune 2017). Khan (2018) noted that "the government of Myanmar therefore has vested interests in clearing land to prepare for further development", suggesting that forced displacement of Rohingyas is a mechanism to facilitate these resource extraction projects and create trading networks with China and India. Debnath et al. (2022) argues that "the persecution and displacement of the Rohingyas may be linked to the resources and geo-strategic factors present in Rakhine". After considering multiple factors, analysts have concluded that "geopolitics and Myanmar's economic interests are more significant than other factors behind the statelessness of the Rohingya minority" (Bhattacharjee 2024).

(Authors have prepared this table from different sources i.e., International Crisis Group Report, 2024; HRW, 2024; Amin, 2024 and Leider, 2023)

Land Confiscation and Dispossession

With systematic land appropriation serving as both a driver and consequence of the Rohingya crisis, land ownership and control is one of the most contentious resource conflicts in Rakhine State. The Rohingya have historically relied on agricultural land for subsistence farming. However, they have faced arbitrary taxation, land confiscation, and restrictions on property ownership that have systematically diluted their economic security (Mohajan 2020). An investigation by the United Nations Independent Investigative Mechanism for Myanmar (IIMM) documented how during the 2017 clearance operations, Rohingya homes, mosques, shops, and farmland were systematically destroyed after residents fled, and the land was subsequently repurposed for Border Guard Police (BGP) bases and related infrastructure (United Nations 2025b). In the Myo Thu Gyi village tract alone, more than 800 structures including homes, shops, markets, and mosques existed before the violence; by 2018, over 411 acres (166 hectares) had been burned and flattened, with a sprawling BGP base constructed in their place (Dönmez 2025). Evidence shows that Myanmar authorities harvested 5,549 acres of paddy fields that had become "ownerless" and "belonging to farmers who fled

Table 5.1 Key Conflicts and Impacts of Different Ethnic and Religious Groups.

Resource Type	*Location in Rakhine*	*Involved Groups*	*Key Conflicts and Impacts*
Agricultural land (rice fields)	Northern Rakhine (Maungdaw, Buthidaung)	Rohingya vs. Rakhine/State Forces	Price spikes lead to increase in state violence; considerable Rohingya refugees report land loss
Oil and gas pipelines	Kyaukphyu to Bay of Bengal	Rohingya vs. Military/Chinese Investors	771-km pipeline displaces communities; 70,000 acres confiscated in 2010
Hydropower and infrastructure	Tha Htay Plant, Kaladan Project	Rakhine (AA) vs. Rohingya/Military	AA captures sites; forced labor and village burnings displace 300,000+ since 2023
Timber, rubber, crude oil	Statewide, including coastal areas	Ethnic Minorities vs. Central Government	Predatory extraction in ethnic states; fuels insurgencies and poverty

Source: Prepared by the authors from different sources.

to Bangladesh" using machinery provided by the Mechanized Agriculture Department (United Nations 2025b). Rohingya witnesses reported being evicted from hundreds of acres of farmland, with seized areas marked by red flags, and entire families displaced when their land was confiscated and razed (United Nations 2025b).

Fishing Rights and Marine Resource Competition

Fishing constitutes a major livelihood for coastal communities in Rakhine, with most of the catch transported to Yangon and some exported internationally (Htun and Swe 2023; Naing 2022). However, the sector has been branded by highly exploitative governance structures that have impoverished small-scale fishermen while enriching government-connected elites. In Maungdaw and Buthidaung townships, Rohingya fishermen have been denied fair access to marine resources and forced to pay discriminatory fees to Rakhine Buddhist license holders. Recent developments have further intensified fishing-related resource conflicts. Since the Arakan Army (AA) gained control of significant portions of Rakhine State, Rohingya fishermen report being compelled to surrender nearly half their catch to local representatives of the United League of Arakan/Arakan Army to access fishing zones (Rohingya Khobor 2025).

Contemporary Political Dynamics: The 2021 Coup, Authoritarianism, and Democratic Fragility

The trajectory of Myanmar's political landscape experienced a catastrophic reversal on February 1, 2021, when Senior General Min Aung Hlaing and the Tatmadaw orchestrated a military coup that abruptly terminated the country's brittle democratic experiment. The coup triggered an unprecedented mass mobilization. Within days of the seizure of power, healthcare workers and civil servants across Myanmar launched the Civil Disobedience Movement (CDM), a nationwide campaign of non-cooperation that attracted over 230,000 followers through social media coordination. By December 2023, more than 210,635 civil service personnel actively participated in the CDM, facing systematic persecution including arrest, detention, property confiscation, and threats against family members in retaliation for their refusal to serve the junta (Win 2024). This civil resistance evolved beyond peaceful protest when the NUG announced the formation of the People's Defense Force (PDF) on May 5, 2021, and declared a "defensive war" against the military regime in September 2021, marking the shift from civil disobedience to armed insurgency (Ware and Skidmore 2023). The junta's response has been brutally authoritarian, characterized by mass killings, arbitrary detentions, and aerial bombardments that amount to crimes against humanity. Judicial executions have resumed, and torture in detention remains rampant, fueling a humanitarian crisis that has displaced 3.5 million people internally (Amnesty International 2025b).

The Emergence of Armed Non-State Actors

The Rohingya themselves are not passive victims in this conflict. Several armed groups claim to represent their interests, most notably the Arakan Rohingya Salvation Army (ARSA), the Rohingya Solidarity Organization (RSO), and the Arakan Rohingya Army (ARA). These groups have a complex and often fraught relationship with both the Myanmar military and the AA. ARSA, led by Ataullah abu Ammar Jununi, emerged as a significant insurgent force in northern Rakhine State in the mid-2010s (Romaniuk and Roul 2024). Its attacks on Myanmar security forces in August 2017 were cited by the military as justification for the brutal campaign of violence that drove hundreds of thousands of Rohingya into Bangladesh. ARSA claims its main purpose is to defend Rohingya rights, but it has been accused of violence against other Rohingya, particularly community leaders in refugee camps. Myanmar and Malaysia have designated ARSA as a terrorist organization, though evidence of foreign Islamist support remains unsubstantiated (Romaniuk and Roul 2024). The AA's territorial gains in 2024 provoked a dramatic realignment. The Myanmar military, previously responsible for atrocities against the Rohingya, began to mobilize Rohingya men and collaborate with ARSA and other groups to slow the AA's advance (Brenner 2025). This alliance was pragmatic, aimed at defending key townships, but deeply unpopular among many Rohingya, who viewed the military as their primary oppressor. As the AA's rhetoric and abuses intensified, Rohingya armed groups paused their infighting in Bangladesh's refugee camps and ramped up recruitment, framing their struggle as a jihad against the AA (Brenner 2025). However, a November 2024 "harmony" agreement among Rohingya groups led to a large unity rally in the camps, with religious leaders legitimizing the campaign to retake northern Rakhine by force. The RSO and ARA also began forced recruitment campaigns, sending new fighters to Maungdaw for military training. The AA's takeover of Maungdaw in December 2024 marked a turning point, with thousands of fighters from all sides killed or injured in the ensuing battles (see Figure 5.1, International Crisis Group 2025).

Non-State Actors: As Gatekeepers or Spoilers to Rohingya Repatriation

The rise of the AA and the strengthening of inter-group conflict have profoundly complicated the prospects for Rohingya repatriation. The AA's control over northern Rakhine State means that any future repatriation process will require its cooperation or acquiescence. However, the AA's policies toward the Rohingya have mirrored many of the discriminatory practices long imposed by the Myanmar military, including movement restrictions, forced labor, and arbitrary detention (Uddin 2024). Moreover, the AA's suspicion of Rohingya collaboration with ARSA or the military has led to further abuses and deepened communal tensions. The forced recruitment of Rohingya villagers by both the AA and Rohingya armed groups has inflamed divisions, making the region even more volatile (Human Rights Watch 2025). The mounting attacks by Rohingya armed groups on AA positions threaten to undermine these talks and heighten anti-Rohingya sentiment in Myanmar, further diminishing the prospects for safe and voluntary repatriation.). The humanitarian situation in northern Rakhine State has deteriorated sharply. The AA's restrictions on livelihoods and agriculture, compounded by extortion and exorbitant prices, have exacerbated food shortages. The junta's blockade on aid since late 2023 has left many Rohingya dependent on remittances from relatives abroad or on precarious day labor for the AA, often unpaid. Families fleeing forced recruitment and abuse have joined the growing ranks of refugees in Bangladesh, while those remaining face constant fear and deprivation (Human Rights Watch 2025).

The emergence of the AA as a territorial authority and the mobilization of Rohingya armed groups have altered the conflict in Rakhine State from a binary struggle between the state and an oppressed minority into a multi-polar contest involving ethnic, religious, and political actors (Ware and Laoutides 2018). The AA, despite its rhetoric of inclusive governance, has perpetuated many of the same abuses as the Tatmadaw, undermining its legitimacy among the Rohingya and complicating any future repatriation process. Rohingya armed groups, while claiming to defend their people, have contributed to instability through forced recruitment and violence, sometimes targeting their own community members (Ware and Laoutides 2018). In this context, non-state actors mean both as gatekeepers, controlling access to territory and the terms of repatriation, and as spoilers, capable of derailing peace initiatives and perpetuating cycles of violence. The prospects for Rohingya repatriation now hinge not only on the policies of the Myanmar state and military, but also on the willingness of the AA to respect minority rights and the ability of Rohingya groups to unify around a non-violent, rights-based agenda. Without meaningful change in the behavior of these actors, the process of repatriation will remain stalled, and the Rohingya will continue to face systematic denial and statelessness.

International Accountability and Myanmar's Selective Engagement

Since the 2017 military operations, Myanmar's authorities have navigated global pressure with calculated ambiguity. They signed repatriation agreements while undermining accountability mechanisms (Amnesty International 2025a). The result is a stalled repatriation process that left over one million refugees in limbo. However, international accountability efforts began escalating after the 2017 clearance operations. The UN described it as a textbook example of ethnic cleansing (United Nations 2017). The Independent International Fact-Finding Mission on Myanmar (IIFFMM), established by the UN Human Rights Council in 2017, documented widespread atrocities including killings, rapes, and village burnings, recommending prosecutions for genocide (UN News 2019). This evidence was handed over to the Independent Investigative Mechanism for Myanmar (IIMM) in 2019 (IIMM 2025a). Yet, Myanmar's response has been one of denial and non-engagement; the military regime has dismissed these bodies as biased, refusing to cooperate and even restricting access to Rakhine State.

In September 2025, during a high-level UN conference, the US representatives criticized Myanmar's military for escaping accountability, noting how the regime's atrocities continue amid civil war, further thwarting repatriation (Harder 2025).

A pivotal avenue for accountability is the International Court of Justice (ICJ), where The Gambia filed a case against Myanmar in 2019 on behalf of the Organisation of Islamic Cooperation. The ICJ issued provisional measures in January 2020, ordering Myanmar to avert genocidal acts against the Rohingya and preserve evidence (ICJ 2020). In its 2022 judgment on preliminary objections, the court affirmed jurisdiction, rejecting Myanmar's arguments that The Gambia lacked standing (ICJ 2022). However, Myanmar's selective engagement is evident here too. While it participated in hearings perhaps to maintain a facade of legitimacy, it has failed to comply substantively, with reports demonstrating ongoing destruction of Rohingya land and property (United Nations 2025a). Critics argue that the geopolitics surrounding the case reveal how Myanmar leverages alliances with China and Russia to shield itself from UN Security Council referrals (Jeffrey 2023).

Similar to the ICJ, the International Criminal Court (ICC) has pursued investigations into crimes against the Rohingya. In November 2019, ICC judges authorized the Prosecutor to investigate, despite Myanmar not being a party to the Rome Statute, based on Bangladesh's membership (United Nations, 2019). Yet, Myanmar's response was selective engagement: it has ignored ICC summons, labeling the court as illegitimate, while selectively cooperating with the Association of Southeast Asian Nations (ASEAN) on humanitarian aid corridors that avoided addressing root causes (Fortify Rights 2024). In addition, Myanmar's creation of its own Independent Commission of Enquiry in 2018 was another dimension of its selective engagement strategy. In January 2020 just days before Myanmar's response to the ICJ's provisional measures order, the Commission's final report, released, acknowledged that members of Myanmar's security forces committed war crimes and serious human rights violations against "Muslims" in northern Rakhine State. However, the report strategically denied evidence of genocidal intent, rejected documented patterns of systematic rape by security forces despite extensive documentation by UN investigators. The Union Attorney General's Office claimed it would coordinate investigations and prosecutions based on the Commission's findings, but no meaningful accountability has materialized. The domestic military justice system remained firmly under Tatmadaw control. This instrumentalization of domestic accountability processes served Myanmar's dual purposes of demonstrating ostensible responsiveness to international concerns while ensuring that no genuine threat to military impunity would emerge.

Regional mechanisms, particularly those coordinated through the ASEAN, were equally ineffective in securing accountability or meaningful humanitarian access to Rohingya populations. ASEAN's foundational principle of non-interference in member states' internal affairs has fundamentally constrained the organization's aptitude to address the Rohingya crisis. The ASEAN Five-Point Consensus, agreed upon in April 2021 following the military coup and calling for immediate cessation of violence, constructive dialogue, humanitarian access, and appointment of a special envoy, has been systematically ignored by Myanmar's junta with minimal consequences (Haacke 2025). Myanmar has selectively engaged with ASEAN by allowing limited visits by the bloc's emergency response teams and participating in discussions about the repatriation of Rohingya refugees from Bangladesh. Multiple attempted repatriations since 2018 have failed completely, with not a single Rohingya refugee voluntarily returning due to well-founded fears regarding safety, lack of citizenship guarantees, and absence of accountability.

In this regard, recent legislative efforts, particularly the BURMA Act (Burma Unified through Rigorous Military Accountability Act) and its expanded iterations such as the BRAVE Burma Act and BURMA GAP Act, are the US's mounting strategic interest in Myanmar (Haque 2024). This increasing involvement is Washington's recognition that Myanmar's instability looms over broader Indo-Pacific security and geopolitical balance against Chinese influence. The US legislative framework overtly commits to supporting Myanmar's democratic transition.

Regarding Arakan region stabilization, the US policy increasingly admits that durable peace requires engagement with de facto authorities, particularly the AA. American support for accountability mechanisms and comprehensive transitional justice frameworks intends to make conditions where safe Rohingya repatriation becomes feasible. The BURMA GAP Act specifically authorizes nine million dollars annually for atrocity investigations and transitional justice measures for Myanmar (Foreign Affairs 2025). It directly supports infrastructure necessary for sustainable returns. Furthermore, expanded humanitarian assistance commitments, including a recent $60 million US pledge at the UN High-Level Conference in September 2025, signal Washington's commitment to regional stabilization as a prerequisite for repatriation (The Daily Star 2025). By combining sanctions against junta entities with support for inclusive governance and accountability, the US incentivizes conditions where Rohingya can return voluntarily and safely to their homeland.

Furthermore, in 2017, Myanmar and Bangladesh signed a repatriation agreement, followed by a tripartite mechanism involving China in 2019 to facilitate returns (Ahmed 2024). However, multiple efforts have failed. A 2023 bilateral pilot project was suspended after UN experts cautioned it was unsafe, citing ongoing violence and lack of citizenship assurances (OHCHR 2023). UNHCR has consistently accentuated that returns must be voluntary,

TABLE 5.2 Diplomatic Initiatives between Bangladesh and Myanmar after 2017 Rohingya Crisis

Year	*Key Event*	*Outcome*	*Source*
2017	Myanmar-Bangladesh Repatriation Agreement	No returns; violence continues	(UNHCR 2019b)
2019	Tripartite Mechanism with China	Stalled due to lack of safety guarantees	(Ahmed 2024)
2023	Bilateral Pilot Project	Suspended; UN calls for halt	(OHCHR 2023)
2025	Ongoing Talks Amid Civil War	No progress; atrocities persist	(Amnesty International 2025c)

safe, and dignified. However, Myanmar's military has instead built internment camps in Rakhine, reminiscent of historical forced repatriations in the 1970s and 1990s (Crisp 2018). In this respect, Amnesty International's 2025 report details how Rohingya in northern Rakhine face forced labor, food shortages, and movement restrictions, making repatriation "catastrophic" under current conditions (see Table 5.2) (Amnesty International 2025c).

Eight years on, the absence of justice perpetuates the cycle of denial. UN reports from 2025 emphasize that safe returns are impossible until perpetrators are held accountable and crimes end (IIMM 2025). Rohingya advocates themselves demand accountability as a prerequisite for peace, gathering in camps to voice that "no peace without justice" (Legal Action Worldwide 2025). To break the repatriation impasse, stronger multilateral pressure, including targeted sanctions and support for ICC/ICJ enforcement, is essential. Otherwise, the Rohingya's plight risks becoming a forgotten chapter in the annals of international failure.

Conclusion

This chapter discussed Myanmar's multifaceted role in perpetuating the Rohingya crisis. Resource conflicts in Rakhine State have further fueled intercommunal tensions and positioned the Rohingya as scapegoats in a resource-scarce environment. The 2021 military coup has entrenched authoritarianism. The coup dismantled fragile democratic structures and escalatedviolence, while non-state actors like the AA and Rohingya armed groups such as ARSA and RSO have complicated governance. These imposed restrictions, forced labor, and abuses that mirror the Tatmadaw's atrocities. Internationally, Myanmar's selective engagement gave rise to an "illusion of readiness" that deflected pressure without addressing root causes. These interconnected dimensions show us not only a bureaucratic inertia but also a calculated strategy to maintain exclusion. As a result, this has displaced over 150,000 more Rohingya since 2023, leaving 1.2 million in Bangladesh's camps amid dire conditions. Moving forward, sustainable repatriation is a reorientation toward comprehensive humanitarian assistance frameworks, guided by UNHCR's principles of protection, assistance, and durable solutions.

- First, international actors must strengthen ICC and ICJ enforcement through targeted sanctions and support for the IIMM to prosecute crimes against humanity. This would ensure offenders face justice as a precondition for safe returns.
- Second, ASEAN and the UN should establish secure aid corridors into Rakhine. They would bypass junta blockades to deliver food, healthcare, and education while involving Rohingya representatives in needs assessments to build trust and reduce abuses.
- Third, while voluntary, dignified returns remain ideal, alternatives like third-country resettlement for vulnerable groups (e.g., children comprising 52% of refugees) and local integration in Bangladesh must be expanded, supported by development aid to alleviate host community pressures and prevent social tensions.
- Finally, there should be advocacy for citizenship reforms in Myanmar, potentially through UN-mediated dialogues with all ethnic stakeholders. Also, investment in Rakhine's economic development to mitigate resource conflicts should foster reconciliation initiatives that promote interethnic dialogue and equitable resource sharing.

Without these integrated efforts, the Rohingya's plight jeopardizes indefinite prolongation, underscoring the urgent need for global solidarity to transform denial into genuine resolution.

References

Ahmed. 2024. "The Rohingya Crisis: Eight Potential Pathways to Repatriation." New Lines Institute, August 7. https://newlinesinstitute.org/state-resilience-fragility/the-rohingya-crisis-eight-potential-pathways-to-repatriation/.

Amnesty International. 2025a. "8 Years On: Accountability Needed for Myanmar Atrocities against Rohingya." Amnesty International, August 22. https://www.amnesty.org/en/latest/news/2025/08/8-years-on-accountability-needed-for-myanmar-atrocities-against-rohingya/.

Amnesty International. 2025b. "Myanmar: Four Years after Coup, World Must Demand Accountability for Atrocity Crimes." Amnesty International, January 31. https://www.amnesty.org/en/latest/news/2025/01/myanmar-four-years-after-coup-world-must-demand-accountability-for-atrocity-crimes/.

Amnesty International. 2025c. “Myanmar: Rohingya Repatriation ‘Catastrophic’ under Existing Conditions in Northern Rakhine State.” Amnesty International, September 29. https://www.amnesty.org/en/latest/news/2025/09/myanmar-rohingya-repatriation-catastrophic-under-existing-conditions-in-northern-rakhine-state/.

Bhattacharjee, Mowsume. 2024. “Statelessness of an Ethnic Minority: The Case of Rohingya.” *Frontiers in Political Science* 6 (June). https://doi.org/10.3389/fpos.2024.1144493.

Black, Richard, and Gent, Saskia. 2006. Sustainable Return in Post-Conflict Contexts, International Migration, 44(3):15 – 38.

Brenner, David. 2025. “Rebel Politics after the Coup: Ethnic Armed Organisations and Myanmar’s Spring Revolution.” *Journal of Contemporary Asia*, May 12, 1–24. https://doi.org/10.1080/00472336.2025.2494109.

Burke, Adam, Nicola Williams, Patrick Barron, Kim Jolliffe, and Thomas Carr. 2017. The Contested Areas of Myanmar: Subnational Conflict, Aid, and Development. https://asiafoundation.org/wp-content/uploads/2024/08/ContestedAreasMyanmarReport.pdf.

Crisp, Jeff. 2018. “‘Primitive People’: The Untold Story of UNHCR’s Historical Engagement with Rohingya Refugees.” Humanitarian Practice Network, October 24. https://odihpn.org/en/publication/primitive-people-the-untold-story-of-unhcrs-historical-engagement-with-rohingya-refugees/.

Debnath, Kunal, Souvik Chatterjee, and Afnan Bint Afzal. 2022. “Natural Resources and Ethnic Conflict: A Geo-Strategic Understanding of the Rohingya Crisis in Myanmar.” *Jadavpur Journal of International Relations* 26 (2): 186–207. https://doi.org/10.1177/09735984221120309.

Dhaka Tribune. 2017. The untapped wealth of Rakhine and the persecution of the Rohingya. https://www.dhakatribune.com/world/south-asia/126585/the-untapped-wealth-of-rakhine-and-the-persecution.

Dönmez, Beyza Binnur. 2025. “UN Investigative Body Finds Rohingya Villages Destroyed, Land Seized in Myanmar.” September 29. https://www.aa.com.tr/en/asia-pacific/un-investigative-body-finds-rohingya-villages-destroyed-land-seized-in-myanmar/3702163.

Fortify Rights. 2024. “The ICC’s Action on the Rohingya Is Historic, But the Court Should Go Further on Myanmar.” Fortify Rights, December 9. https://www.fortifyrights.org/mya-inv-oped-2024-12-09/.

Foreign Affairs, House. 2025. “Meeks, McCaul, Bera, Huizenga Introduce Burma GAP Act.” House Foreign Affairs Committee. June 25, 2025. https://democrats-foreignaffairs.house.gov/2025/6/meeks-mccaul-bera-huizenga-introduce-burma-gap-act.

Haque, Md Mahbubul. 2024. “Protracted Conflict in Myanmar and the Role of International Actors”. *SINERGI: Journal of Strategic Studies & International Affairs* 4 (2): 117–26. https://doi.org/10.17576/sinergi.0402.2024.09.

Haacke, Jürgen. 2025. “Reassessing ASEAN’s Five-Point Consensus: On Shifting Boundaries of Legitimate Involvement and a Contested Consensus.” *Asian Politics & Policy* 17 (4): e70050. https://doi.org/10.1111/aspp.70050.

Hansen, Thomas Blom, and Finn Stepputat. 2006. “Sovereignty Revisited.” *Annual Review of Anthropology* 35 (2006): 295–315. https://doi.org/10.1146/annurev.anthro.35.081705.123317.

Harder, Charles. 2025. “Remarks at a High-Level Conference on the Situation of Rohingya Muslims and Other Minorities in Myanmar.” United States Mission to the United Nations, September 30. https://usun.usmission.gov/remarks-at-a-high-level-conference-on-the-situation-of-rohingya-muslims-and-other-minorities-in-myanmar/.

Htun, Nyo, and Mrat Swe. 2023. "Another Year Dawns With Fears Persisting Among Farmers in Kyaukphyu SEZ Project Area." Development Media Group, January 12. true://www.dmediag.com/feature/fpaf.html.
Human Rights Watch. 2025. UN: Support Protection, Justice for Rohingya. September 29. https://www.hrw.org/news/2025/09/29/un-support-protection-justice-for-rohingya.
International Court of Justice. 2022. Summary of the Judgment of 22 July. 178 - Application of the Convention on the Prevention and Punishment of the Crime of Genocide (The Gambia v. Myanmar: 11 States intervening). https://www.icj-cij.org/node/106180.
IIMM. 2025. "Accountability for Crimes Committed against Rohingya Is Critical for Future Peace, Says Head of the Myanmar Mechanism During Bangladesh Visit." January 24. https://iimm.un.org/en/bangladesh-visit-accountability-crimes-committed-against-rohingya-critical-future-peace.
Jeffrey, Alex. 2023. "Geopolitics and Genocide: The Gambia vs. Myanmar at the International Court of Justice." *Environment and Planning C: Politics and Space* 41 (8): 1609–25. https://doi.org/10.1177/23996544231188822.
Khan, Ashrafuzzaman. 2018. "The Strategic Importance of Rakhine State." *The Daily Star*, September 3. https://www.thedailystar.net/news/opinion/perspective/the-strategic-importance-rakhine-state-1628290.
Legal Action Worldwide. 2025. No Peace Without Justice: Rohingya Call for Accountability. September 23. https://legalactionworldwide.org/accountability-rule-of-law/no-peace-without-justice-rohingya-call-for-accountability/.
Mohajan, Haradhan Kumar. 2020. "History of Rakhine State and the Origin of the Rohingya Muslims." *IKAT: The Indonesian Journal of Southeast Asian Studies* 2 (1): 19–46. https://doi.org/10.22146/ikat.v2i1.37391.
Naing, Yan. 2022. "Guest Column | China-Backed Port in Western Myanmar Depriving Locals of Land and Jobs." *The Irrawaddy*, September 13. https://www.irrawaddy.com/news/burma/china-backed-port-in-western-myanmar-depriving-locals-of-land-and-jobs.html.
Oh, Su-Ann. 2013. "Competing Forms of Sovereignty in the Karen State of Myanmar. ISEAS Working Paper #1." Institute of Southeast Asian Studies. https://kecdktl.org/wp-content/uploads/2024/04/Su-Ann-Oh-Competing-forms-of-sovereignty-in-Karen-state-of-Myanmar-2013.pdf.
OHCHR. 2023. "Bangladesh Must Suspend Pilot Project to Return Rohingya Refugees to Myanmar: UN Expert." OHCHR, June 8. https://www.ohchr.org/en/press-releases/2023/06/bangladesh-must-suspend-pilot-project-return-rohingya-refugees-myanmar-un.
Rahman, Mohammad Atique, and Kawsar Uddin Mahmud. 2024. "The Stranded Million: Rohingyas in Bangladesh and Their Repatriation." *Bangladesh Peace Observatory, Centre for Alternatives,(CA Peace Report 2024)* 7 (3): 29–39.
Rohingya Khobor. 2025. "Rohingya Fishermen in Rakhine Forced to Surrender Half Their Catch to Arakan Army." Rohingya Khobor, May 9. https://rohingyakhobor.com/rohingya-fishermen-in-rakhine-forced-to-surrender-half-their-catch-to-arakan-army/.
Read, H. James. 2020. *Power Versus Liberty*. University Press of Virginia.
Romaniuk, Scott N., and Animesh Roul. 2024. "Arakan Rohingya Salvation Army: Spearheading Myanmar's Islamic Insurgency." In *Handbook of Terrorist and Insurgent Groups*, edited by Seth Jones. CRC Press. https://www.taylorfrancis.com/chapters/edit/10.4324/9780429426063-88/arakan-rohingya-salvation-army-scott-romaniuk-animesh-roul.
Sadan, Mandy. 2013. *Being and Becoming Kachin: Histories Beyond the State in the Borderworlds of Burma*. British Academy. https://doi.org/10.5871/bacad/9780197265550.001.0001.

Schendel, Willem. 2005. "The Bengal Borderland: Beyond State and Nation in South Asia." PLOS Biology – PLOS BIOL, January 1.

Smith, Martin John. 1999. *Burma: Insurgency and the Politics of Ethnicity.* University Press.

Taussig, Michael. 1993. *Mimesis and Alterity: A Particular History of the Senses.* Routledge. https://www.routledge.com/Mimesis-and-Alterity-A-Particular-History-of-the-Senses/Taussig/p/book/9780415906876.

The Daily Star. 2025. "US Pledges $60m for Rohingya Refugees in Bangladesh." *The Daily Star.* September 30, 2025. https://www.thedailystar.net/news/bangladesh/news/us-pledges-60m-rohingya-refugees-bangladesh-3998926.

Tun, Aung. 2009. *History of the Shan State: From Its Origins to 1962.* Silkworm Books. http://catalog.hathitrust.org/api/volumes/oclc/244653687.html.

Uddin, Nasir. 2024. "The Fate of the Rohingya May Be in the Arakan Army's Hands." Al Jazeera, July 3. https://www.aljazeera.com/opinions/2024/7/3/the-fate-of-the-rohingya-may-be-in-the-arakan-armys-hands.

UNHCR. 2019a. "Beyond Survival: Rohingya Refugee Children in Bangladesh Want to Learn | UNICEF." August. https://www.unicef.org/emergencies/rohingya-beyond-survival-alert.

UNHCR. 2019b. "UNHCR Statement on Voluntary Repatriation to Myanmar." UNHCR US, August 22. https://www.unhcr.org/us/news/news-releases/unhcr-statement-voluntary-repatriation-myanmar.

UNHCR. 2025a. "Projected Global Resettlement Needs 2025." UNHCR. https://www.unhcr.org/media/projected-global-resettlement-needs-2025.

UNHCR. 2025c. "UNHCR: Bangladesh Has Welcomed 150,000 Rohingya Refugees in Last 18 Months." UNHCR, July 11. https://www.unhcr.org/news/briefing-notes/unhcr-bangladesh-has-welcomed-150-000-rohingya-refugees-last-18-months.

United Nations. 2017. "UN Human Rights Chief Points to 'Textbook Example of Ethnic Cleansing' in Myanmar | UN News." September 11. https://news.un.org/en/story/2017/09/564622-un-human-rights-chief-points-textbook-example-ethnic-cleansing-myanmar.

United Nations. 2019. ICC green-lights probe into violent crimes against Rohingya. UN News, 15 November. https://news.un.org/en/story/2019/11/1051451

United Nations. 2025a. "Myanmar Mechanism Report Identifies Entities Benefitting from Destruction and Dispossession of Rohingya Land and Property in 2017 | Independent Investigative Mechanism for Myanmar." September 29. https://iimm.un.org/en/myanmar-mechanism-report-identifies-entities-benefitting-destruction-and-dispossession-rohingya.

United Nations. 2025b. *The Destruction and Dispossession of Rohingya Land and Property During the 2017 Clearance Operations – Public Summary.* United Nations. https://iimm.un.org/sites/default/files/2025/09/Land%20Report%20Public%20Summary%20EN.pdf.

Ware, Anthony, and Costas Laoutides. 2018. "Recent Violence and Significance." In *Myanmar's 'Rohingya' Conflict*, edited by Anthony Ware and Costas Laoutides. Oxford University Press. https://doi.org/10.1093/oso/9780190928865.003.0002.

Ware, Anthony, and Monique Skidmore. 2023. Post-Coup Myanmar's Political and Humanitarian Crises. https://doi.org/10.22459/AC.2023.01.

Win, Yin Yin. 2024. "Status of the Civil Service Personnel of the Myanmar Civil Disobedient Movement: National and International Legal Perspectives." February 7. https://macmillan.yale.edu/southeast-asia/status-civil-service-personnel-myanmar-civil-disobedient-movement-national-and.

6

DEALING WITH CHINA OVER THE ROHINGYA ISSUE

Bangladesh's Predicaments and Leverages

Md Touhid Hossain

Introduction

Ever since the military took power in Burma in 1962, the Rohingyas have faced atrocities from the state. The Buddhist clergy and the local Rakhine community joined hands with the military in this act. The first large-scale forced exodus of 250,000 Rohingyas took place in 1978. An agreement was signed between the two countries under which repatriation of 'lawful residents' was agreed, and most of them were repatriated, with a handful staying back. The Citizenship Act of 1982 of Myanmar de-legitimized the Rohingyas (AMCHAM Journal 2021). To be considered as citizens, their ancestors had to be continuously resident in the Rakhine State since 1823, and the onus of proof of residency was on the Rohingyas. In view of the provisions of the Citizenship Act of 1982, many of them could not go back. A slow and continuous exodus of the community continued, and at least 300,000 Rohingyas entered Bangladesh before the organized atrocities of 2016. In 2016, 80,000 Rohingyas fled to Bangladesh, and they could not return. Under international pressure, the Kofi Annan Commission was instituted by Myanmar. The report of the Commission, submitted in August 2017, made 88 recommendations and asked for the return of the Rohingyas to Myanmar with rights and security. Ironically, two days after the Kofi Annan Commission submitted its report, on the pretext of terrorist attacks by the Arakan Rohingya Salvation Army (ARSA) on several security posts, the Myanmar military enacted the latest mass expulsion under extreme atrocities (killing, rape, arson). More than 800,000 Rohingyas were forced to flee to Bangladesh. The UN Human Rights Commissioner has termed it a textbook case of 'ethnic cleansing'. Bangladesh accommodated the

DOI: 10.4324/9781003771890-6

Rohingyas in camps in Teknaf and Ukhiya of Cox's Bazar district bordering the Rakhine State of Myanmar (AMCHAM Journal 2021).

Bangladesh's Prime Minister took the issue to the UN General Assembly in 2017. She gave a 5-point plan to repatriate Rohingyas with rights, security, and dignity. Meanwhile, negotiations were opened with Myanmar, and on 23 November 2017, an agreement was signed for repatriation. The agreement, drawn up rather in a hurry ostensibly under Chinese pressure, was similar to the earlier agreements of 1978 and 1992. However, the completely different nature of the 2017 expulsion vis-à-vis previous exoduses was apparently not factored in. In accordance with the agreement, Bangladesh was to submit lists of Myanmar residents who had taken shelter in Bangladesh, Myanmar was to scrutinize and decide on their bona fides, and the approved ones were then to be repatriated in groups. The issue of their rights and security was not addressed. Bangladesh has so far sent a list of 840,000 Rohingyas, of which Myanmar has cleared only 42,000. There were one or two false starts, but not a single Rohingya has so far been repatriated to their homes.

Against this backdrop, (The subsequent sections of) this chapter examine China's pivotal role in shielding Myanmar within UN organs, elucidating Bangladesh's multifaceted predicaments rooted in domestic constraints and regional dynamics. Finally, it outlines strategies to enhance Bangladesh's leverage, from economic diversification to informal engagements with non-state actors, before concluding with implications for regional stability.

An Inventory of Chinese Presence in UN Bodies on Rohingya Issue

China enjoys close, friendly relations with both Bangladesh and Myanmar, and could have played an even-handed role as the crisis unfolded. However, unfortunately, China decided to stand solidly behind Myanmar, shielding it from any censure for the crimes it committed against the Rohingyas. When Western countries and fellow Nobel Laureates of Aung San Su Kyi urged her to stop the violence against the Rohingyas, the Chinese Foreign Ministry spokesperson offered her encouraging words, voicing Chinese support for her government's efforts to 'uphold peace and stability' in Rakhine (Ramcharan et al. 2023). The issue has been discussed at various organs of the United Nations System since the Bangladesh Prime Minister raised it at the UNGA in 2017. Let us look at the Chinese role on the issue in UN organs (Ramcharan et al. 2023).

Chinese Role in the UN System

In the UN Security Council

Immediately following the atrocities and exodus in 2017, Britain and Sweden asked for an urgent Security Council meeting. However, with firm support from China and Russia on Myanmar's side, the UN Security Council was unable to do anything (Hossain 2022). The Council met behind closed doors to discuss the violence, but could not agree on a formal statement because of Chinese opposition. Since then, several attempts have been made to discuss the issue at the Security Council. However, because of Chinese opposition, this could never be included in the agenda. The issue could only be discussed under 'other matters', with no practical consequences. Since 2017, the Security Council has held several open and closed-door meetings, including an Arria-formula meeting on Myanmar, but no action could be taken. From April 28 to May 1, 2018, members of the Security Council visited Bangladesh. After the visit, the Council issued a Press Statement on May 2018 (UN Security Council 2018). The members of the Security Council urged the Government of Myanmar to step up its efforts to create conditions conducive to the safe, voluntary, and dignified return of Rohingya refugees and internally displaced persons to their homes in Rakhine State and to address the root causes of the crisis through implementation of the Rakhine Advisory Commission (Kofi Annan Commission) recommendations, including those related to human rights, citizenship, poverty alleviation, and development. Such statements, however, did not have enforcement provisions (UN Security Council 2018).

In the UN General Assembly

Since August 2017, the UN General Assembly has adopted the following five resolutions, jointly tabled by the EU and the OIC, on the human rights situation of Myanmar to date (Jain 2015).

UNGA Serial	*Resolution Number*	*Title of the Resolution*	*Date of Adoption*	*Total Vote Dynamics*	*The Status of Chinese Vote*
72*nd* UNGA	A/RES/ 72/248	'Situation of human rights in Myanmar'	Adopted by the General Assembly on 24 December 2017	122 countries voted for the motion (yes), 10 against (no), with 24 abstentions	*China voted 'NO'*
73rd UNGA	A/RES/ 73/264	'Situation of human rights in Myanmar'	Adopted by the General Assembly on 22 December 2018	Voting Record was 136-08-22 (Yes-No-Abstention)	*China voted 'NO'*

(*Continued*)

UNGA Serial	*Resolution Number*	*Title of the Resolution*	*Date of Adoption*	*Total Vote Dynamics*	*The Status of Chinese Vote*
74th UNGA	A/RES/ 74/246	'Situation of human rights of Rohingya Muslims and other minorities in Myanmar'	Adopted by the General Assembly on 27 December 2019	Voting Record was 134-09–28 (Yes-No-Abstention)	*China voted* 'NO' (Daily Sun 2021)
75th UNGA	A/RES/ 75/238	'Situation of human rights of Rohingya Muslims and other minorities in Myanmar'	Adopted by the General Assembly on 31 December 2020	Voting Record was 130-09–26 (Yes-No-Abstention)	*China voted* 'NO' (Daily Sun 2021)
76th UNGA	A/RES/ 76/180	'Situation of human rights of Rohingya Muslims and other minorities in Myanmar'	It was only this resolution that was adopted by the General Assembly without a vote on 16 December 2021(Dhaka Tribune 2019).		

However, UNGA Resolutions, even if passed with an overwhelming majority, can only have a moral value. There is no mechanism to enforce the decisions (Rütte 2022).

At the UN Human Rights Council

At the UN Human Rights Council, various resolutions on the human rights situation in Myanmar and on the Rohingya Muslims were adopted without a vote between 2007 and 2016 (Ramcharan 2022). However, from 2017 onwards (after the current Rohingya crisis started) until the 43rd Session in 2020, the resolutions, though adopted overwhelmingly, were put to vote mostly by China (once by Venezuela) (Ramcharan 2022). Needless to say, China consistently voted against the resolutions. The list runs like this:

Session	*Resolution Symbol*	*Title*	*Adoption Date*	*In Favor*	*Against*	*Abstentions*	*Vote Type*
27th Special Session	S-27/1	Situation of human rights of Rohingya Muslims and other minorities in Myanmar	5 December 2017	33	3	9	Recorded vote
37th Regular Session	37/32	Situation of human rights in Myanmar	23 March 2018	32	5	10	Recorded vote
39th Regular Session	39/2	Situation of human rights of Rohingya Muslims and other minorities in Myanmar	27 September 2018	35	3	7	Recorded vote
40th Regular Session	40/29	Situation of human rights in Myanmar	22 March 2019	37	3	7	Recorded vote (GICJ Report 2019)
42nd Regular Session	42/3	Situation of human rights in Myanmar	3 October 2019	37	2	7	Recorded vote
43rd Regular Session	43/18	Situation of human rights in Myanmar	7 October 2020	37	2	8	Recorded vote
29th Special Session	S-29/1	Human rights implications of the crisis in Myanmar	12 February 2021	Consensus	–	–	Consensus
46th Regular Session	46/21	Situation of human rights in Myanmar	23 September 2021	–	–	–	Without vote
47th Regular Session	47/1	Situation of human rights of Rohingya Muslims and other minorities in Myanmar	23 September 2021	–	–	–	Without vote (UN Geneva 2022)
52nd Regular Session	52/31	Situation of human rights in Myanmar	11 May 2023	–	–	–	Without vote

Bangladesh's Predicaments

Bangladesh's predicaments in its dealings with China emanate from its domestic weaknesses and regional realities. While Bangladesh has its strengths and achievements, certain factors severely limit its bargaining power.

Domestic Realities

Bangladesh is one of the most homogeneous countries in the world in terms of ethnicity, language, and culture (Baker et al. 2013). There are religious minorities, but the culture transcends religious barriers. The people of Bangladesh are traditionally freedom-loving and have a democratic, secular ethos. The country has a youthful population that is hardworking, enterprising, and adventurous. The country has come a long way from the predicaments of the '80s when it was extremely aid-dependent. It has had a sustained economic growth of more than 6% for the last 25-plus years (Hossain 2022). Even during the pandemic, when most major economies experienced contraction, Bangladesh grew at a healthy 3.5%.

There are, however, constraints. Bangladesh's unique geography imposes certain limitations on its external dealings. It is almost India-bound on three sides, except for a small stretch of boundary with Myanmar. The India factor, thus, becomes pivotal. Its rivers—the lifeblood of Bangladesh's economy—have their catchments in India and beyond. The cone-shaped coastline has limited the extent of its exclusive economic zone and would give it a very small continental shelf. Acute population pressure on a relatively small territory, coupled with limited physical resources, restricts its maneuverability in external relations. The low quality of human resources makes Bangladeshi workers some of the lowest paid in the world.

On the domestic front, a complete lack of political consensus on issues of national interest often becomes a serious handicap for Bangladesh. The relative weakness of military power, particularly in the regional context, often makes pursuing its interests difficult. In the Global Firepower Index 2021, Bangladesh at 45 (score 0.7473) is below Myanmar at 38 (score 0.6521, lower score denotes stronger military).

Regional Dynamics

The domestic soft underbelly is weakened further by regional dynamics. The two most important countries of the greater region are China and India, apart from the interests of the global power, the USA. The overwhelming factor in the emerging security environment in the region is the inevitable rise of China and the determination of its adversaries to stop, or at least stymie, that process.

The military modernization program that China started in the 1990s has now reached a state of maturity where some of the hardware in its arsenal can match that of its US counterparts. Chinese strategic thinking has also undergone a sea change. As Prof. Aminul Karim points out: ‘China’s naval strategy is undergoing a paradigm shift from coastal defense of the mainland to active defense of maritime economic resources and strategic interests, asserting China’s sovereignty over the South China Sea islands in the face of other claimants, possibly affecting Taiwan’s forceful unification and curtailing Japanese rearmament.” (; Karim 2018).

On PPP terms, China is already the world’s largest economy, surpassing the USA. As per PWC predictions, China will also become the largest economy on the market exchange rate by the middle of the century (Till and Chan 2013). China is using its economic muscle to further its strategic and economic gains (Mya Thida 2023). Through development partnerships (often laced with rampant corruption) and the Belt and Road Initiative (BRI), China has extended its sway over much of Africa and Asia (Mya Thida 2023; Mahmud 2024a). Her weak point strategically had been the dependence on the Malacca Strait for the import of energy and raw materials, and the export of finished goods to Africa, Europe, and the Middle East (Till and Chan 2013). She is already on its way to resolving this handicap by way of connectivity to the Bay of Bengal through Myanmar (Zou et al. 2019). Chinese naval ambitions in the Indian Ocean are also evident, and it has achieved its first foothold in Djibouti, at the mouth of the strategic Bab-el-Mandeb (Zou et al. 2019). She also has a long-term lease of the Hambantota port in Sri Lanka (Mya Thida 2023). Chinese officials and academics who used to politely deny any ambitions even ten years back now proclaim emphatically that the rise of China is unstoppable (ANU 2024).

Bangladesh had earlier joined the Chinese-led BRI, but did not agree to join the IPS or an extended Quad. This was a logical step considering that while BRI was ostensibly a communication project to facilitate international trade, the anti-China intent of IPS was rather apparent (Mahmud 2024a). India particularly wants Bangladesh beside it in the evolving geostrategic game. However, Bangladesh neither desires nor can afford to take sides in the China-India animosity. While it adheres to the policy of remaining neutral, it also needs Chinese partnership in pursuing its developmental goals (Bhattarai 2022). Curiously, speaking at a program of the Diplomatic Correspondents’ Association of Bangladesh (DCAB) on 10 May 2021, the Chinese Ambassador to Bangladesh openly spelled out the obvious that relations with China will be damaged if Bangladesh joins the US-led Quad (Bhattarai 2022). He also termed Quad as ‘a military alliance’ aimed against China’s resurgence (Star Digital Report 2022). Bangladesh remains committed to the peaceful settlement of disputes, to refraining from any threat of use of force, and to the importance of maintaining the security and freedom of navigation and overflights in all seas and oceans. Bangladesh's position demonstrates its resolve to stay clear of taking any side in the regional geopolitical face-off, and it does so in accordance with its vital national interest. However, as the global and regional situation evolves, maintaining its neutral stance may become increasingly difficult.

Chinese Priorities Paradoxically Align with Myanmar's Advantages

Relating to the Rohingya issue, any advantage of Myanmar constitutes a predicament for Bangladesh, and there are many such advantages of Myanmar (Rahman and Mahmud 2024). While human rights or atrocities against minorities are issues of lesser priority for China, there are also practical reasons why China is strongly backing the Myanmar regime. China's most critical interests in Myanmar center on securing direct access to the Indian Ocean through energy infrastructure and bypassing strategic vulnerabilities in its energy supply chain. The China-Myanmar oil and gas pipeline system is the foundation of Beijing's strategic relationship with Myanmar (Offshore Technology 2013). It is considered China's fourth major energy import channel after Central Asia, Russia, and Middle East routes. This dual pipeline infrastructure, operational since 2013 for gas and 2014 for oil, transports crude oil and natural gas from Myanmar's Rakhine State directly to China's Yunnan Province, covering 2,520 kilometers with 793 kilometers within Myanmar territory (Offshore Technology 2013). The gas pipeline alone has the capacity to transport 13 billion cubic meters annually, while the oil pipeline can handle 22 million tons of crude oil per year. For China, this infrastructure addresses what former President Hu Jintao termed the 'Malacca Dilemma'—the strategic vulnerability of having approximately 80% of China's oil imports transit through the narrow Strait of Malacca, which could potentially be blockaded by hostile forces during conflicts (Mosyakov et al. 2024).

Beyond energy security, Myanmar appears to be China's gateway to the Indian Ocean through the ambitious China-Myanmar Economic Corridor (CMEC) under the BRI (Mosyakov et al. 2024). The centerpiece of this strategy is the Kyaukpyu Deep-Sea Port project, a $7.3 billion investment that grants China a 70% stake in a strategically positioned port facility on the Bay of Bengal. This port, combined with the accompanying $2.7 billion Special Economic Zone, represents China's most significant infrastructure investment in Myanmar and provides Beijing with direct maritime access to the Indian Ocean. The strategic importance of Kyaukpyu extends beyond commercial considerations as it potentially offers China dual-use capabilities for military purposes, allowing Chinese naval vessels to operate in the Indian Ocean region and potentially challenge India's traditional maritime dominance. This development is particularly concerning for India, as the

Kyaukpyu port is located less than 60 kilometers from India's Andaman and Nicobar Islands, effectively placing Chinese-controlled infrastructure in India's immediate maritime neighborhood (Mosyakov et al. 2024). Besides, China's investments in Myanmar's energy and port infrastructure totaling over $15 billion have created significant economic dependence, with Myanmar's military junta particularly reliant on Chinese support since the 2021 coup, making it difficult for Myanmar to resist Chinese strategic interests.

Bangladesh–China Growing Friendship: How to Effectively Capitalize on It?

China was on the side of the genocidal Pakistan regime during the 1971 war of liberation of Bangladesh. It recognized Bangladesh only after the regime change following the killing of Sheikh Mujibur Rahman in 1975. Ever since, Bangladesh-China relations have remained vibrant irrespective of the ruling government in Bangladesh. Trade and economic relations have grown, and today, China is an important source of development finance, as well as the largest trading partner in official figures.

China almost has a monopoly over the supply of military hardware to the armed forces of Bangladesh. Bangladesh has consistently supported China on issues sensitive to it, such as Tibet and Taiwan. China was considered a trusted friend on political issues, but on the Rohingya crisis, it has again taken the side of the genocidal regime. There are vested interest groups within Bangladesh who would work for China for their own financial benefits. Bangladesh needs to achieve Chinese even-handedness on the Rohingya issue, winning even-handedness on the Rohingya issue, winning it away from unconditional support to Myanmar, with no visible success so far. A tripartite process for the repatriation of Rohingyas was initiated, involving China as the facilitator, and the first meeting took place virtually on 19 January 2021(Hasan et al. 2022). The second meeting has not been held since the military coup of 01 February 2021 altered the political situation in Myanmar, and the priorities of the military regime have changed.

How Could Bangladesh's Leverage Be Improved

It would appear from the discussion above that Bangladesh has few levers vis-à-vis China in the current state of affairs. There is a pervading belief that Bangladesh has no alternative to China on most issues and that we have to keep China happy at any cost. Even the huge trade surplus that China has with Bangladesh does not act as leverage; rather, it is looked upon as dependence since Bangladesh needs to source those materials from China to run its manufacturing and export sectors. Bangladesh will need to come out of the sense of overwhelming dependence on China in order to gain some leverage vis-à-vis China. It must be kept in mind that leverage cannot be achieved overnight, and it takes long, well-planned, and painstaking work to gain and improve leverage. Considering the goals, the future strategies can be planned into phases: short-term, mid-term, and long-term goals.

Short-Term Goals

a. **Cooperating with the NUG:** While maintaining formal channels with the military government of Myanmar, Bangladesh should open informal channels of communication with the Government of National Unity (NUG). Cooperation with the NUG may include financial support, technical help, and getting a section of Rohingya refugees to become part of the NUG establishment. This will not only reduce dependence on China but will also open a second line of support in any future negotiated settlement.
b. **Explore possibilities of helping Rohingya participation in the resistance:** There are myriad ethnic insurgencies operating in at least two-thirds of the territories of Myanmar. Many of the ethnic groups are much smaller than the Rohingya and are facing fewer atrocities. Yet this most persecuted of all ethnicities had never had a substantive insurgency. The right of an ethnic group facing annihilation to take up arms to protect itself is universally recognized. Bangladesh, in coordination with the NUG, may explore possibilities of Rohingya participation in the armed resistance against the Myanmar military regime (Mahmud , 2024b). The NUG has invited the Rohingyas to join them in their fight against the military. Bangladesh should encourage and facilitate the process. The outcome, however, should not be an outfit like ARSA, whose purpose is to resist repatriation and perpetuate the refugee problem.
c. **Developing communication with the Arakan Army (AA):** The Arakan Army (AA) is one of the most potent insurgencies in Myanmar (Mizzima 2022). It is believed to have a well-trained force of 20,000 fighters. In any future resolution of the Myanmar crisis, be it on the battlefield or at the negotiating table, AA is going to be a major player in determining the future makeup of Arakan. If a federal structure finally evolves in Myanmar, it will be the AA and its political wing, the United League of Arakan, that will call the shots in the Rakhine State. The return of the Rohingyas to their homes with rights and security will require, among others, the goodwill of this organization. Bangladesh needs to open up to this outfit and create a working relationship with them. The AA is known to be anti-Rohingya as much as the Tatmadaw. However, in recent times, they have mentioned the possibility of including the Rohingyas in their future administration of Arakan. This needs to be built upon, and a rapprochement between the two needs to be developed, however difficult that may be (Mizzima 2022).

Mid-Term Goals

a. **Understanding public opinion in Bangladesh:** The fact that the popular perception of China in Bangladesh was mostly positive serves as a differentiating support ground to translate the passive acceptance into action by formalizing the demand to end the Rohingya crisis. According to the National Image Survey held in 2024, the number of those who express positive attitudes toward China is about 90 percent in Bangladesh, and two-thirds rate the level of bilateral relations as 'good' or 'rather good' (Xinhua 2025). The goodwill that builds up can be diverted toward Beijing via organized grassroots efforts carried out by civil society organizations and ratchet up the pressure on China to leverage to its advantage its capacity to influence Naypyidaw. At the same time, these initiatives should proceed toward official reassurances to the Rohingya on citizenship, security, and long-term infrastructure commitment in Rakhine. The use of public forums, social media alliances, and opinion editorials should place the participation of Beijing as the key focus to the prevalence of peace in the region, alongside achieving the moral obligation of protecting the victimized populace. Coherent natures of messages in different demographic groups can be achieved with strategic partnerships with student associations, professional guilds, faith networks, and so forth, to emphasize that continued pressure on the Myanmar junta by all the great powers, including China, is necessary.

Long-Term Goals

a. **Reducing dependence on China for project finance and vital imports by diversifying sources:** This is certainly easier said than done. Looking a little deeper would, however, show that dependence on China for financing mega projects is somewhat overrated. In the two biggest projects, the Padma Bridge and the Nuclear Power project, no financing from China is involved. Rather, a Chinese company is the main contractor for the Padma bridge, where costs have gone up exponentially to the benefit of the Chinese company, among others. The Dhaka Metro rail project is being financed by Japan, and so is the Matarbari power project. In the ranking of 2020–2021 in foreign aid (mostly loans) disbursement to Bangladesh, China stands at 5th position with disbursement of US$ 244.5 million only, behind Japan (1,926 m), World Bank (1,577 m), ADB (1,261 m), and Russia (1029.6 m) (Economic Relations Division, Ministry of Finance, Government of Bangladesh). Also, it is worth noting that Chinese loans are on much harder terms than the first three.

China being the 'factory of the world', the whole world is dependent on China for consumer as well as intermediate goods. Post-COVID-19, the world is trying to come out of this vulnerability. Bangladesh should carefully plan a way to source some of its vital imports from alternative sources. Particularly for capital machinery, there are alternate sources, albeit at higher prices. However, the extra investment is often offset by quality and durability. This will not be quick and easy, but sustained efforts can show good results. Many of the consumer goods imported from China can also be manufactured in Bangladesh.

b. **Encourage China to stand against Rohingya oppression:** Bangladesh so far has not shown any strong reaction to the untenable Chinese position of unswerving support for the crimes committed by the Myanmar regime. It is time to politely and firmly emphasize the gravity of the Rohingya issue in terms of the economic, social, and military security of Bangladesh. Bangladesh may also make it clear to China that if the Rohingya refugee issue remains unresolved, the situation may become intolerable for Bangladesh, and then there could be no option but to push them back into Myanmar to fight for their rights. In such an eventuality, regional security will be disturbed, and the situation in Rakhine will not remain conducive for investment by outsiders, including China.
c. **Developing closer ties with the West:** On the surface, Bangladesh generally enjoyed good relations with Western countries. Most of its exports go to the West, and it enjoys a substantial trade surplus with these countries. In the EU, Bangladeshi products enjoy preferential access under Everything but Arms (EBA). There is also a sizable Bangladeshi diaspora in Europe and North America, and remittances sent by them are substantial. However, Bangladesh is yet to develop a truly strategic partnership with the West. There are also issues on which the West has concerns, such as democracy, human rights, the rule of law, and human trafficking. Particularly on the issue of Election 2024, the relations with the West in general and with the USA in particular are under stress. For practical reasons, Bangladesh cannot participate in any overtly anti-China construct. However, to raise relations to the level of a strategic partnership with the West, Bangladesh needs to mitigate these concerns of the West. There is, however, a conflicting signal from various levels of political leadership about improving relations with the West. Attracting Western investment could also reduce dependence on China.
d. **Opening up to Taiwan:** Bangladesh is committed to a one-China policy, repeating time and again that Taiwan and Tibet are integral parts of China. However, that should not mean it cannot engage with Taiwan. Sixty countries that do not have diplomatic relations with Taiwan have de facto consulates or missions with other names in Taipei, which virtually work as diplomatic missions. The list includes such close friends of China as Myanmar. Likewise, Taiwan has formal embassies in

only 14 countries that recognize it as a sovereign country. However, Taiwan's foreign ministry runs informal missions and consulates in 81 countries, including Thailand, Myanmar, Turkey, Saudi Arabia, and Indonesia. Bangladesh should open a consulate in Taiwan under whatever name, and increase interaction in trade, investment, employment, and technology.

e. **Diversify sources for procuring military hardware:** This is imperative not only for gaining leverage over China but also to reduce vulnerability in supplies in times of crisis. Although figures are shrouded in secrecy, China evidently is the overwhelming supplier of military hardware procurement for Bangladesh. The only possibility, though remote, of Bangladesh getting entangled in a military conflict is with Myanmar. In such a scenario, Bangladesh can hardly rely on Chinese supplies, China being the chief backer of the Myanmar regime. Bangladesh needs to develop relations with the West as an alternate source of military hardware. Here again, higher prices could be offset by better quality.
f. **Build up credible military deterrence:** Bangladesh's military strength is not commensurate with its size and economy. While the issue of guns vs. butter is relevant, often the gun becomes important to guard your butter. The behavior of the Myanmar junta during the past years has brought the issue to the fore. Bangladesh needs to develop and execute a mid-term program to build a credible minimum military deterrence. While a wise implementation of the forces' goal 2030 can be helpful in the sphere of procurement, more important is the proper training and indoctrination of the military, and their reorientation toward their real purpose, away from the multifarious economic activities that they are engaged in.

Conclusion

Bangladesh has no territorial or hegemonic ambitions. It wants to live in peace, pursuing developmental goals for its people, and contribute to global and regional peace and stability. A serious problem in the form of the Rohingya issue has been thrust upon it from beyond the borders. Bangladesh by all accounts is an innocent victim and should have been dealt with on those counts. So are the Rohingyas. Rohingyas must be recognized as full citizens with equal rights and dignity, and be allowed to return to their homes. Arrangements must be made to ensure their security in the Rakhine State. Atrocities against them by the establishment and others must stop. Bangladesh entered into a bilateral agreement for repatriation rather in a hurry, ostensibly at the behest of China. Such a bilateral arrangement with Myanmar is likely to be futile, since the military's game plan is the complete expulsion of the Rohingyas, which they have almost succeeded in doing.

Bangladesh, however, has to keep the bilateral window open and continue with the trilateral setting with China as the facilitator. China is one country that may have some influence on the Myanmar junta. Bangladesh, however, needs to decrease its overdependence on China and improve other leverage points in order to actively engage China in using its influence on Myanmar.

While continuing the futile bilateral efforts with the military regime, she must also find ways to informally connect to the NUG and the Arakan Army, as that might become very important in any future settlement. The Rohingya problem will be long-drawn, will have unforeseen ramifications—political, social, economic, and security, for Bangladesh as well as for the region. As of now, Bangladesh seems to be ill-prepared for the upcoming challenges. She will need to multiply her capabilities and look for new friends and allies beyond her neighborhood in the geo-economic and geopolitical context. Lastly, history says, such problems involving genocide and ethnic cleansing have never been resolved peacefully. Bangladesh will have to be prepared with deterrence and enhanced capabilities for any possible eventualities.

References

AMCHAM Journal. 2021. "Tribute to War Heroes on the 50th Anniversary of Bangladesh." *AMCHAM Journal* 15 (4). https://www.amchambd.org/wp-content/uploads/2022/03/AmCham-Journal-December-2021-Issue.pdf.

ANU. 2024. "After the Coup: Myanmar's Political and Humanitarian Crises 1760466131, 9781760466138." Ebin.Pub, March 3. https://ebin.pub/after-the-coup-myanmars-political-and-humanitarian-crises-1760466131-9781760466138.html.

Baker, Christopher, Simone Battiston, and Bruno Mascitelli. 2013. "Diaspora Philanthropy in Australia: A Preliminary Critique." *Diaspora* 16 (3): 323–36. https://doi.org/10.3138/diaspora.16.3.323.

Bhattarai, Gaurav. 2022. "Rise with Responsibilities." In *Nepal Between China and India: Difficulty of Being Neutral*, edited by Gaurav Bhattarai. Springer International Publishing. https://doi.org/10.1007/978-3-030-99974-2_7.

Global Firepower Index. 2021. https://www.globalfirepower.com/countries.php#google_vignette.

Hasan, Manzoor, Syed Mansoob Murshed, and Priya Pillai, eds. 2022. *The Rohingya Crisis: Humanitarian and Legal Approaches*. Routledge. https://doi.org/10.4324/9781003304883.

Hossain, Md. Touhid. 2022. "Prospects and Challenges in Bangladesh's Relationship with Germany and the European Union, on Its 50th Anniversary of Independence." CGS, June 30. https://cgs-bd.com/article/9140/Prospects-and-Challenges-in-Bangladesh%E2%80%99s-Relationship-with-Germany-and-the-European-Union%2C-on-its-50th-Anniversary-of-Independence.

Jain, Abhimanyu George. 2015. "Indian Practice Relating to International Law." *Indian Journal of International Law* 55 (2): 265–88. https://doi.org/10.1007/s40901-015-0014-z.

Karim, Mohd. 2018. *Geopolitics of the South China Sea in the Coming Decades*. Nova Science Publishers. https://novapublishers.com/shop/geopolitics-of-the-south-china-sea-in-the-coming-decades/.

Mahmud, Kawsar Uddin. 2024a. "BRI and Beyond: Strengthening Bangladesh-China Relations Amid Political Change." *The Business Standard* (Bangladesh), December 21. https://www.tbsnews.net/thoughts/bri-and-beyond-strengthening-bangladesh-china-relations-amid-political-change-1023916

Mahmud, Kawsar Uddin. 2024b. "Myanmar: A Move to Ban Its Male Citizens from Going Abroad for Work." *The KRF Center for Bangladesh and Global Affairs (CBGA)*, June 2, 1–5. https://doi.org/10.2139/ssrn.5110439.

Mizzima. 2022. "The Rapid Rise of the Arakan Army." *Mizzima Myanmar News and Insight*, July 21. https://www.mizzima.com/article/rapid-rise-arakan-army.

Mosyakov, Dmitry V., Мосяков Дмитрий Валентинович, Marina A. Shpakovskaya, Шпаковская Марина Анатольевна, Tatiana I. Ponka, and Понька Татьяна Ивановна. 2024. "Myanmar's Role in China's Belt and Road Initiative." *Vestnik RUDN. International Relations* 24 (3): 3. https://doi.org/10.22363/2313-0660-2024-24-3-439-449.

Mya Thida, Hnin. 2023. "Myanmar-China Asymmetrical Relations: The Case Study of Myitsone Hydropower Dam Project through the Lens of Small Power's Strategies." Phd, Budapesti Corvinus Egyetem. https://phd.lib.uni-corvinus.hu/1266/.

Offshore Technology. 2013. "Myanmar-China Pipelines." Offshore Technology, October 28. https://www.offshore-technology.com/projects/myanmar-china-pipelines/.

Rahman, Mohammad Atique, and Kawsar Uddin Mahmud. 2024. *The Stranded Million: Rohingyas in Bangladesh and Their Repatriation*. Scholarly Paper. CA Peace Report 2024. Bangladesh Peace Observatory. https://dx.doi.org/10.2139/ssrn.5341037.

Ramcharan, Bertrand G. 2022. *The Protection Role and Jurisprudence of the United Nations Human Rights Council*. Brill. https://brill.com/display/title/61479.

Ramcharan, Bertrand G., Theodoor C. van Boven, Abdul G. Koroma, and Inès French. 2023. *The Universality of Human Rights*. Brill. https://brill.com/display/title/65020.

Rütte, Barbara. 2022. *The Human Right to Citizenship*. Brill. https://brill.com/display/title/62482.

Star Digital Report. 2022. "China Tells Bangladesh to 'Reject Bloc Politics.'" *The Daily Star*, June 2. https://www.thedailystar.net/news/bangladesh/diplomacy/news/china-tells-bangladesh-reject-bloc-politics-indian-media-reports-3038046.

Till, Geoffrey, and Jane Chan, eds. 2013. *Naval Modernisation in South-East Asia: Nature, Causes and Consequences*. Routledge. https://doi.org/10.4324/9780203406830.

UN Security Council. 2018. "Security Council Press Statement on Security Council Visit to Bangladesh, Myanmar | Meetings Coverage and Press Releases." May 9. https://press.un.org/en/2018/sc13331.doc.htm.

Xinhua. 2025. "Around 90 Pct of Bangladeshi Respondents Stand in Favor of China: Survey-Xinhua." March 12. https://english.news.cn/20250312/86d0db337ad94ccf949542b2f8181903/c.html.

Zou, Keyuan, Shicun Wu, and Qiang Ye, eds. 2019. *The 21st Century Maritime Silk Road: Challenges and Opportunities for Asia and Europe*. Routledge. https://doi.org/10.4324/9780429058585.

7

RETHINKING INDIA'S APPROACH TO THE ROHINGYA CRISIS

Raymond Kwun-Sun Lau

Introduction

Since the largest exodus of some 700,000 Rohingya refugees into Bangladesh began in August 2017, the government of Bangladesh made fervent appeals to the international community to put pressure on Myanmar to take back the Rohingya refugees. Such requests were made to Bangladesh's closest and most powerful neighbors like India, given India's significant influence over Myanmar. Yet, apart from providing temporary humanitarian assistance to Bangladesh (India Today 2017), India did not show any tangible willingness so far to facilitate the repatriation of Rohingya refugees. In fact, despite 'a multidimensional fraternal relationship' existing between India and Bangladesh (Ahmed 2022), India's foreign policy position on the Rohingya issue has consistently been aligned with Myanmar (Gao 2017). Indian Prime Minister's joint statement issued after Narendra Modi's visit to Myanmar in September 2017 is a testimony to the pro-Myanmar leanings of India (Mitra 2017). Such leanings became more pronounced in India's relations after the February 2021 coup with the army general Min Aung Hlaing and his State Administration Council (SAC).

Given that India has traditionally been a 'safe haven' for refugees by hosting a large number of Sri Lankan Tamils, Afghans, Tibetans, Chakma, and Hejong refugees, what explains New Delhi's unwillingness to proactively resolve the Rohingya crisis? What role can and should India play as this Rohingya refugee crisis drags on for nearly a decade? What can Bangladesh expect from India for assisting with the repatriation of the Rohingya refugees to Myanmar?

In addressing the above-mentioned questions, this chapter starts with a brief sketch of India's refugee policy in general in a bid to put its approach to

DOI: 10.4324/9781003771890-7

the Rohingya crisis in contrasting light. With India priding itself as 'indeed the mother of democracy' (Haidar 2023), its hesitancy on addressing the Rohingya crisis and its arbitrary arrest and detention of the Rohingya refugees (Al-Jazeera 2023) could undermine India as a regional power with global aspirations (Fawcett and Jagtiani 2024). Also, while India is one of the largest Rohingya-hosting countries outside Bangladesh, New Delhi has a vested interest in stemming the influx of Rohingya refugees by ensuring their peaceful repatriation. This chapter, therefore, argues that a more assertive role and policy approach adopted by India to resolve the Rohingya crisis would enhance India's regional influence, promote its long-term strategic interest and counter-balance China's growing influence in the Indian Ocean region.

India's Refugee Policy and Its Response/Approach to the Rohingya Crisis

India, since its independence in 1947, has adopted a democratic 'open door' policy by hosting refugees and asylum seekers from various neighboring countries as well as the Middle East and Africa. These include Tibetans persecuted by the Chinese government in 1959, Bangladeshis (People of East Pakistan before 1971) bearing the brunt of the brutal violence initiated by West Pakistan's army in 1971, Sri Lankan Tamils escaping violence during the civil war (1983–2009), Afghans seeking refuge in India during the Soviet–Afghan War in the late 1970s and early 1980s (Rana 2022, p. 144).

Yet, even though there are a total of more than 213,000 refugees and asylum seekers in India (Seth 2022), the country is not a party to the 1951 Convention Relating to the Status of Refugees (1951 Refugee Convention) and its 1967 Protocol, nor does it have a national legal protection framework that deals with refugee and asylum seeker protection. Therefore, the Indian government has to rely on laws dealing with entry, stay, and exit (or removal) of foreigners for refugees and asylum seekers. The first piece of legislation is the Passport (Entry into India) Act, 1920. This Act requires that persons entering India shall be in possession of passports. And in supersession of the Indian Passport Rules, 1921, the Indian government enacted the Passport (Entry into India) Rules, 1950, which extend to the whole of India, requiring a proper visa to enter India.

The second piece of legislation is the Registration of Foreigners Act, 1939, which, for the first time, defines foreigners as a person who is not a citizen of India and was enacted to provide for the registration of foreigners entering, being present in, and departing from, British India. The Foreigners Act, 1946 is another piece of widely used legislation for dealing with foreigners in India. Under this Act, the (Indian) Central government is equipped with the power to issue orders by prohibiting, regulating, or restricting the entry of foreigners into India or their departure. The Registration of Foreigners

Rules, 1992, which is a supersession of the Registration of Foreigners Rules, 1939, requires every foreigner who enters India on a visa valid for a stay for a period of more than 180 days to present a registration report to the Registration Officer having jurisdiction in the place.

Since the Indian government has never formulated any well-defined asylum seekers and refugee protection law, those refugees and asylum seekers are also governed by that above-mentioned old colonial legislation and, therefore, are classified into the same category as foreigners, meaning that those who are found without valid documents, such as passports and visas, are considered 'illegal immigrants' and subject to detention and deportation from India. While the passage of the Citizenship (Amendment) Act, 2003 and Citizenship (Amendment) Act, 2019 has made a certain class of illegal immigrants eligible to be granted Indian citizenship, these new citizenship laws, however, are not applicable to Muslim minorities including the Ahmadiyya from Pakistan and the Rohingya from Myanmar (Winchester 2020). By dividing alleged migrants into Muslims and non-Muslims, those Acts are criticized for protecting 'only the rights of non-Muslim irregular immigrants from the neighboring Muslim-majority countries of Afghanistan, Bangladesh, and Pakistan' (Human Rights Watch 2019).

The absence of clearly defined statutory standards on refugee and asylum seeker protection has resulted in the formation of inconsistent and arbitrary government policies. This administrative *ad hocism*, therefore, has made different refugee communities subject to varying standards of protection (Raj 2020, pp. 32–4). The Indian government's selective way of treating certain refugee publics differently is also evident in its response/approach to the Rohingya refugees fleeing to India.

India's Response/Approach to the Rohingya Crisis

While India has already experienced the Rohingya refugee movement following a mass exodus of some 250,000 Rohingya fleeing persecution in the Rakhine State between December 1991 and March 1992, it was not until 2012 that India started witnessing a steady influx of Rohingya into various regions of the country including Jammu and Kashmir, West Bengal, Delhi, Hyderabad, among others (Verma 2022, p. 7). According to a 2019 UNHCR estimate, there are approximately 43,000 Rohingya living in various regions of the country, whereas some 17,500 of them were registered with the United Nations High Commissioner for Refugees (UNHCR) until 2018 (Tay and Ventevogel 2018).

The approach taken by India toward the Rohingya crisis can be divided into four phases (Yasmin 2022). In the first phase, the Indian government avoided making comments on the conflict pitting ethnic Rakhine Buddhists against Rohingya Muslims since June 2012 as New Delhi considered the conflict an 'internal affairs' of Myanmar. Still, the Rohingya asylum seekers could manage to get refugee status (by the UNHCR) and long-term visas (LTVs) yearly by the Foreigners Regional Registration Office (FRRO) for their continuous residence in India (Verma 2022, p. 485). However, with Narendra Modi and his Bharatiya Janata Party (BJP) coming into power in 2014, India started considering the Rohingyas as 'illegal immigrants' and halted the renewal of their LTVs: only fewer than 500 of them out of roughly 40,000 Rohingyas residing in India have been granted long-term visas by the Indian government (The Times of India 2017).

India's Rohingya policy in the second phase, which roughly began in mid-2017, was characterized by a further toughening of the Modi government's policy toward the Rohingyas and its one-sided support to the Myanmar government in combating terrorism amidst the ongoing violence in Myanmar's northern Rakhine State (The Irrawaddy 2017). On the 9th of August, Kiren Rijiju, the then Minister of State for Home Affairs, announced that all Rohingyas, as illegal immigrants, have no basis to live in India and could be subject to deportation (Hindustan Times 2017). Also, the India-Myanmar joint statement issued after Prime Minister Narendra Modi's visit to Myanmar in September 2017, for instance, condemned the August 2017 terrorist attacks on police and army outposts in the northern Rakhine State by the Arakan Rohingya Salvation Army (ARSA), a Rohingya insurgent group founded in 2013, but remained silent on the Rohingya refugee crisis (Yhome 2018, p. 4).

The third phase of India's response saw a dramatic change in its Rohingya policy. In stark contrast to its (somewhat) passive attitude toward the 'internal affairs' of Myanmar, New Delhi stepped up its efforts to help solve the refugee crisis through using 'quiet diplomacy' (Yhome 2018, p. 5). A Memorandum of Understanding (MoU) signed between India's then Foreign Secretary S. Jaishankar and Myanmar's Deputy Minister for social welfare, relief and resettlement U Soe Aung, during Jaishankar's visit to Myanmar in December 2017 (The Indian Express 2017), is the first government-to-government (G2G) agreement that focuses on socio-economic development and livelihood initiatives in Rakhine State (Mohan 2017).

In the fourth and also the ongoing phase since mid-2020, India has stepped up its efforts to conciliate Bangladesh by endorsing Dhaka's urge to the wider international community in increasing pressure on Myanmar to take back the Rohingyas (Yasmin 2022, p. 128). In his letter issued in July 2020 to Bangladesh's foreign minister, India's current External Affairs Minister Subrahmanyam Jaishankar highly praised Bangladesh 'for showing generosity and humanity by sheltering the Rohingya' and suggested that 'a quick, safe and sustainable repatriation of the refugees in Bangladesh will benefit all parties' (The Business Standard 2020). India's Foreign Secretary Harsh Vardhan Shringla reiterated his country's fullest support for 'any mutually-acceptable solution that would enable earliest possible return of displaced persons' to Myanmar's Rakhine State (The Economic Times 2020).

Yet, despite its efforts to conciliate Bangladesh, it is obvious that India's policy approach is still largely focused on apprehending Rohingya Muslims on Indian soil, shifting them to detention centers and deporting them to Myanmar, other than offering them asylum (Ara 2023). The Uttar Pradesh Police's Anti-Terror Squad (ATS), for instance, has arrested 74 Rohingya Muslims who, as the police said, had entered India from Bangladesh and Myanmar illegally in July 2023 (Sharma 2023). This policy of detention and (forced) deportation suggests that while other refugee groups, such as Afghan, Bengali, Tamil, and Tibetan, have been positively received in the country, New Delhi, however, 'seems to be very intolerant towards its relatively small Rohingya population of 40,000' (Bais 2020, p. 2). The dramatic change of New Delhi's attitude and policy approach toward the Rohingya crisis, as will be discussed below, indicates that India's response/approach toward the Rohingya crisis has been driven by the interplay of various factors.

Factors Motivating India's Response to the Rohingya Crisis and Their Implications

In light of the *ad hoc* and arbitrary nature of India's policy approach toward refugee groups, New Delhi's response to the Rohingya crisis has been governed by geopolitical and diplomatic incentives, domestic electoral mandates, and local socio-cultural dynamics (Khosla 2022). These factors include i) New Delhi's strategic and economic interests in Myanmar; ii) China's growing influence in Myanmar and South Asia; iii) New Delhi's security interest in its North Eastern Region (NER); iv) New Delhi's balancing act between Bangladesh and Myanmar and v) India's domestic politics and especially the rise of Hindu nationalism under Modi.

New Delhi's Strategic and Economic Interests in Myanmar

In acknowledging the strategic and economic importance of the Southeast Asian region, India, during the Indian National Congress (INC) government under Prime Minister P. V. Narasimha Rao (1991–1996), employed the Look East Policy (LEP) in 1991 to seek greater economic alignment with the Association of Southeast Asian Nations (ASEAN). Subsequently, India has become the sectoral dialogue partner (1992) and the full dialogue partner (1996) of the ASEAN and a member of the ASEAN Regional Forum (ARF).

With ASEAN (as a regional entity) becoming a corridor for India's outreach to Southeast Asia, Prime Minister Narendra Modi, during his attendance at the 12th ASEAN-India Summit held in Naypyidaw, Myanmar in November 2014, announced that "India's "Look East Policy" would become 'Act East Policy'" (Parameswaran 2014). This Act East Policy (AEP), which can be considered the upgraded LEP, is built on the three Cs (Commerce, Culture, and Connectivity), and aimed to 'serve the twin purposes of stronger trade and business ties with South East Asia and other Indo-Pacific countries and to create development opportunities for the North East States of India' (Wadhwa 2019).

Since developing and strengthening connectivity of India's North Eastern Region (NER) with ASEAN, as will be discussed below, has been acknowledged as a priority of the AEP, Myanmar is, both strategically and economically speaking, significant to India because it is the only ASEAN country that shares a land border with Northeast India, stretching some 1,624 kilometers (Atmakuri and Izzuddin. 2020), and the only country that 'sits at the intersection of India's "Neighborhood First" policy and "Act East" policy' (Ramaswamy and Maini 2014).

This suggests why India has started to pursue a policy of realpolitik engagement with Myanmar's military junta from the mid-1990s onwards, as India's economic and connectivity interests in Myanmar are evidenced by its large-scale investments and infrastructure projects carried out in this ASEAN country. These projects include the construction of the Kaladan Multi-Modal Transit Transport project (KMMTP) and the Trilateral Highway Project connecting our Northeast with Myanmar and Thailand (Ministry of External Affairs, Government of India 2024a). Therefore, Myanmar's importance to LEP and India's gateway to Southeast Asia has driven New Delhi to engage with the central authority in Myanmar 'irrespective of the nature of the government' (Chaudhury 2024), as the Modi government has tried to stick with the 'pro-engagement, anti-sanctions' strategy with the Myanmar military in the aftermath of the February 2021 coup, which returned Myanmar to military rule and dashed hopes of democratic reforms since 2011 (Jaffrey 2021).

China's Growing Influence in Myanmar and South Asia

While India has actively engaged Myanmar by including this ASEAN country into sub-regional groupings such as the Bangladesh-India-Myanmar-Sri Lanka-Thailand Economic Cooperation (BIMSTEC) in 1997, China has also shown an increasing interest in strengthening its relations with countries in South Asia including Myanmar in the 1990s. Known as the 'Kunming Initiative', this idea of establishing an economic corridor was first developed by Chinese scholars and later converted into a sub-regional initiative for economic cooperation in 1999: the Bangladesh-China-India-Myanmar (BCIM) Forum for Regional Cooperation (Bhattacharjee 2016).

What is worth highlighting is this BCIM, since Chinese President Xi Jinping launched a massive China-led infrastructure project known as the Belt and Road Initiative (BRI) in 2013, has been transformed from a Track II exercise into a Track-I initiative, with Beijing proactively incorporating this regional grouping into its BRI for the revival of the ancient Southern Silk Road trade route (Marchang 2021). As a result, the BCIM is increasingly recognized as the Southern Silk Road (as part of the BRI), as its ownership, therefore, is shifted largely to China (Oysharja 2017).

Among all the countries in Southeast Asia, Myanmar is, above all, the country where China and India have been waging 'an open and determined struggle for influence and domination' (Malik 1994, p. 137). Beijing's growing activism in South Asia and its inroads into Myanmar since the 1990s have been perceived, from New Delhi's perspective, as constituting a threat in India's sphere of influence (Malik 1994). Myanmar's post-1988 alignment with China, on the other hand, is equally worrying to India: Faced with growing international isolation after its brutal suppression of the pro-democracy protest movements in 1988, the military junta in Yangon sought to develop stronger military and diplomatic ties with China, a country which also found itself in a similar situation following the 1989 Tiananmen Square massacre (Malik 1994, p. 139).

In this context, New Delhi is actively 'seeking to balance China's influence by deepening its ties with Myanmar and undertaking collaborative infrastructure projects', as its imperative is to 'wean Myanmar from dependence on China' (Pande 2023). The above-mentioned Kaladan Multi-Modal Transit Transport project, therefore, 'serves as a strategic counterbalance to China's regional dominance' (Peter 2023).

New Delhi's Security and Connectivity Interest in Its North Eastern Region (NER)

The North Eastern Region, the easternmost region of the country, 'is', in the words of the then Minister of External Affairs Pranab Mukherjee, 'one region into whose progress and development we can dovetail India's Look East Policy' (Quoted in Thomas and Freddy 2023, p. 315). A major thrust area identified by the North Eastern Region Vision 2020 (NER2020) Document, which was unveiled by the Indian government in July 2008, is in 'build[ing] the required infrastructure right up to the border areas, establishing connectivity and communication links to the cross-border points through which trade and economic exchanges with the countries neighboring the North Eastern Region are proposed to be promoted under the Look East Policy' (Ministry of Development of North Eastern Region, North Eastern Council, Government of India 2008).

This 'Northeast Development Concern' of the LEP is, in nature, 'look east through northeast' (Bhaumik 2014). Given that four northeastern states

– Mizoram, Manipur, Nagaland and Arunachal Pradesh – share a total of 1624 km international border with Myanmar, Myanmar is a strategic bridgehead for India's upgraded AEP as this ASEAN country could provide the Northeast with an outlet to the sea, a route that is shorter than the Siliguri corridor, the only transportation chokepoint, known as the 'Chicken's Neck', connecting the eight northeastern states of India with the rest of the country (Fazl-E-Haider 2020). The Kaladan Project implemented by the Indian government in Myanmar, as mentioned above, could create an alternative route to the NER via the Sittwe Port in Rakhine State, Myanmar, thereby providing connectivity between India and Myanmar and accelerating infrastructure and economic development of the two countries.

Apart from realizing Myanmar's importance to India's regional connectivity efforts, New Delhi is also convinced that maintaining good relations with Naypyidaw (Myanmar's military junta) is crucial for its counterinsurgency operations in the Northeast: The Tatmadaw, in New Delhi's eyes, has the capacity to deal with those anti-India insurgency groups whose bases are located in Myanmar's jungles (Ramachandran 2021). This explains the rationale behind New Delhi's continued engagement with the Tatmadaw since the Myanmar military coup in February 2021, and, in particular, its decision to abstain from a 2022 UN Security Council resolution, the first of its kind in 74 years, demanding an immediate end to violence in Myanmar while commending Bangladesh's efforts for hosting and providing humanitarian support to the Rohingyas (The Business Standard 2022), since New Delhi is desperate to deliberately keep the option of engaging with Myanmar's military junta open.

New Delhi's Balancing Act between Bangladesh and Myanmar

Just as Myanmar, despite being the only ASEAN country, shares a land border of some 1624 km with the NER, Bangladesh also shares a 4096 km border, the world's fifth longest land border, with India, and a 1879 km border with four North-east Indian states (Banik 2011). Economically speaking, while India is the fourth largest trading partner of Myanmar, Bangladesh is, in fact, India's biggest trade partner in South Asia. Also, along with being the second biggest trade partner of Bangladesh in Asia, India is also Bangladesh's largest export destination in Asia (Ministry of External Affairs, Government of India 2024a).

Apart from economic ties, the NER, to the surprise of New Delhi, has witnessed a dramatic decline in terrorist activities and this is largely because of some significant steps taken by Bangladesh under Sheikh Hasina's government in addressing the security concerns of India. The signing of a landmark extradition treaty in 2013 and the land boundary agreement in 2015 between India and Bangladesh, in particular, have effectively prevented those insurgent/terrorist groups from getting shelter within Bangladesh or operating in the NER (Ashrat 2022). Bangladesh, in the words of a former Director General of India's National Security Guard (NSG), 'has so far been an outstanding and amazing partner of India on security issues' (The Daily Star 2022).

With both countries being perceived by India as important economic and security partners, New Delhi cannot afford to alienate either Myanmar or Bangladesh, which it relies on for commerce and trade, security, and connectivity. Therefore, India's then External Affairs Minister Sushma Swaraj's visit to Myanmar in 2018 and her emphasis on India's desire for 'safe, secure sustainable return of the Rohingyas' (The Times of India 2018) does not represent a fundamental shift of New Delhi's Rohingya policy. Instead, it is India's attempt to strike a careful balance between Myanmar and Bangladesh, thereby explaining that New Delhi will neither make any explicit commitments to Bangladesh's government nor take any bold stance against Myanmar's military junta.

India's Domestic Politics, Especially the Rise of Hindu Nationalism under Modi

The Rohingyas, at least before 2014, could still manage to reside in India continuously by getting long-term visas (LTVs) issued by the Indian government. Yet, as mentioned earlier, there has been a dramatic shift in New Delhi's policy toward the Rohingya since Narendra Modi's BJP came into power in 2014. Instead of letting them continuously reside in India by granting them LTVs, the Modi government officially labeled the Rohingyas as 'illegal immigrants'. As a result, their freedom of movement and access to education, basic health and legal services as well as formal employment opportunities are severely restricted.

By and large, the Modi government's dramatic policy shift and its increasingly hostile attitudes toward the Rohingyas are largely attributed to its anti-Muslim mentality and its vote-bank politics (Verma 2024, p. 18–20). This anti-Muslim mentality is derived from the ideological guiding principle of the ruling BJP: Hindutva (meaning 'Hindu-ness')—a term coined in the 1920s by a Hindu right-wing Indian politician and activist Vinayak Damodar Savarkar meaning 'Hindu-ness'. It represents a belief in i) the interconnection between Indian national identity, culture, and religion; and ii) the establishment of a Hindu, rather than secular, state of India. Accordingly, there are three essentials of Hindutva: namely, a common nation (Hindu Rashtra), a common race (jati), and a common civilization (sanskriti) (Dena 2022). In this context, Muslims are portrayed as 'outsiders', 'invaders', 'internal enemies', or even a national security threat to India. By using this narrative, the BJP executes its time-bound plan to deport all Rohingyas and other illegal immigrants (The Times of India 2023), since the Rohingyas are the Muslim ethnic minority group who 'infiltrated India through Bangladesh' and 'came from Myanmar', and therefore, they 'will never be accepted as citizens of India' (The Statesman 2019).

Providing Proactive Leadership in Resolving the Rohingya Crisis: Why It Matters for India?

It is worth noting that there are three important developments that are, more or less, caused by New Delhi's current Rohingya policy: i) New Delhi's deportation of the first group of Myanmar refugees who sought shelter in India after the 2021 military coup (Nikkei Asia 2024); ii) Bangladesh government's decision not to allow any more Rohingya refugees from Myanmar to enter the country (Paul and Ganguly 2024); and iii) Beijing's pledge to support Bangladesh in repatriating Rohingya refugees to Myanmar (DW News 2022). Therefore, considering the evolving situation and the future prospects of Rohingya repatriation, New Delhi has to urgently rethink its balancing act in Myanmar and Bangladesh, as there is a danger that this balancing approach is undermining India's image as a regional power with global aspirations and will do more harm than good for its determination to become a superpower that could surpass China (Allison 2023).

If India is serious about strengthening its reputation as not only an emerging economic superpower but also as a leading voice of the developing world, New Delhi's policymakers must understand that providing proactive leadership in resolving the Rohingya crisis is both a moral imperative and a matter of hard-headed national interest for India. There are three important reasons why it is in India's national interest to side with Bangladesh in resolving the Rohingya crisis proactively. First, by accommodating Dhaka's request to peacefully repatriate the Rohingya refugees, India could make it clear that not only will the Modi government continue with the Gujral doctrine of non-reciprocity (as spelled out by Inder Kumar Gujral since the 1990s) by extending vital support to its close neighbors like Bangladesh but will also ensure that New Delhi's desire of advancing friendship and cooperation with her neighbors remains unchanged. It stands to reason that Modi's India needs to acknowledge Bangladesh, not Myanmar, as India's closest, most reliable and trustworthy partner. After all, the shared heritage of the Indic civilization, history, language, culture and a common border between India and Bangladesh and, in particular, India's involvement in Bangladesh's War of Independence of 1971 form a special bond and the bedrock for ties between the two countries (The Hindu 2023).

While Sheikh Hasina's sudden exit from Bangladesh politics (following the ouster of her government in August 2024) could generate uncertainty in many aspects of India-Bangladesh relations, it is not in New Delhi's interest to alienate its most trustworthy partner/neighbor by ignoring Bangladesh's urge to India for playing a bigger role in resolving the Rohingya crisis. Instead of blindly siding with Myanmar's junta, the Modi government must prioritize its cordial bilateral relations with a post-Hasina Bangladesh, seize the opportunity to mitigate the socio-economic and national security impact of the Rohingya crisis on Bangladesh, and reciprocate Dhaka's ongoing request to ensure safe, voluntary, and sustainable Rohingya repatriation to Myanmar.

Second, by taking more proactive actions in pressurizing Myanmar to take back the Rohingyas from Bangladesh, India can not only retain its leadership position in resolving the Rohingya crisis but also foreclose the possibility of a successful Chinese mediation diplomacy between Myanmar and Bangladesh over the issue of Rohingya repatriation (Rumi 2022). And perhaps somewhat coincidentally, China's initiative was followed by Bangladesh's then foreign minister AK Abdul Momen's proposal of a Bangladesh-Myanmar-China 'tripartite joint working mechanism' for overseeing the repatriation process of Rohingya to Myanmar (APN News 2019). This indicates Dhaka's lost patience (and perhaps, faith) in New Delhi over the issue of Rohingya repatriation.

Considering the fact that China has identified this opportunity to make Myanmar and, especially Bangladesh go deeper into its orbit and to weaken India's influence in the region, it would be foolhardy for India to compete with China on Myanmar by attempting to remove Myanmar from China's orbit or sphere of influence. Instead of siding with Myanmar's military junta (and hoping for reducing Myanmar's dependence on China), it is more important for India to maintain its special relationship with Bangladesh. The reason is simple: India's proactive leadership in the repatriation of Rohingyas could provide disincentives to Bangladesh for seeking China's help.

Third, by adopting a more tolerant attitude toward the Rohingya refugees, the Modi government can plausibly argue that BJP's Hindutva politics/Hindu nationalism in India is not necessarily a reflection of anti-Muslim prejudice and bigotry. Instead of shifting all Rohingyas to detention centers and deporting them to Myanmar straight away, being more tolerant of the Rohingya Muslims by making the CAA more inclusive and less discriminatory toward them can bring numerous advantages to the Indian government, provided that Modi's BJP has the courage and enthusiasm to do so. The first advantage is that it could help restore the (somewhat) negative national image of India as a major hub of Islamophobia (Sen 2022).

Adopting a less hostile and more Muslim-friendly Rohingya refugee policy could forestall the possibility of the Muslim-dominated countries playing the anti-India card, thereby retaining its influence in its neighboring countries. Third, it could give India the flexibility to engage other political parties (including those Islamist parties) in Bangladesh, especially after the removal of the ruling Awami League (AL) from power in August 2024. Given the continued existence of Islamist political parties in Bangladesh, India needs to rethink its long-term strategy of giving all-out support for the AL. Adopting a Muslim-friendly Rohingya refugee policy could help India get itself better prepared for engaging with different political parties in Bangladesh.

Conclusion

There is no doubt that the 2017 influx of Rohingyas and their prolonged presence in Bangladesh, the largest and fastest one so far, has imposed a heavy burden on the government of Bangladesh. Apart from the financial burden of providing temporary shelter, food, and medical assistance to over one million Rohingyas, the protracted nature of the crisis, as admitted by former Prime Minister Hasina, has become a threat to the security not only for Bangladesh but also for the region' (The Times of India 2019). Also, along with the presence of some 40,000 Rohingyas, the '[c]ontinuance of Rohingyas' illegal migration to India and their stay in India, apart from it being absolutely illegal', as highlighted by the Indian government, 'is fraught with serious security ramifications' (Tripathi 2024).

The fact that the prolonged presence of the Rohingyas in both Bangladesh and India could generate threats to national security for the two countries suggests that a stronger India-Bangladesh partnership in resolving this protracted Rohingya crisis could have been mutually beneficial. For Bangladesh, even though China seems to be a useful counterweight to New Delhi (Kanunjna 2024; Azcárate 2024), India is nonetheless a 'major neighbour, trusted friend, and regional partner' (The Business Standard 2024) since its independence in 1971. For India, Bangladesh is 'a close and valued neighbour with rapidly growing capabilities' and, perhaps more importantly, 'an indispensable partner in the development of India's northeastern region' (Ministry of External Affairs, Government of India 2024b), Therefore, notwithstanding that New Delhi is concerned with Dhaka's growing economic and military ties with Beijing, the key question in relation to India's role and policy approach in the context of the geopolitical competition between India and China for influence in South Asia (Baruah, Madan and Xavier 2023) in general and the Rohingya crisis in particular relates to how far India can seize the opportunity and propel itself to become a more trustworthy and reliable partner to Bangladesh than China.

If the India-Bangladesh bilateral ties are, notwithstanding the ouster of Sheikh Hasina's government in August 2024, still what India describes as 'an all-encompassing partnership that transcends a strategic partnership' (Ministry of External Affairs, Government of India, 2024b), then New Delhi must recognize that continuing to maintain its special relationship with Dhaka and preventing a post-Hasina Bangladesh from tilting toward China is far more important than siding with Myanmar's military junta by making efforts to reduce Myanmar's dependence on China. Since Bangladesh has high hopes for India's proactive leadership role in resolving the Rohingya crisis, India needs to make good use of this opportunity to restore trust with Bangladesh by demonstrating its willingness to respond helpfully, forcefully, and clearly to the critical needs of the government of Bangladesh: pressurizing Myanmar to begin safe, sustainable, and dignified repatriation of the Rohingyas. After all, New Delhi's proper handling of the Rohingya crisis is both necessary and desirable for strengthening India's reputation (regional and global) as well as re-establishing strong and close ties with Bangladesh after Hasina.

References

Ahmed, Kazi Fahim. 2022. 'Why Is Bangladesh Important to India?', *The Geopolitics*, 31 August. Available at https://thegeopolitics.com/why-bangladesh-is-important-to-india/

Allison, Graham. 2023. 'Will India Surpass China to Become the Next Superpower?', *Foreign Policy*, 24 June. Available at https://foreignpolicy.com/2023/06/24/india-china-biden-modi-summit-great-power-competition-economic-growth/

Al-Jazeera 2023. 'India Police Arrest 74 Rohingya Refugees in Latest Crackdown', 25 July. Available at https://www.aljazeera.com/news/2023/7/25/india-police-arrest-seventy-four-rohingya-in-latest-crackdown-on-refugees

APN News 2019. 'Bangladesh, Myanmar & China to Form Tripartite Mechanism for Rohingya Repatriation', 25 September. Available at https://www.apnnews.com/bangladesh-myanmar-china-to-form-tripartite-mechanism-for-rohingya-repatriation/

Ara, Ismat. 2023. 'Government toughens stance against Rohingya refugees', The Hindu, 26 July.Available at https://frontline.thehindu.com/news/govt-toughens-stance-against-rohingya-refugees/article67123774.ece

Ashrat, Samara. 2022. 'Bangladesh's Role in the Security of Northeastern States of India', *Euroasia Review*, 20 December. Available at https://www.eurasiareview.com/20122022-bangladeshs-role-in-the-security-of-northeastern-states-of-india-oped/

Atmakuri, Archana and Mustafa Izzuddin. 2020. 'Why Myanmar Should Matter to India', *The Diplomat*, 8 January. Available at https://thediplomat.com/2020/01/why-myanmar-should-matter-to-india/

Azcárate, Cristina. 2024. 'Bangladesh: Close to India But Expecting Benefits from China', Center for Global Affairs & Strategic Studies (GASS), Universidad de Navarra, 16 April. Available at https://www.unav.edu/en/web/global-affairs/bangladesh-close-to-india-but-expecting-benefits-from-china

Bais, Devasheesh. 2020. 'Understanding Indian Responses to the Rohingya Crisis' Policy Brief Series No 117.

Banik, Ashish. 2011. 'Bangladesh and India's Northeast: A security perspective', *The Daily Star*, 15 October. Available at https://www.thedailystar.net/news-detail-206537

Baruah, Madan and Xavier 2023. 'How India and China Compete in Non-Aligned South Asia and the Indian Ocean', *Brookings Commentary (Podcast)*, 18 October. Available at https://www.brookings.edu/articles/how-india-and-china-compete-in-non-aligned-south-asia-and-the-indian-ocean/

Bhattacharjee, Rupak. 2016. 'Bangladesh, China, India and Myanmar-Economic Corridor: Ushering a New Era of Interconnectedness', *India Defence Review*, 18 September. Available at https://www.indiandefencereview.com/spotlights/bangladesh-china-india-and-myanmar-economic-corridor-ushering-a-new-era-of-interconnectedness/

Bhaumik, Subir. 2014. 'Look East Through Northeast': Challenges and Prospects for India', ORF Occasional Paper #51, *Observer Research Foundation*, 25 June. Available at https://www.orfonline.org/research/look-east-through-northeast-challenges-and-prospects-for-india

Chaudhury, Dipanjan Roy. 2024. 'India Mulls Changes in Its Myanmar Strategy as Junta Faces Setback', *The Economic Times*, 15 January. Available at https://economictimes.indiatimes.com/news/india/india-mulls-changes-in-its-myanmar-strategy-as-junta-faces-setback/articleshow/106843037.cms?from=mdr

DW News. 2022. 'China to Help Bangladesh Repatriate Rohingya', 8 August. Available at https://www.dw.com/en/china-to-help-bangladesh-repatriate-rohingya-refugees/a-62737442

Dena, Lal. 2022. 'Hindutva and the Question of Who Owns India', *The Wire*, 19 February. Available at https://thewire.in/communalism/hindutva-and-the-question-of-who-owns-india

Fawcett, Louise and Sharinee L. Jagtiani. 2024. 'Regional powers, global aspirations: lessonsfrom India and Iran', International Politics Vol. 61, pp. 215-238.

Fazl-E-Haider, Syed. 2020. 'Twisting India's Chicken's Neck', *The Interpreter*, 25 July. Available at https://www.lowyinstitute.org/the-interpreter/twisting-india-s-chicken-s-neck

Gao, Charlotte. 2017. 'On Rohingya Issue, Both China and India Back Myanmar Government', *The Diplomat*, 13 September. Available at https://thediplomat.com/2017/09/on-rohingya-issue-both-china-and-india-back-myanmar-government/

Haider, Suhasini. 2023. 'India is indeed the mother of democracy, says PM Modi citingMahabharata and Vedas', The Hindu, 29 March. Available athttps://www.thehindu.com/news/national/india-mother-of-democracy-home-to-idea-of-elected-leaders-much-before-rest-of-world-pm-modi/article66675267.ece

Hindustan Times. 2017. 'Rohingyas to Be Deported, India Doesn't Need Lessons on Refugees: Kiren Rijiju', 5 September. Available at https://www.hindustantimes.com/india-news/rohingyas-to-be-deported-don-t-preach-india-on-refugees-kiren-rijiju/story-fNUJ82lpThO61wlQFUhZ6J.html

Human Rights Watch. 2019. 'India: Citizenship Bill Discriminates Against Muslims', 11 December. Available at https://www.hrw.org/news/2019/12/11/india-citizenship-bill-discriminates-against-muslims

India Today. 2017. 'Operation Insaniyat: India to Send Relief to Bangladesh to Help with Rohingya Influx', 14 September. Available at https://www.indiatoday.in/world/story/india-sends-humanitarian-relief-to-bangladesh-rohingya-muslims-influx-un-myanmar-1044417-2017-09-14

Jaffrey, Sana. 2021. 'End of Myanmar's Rocky Road to Democracy?', *Carnegie Endownment For International Peace*, 2 February. Available at https://carnegieendowment.org/2021/02/02/end-of-myanmar-s-rocky-road-to-democracy-pub-83774

Kanunjna, Anupam Deb. 2024. 'Bangladesh Seeks Careful Balance Between China and India', *DW News*, 18 January. Available at https://www.dw.com/en/bangladesh-seeks-careful-balance-between-china-and-india/a-68023417

Khosla, Mahika. 2022. 'The Geopolitics of India's Refugee Policy', *South Asian Voices*, 22 September. Available at https://southasianvoices.org/the-geopolitics-of-indias-refugee-policy/

Malik, J. Mohan. 1994. 'Sino-Indian Rivalry in Myanmar: Implications for Regional Security', *Contemporary Southeast Asia*, Vol. 16, No. 2 (September), pp. 137–156.

Marchang, Reimeingam. 2021. 'BCIM Economic Corridor an Integral Part of BRI for Regional Cooperation: Positioning India's North-East and Act East Policy', *Journal of Asian Security and International Affairs*, Vol. 8, No 2, pp. 249–269.

Ministry of Development of North Eastern Region, North Eastern Council, Government of India, 2008. 'North Eastern Region Vision 2020', 13 May. Available at https://necouncil.gov.in/sites/default/files/Vision_2020.pdf

Ministry of External Affairs, Government of India, 2024a. 'India-Bangladesh Bilateral Relations', 15 February. Available at https://www.mea.gov.in/Portal/ForeignRelation/Bilateral-Brief-Bangladesh-February-2024.pdf

Ministry of External Affairs, Government of India, 2024b. 'India-Bangladesh Shared Vision for Future: Enhancing Connectivity, Commerce and Collaboration for Shared Prosperity', 22 June. Available at https://www.mea.gov.in/bilateral-documents.htm?dtl/37897/IndiaBangladesh+Shared+Vision+for+Future+Enhancing+Connectivity+Commerce+and+Collaboration+for+Shared+Prosperity

Mitra, Devirupa. 2017. 'Exclusive: Public Anger Brews in Bangladesh Over India's Stance on Rohingya Crisis', *TheWire*, 10 September. Available at https://thewire.in/uncategorised/bangaldesh-rohingya-crisis-myanmar-india

Mohan, Geeta. 2017. 'India Signs MoU with Myanmar, to Help Bring Normalcy to Strategic Region Amid Rohingya Crisis', *India Today*, 20 December. Available at https://www.indiatoday.in/india/story/india-myanmar-mou-rohingya-1113632-2017-12-20

Nikkei Asia. 2024. 'India Begins Deporting 1st Group of Myanmar Refugees Who Fled Coup', 10 March. Available at https://asia.nikkei.com/Spotlight/Myanmar-Crisis/India-begins-deporting-1st-group-of-Myanmar-refugees-who-fled-coup

Oysharja, Orpita. 2017. 'BCIM: In the Shadow of Belt and Road Initiative', *The Financial Express*, 17 November. Available at https://today.thefinancialexpress.com.bd/anniversary-issue-3/bcim-in-the-shadow-of-belt-and-road-initiative-1511942258

Pande, Aparna. 2023. 'India's Realpolitik Myanmar Policy', Geopolitical Intelligence Services, 26 October. Available at https://www.gisreportsonline.com/r/india-myanmar-2/

Parameswaran, Prashanth. 2014. 'Modi Unveils India's 'Act East Policy' to ASEAN in Myanmar', 17 November, *The Diplomat*. Available at https://thediplomat.com/2014/11/modi-unveils-indias-act-east-policy-to-asean-in-myanmar/

Paul, Ruma, and Sudipto Ganguly. 2024. 'Bangladesh Will Not Let in Any More Rohingya Refugees - inister', *Reuters*, 7 February. Available at https://www.reuters.com/world/asia-pacific/bangladesh-will-not-let-any-more-rohingya-refugees-minister-2024-02-07/

Peter, Zsombor. 2023. 'India Opens Myanmar Port with Wary Eye on China', *VOA News*, 27 May. Available at https://www.voanews.com/a/india-opens-myanmar-port-with-wary-eye-on-china/7111753.html

Raj, Prachi. 2020. 'Understanding Citizenship and Refugees' Status in India', *Economic & Political Weekly* Vol. 55, No. 23 (June 6), pp. 31–34.

Ramachandran, Suhda. 2021. 'India's Dangerous Myanmar Policy' *The Diplomat*, 26 March. Available at https://thediplomat.com/2021/03/indias-dangerous-myanmar-policy/

Ramaswamy, Sridhar, and Tridivesh Singh Maini. 2014. 'The Strategic Importance of Myanmar for India', *The Diplomat*, 12 August. Available at https://thediplomat.com/2014/08/the-strategic-importance-of-myanmar-for-india/

Rana, Hemaadri Singh. 2022. 'India's Refugee Law and Politics of Hospitality Since Independence', in S. Irudaya Rajan (ed.), *The Routledge Handbook of Refugees in India*, pp. 135–156. London and New York: Routledge.

Rumi, Aoyama. 2022. 'China's Mediation Diplomacy in Myanmar', The Japan Institute of International Affairs Research Report, 15 July. Available at https://www.jiia.or.jp/en/column/2022/07/china-fy2021-07.html

Sen, Somdeep. 2022. 'Analysis: Islamophobia Is the Norm in Modi's India', *Al Jazeera*, 10 June. Available at https://www.aljazeera.com/features/2022/6/10/analysis-islamophobia-is-the-norm-in-modis-india

Seth, Shivangi. 2022. 'Why India Needs a Refugee Law', *The Interpreter*, 25 July. Available at https://www.lowyinstitute.org/the-interpreter/why-india-needs-refugee-law

Sharma, Amit. 2023. '74 Rohingya Held from UP for Staying Without Valid Papers', *The Indian Express*, 25 July. Available at https://indianexpress.com/article/cities/lucknow/plice-crackdown-on-rohingyas-rohingya-arrests-up-ats-illegal-rohingya-migrants-8858326/

Statesman. 2019. 'Rohingya Muslims will never be accepted as Indian citizens: Amit Shah clarifies in LS', Available at https://www.thestatesman.com/india/rohingya-muslims-never-accepted-indian-citizens-amit-shah-ls-1502831850.html

Tay, Alvin K., and Peter Ventevogel, eds. 2018. *Culture, Context and Mental Health of Rohingya Refugees: A Review for Staff in Mental Health and Psychosocial Support Programmes for Rohingya Refugees.* Geneva: United Nations High Commissioner for Refugees.

The Business Standard. 2020. 'India Wants Quick Repatriation of Rohingya Refugees in Bangladesh', 8 July. Available at https://www.tbsnews.net/rohingya-crisis/india-wants-quick-repatriation-rohingya-refugees-bangladesh-103702

The Business Standard. 2022. 'UN Security Council Adopts First-Ever Resolution on Myanmar; China, Russia and India Abstain from Voting', 22 December. Available at https://www.tbsnews.net/bangladesh/un-security-council-adopts-first-ever-resolution-myanmar-china-russia-and-india-abstain

The Business Standard. 2024. 'Both Sides Agreed on 'Green Partnership for a Sustainable Future': Hasina', 22 June. Available at https://www.tbsnews.net/bangladesh/dhaka-delhi-agrees-about-shared-vision-sustainable-future-pm-881566

The Daily Star. 2022. 'None Did as Much for India's Northeast as Bangladesh: Ex-NSG Chief', 8 June. Available at https://www.thedailystar.net/news/asia/south-asia/news/none-did-much-indias-northeast-bangladesh-ex-nsg-chief-3042396

The Economic Times. 2020. 'Committed to Support Mutually-Acceptable Solution to Enable Return of Rohingya Refugees: India', 2 March. Available at https://economictimes.indiatimes.com/news/politics-and-nation/committed-to-support-mutually-acceptable-solution-to-enable-return-of-rohingya-refugees-india/articleshow/74439286.cms

The Hindu. 2023. 'Bangladesh War of Liberation Is the Bedrock of Its Ties with India, Says Indian Envoy', 18 December. Available at https://www.thehindu.com/news/national/bangladesh-war-of-liberation-is-the-bedrock-of-its-ties-with-india-says-indian-envoy/article67647826.ece

The Indian Express. 2017. 'India, Myanmar Sign MoU for Development of Rakhine', 21 December. Available at https://indianexpress.com/article/india/india-myanmar-sign-mou-for-development-of-rakhine-4992187/

The Irrawaddy. 2017. 'India Supports Myanmar in Tackling Terrorism', 7 September. Available at https://www.irrawaddy.com/news/burma/india-supports-myanmar-in-tackling-terrorism.html

The Times of India. 2017. '486 Rohingyas in India on Long-Term Visa, 40,000 Residing Illegally: Rijiju', 27 December. Available at http://timesofindia.indiatimes.com/articleshow/62273043.cms?from=mdr&utm_source=contentofinterest&utm_medium=text&utm_campaign=cppst

The Times of India. 2018. 'India for Safe, Sustainable Return of Rohingyas: Swaraj', 11 May. Available at https://timesofindia.indiatimes.com/india/india-for-safe-sustainable-return-of-rohingya-swaraj/articleshow/64125424.cms

The Times of India. 2019. 'Rohingyas "Threat" to National and Regional Security: Bangladesh PM Hasina', 19 November. Available at https://timesofindia.indiatimes.com/world/south-asia/rohingyas-threat-to-national-and-regional-security-bangladesh-pm-hasina/articleshow/72009641.cms

The Times of India. 2023. 'BJP Promises to Deport All Illegal Immigrants in Time-Bound Manner', 19 November. Available at https://timesofindia.indiatimes.com/city/hyderabad/bjp-time-bound-plan-deport-illegal-immigrants/articleshow/105323546.cms

Thomas, C. Fre, and Haans J. Freddy. 2023. 'Look East Policy', in Jelle J. P. Wouters and Tanka B. Subba (eds.), *The Routledge Companion to Northeast India*, pp. 312–317. London and New York: Routledge.

Tripathi, Ashish. 2024. 'Illegal Rohingya Migrants Don't Possess Fundamental Right to Reside in India, Centre tells SC', *Deccan Herald*, 20 March. Available at https://www.deccanherald.com/india/illegal-rohingya-migrants-dont-possess-fundamental-right-to-reside-in-india-centre-tells-sc-2945401

Verma, Monika. 2024. 'Hindutva Politics and the Making of Extreme Precarity', *Innovation in the Social Sciences*, Vol. 2, No. 1 (2024), pp. 3–31.

Verma, Monika. 2022. 'The Plight of Rohingya Refugees in India: Living in Denial', *Asia Review*, Vol. 12, No. 3, pp. 479–504.

Wadhwa, Amb (Retd) Anil. 2019. 'India's Act East Policy', 9 August. Ministry of External Affairs, Government of India. Available at https://www.mea.gov.in/distinguished-lectures-detail.htm?840#:~:text=The%20Act%20East%20Policy%20is,North%20East%20States%20of%20India

Winchester, Nicole. 2020. 'India's Citizenship (Amendment) Act 2019', 12 February. House of Lords Library Research Briefing. Available at https://lordslibrary.parliament.uk/research-briefings/lln-2020-0058/

Yasmin, Lailufar. 2022. 'From Disorganized Hypocrisy to Political Neo-Medievalism: Rohingya Crises in Bangladesh', in Imtiaz A. Hussain (ed.), *Rohingya Camp Narratives: Tales From the 'Lesser Roads' Traveled*, pp. 113–142. Singapore: Springer Nature Singapore.

Yhome, K. 2018. 'Examining India's Stance on the Rohingya Crisis', ORF Issue Brief, IssueNO. 247, July. Available at https://www.orfonline.org/research/examining-india-s-stance-on-the-rohingya-crisis

8

THE ROHINGYA QUAGMIRE

US Policy, Myanmar's Resistance, and the International Response

Mohammad Jalal Uddin Sikder, Selim Reza, and Sumaya Halim

Introduction

The most powerful military and political force in the world, the United States (US), is anticipated to be a key player in the complicated Rohingya situation, but its political influence has been conspicuously weaker than projected thus far. While the humanitarian response to the crisis has thrived over the last ten years, the problem's inherently political nature has been overshadowed by the lack of strong political pressure from the US toward Myanmar. In order to understand why the US appears to be unresponsive when it comes to proposing workable political solutions to the Rohingya crisis, this paper examines the intricate web of political, economic, and strategic issues, and explores why there has not been any progress in the situation. It also highlights the reasons why the United States' crisis management policy positions have been ineffectual in light of the shifting geopolitical interests in Asia and the dynamics of America-China relations.

Contemporary US Responses to the Rohingya Crisis

Given the extensive implications of the Rohingya crisis, it is vital to understand how the world is reacting to it, especially in relation to US policy and the extent to which it adheres to the Responsibility to Protect (R2P)[1] theory. It not only highlights the humanitarian need to lessen the suffering of Rohingya refugees but also reflects the moral responsibility to stop atrocities and respond to them. The interaction between political dynamics, diplomatic links, and strategic objectives that influence the international responses to mass crimes is further illuminated through examining

DOI: 10.4324/9781003771890-8

US policy within the context of R2P. Furthermore, how the Rohingya issue is handled will establish guidelines for similar humanitarian operations in the future and emphasize how vital it is to hold those responsible for these crimes accountable and bring them to justice. To address the situation holistically and prevent similar tragedies from occurring in the future, it is therefore crucial to understand the level of commitment and actions of important actors like the United States. Therefore, an examination of the historical trajectory of US-Burma (now Myanmar)[2] ties is necessary in order to make sense of US contemporary policy toward the Rohingya crisis.

The United States of America has been actively attempting to restore democracy in Myanmar ever since the coup in 1962. In order to urge the Burmese military (Tatmadaw) to clear the path for the creation of democracy, restrictions were placed on bilateral relations during the military regime (1962 to date). However, the foreign policy goals and strategies of the Ronald Reagan, George H.W. Bush, Bill Clinton, George W. Bush, Barack Obama, Donald Trump, and Joe Biden administrations regarding Burma varied significantly.

The US policy toward Myanmar was characterized by military engagement and economic collaboration up until the late 1980s. Myanmar was awarded Most Favored Nation (MFN) status for trade, although this was not directly related to General Agreement on Tariffs and Trade (GATT) obligations, but rather represented bilateral trade agreements and geopolitical issues. It also held a beneficiary status under the Generalized System of Preferences (GSP) program, and so also enjoyed access to international financial institutions' developmental aid, and close military-to-military ties, as evidenced by the participants in the International Military Education and Training (IMET) program (Myat, 2016; Rieffel, 2016; Herfindahl, 2016). The objectives of these actions were to advance bilateral cooperation and economic development, but during the late 1980s, diplomatic relations chilled as worries about human rights abuses and political changes in Myanmar grew (Martin, 2010: 3).

The international world first became aware of the Rohingya situation during the early 2000 administrations, most notably that of Barack Obama and his successors. Since then, more has been done to address the humanitarian catastrophe and condemn Burma's treatment of the Rohingya population. As soon as Obama's administration entered office in 2009, its political strategy drastically shifted, however. Rebalancing the US posture in the Asia-Pacific area was the main goal of Obama's Burma Policy, which took into account the geopolitical shifts in East Asia, particularly the growth of China (Haacke, 2015). As part of a larger strategy to push for democratic reforms, open Burma up to the outside world, and promote stability in the region, the Obama administration adopted an engagement policy with Suu Kyi and the Burma government. This strategy involved tactful, diplomatic attempts to resolve human rights concerns and urge Burma's government to implement democratic changes (CBS, 2014). The Obama administration established an ambassador to Rangoon as part of that initiative, removing the investment prohibition and restricting humanitarian aid in order to launch a more diplomatic interaction with Burma (Nguyen, 2018: 58; Lubina, 2021: 261).

In 2012, Obama made his first visit to Burma as US president. The Obama administration has been subject to strong criticism by both the domestic and international community for not doing enough to address the Rohingya situation. Several detractors stated that the administration failed to act sufficiently to forcefully stop the violations of the Rohingya population's human rights. The administration adopted a careful stance, weighing interaction with Burma's government against worries about escalating tensions or jeopardizing the delicate democratic transition, despite demands for more forceful steps from human rights organizations and certain members of Congress (Stearns, 2012; Campbell, 2014; Yan and Watson, 2014; Boghani, 2018).

Since certain developments following 2016, several members of Congress have questioned the appropriateness of the US policy toward Burma and suggested the reinstatement of some waived sanctions and/or the implementation of new limitations on relations with Burma. Owing to Suu Kyi's status and influence in Burma, the Obama administration was hesitant to criticize her openly or take any other steps that would compromise the delicate electoral process. Moreover, the administration was hoping that positive interactions with Suu Kyi and the government of Burma would result in greater respect for human rights and democratic governance.

Under President Barack Obama, the US took the first steps toward restoring relations with Burma in response to reforms that had started to take root in Southeast Asian countries. Nonetheless, an inquiry into the murders of Rohingya Muslims in 2017 and their forcible transfer from Burma to Bangladesh was initiated by the Trump administration. The US State Department carried out this inquiry with the intention of gathering information and determining whether the acts of violence that had been committed against the Rohingya population should be classified as crimes against humanity or genocide. Officials from the Trump administration, including former Secretary of State Rex Tillerson and UN Ambassador Nikki Haley, denounced the atrocities against the Rohingya people and demanded that those accountable for violations of human rights be held accountable.

Targeted sanctions were also imposed by the Trump administration on military personnel and organizations in Burma that are alleged to have violated the human rights of the Rohingya people. These sanctions formed part of larger campaigns to make those guilty of committing atrocities answerable for them, and to put pressure on the Burmese government to resolve the Rakhine State humanitarian catastrophe. Through diplomatic measures and multilateral forums, the Trump administration collaborated with both regional and global allies to solve the Rohingya crisis. In an effort to aid Rohingya refugees and promote a peaceful settlement to the conflict, the US administration backed initiatives taken by the UN and other international organizations (Parameswaran, 2019; Martin et al., 2017; Haque and Islam, 2023).

In 2019, a leader of the Rohingya community named Mr Mohibullah received an invitation to the White House, where he met and talked with President Donald Trump and other survivors of religious persecution, including Rohingya Muslims (Solomon, 2021). Even though the meeting itself did not result in any quick changes to policy or resolve the Rohingya issue, it did help to increase awareness of the situation and give voice to those who had survived it. In addition to highlighting the necessity of taking international action to address the crisis's underlying causes, it emphasized the significance of tackling religious persecution and human rights violations, particularly those committed against the Rohingya minority.

Even though the brutality that was committed against the Rohingya community was widely discussed and condemned, the Trump administration chose to avoid officially labeling the atrocities carried out against the Rohingya as acts of genocide. Recently, in July 2025, the US Treasury removed sanctions against a number of Myanmar-affiliated individuals and businesses that had been placed on a blacklist by earlier administrations, such as Suntac Technologies, the MCM Group, and KT Services & Logistics. Many analysts believe that this decision marks a change in Washington's approach to Myanmar (Reuters, 2025). It is possible that President Trump was not interested in the Rohingya or Burma issues since he focused on other issues like North Korea's nuclear threat and the US's shifting relationship with China.

It took until March 2022 for the Biden administration to declare formally that the crimes that were committed against the Rohingya constituted genocide. This decision highlights the seriousness of the violations of human rights against the Rohingya population and demonstrates a commitment to justice, truth, and accountability (Hansler, 2022; Jakes, 2022; Garrido, 2022). This acknowledgment not only shows the world communities' desire to stop and punish genocide, but it also has moral and legal ramifications. It also shows solidarity with the Rohingya population. Although the timing of the Biden administration's decision might have been influenced by concerns about Burma's relations with China, it is crucial to remember that the main factors were probably legal evaluations, diplomatic discussions, and continuous efforts to address the Rohingya crisis in its entirety.

President Biden's leadership has brought the Rohingya population's situation and the necessity of forceful international action to solve the problem back into the public eye. In this instance, a legislative measure known as the *Burma Unified through Rigorous Military Accountability Act of 2021* (Congress.gov, 2021) was presented in reaction to the military coup that occurred in Myanmar in February 2021. It expands upon earlier initiatives, including the *Burma Human Rights and Freedom Act of 2017* (S.2060) (Congress.gov, 2018) and the *Burma Unified through Rigorous Military Accountability Act of 2017* (H.R. 4223) (Congress.gov, 2017), which were introduced in the 115th Congress in response to the August 2017 attack on Rohingyas by the Burmese military. The significance of these two laws lies in their proposal of various policy measures that aim to hold human rights offenders in Myanmar accountable. They contain clauses that target the top military commanders who were implicated in violations of human rights, impose sanctions, prohibit visas, and limit security assistance (Martin, 2023; Naing, 2024).

In spite of these developments, aid organizations, affected nations, and the Rohingya population were optimistic that the Burma Act of 2022, which was also integrated into the National Defense Authorization Act (NDAA) for the fiscal year 2023, would put meaningful political pressure on Myanmar. The way in which the bills are written, however, and especially the way they utilize language that is conditional, such as "may" or "shall," makes one wonder how the US is tackling Myanmar policy.

Section 570, for example, imposes fines on "senior leaders of the Burmese military or security forces" who violate human rights. However, the usage of the word "may" in clauses dealing with entities such as the Myanmar Oil and Gas Enterprise (MOGE) allows for presidential discretion, thereby undermining the enforcement and limiting the Act's influence in terms of pushing Myanmar's military administration. This legislative uncertainty raises the possibility of constraints being placed on the US government's capacity to take significant action against the military rule in Myanmar (Tucker and Thang 2017). Martin (2023) argues that the Act lacks strong enforcement tools. There are no defined standards or timetables for executing the punishments, and no penalties are specified for noncompliance. The lack of enforcement detail makes it difficult to ensure that the necessary pressure is applied to the Myanmar military regime.

It seems that the US response to human rights crimes in Myanmar has been limited, as demonstrated by its careful handling of the death of Rohingya leader Mohibullah. Following this event, the US administration failed to take immediate action, which reveals a larger trend of insufficient involvement with the Rohingya situation. Even though Mohibullah's murder was denounced in a press release by Secretary of State Antony J. Blinken, no further significant steps were taken. The US government's commitment to resolving human rights breaches and political persecution in Myanmar is called into question by this lack of a firm reaction. It also emphasizes how difficult it will be to resolve the Rohingya issue through international channels and how important it is for the US and other parties to make consistent, proactive efforts.

The Real US Approach: Humanitarian Aid or Political Strategy?

The US has only provided financial support in response to the Rohingya crisis since it began in August 2017. According to the US Department of State's Bilateral Relations Fact Sheet, the US government has contributed more than \$1.9 billion. This assistance was provided by the US government through public international organizations (PIOs), such as UN agencies as well as international non-governmental organizations (NGOs) (USAID, 2024). The US has not acted decisively enough in Myanmar to hold the Burmese military responsible for its crimes against the Rohingya, despite having engaged militarily or imposed sanctions in crises such as Kosovo, Iraq, Syria, Iran, and Afghanistan. There may be several reasons for this.

First, geopolitical factors and strategic interests in the area may be one cause of this discrepancy. Myanmar, which borders China, India, and Thailand, is situated in a strategically significant area of Southeast Asia. Due to its natural resources and close proximity to crucial marine trade routes, it plays a significant role in the regional geopolitics (Haacke, 2012). Particularly with regard to infrastructure and port access, China and India have substantial strategic and commercial interests in Myanmar. The Kyaukpyu Deep-Sea Port and the Kyaukpyu Special Economic Zone (SEZ) in Rakhine State are two notable examples. This port represents a vital part of China's Belt and Road Initiative (BRI), giving China direct access to the Indian Ocean and a different path for oil imports that avoids the Strait of Malacca.

An additional, noteworthy project that involves both China and Myanmar is the China-Myanmar Oil and Gas Pipeline Project. Both the Myanmar-China Natural Gas Pipeline and the Myanmar-China Crude Oil Pipeline form parts of this project. The pipeline transports crude oil from Kunming in China's Yunnan Province to Kyaukpyu, a deep-water port in Rakhine State, Myanmar. In order to avoid the crowded, strategically dangerous Strait of Malacca, crude oil will be transported from the Middle East and Africa to China. In contrast, Kunming is where the natural gas pipeline ends, after also beginning in Kyaukpyu. Through this transportation, China will receive a fresh supply of energy from Myanmar's offshore fields in the Bay of Bengal. These pipelines are a component of China's larger plan to diversify its energy delivery channels and secure its energy supplies.

A further major infrastructure project that will connect India and Myanmar is the Kaladan Multi-Modal Transit Transport Project, which seeks to establish a land and river connection between the seaports of Sittwe in Rakhine in Myanmar and Kolkata in eastern India. To improve the connections and business dealings between the two countries, the project calls for the building of highways and inland water terminals. Complicated geopolitical factors are at work in Myanmar, where conflicting national political objectives collide with those of powerful nations like China, India, and the US. In terms of economic investments, access to resources, and geopolitical influence, it is true that China and India have major strategic interests in the Myanmar crisis; (Hansler 2022). Consequently, they might be wary of US intervention in the area, especially if this compromises their own respective stances. Understanding these dynamics, the US finds it challenging to exert political pressure on Myanmar to address issues like the Rohingya.

Second, in terms of foreign policy, the US is frequently compelled to strike a difficult balance, especially in areas like Southeast Asia, where strategic considerations collide with human rights issues. The US may have strategic goals related to Myanmar, including fostering economic relations, preserving regional stability, and containing the dominance of countries like China, but these interests must be weighed against the necessity of preserving democracy and human rights. Strong punitive measures against the military rule in Myanmar, including the imposition of all-encompassing sanctions or diplomatic isolation, may have far-reaching effects. It might worsen Myanmar's already unstable situation, push the country closer to other superpowers like China, and possibly endanger the general populace, especially the Rohingya refugees (Myers, 2022; Parameswaran, 2022). Furthermore, there is no assurance that taking such steps would result in a significant shift in Myanmar's behavior.

Third, the internal dynamics of Myanmar, such as its government which is ruled by the military and its intricate ethnic disputes, could make US engagement more difficult. With a long history of military control, the Tatmadaw, the Myanmar military, holds considerable political sway. The military's hold over the country's institutions and economy makes it difficult for outside players to effect political change. The ethnic composition of Myanmar is diverse, with several ethnic minority groups fighting for greater sovereignty or independence (Brenner, 2024; Wason, 2023) The Rohingya issue is merely one facet of the larger ethnic conflicts in Myanmar, which are characterized by intricate political, social, and historical processes.

Fourth, the international community has not reached the same level of unanimity regarding the Rohingya situation as it achieved with regard to crises like Kosovo or Iraq, where there was widespread support for intervention. Concerted action is impeded by divisions among key countries, including inside the UN Security Council. The Rohingya humanitarian crisis is widely acknowledged, but the opinions on how to address the underlying structural and political problems that are causing the issue are more diverse. Humanitarian aid may take precedence over political pressure in certain countries.

Fifth, instead of using force to push for political change and human rights compliance in Myanmar, the US and other countries may choose to engage diplomatically. Even if the progress is sluggish, dialogues and discussions may end up being more successful in the long term. It may be feared that harsh actions by the US government will incite a reaction or worsen the existing tensions. Engagement with regional partners like ASEAN and the appointment of a US Special Envoy for Myanmar are examples of diplomatic efforts that show a preference for diplomatic solutions over military intervention. These efforts may concentrate on ways to reward positive behavior rather than applying punitive measures.

International Responses to the Rohingya Crisis

The role played by several international organizations, including the Association of Southeast Asian Nations (ASEAN), the Organization of Islamic Cooperation (OIC), the United Nations (UN), and the European Union (EU), must be taken into account when analyzing the political dynamics surrounding the Rohingya crisis. These groups are essential for resolving international humanitarian emergencies and advancing safety and security, but their success in terms of settling disputes and stopping crimes has not always been consistent. Following Myanmar's independence from British colonial authority, the country has been affected by complicated political and socioeconomic factors that lie at the heart of the Rohingya conflict. That being said, after the military junta took power in Myanmar in 1962, the targeted persecution and discrimination against the Rohingya minority intensified.

Although the scope and intensity of the Rohingya crisis increased dramatically in the following years, the UN has been involved in seeking to resolve this issue since its inception. Over the years, numerous UN agencies and human rights organizations have compiled evidence of discrimination, violence, and human rights breaches being committed against the Rohingya. The UN Security Council and General Assembly have both adopted resolutions and declarations in an attempt to address the situation in Myanmar using diplomatic means. These diplomatic initiatives represented an attempt to exert pressure on the Myanmar government to uphold human rights and resolve the minority Rohingyas complaints. The following significant occasions and UN activities are connected to the Rohingya crisis and highlight specific UN actions:

Date/Year	*Description*
August 2017	Following a military crackdown that sent hundreds of thousands of Rohingya fleeing to Bangladesh, United Nations High Commissioner for Human Rights refers to the situation in Rakhine State, Myanmar, as a "textbook example of ethnic cleansing." (UN, 2017)

Date/Year	*Description*
September, 2017	A presidential statement denouncing the violence in Rakhine State was released by the UN Security Council, which met for the first time in public to discuss the Rohingya crisis. (UN, 2017)
September 2017	A resolution expressing "grave concern" about reports of Rohingya human rights atrocities and demanding accountability for those guilty was adopted by the UN General Assembly. (UN, 2017)
September 2017	An Independent International Fact-Finding Mission on Myanmar was established by the UN Human Rights Council to investigate claims of violations of human rights, particularly those in Rakhine State. (UN, 2017)
September 2018	The Fact-Finding Mission's final report was released, which stated that war crimes, crimes against humanity, and genocide against the Rohingya and other ethnic minorities by Myanmar's military officials should be investigated and prosecuted. (HRC, 2018)
August 2023	The Secretary-General and special rapporteurs on human rights, among other UN representatives, denounced the persecution of the Rohingya and demanded a resolution to this situation. (UN, 2023)

These are but a handful of the initiatives being launched by the UN to resolve the Rohingya issue although, due to political differences among the member states, obstruction by the Myanmar government, and the complexity of the situation, the UN has struggled to make significant progress despite these measures. For instance, claiming concerns about sovereignty and noninterference in domestic issues, certain nations, like China and Russia, have blocked the Security Council from taking wider action. Delivering help and conducting independent investigations has become challenging due to the Myanmar government's resistance to international participation and restrictions on access for UN agencies and humanitarian organizations (Al Jazeera, 2018; Zahed, 2021).

The Prosecutor was given permission to investigate the alleged crimes against the Rohingya people by the Pre-Trial Chamber III of the International Criminal Court (ICC) in July 2019. This ruling gave the International Criminal Court (ICC) the authority to investigate possible war crimes, crimes against humanity, and genocide that may fall under its purview. The ICC Prosecutor's request was granted authorization to conduct an investigation. In order to investigate the alleged deportation of Rohingya persons from Myanmar to Bangladesh, the Prosecutor filed this request in April 2018. In the fight for victims' justice and to hold those responsible for crimes against the Rohingya community accountable, this ruling represented a major step forward (ICC, 2019).

In November 2019, Gambia filed a lawsuit with the International Court of Justice (ICJ), claiming that Myanmar had violated the 1948 Convention on the Prevention and Punishment of the Crime of Genocide (Genocide Convention) by intending to wipe out the Rohingya people, either entirely or partially. Myanmar rejected Gambia's accusation of genocide, claiming that the military's actions were designed to force the Rohingyas into Bangladesh rather than cause them physical harm (HRC, 2022a). Even though there was a lot of evidence in the case that went before the ICJ, the majority of it was willfully destroyed by the Myanmar government.

Despite its substantial power and resources, the Organization of Islamic Cooperation (OIC) has encountered difficulties in handling the Rohingya issue. The OIC's member countries' disparate interests and goals are one factor that contributes to its inefficiency. Although many member states offer sympathy and express concern for the Rohingya, their responses are frequently influenced by domestic political dynamics, economic interests, and geopolitical concerns. It may be challenging to reach an agreement on important decisions due to differences in commitment and collaboration among the members of the organization as a result of this diversity. Furthermore, the OIC's organizational structure and mandate place restrictions on its capacity to participate directly in hostilities or humanitarian emergencies.

While diplomatic efforts are crucial for resolving the issue, ASEAN's strategy has frequently placed a higher priority on the non-interference in the domestic affairs of its member states than on undertaking forceful action to stop human rights violations (Connors, Davison and Dosch, 2018). Although the Rohingya problem was discussed by leaders at the ASEAN Summit in Manila, the Philippines, no real steps were taken to alleviate the situation. The Rohingyas were not expressly mentioned in the August 2018 ASEAN statement, which also failed either to blame Myanmar's military or to express "deep concern" about the bloodshed in Rakhine State. However, ASEAN's special meeting of foreign ministers in October 2020 neither called for the return of civilian rule nor denounced the military's conduct (Aljazeera, 2020; HRC, 2022b; APR2P, 2022). Critics argue that ASEAN's stance has given Myanmar license to ignore responsibility for its deeds and continue violating the human rights of the Rohingya people.

Since 1988, the European Union (EU) has promoted democracy in Myanmar, based on the assumption that a democratic government would protect the Rohingyas. This approach has been more reactive than strategically planned (Dosch & Sidhu, 2015), however, it clearly reflects how the EU formulates its policies toward Myanmar. In 1991, the EU levied sanctions in an effort to support Aung San Suu Kyi's release and restore democracy in Myanmar (Hufbauer et al., 2008). Targeted sanctions have also been imposed on Myanmar by the European Union (EU) in reaction to violations of international law and abuses of human rights, especially those directed toward the Rohingya people. The EU imposed sanctions on seven senior military leaders from Myanmar in April 2018, alleging their complicity in human rights violations targeting the Rohingya population. Asset freezes and travel restrictions were two of these penalties.

Additionally, the EU placed an arms embargo on Myanmar, making it illegal to export, transfer, buy, or sell weapons or related equipment to the nation. In October 2018, the European Union broadened the scope of its sanctions to encompass more persons and organizations accountable for transgressions against human rights in Myanmar. This included imposing sanctions on prominent General Min Aung Hlaing, the head of the Myanmar military, as well as several other senior officials. The EU placed sanctions on 11 persons and four businesses in Myanmar in April 2021, intended to target those accountable for the military coup that occurred in February 2021 (European Council, 2021; Caine et al., 2021).

The EU's response, however, to the Rohingya issue has been constrained by divergent institutional agendas and a lack of coordination among the member states. The EU's capacity to voice a unified position on the matter and exhibit unity in its interactions with Myanmar has been compromised by this lack of coherence. Some opponents contend that, in comparison to other global crises or geopolitical issues, the EU has given the Rohingya problem insufficient prominence on its foreign policy agenda (Poletti & Sicurelli, 2022: 47). In addition to a general propensity to prioritize stability and economic interests over human rights concerns when making foreign policy decisions, this approach may also result from conflicting interests and priorities inside the EU.

While democratic ideals have a huge influence on the EU, China and Russia's veto power in the UNSC continues to present challenges for institutions like the ICC, ICJ, and OIC. However, by putting individual national interests first and adopting a non-interference strategy, ASEAN is avoiding having to deal with the current problems and has not made any notable progress in this regard. Hence, it is clear that the international organizations are not coordinating their efforts toward the Rohingya issue in a consistent manner, which is impeding the effectiveness of such measures.

Conclusion

The Rohingya issue highlights the complexity of international involvement and diplomacy by posing a diverse problem. In lieu of taking strong political action, the United States' approach to Myanmar has primarily been humanitarian in nature, striking a careful balance between strategic objectives and human rights concerns. Aung San Suu Kyi's fluctuating role and the military junta's hold on power are two examples of the resistance within Myanmar that have made the efforts to resolve the situation more difficult.

Concurrently, political dynamics, regional interests, and institutional limitations have impeded the international responses, such as those by the United Nations, the EU, ASEAN, and other organizations. The Rohingya people have continued to face persecution and displacement in spite of strong condemnations and requests for action. In fact, the ongoing Rohingya crisis is a sobering reminder of the boundaries of international action and the difficulties involved in balancing geopolitical concerns while simultaneously responding to humanitarian crises. In order to address the underlying causes of the crisis successfully and offer the Rohingya community long-term remedies, coordinated action is required which should prioritize human rights and promote increased collaboration among the various stakeholders.

Notes

1 The notion of R2P, or Responsibility to Protect, emerged in response to the widespread crimes carried out in Rwanda and the former Yugoslavia throughout the 1990s, to which the international community was unable to react adequately. The notion of a Responsibility to Protect was founded in 2001 by the International Committee on Intervention and State Sovereignty. Retrieved from https://www.un.org/en/genocideprevention/about-responsibility-to-protect.shtml

2 Burma was renamed "Myanmar" on 18 June 1989, and Rangoon was renamed as the country's capital, "Yangon." The reigning military government made this decision with the intention of promoting national identity and launching political reforms. Not every nation and group, however, agreed with this shift because of the controversy it caused. Owing to historical or political reasons, some people still refer to the nation as "Burma."

References

Al Jazeera. (2018, 29 Aug 2018). Myanmar rejects UN findings in Rohingya genocide report, *Al Jazeera*. Retrieved from https://www.aljazeera.com/news/2018/8/29/myanmar-rejects-un-findings-in-rohingya-genocide-report

Al Jazeera. (2020, 20 October 2020). Myanmar's Rohingya crisis exposes ASEAN weaknesses: Report, *Al Jazeera*. Retrieved from https://www.aljazeera.com/news/2020/10/20/myanmars-rohingya-crisis-exposes-asean-weaknesses-report

APR2P. (2022). *ASEAN and the Rohingya crisis since 2017*. Asia-Pacific Centre for the Responsibility to Protect (APR2P), School of Political Science and International Studies, The University of Queensland, Queensland. Retrieved from https://r2pasiapacific.org/files/9005/2022_ASEAN__Rohingya_Crisis_Since_2017.pdf.

Boghani, P. (2018, 10 May 2018). As Obama eased Myanmar sanctions, some saw warnings of a massacre, *Frontline*. Retrieved from https://www.pbs.org/wgbh/frontline/article/as-obama-eased-myanmar-sanctions-some-saw-warnings-of-a-massacre/

Brenner, D. (2024). Misunderstanding Myanmar through the lens of democracy. *International Affairs, 100*(2), 751–769.

Caine, K., Fardelmann, K., McDougall, K., Nattrass, S., & Gollish, S. (2021). *New sanctions and export restrictions imposed targeting Burma: Updated positions of the United States, Canada, United Kingdom and European Union*. Norton

Rose Fulbright, Texas. Retrieved from https://www.nortonrosefulbright.com/en-us/knowledge/publications/ac28ff93/new-sanctions-and-export-restrictions-imposed-targeting-burma.
Campbell, C. (2014, 13 November 2014). If Obama only talks about one thing in Burma it must be the Rohingya. *The Time*. Retrieved from https://time.com/3582611/obama-rohingya-burma-myanmar/
Congress.gov. (2017). *Unified through Rigorous Military Accountability Act of 2017 (H.R. 4223)*. United States Congress. Retrieved from https://www.congress.gov/bill/115th-congress/senate-bill/2060/cosponsors?r=69&s=1&q=%7B%22party%22%3A%22Democratic%22%7D
Congress.gov. (2018). *S.2060 - Burma Human Rights and Freedom Act of 2018*. United States Congress. Retrieved from https://www.congress.gov/bill/115th-congress/senate-bill/2060/cosponsors?r=69&s=1&q=%7B%22party%22%3A%22Democratic%22%7D
Congress.gov. (2021). *H.R.5497 - BURMA Act of 2021*. United States Congress, Washington, D.C. Retrieved from https://www.congress.gov/bill/117th-congress/house-bill/5497/text
Connors, M. K., Davison, R., & Dosch, J. (2018). *The new global politics of the Asia-Pacific: Conflict and cooperation in the Asian century*. Routledge.
Dosch, J., & Sidhu, J. S. (2015). The European Union's Myanmar policy: Focused or directionless? *Journal of Current Southeast Asian Affairs*, *34*(2), 85–112.
European Council. (2021). *Myanmar/Burma: EU sanctions 11 people over the recent military coup and ensuing repression*. European Council of the European Union, Brussels. Retrieved from https://www.consilium.europa.eu/en/press/press-releases/2021/03/22/myanmar-burma-eu-sanctions-11-people-over-the-recent-military-coup-and-ensuing-repression/
Garrido, C. R. (2022). The state-sponsored genocide of the Rohingya community from a constructivist perspective. *Comillas Journal of International Relations*, 24. Retrieved from https://revistas.comillas.edu/index.php/internationalrelations/article/view/18728/16558
Haacke, J. (2012). Myanmar. In N. Kitchen (Ed.), *The new geopolitics of Southeast Asia* (pp. 53–60). IDEAS, LSE.
Haacke, J. (2015). The United States and Myanmar: From antagonists to security partners? *Journal of Current Southeast Asian Affairs*, *34*(2), 55–83.
Hansler, J. (2022, 22 March 2022). Biden administration formally determines Myanmar's military committed genocide, *CNN*. Retrieved from https://edition.cnn.com/2022/03/20/politics/biden-administration-myanmar-military-genocide/index.html
Haque, E., & Islam, T. (2023). Bangladesh's endeavors for Rohingya repatriation and challenges: A critical analysis. *Dumlupınar Üniversitesi Sosyal Bilimler Dergisi*, *76*, 80–93.
Herfindahl, E. (2016). *Expanding Myanmar's exports through the Generalized System of Preferences (GSP) program*. United States Trade Representative (USTR). Retrieved from https://ustr.gov/sites/default/files/Burma-GSP-PP-English-December-2016.pdf
HRC. (2018). *Situation of human rights of Rohingya Muslims and other minorities in Myanmar: Report of the Independent International Fact-Finding Mission on Myanmar (A/HRC/39/64)*. Human Rights Watch (HRC). Retrieved from https://www.ohchr.org/sites/default/files/Documents/HRBodies/HRCouncil/FFM-Myanmar/A_HRC_39_64.pdf
HRC. (2022a). *Developments in the Gambia's case against Myanmar at the International Court of Justice*. Human Rights Watch (HRC). Retrieved from https://www.hrw.org/news/2022/02/14/developments-gambias-case-against-myanmar-international-court-justice.

HRC. (2022b). *Myanmar: ASEAN's failed '5-point consensus' a year on*. Human Rights Watch (HRC). Retrieved from https://www.hrw.org/news/2022/04/22/myanmar-aseans-failed-5-point-consensus-year.

Hufbauer, G. C., Schott, J. J., Elliott, K. A., & Oegg, B. (2008). Case 88-1: US/EU/Japan v. Burma (1988: Human rights, democracy, narcotics). Peterson Institute for International Economics (PIIE). Retrieved from https://www.piie.com/commentary/speeches-papers/case-88-1

ICC. (2019, 14 November 2019). *ICC judges authorise opening of an investigation into the situation in Bangladesh/Myanmar*. International Criminal Court (ICC) News Center. Retrieved from https://www.icc-cpi.int/news/icc-judges-authorise-opening-investigation-situation-bangladesh/myanmar

Jakes, L. (2022, 21 May 2022). Myanmar's military committed genocide against Rohingya, U.S. says. *The New York Times*. Retrieved from https://www.nytimes.com/2022/03/21/us/politics/myanmar-genocide-biden.html

Lubina, M. (2021). *An unfulfilled relationship: US–Burma/Myanmar political relations*. Jagiellonian University. Retrieved from https://dspace.uni.lodz.pl/xmlui/bitstream/handle/11089/42157/247-268-lubina.pdf?sequence=1&isAllowed=y

Martin, M. F. (2010). *U.S. sanctions on Burma*. Congressional Research Service (CRS), CRS Report for Congress. Retrieved from https://www.everycrsreport.com/files/20100716_R41336_6c33f8d2af751723e4f7f07b58ea8d5e5fafbe33.pdf

Martin, M. F. (2023). *What the BURMA Act does and doesn't mean for U.S. policy in Myanmar*. Center for Strategic and International Studies (CSIS). Retrieved from https://www.csis.org/analysis/what-burma-act-does-and-doesnt-mean-us-policy-myanmar

Martin, M. F., Margesson, R., & Vaughn, B. (2017). *U.S. sanctions on Burma*. Congressional Research Service (CRS), CRS Report for Congress. Retrieved from https://sgp.fas.org/crs/row/R45016.pdf

Myat, S. S. (2016). *The US-Myanmar rapprochement reconsidered: Realignment or non-alignment?* PhD Program, Graduate School of Asia-Pacific Studies, Waseda University, Tokyo. Retrieved from https://www.waseda.jp/inst/oris/assets/uploads/2016/12/5619dfe6cc048d475a7e654872d32135.pdf

Myers, L. (2022). *Balancing acts in U.S. Southeast Asia policy*. Woodrow Wilson International Center for Scholars. Retrieved from https://www.wilsoncenter.org/blog-post/balancing-acts-us-southeast-asia-policy

Naing, I. (2024, 23 April 2024). Myanmar junta slams US aid plan. *VOA News*. Retrieved from https://www.voanews.com/a/myanmar-junta-slams-us-aid-plan/7581977.html

Nguyen, V. (2018). *The Rohingya crisis in Myanmar: Rethinking international engagement toward better humanitarian protection*. Special Honors, The University of Texas. Retrieved from https://core.ac.uk/download/pdf/211330385.pdf

Parameswaran, P. (2019). *US-Myanmar policy under Trump in the spotlight with new sanctions*. The Diplomat. Retrieved from https://thediplomat.com/2019/07/us-myanmar-policy-under-trump-in-the-spotlight-with-new-sanctions/

Parameswaran, P. (2022). *US Southeast Asia strategy: A balance of commitment approach under Biden and beyond*. The Diplomat. Retrieved from https://thediplomat.com/2022/01/us-southeast-asia-strategy-a-balance-of-commitment-approach-under-biden-and-beyond/.

Poletti, A., & Sicurelli, D. (2022). The political economy of the EU approach to the Rohingya Crisis in Myanmar. *Politics and Governance*, *10*(1), 47–57.

Rieffel, L. (2016). *Myanmar: A little trade issue with big consequences*. Brookings Institution. Retrieved from https://www.brookings.edu/articles/myanmar-a-little-trade-issue-with-big-consequences/

Reuters. (2025, July 26). *U.S. lifts some Myanmar sanctions, says no link to generals' letter to Trump.* Retrieved from https://www.reuters.com/world/asia-pacific/us-lifts-some-myanmar-sanctions-says-no-link-generals-letter-trump-2025-07-25/

Solomon, F. (2021, 30 September 2021). Rohingya civil-rights leader Mohib Ullah killed in Bangladesh. *The Wall Street Journal.* Retrieved from https://www.wsj.com/articles/rohingya-civil-rights-leader-mohib-ullah-killed-in-bangladesh-11632993271

Stearns, S. (2012, 17 May 2012). US suspends all economic sanctions on Burma. *Voice of America.* Retrieved from https://www.voanews.com/a/clinton-bruma-fm-meet-in-washington/667077.html

Tucker, S., & Thang, L. B. (2017). *Is Myanmar still hopeful about the NDAA Burma Act?* Stimson. Retrieved from https://www.stimson.org/2023/is-myanmar-still-hopeful-about-the-ndaa-burma-act/.

UN. (28 September 2017). *Amid 'humanitarian and human rights nightmare' in Myanmar, Secretary-General urges full access fora Aid, safe return of displaced Rohingya, end to military operations.* United Nations (UN) News Center. Retrieved from https://press.un.org/en/2017/sc13012.doc.htm

UN. (10 August 2023). *UN rights office calls for action to address root causes of Rohingya crisis.* United Nations (UN) News Center. Retrieved from https://news.un.org/en/story/2023/08/1140032

USAID. (2024). *Rohingya crisis: Ongoing challenges limit USAID's ability to move from humanitarian to development assistance.* U.S. Agency for International Development (USAID). Retrieved from https://oig.usaid.gov/sites/default/files/2024-01/5-000-24-001-P_1.pdf.

Wason, K. (25 December 2023). Examining Myanmar's progression: Past to present. *The Hindustan Times.* Retrieved from https://www.hindustantimes.com/ht-insight/international-affairs/examining-myanmar-s-progression-past-to-present-101703508829160.html

Yan, H., & Watson, I. (13 November 2014). Obama in Myanmar: Rohingya crisis could dim ASEAN summit. *CNN.* Retrieved from https://edition.cnn.com/2014/11/13/politics/myanmar-obama-asean-visit/index.html

Zahed, I. U. M. (2021). Responsibility to protect? The international community's failure to protect the Rohingya. *Asian Affairs*, *52*(4), 934–995.

9

ROADBLOCKS TO ROHINGYA REPATRIATION

Can the R2P Help Remove Them?

Mahbubur Rahman

Introduction

Rohingyas, an ethnic minority of Myanmar, have been subjected to systematic persecution and marginalization decade after decade, resulting in multiple waves of forced displacement. The latest and largest exodus of displacement took place in 2017, when hundreds of thousands of Rohingya were ruthlessly expelled by Myanmar's military, compelling them to take refuge in neighboring Bangladesh. Since then, Bangladesh has taken in more than a million Rohingya refugees, placing a tremendous burden on its infrastructure and resources. Notwithstanding Bangladesh's attempts to manage the crisis amicably, the protracted refugee crisis has raised tensions due to worries about insecurity, organized crime, and drug and human trafficking. Their safe return is further hampered by Myanmar's unwillingness to establish a welcoming environment for them to return and to address their rights-related concerns, such as providing them with a route to citizenship, returning to their ancestral home, and assuring their safety and security. Although there have been occasional attempts at repatriation, first bilaterally and later through a tripartite arrangement comprising China, Myanmar, and Bangladesh, real progress has not been made. The Rohingya, Bangladesh, and the bulk of foreign parties have expressed dissatisfaction with the circumstances Myanmar has demonstrated in accepting their return. Meanwhile, after the military seized control of Myanmar and encountered hitherto unseen opposition from both the Bamar majority and other ethnic groups, the country's political landscape underwent a dramatic shift. With the rise of the Arakan Army as the primary force in Rakhine and the equation between the Rakhines, Rohingya, and Tatmadaw

DOI: 10.4324/9781003771890-9

remaining extremely unstable, the situation in Rakhine saw a significant upheaval.

The Responsibility to Protect—known as R2P—is an international norm or standard that aims to make sure that the international community never again fails to put an end to mass atrocity crimes, including ethnic cleansing, war crimes, genocide, and crimes against humanity. Bangladesh's long efforts for Rohingya repatriation did not materialize because of Myanmar's non-cooperation with Bangladesh and geostrategic-economic interests, as well as the application of vetoes mainly by Russia and China. While Myanmar bears the responsibility for safeguarding the rights of the Rohingyas, collective efforts are essential to reach a just resolution to the Rohingya crisis. This chapter seeks to explore whether R2P is applicable to this crisis, and if so, how the doctrine can be implemented and how Rohingya repatriation can be facilitated. Utilizing qualitative analysis of existing literature and the scholarly debate on the principle, the chapter seeks to determine if there is any conceptual ambiguity or inherent institutional shortcomings in the implementation of this principle. The chapter argues that the R2P doctrine, if effectively applied, can address legal, political, and logistical roadblocks to Rohingya repatriation by mobilizing international action, ensuring Myanmar's accountability, and facilitating a secure environment for returnees.

To discuss the dynamics in detail, apart from introduction and conclusion, the chapter consists of four more sections. In the first section, the chapter discusses the principles, policies or framework, and checkered history of the R2P identifying its doctrinal strengths and challenges. The second section sheds light on some cases from regional instances such as Africa. It also discusses how Chinese and Russian "vetoes" inhibited measures for safe Rohingya repatriation from Bangladesh to their homeland. The third section delineates the Rohingya crisis in light of R2P. The fourth section confers the prospects for regional R2P implementation, giving focus on SAARC, ASEAN, and the Rohingya protection. Finally, the study concludes invoking the reform measures that are warranted for overcoming the current impasse and making R2P work for removing the roadblocks to Rohingya repatriation.

Understanding the Responsibility to Protect (R2P) and Its Framework

The Responsibility to Protect (R2P), which is a global political commitment, rests upon three pillars: (1) State responsibility to protect its citizens; (2) International responsibility to assist states in protecting their populations; (3) Global community's duty to intervene if a state fails to protect. The doctrine states that the state bears the primary responsibility for safeguarding a population against crimes against humanity, war crimes, ethnic cleansing, and genocide. It then speaks for the responsibility of the international community to support states in safeguarding their populations. It further states that if a state is incapable or unwilling to carry out its duty, the international community has a secondary duty to step in and use diplomatic, humanitarian, or even military means as a last resort. In other words, the R2P consists of three responsibilities: prevent, react, and rebuild; "prevent" being the most significant pillar for R2P norm refers to the root cause of conflict when human security is at high risk; "react" includes economic, political, and diplomatic tools, even military actions, and "rebuild" focuses on reconstruction and reconciliation in response to humanitarian crisis (Bellamy 2023). According to the R2P principle, the UN Security Council is "the critical body ultimately responsible for discharging the international response" (Genser 2018).

The idea of R2P came about as a result of the international community's inability to appropriately address the widespread crimes carried out in the 1990s in Rwanda and the former Yugoslavia. The notion of Responsibility to Protect was developed in 2001 by the International Committee on Intervention and State Sovereignty (ICISS). It was unanimously adopted in 2005 at the UN World Summit, the largest gathering of Heads of State and Government in history. The doctrine is articulated in paragraphs 138 and 139:138. Each individual State has the responsibility to protect its populations from genocide, war crimes, ethnic cleansing and crimes against humanity. This responsibility entails the prevention of such crimes, including their incitement, through appropriate and necessary means. We accept that responsibility and will act in accordance with it. The international community should, as appropriate, encourage and help States to exercise this responsibility and support the United Nations in establishing an early warning capability.

The international community, through the United Nations, also has the responsibility to use appropriate diplomatic, humanitarian and other peaceful means, in accordance with Chapters VI and VIII of the Charter, to help to protect populations from genocide, war crimes, ethnic cleansing and crimes against humanity. In this context, we are prepared to take collective action, in a timely and decisive manner, through the Security Council, in accordance with the Charter, including Chapter VII, on a case-by-case basis and in cooperation with relevant regional organizations as appropriate, should peaceful means be inadequate and national authorities are manifestly failing to protect their populations from genocide, war crimes, ethnic cleansing and crimes against humanity. We stress the need for the General Assembly to continue consideration of the responsibility to protect populations from genocide, war crimes, ethnic cleansing and crimes against humanity and its implications, bearing in mind the principles of the Charter and international law. We also intend to commit ourselves, as necessary and appropriate, to helping States build capacity to protect their populations from genocide, war crimes, ethnic cleansing and crimes against humanity and to assisting those that are under stress before crises and conflicts break out.

The strategy for implementing R2P within the UN system was later articulated and fine-tuned by Secretary-General Ban Ki-moon in his 2009 report, *Implementing the Responsibility to Protect*. The strategy consisted of three pillars drawn from the framework of the relevant World Summit Outcome Document paragraphs: the protection responsibilities of the state (Pillar I), international assistance and capacity-building (Pillar II), and the timely and decisive response of the international community once a state has failed to protect its own civilian population (Pillar III).

The World Summit Outcome Document and Secretary-General's reports outline the obligations of UN member states to respond collectively in a timely and decisive manner when a state is manifestly failing to protect its population. In implementing R2P, the Security Council serves an integral role. While there are numerous ways for the Secretary-General and other UN agencies to engage to prevent mass atrocity crimes, R2P calls on the Security Council to use the full range of its powers under Chapter VI to VIII of the UN Charter, if and when other actions are insufficient. The Security Council's leadership and engagement with implementing R2P is therefore essential to the ultimate success or failure of R2P.

To be precise, two contrasting interpretations exist regarding the journey of R2P. There are scholars who maintain that R2P is making progress point out that R2P was endorsed by all states at the 2005 UN World Summit, and then in 2009, when the General Assembly held an "Interactive Dialogue" to discuss the concept, it clearly marked its major achievement. In 2011, when the UN Security Council passed Resolution 1973 sanctioning a military response to the situation in Libya (the Resolution recognized "the responsibility of the Libyan authorities to protect the Libyan population"), it was cited and even celebrated as conclusive proof that R2P had progressed through the various stages of the norm life-cycle model and had compelled the permanent members of the UN Security Council to re-orient their focus away from narrow national interests to "a new politics of protection" (Thakur 2016).

On the other hand, the scholars who hold the opposite view are of the opinion that R2P's so-called "profound influence" has been sustained by a highly selective reading of the evolution and impact of this norm. They suggest that R2P was not working and would never work because it would not significantly alter the international response to intra-state mass atrocities (Hehir 2015) R2P is merely a new slogan enthusiastically avowed by states but one devoid of substance, rendering it a "hollow norm" (Hehir 2015)

As far as the practice is concerned, the UN Security Council has acted on its R2P mandate at various times, both successfully and unsuccessfully.

Despite the assurances made time and time again, attempts to safeguard communities from atrocity crimes are manifestly failing. Atrocity crimes are still being committed in Afghanistan, Ethiopia, Syria, Myanmar, Ukraine, and other places, according to reliable information. Even if numerous states have made efforts in accordance with their R2P obligations, viewed as a whole, these actions have not been sufficient to stop these crimes, much less stop them from happening in the first place.

Nevertheless, R2P has traveled a long way in an extremely short space of time, even though its effectiveness in eliciting responses to mass atrocities around the world is checkered. There is no denying that R2P is no panacea; rather it is a political principle that generates a set of expectations around practical efforts to prevent and halt mass atrocity crimes. As such, it is part of a set of norms that seek to regulate behavior toward civilians and put in place mechanisms to ameliorate their suffering. R2P works in tandem with a range of other contiguous normative agendas that enable and reinforce, or inhibit and undermine, its efficacy.

Ever since the R2P was adopted and implemented, it has often come under fire for various reasons. Sometimes it is accused of being a continuation of postcolonial logics, supporting the interference of the powerful in the affairs of the weak. Sometimes it is viewed as being too militaristic, supporting the use of force for spurious humanitarian ends. Sometimes R2P is criticized for failing to produce adequate solutions to ongoing cases of mass atrocity violence (Hehir 2015). Jared Genser (2018) in his land-mark study titled, "*The UN Security Council's Implementation of the Responsibility to Protect: A Review of Past Interventions and Recommendations for Improvement*," has examined eleven country-specific case studies, which demonstrate that the presence of certain conditions enables the UN Security Council to successfully implement its R2P mandate. In this study, he identifies three conditions that generally need to be present for the Security Council to successfully implement its R2P mandate:

(1) there must be no government obstruction from the state in which mass atrocity crimes are being perpetrated, or, if government obstruction exists, one of the five permanent members of the Security Council (P5 member) must provide political will to overcome obstruction;
(2) there must be cooperation between regional organizations and the Security Council; and
(3) the Council must have the capacity to respond rapidly to the unfolding situation.

He maintains that all three conditions are necessary for successful implementation, while the absence of these conditions is more likely to lead to unsuccessful R2P implementation by the Security Council.

Regional Organizations and the UN: A Critical Analysis of Some Cases Regarding R2P Implementation

The African Union and Darfur

The R2P doctrine relished its most significant early test in Sudan's Darfur region. The African Union's (AU) Article 4(h) provision for direct intervention authorization encountered severe implementation challenges. Although the AU's constitutional mandate was to intervene in cases of genocide, war crimes, crimes against humanity, and ethnic cleansing, the organization's response to Darfur exposed fundamental structural and political limitations that brought about critical questions to R2P implementation across Africa. The AU deployed the African Mission in Sudan (AMIS) in 2004. It was initially with a mandate limited to monitoring a fragile ceasefire agreement between the Sudanese government and rebel groups (Verhoeven et al. 2016). However, as violence escalated and an estimated 300,000 people died, with over 2.7 million displaced, the AU's capacity proved woefully inadequate.

ECOWAS Interventions: Mixed Results in West Africa

With both notable successes and significant limitations in its humanitarian interventions in Liberia and Sierra Leone, the Economic Community of West African States (ECOWAS) has experienced a more complex picture of R2P implementation. Its deployment of the Economic Community of West African States Monitoring Group (ECOMOG) in Liberia (1990–1997) and Sierra Leone (1997–2000) has been regarded as important precedents for regional humanitarian intervention (Enuka 2012). However, in Liberia, ECOWAS intervened during the brutal civil war (1989–1996). During the period, an estimated 150,000 people were killed and displaced, over half of the total population (Amaraegbu 2013). The intervention, while eventually successful in ending the immediate violence, also faced notable challenges. These include unclear mandates, insufficient resources, and accusations of bias toward particular factions. The intervention marked the first major "interference" of an African sub-regional body in the internal affairs of a member state (Amaraegbu 2013). This defied the traditional notions of "state sovereignty" within the region.

ASEAN: Non-Interference versus Protection Dilemmas

The Association of Southeast Asian Nations (ASEAN) underwent tensions between its foundational "non-interference principle" and emerging R2P obligations. It notably happened during Myanmar's Cyclone named Nargis 2008 and the ongoing Rohingya crisis (Quint and Pareja-Alcaraz 2023). During Cyclone Nargis, which killed over 140,000 people, Myanmar's military junta initially repudiated international humanitarian assistance, giving rise to what some scholars considered "a crime against humanity" (Langmore and McLachlan-Bent 2011). ASEAN found itself caught between international pressure to invoke R2P and its own non-interference principles. As then-Secretary-General Surin Pitsuwan stated, he was "baptized in Nargis" as ASEAN took unprecedented steps to coordinate international relief efforts (Heyzer 2017).

By the way, ASEAN's response was with both innovation and limitation. The organization successfully established the Tripartite Core Group with the UN and Myanmar government, facilitating humanitarian access that might otherwise have been impossible. However, it did so at the expense of adding weight to Myanmar's sovereignty claims and precedent that would later appear in some responses to crimes against humanity targeted at the Rohingya. In this sense, the contradictions were exposed more clearly by the Rohingya crisis. Even though there were strong elements of ethnic cleansing and crimes against humanity that took place in 2016–2017, ASEAN's response was less than effective with economic aid and expressions of diplomatic concern (Serey et al. 2024). As one ASEAN official noted, "No Member State in ASEAN supports the idea [of R2P]...There is a fear that once you use it, it will come back at you" (Barber 2023). This reticence reveals underlying structural problems within ASEAN. In this respect, decision-making processes based on consensus and sovereignty considerations acted as institutional impediments to the implementation of R2P. There has been some improvement in the organization's response to Myanmar's military coup of 2021, with ASEAN taking an unprecedented step by excluding from critical meetings that country's junta. Yet these fall short of R2P's standards to safeguard civilian populations (Barber 2023).

R2P in Solving the Protracted Rohingya Crisis

R2P applies to the Rohingya crisis in many ways. First, Myanmar's ongoing violations of human rights are causing at least one of the four atrocity crimes specified in the R2P framework. They include genocide, ethnic cleansing, and crimes against humanity. Most researchers (Gepp 2021; Adams 2019) specifically cite the UN High Commissioner for Human Rights' 2017 statement that described the Rohingya problem as a "textbook example of ethnic cleansing." The 2017 UN Fact-Finding Mission on Myanmar (IFFMM) report is used by Gepp (2021) as evidence that the state has clearly displayed acts of mass murder and genocidal intent. Mennecke and Stansrud (2021) also explicitly emphasize the government's incapacity and unwillingness to stop the abuses. This suggests that Pillar I, which lays the burden of responsibility on the international community, has not been met by the government.

The second pillar pertains to the responsibility of the international community to support states in safeguarding their populations. However, before 2017, the international community focused primarily on promoting democratic reforms and economic development in Myanmar, rather than addressing the critical issues of citizenship and statelessness affecting the Rohingya community. Apart from the incidence of crimes against humanity, the overall intensity of the conflict is underscored by the increasing atrocities and the global consequences of this progression (Mennecke & Stensrud 2021).

There is no denying that Myanmar has perpetrated crimes against humanity and ethnic cleansing against the Rohingya. International human rights rules and instruments are in conflict with the atrocities committed against the Rohingya. The Rohingya are currently facing an impending calamity that could endanger their existence both inside and outside of Burma. Burma has failed to shield its own citizens from the horrors (sovereignty as responsibility), and it is even hesitant to do so (duty to prevent). According to the United Nations' "responsibility to protect" standards, the international world is now in charge of protecting the Rohingya because they are reluctant to shield them from the horrors (responsibility to prevent). Consequently, accountability now rests with the international community in accordance with the United Nations' "responsibility to protect" standards.

Myanmar has violated the treaties, conventions, and declarations it has signed, despite being a party to the 1948 Genocide Convention, a member of the United Nations, and the International Court of Justice. The international community is also duty-bound under the R2P to protect populations from genocide, war crimes, and ethnic cleansing, but Myanmar has had impunity for decades. While the United Nations and the global community are supposed to uphold the R2P doctrine, they are found to be ignoring what is occurring on the ground and attempting to resolve issues solely through statements or some financial assistance to the refugees, which is also waning. According to the international human rights principles and policies, refugees' right to dignified return to their homeland, reintegration into their homeland, safety assurances for the Rohingya minority, and the advancement of interethnic harmony should take precedence over any business dealings. Unfortunately, given that Myanmar is dealing with a civil war enmeshed in ethnic tensions and that minorities like the Rohingya are being targeted in an effort to inflame the nationalist feelings of majoritarian groups, the situation is unlikely to improve.

Repatriation of Rohingya: The Challenges

Unfortunately, in the wake of the Tatmadaw's targeted violence against the Rohingya, the response of the international community has largely been limited to condemnation and imposing mere sanctions. The United Nations

Security Council (UNSC) has failed to implement any forceful measures due to opposition from veto-wielding nations such as China and Russia. Despite the global commitment to the R2P principle, most international actors avoided engaging in political confrontations with Myanmar concerning the Rohingya issue, citing norms of Myanmar sovereignty. Indeed, it becomes shockingly clear that if the R2P is about protecting citizens, then the Myanmar government is not liable toward the Rohingya who are rendered stateless in an era of the so-called "absolutist sovereignty" (Bellamy 2009). Here lies the paradox of the current (search for a) response to the Rakhine State crisis: it cannot help but call for the amendment of the contested citizenship law in order for the human rights of the persecuted Rohingya to be properly respected.

Key regional players like China and India prioritize their strategic interests in Myanmar, undermining international efforts to hold Myanmar accountable. This geopolitical state of affairs indicates little hope for a political arrangement for voluntary and safe repatriation of the Rohingya to the Rakhine State of Myanmar. As already mentioned, China has a long history of supporting Myanmar, both politically and economically. Russia and India also have a soft interest in Myanmar. China is building a deep seaport in Kyaukpyu, Rakhine State, and has already invested billions of dollars to establish oil and gas pipelines from the port to the landlocked Chinese province of Yunnan. China considers Myanmar a key gateway to the Bay of Bengal and the Indian Ocean. These geopolitical interests have so far restricted China from taking any decision that goes against Myanmar's favor. This was evident in the 2017 UNSC meeting on Myanmar, where China blocked a resolution to condemn Myanmar for its atrocities against the Rohingya ethnic minority. China has always opted for pursuing a bilateral solution to a global problem and emphasized the necessity of economic development in Rakhine State to resolve the crisis. In addition to the above predicament, international inaction or weak enforcement of international law has also made it impossible to make Myanmar responsible for its atrocities, let alone punishable in court. While the International Court of Justice (ICJ) has issued provisional measures against Myanmar, enforcement mechanisms are limited.

Bangladesh's limited leverage is also another factor that has made the repatriation case weaker. Despite hosting such a huge number of refugees, during the previous regime of Sheikh Hasina, Bangladesh was reluctant to pressure Myanmar or the country practically lacked the strength or will, and diplomatic and economic influence to pressure into action. As a result, regional organizations like ASEAN and South Asian neighbors have been reluctant to play a proactive role in advocating for Rohingya rights and repatriation. Given that Myanmar has failed to provide assurances of safety, citizenship, or basic rights for returnees, all bilateral and trilateral efforts for repatriation have failed. Myanmar refuses to recognize the Rohingya as citizens, labeling them illegal immigrants from Bangladesh. It has consistently denied allegations of genocide and human rights abuses. Even the so-called Pilot project (advised and assisted by China) for convincing a very limited number of Rohingya refugees (after all verification processes) didn't see the light of day.

Calls for the UNSC to voluntarily forego using its veto power in cases of atrocity have gained traction in recent years. In addition to two UN observation missions, more than 120 states have backed proposals for a code of behavior or veto restriction. In order to issue united pleas for caution, the Global Centre for the Responsibility to Protect has been collaborating closely with member nations and civil society organizations, such as the Elders. Jennifer Trahan has also noted that the unbridled use of veto power by the P5 nations is a global issue that necessitates discussion and a different approach (Trahan 2020). She has discussed the legal question of "whether the P5 countries are permitted to exercise their veto in the face of atrocity crimes," which has important implications for both ongoing and future conflicts as well as the lives of all those affected by them. She makes the logical and impassioned request that we all "do our utmost to ensure that the UN Charter's voting provisions are never used in a way that directly or indirectly facilitates or enables the ongoing perpetration of genocide, crimes against humanity, or war crimes." She then draws a connection between the use of the veto power and "continuing death tolls on the ground" (Trahan 2020). It is hoped that raising awareness about this compelling case can increase pressure on governments and international organizations to act.

Removing the Roadblocks to Repatriation: Any Light at the End of the Tunnel?

Given that the United Nations' initiative didn't succeed due to China's veto, China, as part of its "feel good" diplomacy, attempted to mediate the beginning of Rohingya repatriation between Bangladesh and the Myanmar government on multiple occasions before the rise of the Arakan Army (AA) to prominence. The attempts were unsuccessful primarily due to the exclusion of both the Rohingya and the Rakhine.

It is important to mention that Myanmar has been in civil war since the military coup that ousted the democratic government in February 2021. The National Unity Government, the shadow government formed by the political leaders and dozens of other ethnic groups after the 2021 coup, has been fighting the junta since then. Today, the AA, which seeks autonomy in Rakhine, controls the entire 271-kilometer-long border with Bangladesh. It is also worth mentioning that more than a million Rohingyas who have taken shelter in Bangladesh fled from that state. Current events therefore indicate that progress on repatriation and other pressing concerns pertaining to the Rohingya will remain illusory until and unless Bangladesh, China, and the international world recognize the AA's authority. Therefore, more practical strategies are required, such as involving the AA, a non-state actor that is unquestionably the de facto authority in Rakhine.

However, two events have put doubt on the AA's military accomplishments, despite the fact that the group has freed the majority of the state from the Tatmadaw's control. Rakhine is currently in danger of a humanitarian and economic catastrophe as a result of the latest wave of warfare, which started in November 2023. The military of Myanmar has tightened its siege of the state, making it impossible for necessities to enter. Basic commodity prices have soared, and there is even a shortage of currency in areas under AA rule. Serious food shortages and even famine-like circumstances might occur, according to warnings from the UNDP and others.

Furthermore, the conflict has harmed inter-ethnic relationships within the Rakhine community. Even while the Myanmar military has been losing the conflict, it did manage to turn a sizable portion of the Rohingya against the AA's primarily ethnic Rakhine forces by employing its well-proven divide-and-rule tactic. It has accomplished this by working with Rohingya armed groups, such as the Arakan Rohingya Salvation Army and the Rohingya Solidarity Organization, and by actively recruiting Rohingya. Tensions have only increased as all parties have been charged with violating civilians' human rights since April 2024. For a state like Rakhine, where ethnic and communal divisions run deep, what role the Arakan Army will play is yet to be seen.

In these circumstances, engaging AA for negotiating with the Rohingyas for inclusive administration in Rakhine State through the good offices of neighboring Bangladesh and the United Nations could be the best starting point. Bangladesh, meanwhile, has successfully lobbied the UN to hold a high-level conference on the Rohingya in 2025 that aimed at developing "a comprehensive, innovative, concrete, and time-bound plan for the sustainable resolution of the crisis." However, it lacked adequate homework. As an analyst rightly pointed out, "A large conference without prior homework won't be effective. While it may help raise funds, the repatriation process is highly complex." (Billah 2024). He further pointed out that preparatory work needed to be done with countries like China, India, Japan, and the US. Once these bilateral engagements yield progress, the conference could be convened with broader consensus, which would then make it more fruitful. (Billah 2024).

Finally, China and India, as influential regional powers with extensive interests and investments in both Myanmar and Bangladesh, should realize that delaying a sustainable solution to the Rohingya crisis can lead to humanitarian crises and security threats for the entire region in the longer term. A coordinated global and regional commitment to R2P is likely to be more impactful in finding a sustainable resolution to this humanitarian crisis.

Prospects for Regional R2P Implementation and the Rohingya Protection

Prospect for Regional R2P

Bangladesh is considered a bridge between South Asia and Southeast Asia. In the two regions, the evolution of regional R2P mechanisms has both opportunities and significant obstacles. In this regard, the South Asian Association for Regional Cooperation (SAARC) has largely failed to address complex humanitarian crises such as the Rohingya crisis. Former Bangladeshi Foreign Minister AH Mahmood Ali frankly admitted in 2017 that the Rohingya crisis had "no relevance for SAARC" (New Age 2025). This exhibits the organization's structural limitations in confronting politically sensitive humanitarian emergencies. This is a broader institutional weakness that characterizes SAARC as a "dysfunctional, talk-shop, and dead organisation" constrained by bilateral disagreements between member states(Anwar 2022).

However, ASEAN has more hopeful precedents when it comes to regional R2P use, in particular its response to humanitarian crises such as Cyclone Nargis in 2008. The creation of the ASEAN Humanitarian Task Force (AHTF) and the novel Tripartite Core Group process was an indication that regional organizations could move beyond its non-interference principles in face of humanitarian imperatives (Loevy 2015). ASEAN was active in facilitating access into Myanmar for rescue teams and humanitarian aid through the TCG. It created a chance and bridge between the international community and the Government. This successfully brought about normative foundations for applying R2P principles within Southeast Asian frameworks, even though it involved natural disasters rather than mass atrocities.

While Bangladesh can play an important role in reviving the SAARC, it can connect a bridge between it and ASEAN with a view to solving the Rohingya crisis. The theoretical basis for regional R2P remains sound, as scholars have argued that "the norms and objectives of the R2P are not alien to ASEAN." Southeast Asia possesses relevant mechanisms including the ASEAN Intergovernmental Commission on Human Rights (AICHR) and the ASEAN Commission on the Promotion and Protection of the Rights of Women and Children (ACWC). Bangladesh can play a role in the rejuvenation of ASEAN's proactive role to ensure a secured and safe environment in Rakhine for the voluntary repatriation of

Building Relations with ASEAN

With regard to Cyclone Nargis, the creation of the ASEAN-led coordinating mechanism succeeded because it provided Myanmar with assurances that assistance "would not be politicised" while creating space for international humanitarian access. ASEAN's institutional development since 2008 has created additional frameworks relevant to R2P implementation (ReliefWeb 2009). ASEAN's non-interference principle continues to obstruct effective R2P implementation, particularly in the Rohingya case where the principle "manifests selective application favouring powerful member states, and effectively serves to shield authoritarian regimes rather than to defend human rights."

Still, the organization's evolving human rights architecture, including the AICHR, provides a room for institutional foundations that could be leveraged by Bangladesh to discuss the Rohingya atrocity prevention. In this respect, Bangladesh should build strong relations with ASEAN to discuss the urgent need for making a safe environment for Rohingya repatriation. With the Yunus administration's leadership, Bangladesh has already sought the membership of the organization. Bangladesh must continue such involvement and urge the organizational figures to hasten the process of repatriation under the R2P mechanism (Siow 2025).

Coalitions with the UN

The Tripartite Core Group model established during Cyclone Nargis provides a template for UN-ASEAN cooperation. With the new development regarding the Rohingya crisis, such a framework could be adapted for R2P situations in order to ensure the Rohingya repatriation in a safe environment in Rakhine. Contemporary R2P baseline assessments indicate that Asia-Pacific states have "broad constituency within the region for moving the principle from rhetoric to reality at the United Nations" (Khan and Ahmed 2020). The 2023 regional assessment found that the slight increase in the overall score shows R2P implementation in the Asia Pacific is making progress with stronger performance among traditional allies like Australia, New Zealand, and South Korea (Bellamy et al. 2023). The assessment noted continued challenges in states like Myanmar and North Korea. Also, recent analysis notes, "the growth of Chinese capital in the economy of Myanmar and the political influence of Beijing on the military" have become central factors in regional dynamics (Vinogradov 2023).

However, the Global Centre for the Responsibility to Protect has identified specific opportunities for deepening UN-regional cooperation. As already noted above that "the norms and objectives of the R2P are not alien to ASEAN." Bangladesh can play a coordinating role in developing "a commitment of support [that] stands as the foundation for deepening cooperation between ASEAN and the UN" while respecting regional autonomy in implementation approaches to ensure the safe and voluntary repatriation of Rohingya people. Also, Bangladesh can highlight the importance of reviving the High-Level Advisory Panel on the Responsibility to Protect (R2P) in Southeast Asia which was established in April 2013 to support the implementation of R2P in the region (Pitsuwan et al. n.d.).

Motivating China

Beijing's strategic calculations regarding Myanmar are driven by multiple imperatives: securing Belt and Road Initiative (BRI) investments, maintaining energy corridor access to the Indian Ocean, and preventing regional instability that could affect Chinese border provinces (Kobayashi and King 2022). China's resistance to R2P implementation in Myanmar reflects a somewhat blended concern about Western intervention and regime change. However, China's interests are not monolithic, and evolving circumstances in Myanmar have given rise to opportunities for alternative approaches. The post-2021 coup fragmentation of Myanmar has complicated Chinese investments and security concerns. Beijing's transactional approach to ethnic armed groups like the Arakan Army in areas where there are large Chinese investments (for example, a $1.5 billion investment in oil and gas pipelines that go through Rakhine State into Kunming) indicates possible flexibility around support for stabilization mechanisms aimed at protecting the civilian population (Mahmud 2025).

To motivate Chinese cooperation, R2P implementation would have to be seen as congruent with China's most important core interests in the area—stability and economic security in Burma. The crisis over the Rohingya has produced exactly the regional instability that risks Chinese investments and border security. The geopolitical implications of the crisis mean that the fight for regional hegemony makes the Rohingya crisis more vulnerable. China's historical role in facilitating dialogue between Myanmar's government and ethnic armed organizations is a notable example of Beijing's capacity for constructive engagement when its interests align with international objectives. Building on this precedent needs careful diplomatic engagement that acknowledges Chinese concerns while accentuating shared interests in regional stability and civilian protection.

In this respect, Bangladesh can revive the trilateral diplomacy effort involving Bangladesh, Myanmar, and China, which has been underway to facilitate the repatriation of Rohingya refugees to Myanmar (Mahmud 2023). China has been mediating discussions between Bangladesh and Myanmar. It was aimed at a safe and voluntary return of Rohingya refugees to Rakhine State. Such trilateral diplomacy can spur the establishment of diplomatic engagement of China as well as its role to notably contribute to the regional R2P mechanism.

Conclusion

Nations committed to R2P could incorporate policies that take on responsibility sharing. For the Rohingya, currently facing persecution and being forcibly displaced, R2P can incorporate policies that offer physical safe havens to Rohingya refugees fleeing persecution in Myanmar. Not only does this ensure greater protection for a greater number of refugees, but it also alleviates logistical pressure from nations like Bangladesh, which is currently hosting Rohingya refugees at great cost to itself at a social and economic level. Furthermore, this incentivizes more nations to act in favor of resolving the Rohingya situation faster.

In the absence of concrete measures of accountability, these policies are an effective stopgap that ensures human protection. Additionally, because these policies only require the willingness of individual nations, they are unlikely to be blocked by international political machinations. Considering the universal consensus toward R2P and considering that a majority of its concerns for implementation was driven by potential blocks at the Security Council level, this expansion provides a palatable alternative that is not only sustainable but is also likely to be effective at ensuring that human lives are protected. Furthermore, this allows the opportunity for the international community to assist the Rohingya in galvanizing activities and advocating for their demands. By first ensuring their physical safety, global actors in this field are then able to move toward capacity building for the victims of such crimes to push toward policy changes that protect them.

By leveraging the Responsibility to Protect, the global community can address barriers to repatriation, ensuring dignity, safety, and justice for the Rohingya. Sustained action, rooted in international solidarity and accountability, is essential for a durable solution to this humanitarian tragedy. While there are formidable challenges, the international community has a responsibility to keep trying to accomplish whatever is achievable. As the former Secretary-General Ban Ki-moon said:

> [t]he world's people have, nevertheless, kept their faith in the institution, because it never tires of trying to accomplish the impossible. So be it with R2P, which speaks to the things that are most noble and most enduring in the human condition. We will not always succeed in this cardinal enterprise, and we are taking but the first steps in a long journey. But our first responsibility is to try.
>
> *(Ban Ki-moon 2008, SG/SM/11701)*

References

Adams, S. 2019. The Responsibility to Protect and the Fate of the Rohingya, *Global Responsibility to Protect*, 11(4): 435–450.

Amaraegbu, D. 2013. *The African Union Charter and ECOWAS Humanitarian Intervention in Liberia: The Behaviouralist Perspective.* Rochester, NY: Social Science Research Network. Available at: https://papers.ssrn.com/abstract=2246860 (Accessed: 1 August 2025).

Anwar, M.F. 2022. Saarc and Asean: A Comparative Study Success & Failure. *International Journal of Social Sciences*, 11(2), pp. 13–23.

Barber, R. 2023. A Proposal for Advancing Implementation of the Responsibility to Protect. Available at: https://doi.org/10.1163/1875984X-20230007.

Bellamy, A.J. 2009. *Responsibility to Protect: The Global Effort to End Mass Atrocities.* Cambridge: Polity Press.

Bellamy, A.J. et al. 2023. Implementing the Responsibility to Protect Asia Pacific. Available at: https://r2pasiapacific.org/files/12054/R2P%20Baseline%20FINAL%20DRAFT%202024.pdf.

Billah, Masum. 2024. *Rohingya Crisis: Can the Interim Government's 'New Strategy' Break the Deadlock?* Available at: https://bdnews24.com/bangladesh/dfc4db8d621d.

Enuka, C. 2012. *United Nations and ECOWAS Joint Intervention in Sierra-Leonean Conflict: An Analysis of the Problems of Peacekeeping, Peacemaking and Peace Enforcement.* Rochester: Social Science Research Network. Available at: https://papers.ssrn.com/abstract=2172708.

Genser, J. 2018. The United Nations Security Council's Implementation of the Responsibility to Protect: A Review of Past Interventions and Recommendations for Improvement. *Chicago Journal of International Law*, 18(2), 420–501.

Gepp, M. 2021. The Road Not Taken: Failure to Protect from Atrocity Crimes in Myanmar, Groningen. *Journal of International Law*, 9(1), 78–100.

Hehir, A., & Pattison, J. 2015. Introduction: The Responsibility to Protect after the Arab Spring. *Cooperation and Conflict*, 51(2), 141–147. https://doi.org/10.1177/0010836715612853. (Original work published 2016)

Heyzer, N. 2017. Weathering the Storm: ASEAN's Humanitarianism in the Aftermath of Nargis', in 50 Years of ASEAN and Singapore. *World Scientific*, pp. 101–108. Available at: https://doi.org/10.1142/9789813225138_0011.

Khan, M.T. and Ahmed, S. 2020. Dealing with the Rohingya Crisis: The Relevance of the General Assembly and R2P. *Asian Journal of Comparative Politics*, 5(2), pp. 121–143. Available at: https://doi.org/10.1177/2057891119868312.

Kobayashi, Y. and King, J. 2022. Myanmar's Strategy in the China–Myanmar Economic Corridor: A Failure in Hedging?. *International Affairs*, 98(3), pp. 1013–1032. Available at: https://doi.org/10.1093/ia/iiac049.

Langmore, J. and McLachlan-Bent, A. 2011. A Crime Against Humanity? Implications and Prospects of the Responsibility to Protect in the Wake of Cyclone Nargis. Available at: https://doi.org/10.1163/187598411X549477.

Loevy, K. 2015. The Legal Politics of Jurisdiction: Understanding ASEAN's Role in Myanmar's Disaster, Cyclone Nargis (2008). *Asian Journal of International Law*, 5(1), pp. 55–93.

Mahmud, K.U. 2023. The Rohingya Repatriation to Myanmar: The Relevance of the Trilateral Diplomacy. *The Geopolitics*, 8 October. Available at: https://thegeopolitics.com/the-rohingya-repatriation-to-myanmar-the-relevance-of-the-trilateral-diplomacy/ (Accessed: 1 August 2025).

Mahmud, K.U. 2025. Geopolitics Rewritten: The Arakan Army's Unprecedented Rise. *The Daily Star*, pp. 1–6. Available at: https://doi.org/10.2139/ssrn.5267634.

Mennecke, M. and Stensrud, E.E. 2021. The Failure of the International Community to Apply R2P and Atrocity Prevention in Myanmar. *Global Responsibility to Protect*, 13(2–3), 111–130.
Moon, K.B. 2008. Available at: https://press.un.org/en/2008/sgsm11701.doc.htm.
New Age. 2025. No Relevance of Rohingya Crisis for SAARC: FM. Available at: https://www.newagebd.net/article/26413/no-relevance-of-rohingyacrisis-for-saarc-fm (Accessed: 1 August 2025).
Pitsuwan, D.S. et al. n.d. 'High-Level Advisory Panel on the Responsibility to Protect in Southeast Asia', 2014 [Preprint]. Available at: https://www.un.org/en/genocideprevention/documents/responsibility-to-protect/HLAP%20Report_FINAL.pdf.
Quint, K. and Pareja-Alcaraz, P. 2023. ASEAN's Approach to the Responsibility to Protect: Case Analysis of the Rohingya in Myanmar. Available at: https://www.academia.edu/download/111916086/Katharina_Quint_LLM_Thesis.pdf.
ReliefWeb. 2009. A Bridge to Recovery: ASEAN's Response to Cyclone Nargis - Myanmar. Available at: https://reliefweb.int/report/myanmar/bridge-recovery-aseans-response-cyclone-nargis.
Serey, R., Bivens, R.T. and Glas, A. 2024. This Is Not the 90s": Myanmar and Change in ASEAN's Normative Order. *Pacific Affairs*, 97(4), pp. 773–794. Available at: https://doi.org/10.5509/2024974-art5.
Siow, M. 2025. Will Bangladesh's Asean Dream Become a Reality?, *South China Morning Post*. Available at: https://www.scmp.com/week-asia/politics/article/3320334/bangladesh-wants-malaysias-help-join-asean-it-faces-uphill-battle (Accessed: 1 August 2025).
Thakur, R. 2016. The Responsibility to Protect at 15'. *International Affairs*, 92(2): 415–434.
Trahan, J. 2020. *Existing Legal Limits to Security Council Veto Power in the Face of Atrocity Crimes*. Cambridge: Cambridge University Press.
Verhoeven, H., De Oliveira, R.S. and Jaganathan, M.M. 2016. To Intervene in Darfur, or Not: Re-Examining the R2P Debate and Its Impact. *Global Society*, 30(1), pp. 21–37. Available at: https://doi.org/10.1080/13600826.2015.1093464.
Vinogradov, I. 2023. Myanmar – China: Beijing's Strategic Interests and Instruments of Influence. *Asia and Africa Today*, 5, pp. 26–35. Available at: https://doi.org/10.31857/S032150750025705-7.

10

UNITING FOR "PEACE"

The (Missing) Role of the United Nations General Assembly in the Rohingya Crisis

Sayere Nazabi Sayem

Introduction

The Rohingya are the largest stateless population globally, having fled to Bangladesh in 2017 during the biggest exodus to date. As per a study by the Ontario International Development Agency (*Forced Migration of Rohingya: The Untold Experience*, 2018), state forces in Myanmar have killed almost 24,000 Rohingya Muslims since the crackdown on August 25, 2017, raped 18,000+ Rohingya women and girls, and over 115,000 Rohingya homes were burned down, with another 113,000 vandalised. This chapter scrutinises the possible "what-ifs" that could have been implemented by the United Nations (UN) instead, using the Uniting for Peace Resolution, which is well known to be under its ambit for grave violations of peace and security.

The two pivotal organs of the UN, the Security Council (UNSC) and the General Assembly (UNGA), work in tandem to address international disputes. The former maintains international peace and security as one of its primary functions, while the latter serves as the principal policymaking organ of the UN. The UNGA allows multifaceted discussions of Member States on international issues. As enshrined in Article 14 of the Charter of the United Nations, which states:

> [T]he General Assembly may recommend measures for the peaceful adjustment of any situation, regardless of origin, which it deems likely to impair the general welfare or friendly relations among nations, including situations resulting from a violation of the provisions of the present Charter setting forth the Purposes and Principles of the United Nations.

DOI: 10.4324/9781003771890-10

The aforementioned Article can only be implemented by the Assembly without curtailing the powers of the UNSC, as mentioned in Article 12 of the Charter. However, there may be situations when the Council is unable to act, but the matter is so grave that the principal body of the United Nations would have to act in its place to ensure compliance. UNGA can order procedural and substantive measures to maintain international peace and security. Such a practice of intervention in lieu of the UNSC has been documented in UNGA Resolution 377 (V) of 1950, also known as the "Uniting for Peace Resolution."

Over the years, the UNGA has become a special forum to deliberate on policies and practices of various countries, "totally changing its character from a meeting convened to discuss urgent matters to a permanent, but intermittent conference on a topic of paramount interest to the international community" (Tomuschat, 2008).

What Is the Uniting for Peace Resolution of the UNGA?

Resolution 377 (V), also known as the Uniting for Peace (UFP) Resolution or the Acheson Plan, was adopted by the UNGA on 3 November 1950, during the Korean War (United Nations, 1950). It was adopted by 52 votes to 5, with 2 abstentions. The successfully passed Resolution limits the Council's authority to act within the UN system of collective security, allowing the Assembly to interfere in international conflicts. It allows the UNGA to act in cases of deadlock of the UNSC due to the use of a veto by one of its permanent members (China, Russia, the United States of America, France and the United Kingdom). The Assembly can take action, such as using force when necessary, under the UFP Resolution to maintain international peace and security. The resolution allows the Assembly to act in situations that fall under Chapter VII of the UN Charter, such as threats to peace, breaches of peace, or acts of aggression (*International Law*, 2017). The Assembly can also call upon emergency special sessions within twenty-four hours, contrary to the annual meetings, as per Article 20 of the UN Charter. It has become a common practice for "an increasing tendency over time for the General Assembly and the Security Council to deal in parallel with the same matter concerning the maintenance of international peace and security" (International Court of Justice, 2004). The Council can summon an emergency session with a vote of seven members [nine since 1965] or a majority of UN members. An UNSC resolution calling for an emergency special session of the Assembly is a procedural resolution and, hence, cannot be vetoed. The UFP Resolution establishes a way for a majority of the UNSC to transfer a topic to the Assembly when a veto from one of the five permanent members blocks substantive action by the Council.

During the Korean crisis (25 June 1950–27 July 1953), the Union of Soviet Socialist Republics (USSR) used its veto authority in the UNSC, causing additional resolutions to stall. It is then that the United States sought to act through the UNGA, persuading it to claim subsidiary responsibility and the UFP Resolution was formed to achieve this goal, as enshrined in Article 14 of the Charter.

How Did It Work in Prior Cases?

The Uniting for Peace Resolution (Resolution 377) would address this issue by implementing the following six improvements in structure and procedure:

1) The authority to send a peace-and-security issue to the General Assembly if the Security Council was stopped by veto;
2) the ability to call emergency sessions of the Assembly for this purpose, if required;
3) a recommendation that Member States maintain specific UN-designated units in their separate national armed forces;
4) the establishment of a Peace Observation Commission;
5) a Collective Measures Committee; and
6) a panel of military experts.

It has been documented that the UFP Resolution has been invoked several times in the past, in significant instances. Between 1951 and 2022, it has been invoked 13 times, following requests from both the Council and the Assembly themselves.

In 1950, following the USSR's vetoes of S/1653 (6 September 1950), S/1752 (12 September 1950), and S/1894 (30 November 1950), six UNSC members urged the UNGA to investigate the situation in Korea (A/1618, 4 December 1950). The Council removed a procedural issue from its agenda, allowing the Assembly to discuss it freely under Article 11 of the United Nations Charter. In resolution 498 (V) [1 February 1951], the Assembly cited the UFP, stating that the UNSC had failed to fulfil its primary responsibility of maintaining international peace and security due to a lack of unanimity among its permanent members; hence, it had to intervene.

Resolution 377 was used to call an emergency session of the Assembly in 1951 due to a lack of unanimity among UNSC members. It prompted the passage of UN Resolution 498 (V), which stated that China had militarily intervened in the Korean War (Motamedi, 2023). It was the first time the UN viewed a nation as an aggressor during a conflict, and also the only time it allowed the use of force under the UFP Resolution. Resolution 498 did not expressly refer to the UFP resolution, but it did quote its text, "*noting that the Security Council, because of lack of unanimity of the permanent members, has failed to exercise its primary responsibility for the maintenance of international peace and security with regard to Chinese communist intervention in Korea*." It "*called on all States and authorities to continue to lend every assistance to the United Nations' action in Korea*," implying military assistance (Tomuschat, 2008).

Similarly, the Security Council has also requested the General Assembly to intervene in Resolution 119 (1956) since France and the United Kingdom voted against (in S/3710 and S/3713/Rev.1) in the Suez Canal Crisis. The Assembly convened an emergency special session and passed seven resolutions, including Resolution 1000 (ES-I) mandating the UN Emergency Force and calling for the withdrawal of Israeli, British, and French forces from the Egyptian territory.

Following the veto by the USSR (S/3730/Rev.1), the UNGA adopted five resolutions, including Resolution 1004 (ES-II), which mandated a commission of inquiry into foreign intervention in Hungary, condemned the intervention and called for the withdrawal of Soviet forces in Hungary. Later, in 1958, the Third Emergency Special Session on "The Situation in the Middle East" adopted Resolution 1237 (ES-III) since the UNSC was incapacitated due to the veto of the USSR (S/4050/Rev.1, S/4055/ Rev.1). The UNGA called for the early withdrawal of foreign troops from Jordan and Lebanon. Fifthly, in 1960, following the USSR's veto (S/4523), the Fourth Emergency Special Session was convened on "The Situation in the Congo" and adopted Resolution 1474 (ES-IV), confirming the mandate of the UN Operation in the Congo.

Even for Bangladesh, the UNGA previously intervened post USSR's veto (S/10416, S/10423) and opted to discuss the 1971 war under the agenda "UN Assistance to East Pakistan Refugees" (Resolution 303). The Sixth Emergency Special Session took place on "The Situation in Afghanistan" and adopted Resolution ES-6/2, which calls for the immediate, unconditional, and total withdrawal of foreign troops from Afghanistan in 1980, after the veto of the USSR (S/13729). The Ninth Emergency Special Session on "The Situation in the Middle East" adopted Resolution ES-9/1, labelling Israel a non-peace-loving state and urging members to impose various measures on Israel, after the United States vetoed in the UNSC (S/14832).

The Assembly has also requested the implementation of the Resolution, as seen in instances such as the USSR's request (A/6717) after its draft resolution failed to receive nine votes at the UNSC in 1967. The Fifth Emergency Special Session was called on "The Situation in the Middle East," passed six resolutions, including Resolutions 2253 and 2254 (ES-V), urging Israel to end unilateral measures in Jerusalem. After the US's veto (S/13911) in 1980, Senegal requested (A/ES-7/1) to the UNGA for the Seventh Emergency Special Session on "The Question of Palestine." It adopted eight resolutions (ES-7/2–9), asking for Israel's unconditional and comprehensive withdrawal from lands occupied since 1967.

After vetoes from France, the United Kingdom and the United States respectively (S/14459, S/14460/Rev.1, S/14461, S/14462), Zimbabwe requested (A/ES-8/1) the Eighth Emergency Special Session on "The Question of Namibia" and the UNGA adopted Resolution ES-8/2, denouncing South Africa's occupation and urging assistance for the liberation movement. UNGA condemned South Africa's "unprovoked massive armed aggression" against Angola and urged member states to provide "military assistance" to protect the sovereignty of frontline states from further aggression.

The Tenth Emergency Special Session in 1997, as requested by Qatar (A/ES/10/1) after the veto of the United States (S/1997/199, S/1997/241) on "The Question of Palestine." It adopted Resolution ES-10/14, seeking an advisory opinion from the International Court of Justice (ICJ). In March 2022, the Assembly used the "Uniting for Peace" resolution of 1950 to adopt a resolution on aggression against Ukraine (Res. ES11/1). This contribution focuses on the GA's competence to establish a criminal tribunal and refer cases to the International Criminal Court (ICC) within the framework of the UFP resolution.

Role of the United Nations So Far

In April 2017, the Human Rights Council (UNHRC) adopted Resolution 34/22, which established an impartial international fact-finding mission on Myanmar (Martin, 2019). The mission's report, published in September 2018, contains graphic accounts of murder, rape, and assault against the Rohingya (Human Rights Council, 2018).

UNHRC has adopted several other resolutions including the recent five adopted on 14th July 2023: resolution (A/HRC/53/L.24/Rev.1) on the "Implementation of Human Rights Council Resolution A/HRC/RES31/36"; resolution (A/HRC/53/L.30/Rev.1) on the "Situation of human rights of Rohingya Muslims and other minorities in Myanmar"; resolution (A/HRC/53/L.5/Rev.1) on "Accelerating efforts to eliminate all forms of violence against women and girls: preventing and responding to all forms of violence against women and girls in criminal justice detention"; resolution (A/HRC/53/L.26) on the contribution of development to the enjoyment of all human rights; and resolution (A/HRC/53/L.27/Rev.1) on "New and emerging digital technologies and human rights."

The UNGA has also adopted several resolutions; for example, on December 24, 2017 (A/RES/72/248), it adopted a resolution titled "Situation of human rights of Rohingya Muslims and other minorities in Myanmar," urging the Myanmar government to end military attacks against the Rohingyas and calling for the appointment of a UN special envoy despite opposition from China and Russia, by a vote of 122 to 10 with 24 abstentions.

The resolution again with an overwhelming majority of votes was adopted as Res 73/264 on 22 December 2018; Res 74/246 on 27 December 2019; Res 75/238 on 31 December 2020; Res 76/180 on 16 December 2021; Res

77/227 on 15 December 2022; and Res A/C.3/78/L.40/Rev.1 by the Third Committee on 15 November 2023. Resolution titled, "The situation in Myanmar" (A/RES/75/287) on 18 June 2021 and several others. However, such unanimity did not yield results, as resolutions of the UNGA have no binding effect in the operational realm of international peace and security (Öberg, 2005).

The UNSC, the primary organ of the UN responsible for maintaining international peace and security as per Article 24 of the UN Charter, is unable to act on genocide due to several vetoes by China and Russia over the years on several endeavours of the organ. The cat-and-mouse trail began on 12 January 2007, long before the 2017 crackdown, when China and Russia vetoed a draft resolution in the UNSC, marking the first time multiple vetoes had been used in the UNSC since 1989. The resolution called on Myanmar to "release all political prisoners, begin widespread dialogue, and end its military attacks and human rights violations against ethnic minorities" ("China and Russia Veto US/UK-backed Security Council Draft Resolution on Myanmar," 2007).

Starting with vetoes against resolutions to even prevent the Council from issuing statements expressing worry about the violence and dire humanitarian situation in Myanmar, China and Russia have blocked it all (Lederer, 2022) – preventing any little effort to restore peace in Myanmar. Amidst such curtailment, the only effort the UNSC could undertake was to send its delegation to Myanmar in 2018 and hold meetings with State Counsellor Aung San Suu Kyi and Min Aung Hlaing, Commander-in-Chief of the Armed Forces ("Myanmar: Security Council Meets Leaders Face-to-face," 2018).

Since the enforcement of the ICJ's decisions is primarily under the mandate of the Council (as per Article 94 of the UN Charter), similar efforts were evident when the UNSC convened a meeting to devise a strategy for ensuring compliance with the ICJ's provisional measures regarding the Rohingya refugees. The summit, however, was blocked by China and Russia, and therefore, no definitive plan of action could be accomplished.

Another example of China and Russia's constant vetoing is right after the military coup on 1 February 2021; China, backed by Russia, blocked a statement condemning the coup from the UNSC (BBC News, 2021) and again in 2022, when the UNSC wanted to express its concern about the grave humanitarian violations in Myanmar (Lederer, 2022) and so on.

After years, for the very first time, the Council adopted Resolution 2669 (2022) on the situation in Myanmar, marking the first resolution on Myanmar in 74 years. It was adopted with a vote of 12 in favour, none against, and 3 abstentions from China, India, and the Russian Federation on 21 December 2022. Although a minimal but noteworthy initiative by the UNSC, the resolution expectedly came with its shortcomings. It failed to include measures like targeted sanctions against government officials responsible for the genocide, comprehensive arms embargos and a referral of the situation to the ICC (Amnesty International, 2022). It, however, did include the demand for an immediate cessation of all forms of violence throughout Myanmar and advocated caution and de-escalation of tensions, while appreciating the key role of the Association of Southeast Asian Nations (ASEAN), particularly its five-point agreement on Myanmar. The Council also urged the military to immediately release all arbitrarily detained prisoners, including President Win Myint and Ms Suu Kyi, and reiterated its call to uphold democratic institutions and processes, as well as to pursue constructive dialogue and reconciliation in accordance with the will and interests of Myanmar's people in the Report of the Secretary-General (A/78/278). The Council also requested that the Secretary-General, in collaboration with the ASEAN Special Envoy, provide an oral report to the Council by March 15, 2023.

It cannot be, however, that the permanent members (P-5) are not always willing to allow humanitarian intervention in areas that may affect their national interests, especially if the state in question is a close partner of any of them. Although they had not vetoed the recent aforementioned resolution of the UNSC, it was evident that they would continue to block measures that curtail their political interests. Between 1946 and the end of 2018, 202 resolutions on several substantive concerns that required immediate humanitarian attention were vetoed, sometimes by multiple P-5 members (Ahmed and Ahmed,2018). Due to their close economic and geopolitical ties with Myanmar's administration, powerful governments such as China and Russia have helped consolidate the country's position (Islam, 2020, p. 79). Hence, a possible alternative remains the enforcement of the UFP Resolution, which directs the Council and other relevant bodies to take measures within their mandate, as per the Assembly's instructions.

How Could the Uniting for Peace Resolution Have Helped in Mitigating the Rohingya Crisis?

The UFP Resolution clearly states that the GA *shall* consider the matter when the Council fails. It is impractical to keep it aside to avoid simultaneous actions by the organ and the Council. Hence, the UFP is or could have been worth enforcing in the Rohingya crisis, where the Security Council is not working simultaneously in a manner, but is relatively stagnant due to constant vetoing. And even if they were discussing the same agenda (as opposed to Article 12(1) of the UN Charter), the ICJ has formally acknowledged in the *Wall* case that the prohibition of simultaneous actions of the UNGA and the UNSC has been superseded by practice (International Court of Justice, 2004). Moreover, such practices are also standard between the two bodies as Constantin A. Stavropoulos, legal counsel of the United Nations, stated that "the Assembly had interpreted the words 'is exercising' as meaning 'is exercising at this *moment*'; consequently, it had made recommendations on other matters which the Security Council was also considering" (A/C.3/SR.1637). To work on the same agenda, the UNGA would only have to wait a *moment*, which it clearly has since the crackdown or even the coup.

The voting procedure of the Security Council is governed by Article 27 of the UN Charter and Rule 40 of the Provisional Rules of Procedure. UNGA Resolution 267(III) of 14 April 1949 recommended to the Council to consider several types of issues, including the ones listed following as "procedural":

- submission to the General Assembly of any questions relating to the maintenance of international peace and security;
- request to the General Assembly that it make a recommendation on a dispute or situation the Council is seized of;

The "submission to the General Assembly of any questions relating to the maintenance of international peace and security" is subject to a procedural vote by the UNSC. The veto issue from the ends of China and Russia can be resolved by moving the responsibility from the UNSC to the UNGA as a procedural matter rather than through a resolution. However, this in a manner demonstrates the UNSC's inability to reach a compromise (very truly so, in this crisis). The Assembly lacks the authority to enforce decisions in the same manner as the UNSC, i.e., by dispatching military forces. While China and Russia are likely to oppose it, this procedural motion could still achieve a majority vote in the Council. Most UNSC members view it as a last resort and have previously shown willingness to act. There is a need for members to address the Council's shortcomings in preventing severe crimes like genocide.

The UFP Resolution permits the Assembly to hold special meetings outside its usual schedule, following the same rules as annual sessions. The UNGA can convene an emergency session at the request of the Security Council or a majority of its members, recommending collective measures, including the use of armed force if necessary. Additionally, Resolution 377 A (V) established the Peace Observation Commission, which lasted until 1960, and the Collective Measures Committee, which existed for just two years. Neither of these bodies has played a significant role (Tomuschat, 2008).

As for the recommendations of collective measures (the use of force), they are hindered by a shortcoming in their legal applicability. If the enforcement action was required by a separate binding legal norm such as the responsibility to protect (R2P) or the commitment to respond to genocide, the Assembly, rather than the Council, may recommend military action with more limited purposes and projections (Richardson, 2014). The Assembly would be exercising collective authority under international law by making such a recommendation: member states would not be required to act based on its recommendations, but they would most likely be obligated to do so under R2P or other international law (Richardson, 2014, p. 140). If they chose to act, they would do so in accordance with the Assembly's permissive collective authority rather than independently. Klein & Schmahl (2010) define "enforcement action" by its binding nature and conclude that the UNGA is not prevented from recommending coercive measures.

Although it is believed, particularly seen in the *Certain Expenses* case, that the enforcement mechanism is solely confined to the UNSC (International Court of Justice, 1962), and the GA would rather make recommendations only, such practice has been falsified by the GA itself. When it took on versatile roles at different times, it instead established institutional measures. For example, in 2006, Resolution 60/251 created the UNHRC; hence, technically, the General Assembly performed as the driving proponent of the fact-finding mission in Myanmar in 2017. UNHRC's resolution 39/2 (A/HRC/RES/39/2) was endorsed in G.A. Res. 73/264, where it created a collaborative investigative commission with the Council's mission of investigating the situation in Myanmar in 2018 as well. It also formally took over the responsibility for the Council's accountability-related commissions of inquiry and investigative missions ("UN Commissions of Inquiry and Fact-finding Missions," 2014). Moreover, the subject matter of the term "genocide" gained wider acceptance due to the UNGA, which approved the Convention on the Prevention and Punishment of the Crime of Genocide (The Convention on the Prevention and Punishment of the Crime of Genocide, 1948)and proposed it for signature, ratification, or accession by states in UNGA Resolution 260 A (III) in 1950.

Keeping such precedents in mind, the Assembly could rely on the UFP resolution to "set up an ad hoc International Tribunal," which would operate on the basis of delegated universal jurisdiction (Human Rights Council, 2014) as it did with the Special Court for Sierra Leone, and the establishment of the Group of Experts, resulting in the formation of the Extraordinary Chambers in the Courts of Cambodia, a well-recognised and accepted criminal tribunal to prosecute the international crimes committed during the Khmer Rouge era. UNGA also created a quasi-prosecutorial investigative body to facilitate prosecution, the International, Impartial and Independent Mechanism for Syria (G.A. Res. 71/248). The Assembly has been seen taking such proactive stances on creating institutional frameworks when in need to restore humanitarian law, but refrained from maximising such authority extensively to date (considering that the quantity of available examples remains comparatively limited). The Assembly has not simply viewed its powers as recommendatory; instead, it has interpreted them to include the establishment of various bodies necessary for maintaining peace and security, especially when the Security Council is not fulfilling this role (Barber,

2019). There is no reason the General Assembly could not take a further step and establish an ad hoc criminal tribunal.

In 2014, the Commission of Inquiry on Human Rights in the Democratic People's Republic of Korea suggested (U.N. Doc. A/HRC/25/CRP.1) that the UNGA could rely on the UFP resolution to "set up an ad hoc International Tribunal for the Democratic People's Republic of Korea." The Commission stated that in the event that the Security Council fails to refer the situation to the ICC or set up an ad hoc tribunal, the Assembly could establish a tribunal [to fill in the vacuum to ensure justice]. In this regard, the UNGA could rely on its residual powers, recognised inter alia in the "Uniting for Peace" resolution and the combined sovereign powers of all individual Member States, to try perpetrators of crimes against humanity on the basis of the principle of universal jurisdiction (Stahn, 2023).

During previous emergency special sessions, the Assembly has proposed various measures for Myanmar, including ceasefires, sanctions, and peacekeeper deployments (Smith, 2021). Another potential action is establishing a criminal tribunal to prosecute crimes committed by Myanmar. In the Prosecutor v. Tadić decision, it was ruled that the UNGA does not "have to be a judicial organ possessed of judicial functions and powers in order to be able to establish" a tribunal. The Assembly could also pass a resolution to condemn the Council's inaction and request a report on its response to the coup. While not legally binding, resolutions would reflect the collective will of UN Member States and compel the UNSC to consider its responsibilities (Nartey, 2022).

Countries such as the United States, the United Kingdom, Canada, and several others have implemented targeted sanctions against Myanmar and its officials; however, no sanctions have been imposed by the UN. The UNGA could impose targeted sanctions and recommend that the Council do so on senior military officials of the Myanmar government (Islam, 2017), in compliance with its Draft Declaration on Unilateral Measures and the Rule of Law, and influence other states to do the same. It is worth noting that since the coup, Russia and China have been the primary suppliers of modern weapons systems to the Myanmar military, accounting for more than $400 million and $260 million, respectively (Human Rights Council, 2023). To limit such an exponential spurt of commerce, trade embargos are an option. GA has made such recommendations of embargos in the past in Resolution 31/6 of 1976 during the apartheid in South Africa. The embargo would apply to all types of weapons and halt imports of military supplies made in or with Myanmar, terminating existing military agreements, and preventing new arrangements. This would not be legally binding, but would create intense political pressure after the UNGA directives.

The Assembly could also suggest the deployment of peacekeeping forces on the Bangladesh-Myanmar border, which would meet a long-standing request from the Rohingya, who are particularly vulnerable in the current scenario. The UFP strategy can be used once again to send the force to help the Rohingya return to their native countries (Islam & Ferdous, 2021). The UNGA could also implement various measures to exert political pressure on Myanmar's military, such as calling for the restoration of a democratically elected government by rescinding the state of emergency. In a press conference in 2021, the Secretary-General of the UN emphasised "a return to democracy, respect for the results of the November parliamentary elections, and release of all people detained by the military"; "I believe we need to have all possible areas of pressure to make it happen," said Antonio Guterres (*AP News*, 2021). The GA could deny the credentials of the representative of the Member State, similar to those mentioned in Res. 31/6, during the apartheid era in South Africa.

If they continue to ignore the pressure, a drastic but viable option could be to remove Myanmar from the UN. Article 6 of the Charter clearly states, "a Member of the United Nations which has persistently violated the Principles contained in the present Charter may be expelled from the Organisation by the General Assembly upon the recommendation of the Security Council." However, superpowers like Russia and China would likely prevent or attempt to prevent such an occurrence. Instead, or subsequently, a resolution seeking the expulsion or suspension of Myanmar's membership would have to be referred to the UNGA from the UNSC, as per Article 12(1) of the UN Charter. The next option would be to explore Article 18(2) of the Charter, which states that the Assembly shall decide important questions, such as the expulsion of Members, by a two-thirds majority of the members present and voting. Such options were even explored while trying to remove the Russian Federation from the UN to impose accountability on a permanent Member going rogue towards Ukraine in 2022.

UNGA Resolution 396(V) titled "Recognition by the United Nations of the Representation of a Member State," adopted on 14 December 1950, provides in its paragraph 1 that "whenever more than one authority claims to be the government entitled to represent a Member State in the United Nations, the question should be considered in the light of the Purposes and Principles of the Charter and the circumstances of each case." The constant violations of fundamental principles and peremptory norms of international human rights law pose questions to the credibility of the military junta of Myanmar. On such a basis, several inventive solutions were proposed for Myanmar:

> [V]arious steps unpleasant to a member state may be taken to make clear to it that it is no longer welcome and should withdraw; or an amendment to the constitution of the organization may be adopted to enable the organization to expel a member, and the amendment itself may constitute an especially strong hint that the member should grace- fully leave the

> organization now to avoid ignominy later... The blow may be softened by adopting the pretense that the state involved is not deprived of membership, but that only its government is being excluded, temporarily and conditionally. In such a case, should the government mend its way, or should a new government, more willing to cooperate, replace the old reprobates, the state would again be permitted to take its rightful place without the painful process of readmission. Finally, there is expulsion [...], an act by which an organization unequivocally severs all ties with a member which has outraged the community by a serious violation of the constitution of the organization.
>
> *(Sohn, 1964, p. 1421)*

Such steps can be taken by any international organ, including the Assembly, holding such institutional authority, which would not be required to wait for any supposed amendment to the Charter, but can use the voting power in its called-upon session after invoking the UFP Resolution to oust a member or use other forms of inducements.

Conclusion

There remains a lack of explicit text that legitimises UN Resolution 377 A (V). When discussing the powers of the Assembly, neither UN Resolutions nor the ICJ has referred to using the "Uniting for Peace" Resolution, even though it has been invoked several times in the past. The Resolution affirms that the GA can recommend collective action, e.g. use of force. It has been implemented, for instance, in Resolution 498 (V) of 1 February 1951 to provide military assistance to Korea, the only time. But not once did the organ explicitly mention Resolution 377 A (V).

In every other case, it has been a standard element of UNGA resolutions on armed conflicts to urge the parties to cease hostilities and remove their troops to their own borders. However, such requests cannot be assumed to be a particular validation of the "Uniting for Peace" Resolution. The lack of reference to the Resolution has, in a way, curtailed its wide recognition, legitimisation and overall usage.

The Assembly cannot take action if permanent members choose to remain inactive in a conflict. Any UNGA resolution aimed at peace and security requires a two-thirds majority of Member States, which complicates effectiveness, especially when other Member States may intervene after a veto. This reluctance often stems from fears of escalating tensions with the vetoing nation, and differing priorities make achieving consensus difficult.

However, the preamble of the UFP Resolution states "failure of the Security Council to discharge its responsibilities on behalf of all the Member States [does not] deprive the General Assembly of its rights or relieve it of its responsibilities under the Charter in regard to the maintenance of international peace and security." Despite several risk factors and shortcomings, the Uniting for Peace Resolutions allow a ray of hope in the humanitarian turmoil of the Rohingya Crisis, which has not only affected Myanmar and Bangladesh but the international community as a whole, and looks up to the efficacy of the United Nations. The UN cannot remain dormant due to the political manoeuvring of a few of its Members at such significant times of humanitarian crisis.

References

AP News. 2021. "UN Chief: UN Will Seek to Unite World, Reverse Myanmar Coup | AP News," April 20, 2021. https://apnews.com/article/aung-san-suu-kyi-global-trade-myanmar-elections-antonio-guterres-e15c06b4fce06621f465146 6cad6e458.

Barber, R. (2019). Accountability for Crimes against the Rohingya. *Journal of International Criminal Justice* 17(3): 557–84. https://doi.org/10.1093/jicj/mqz031.

BBC News. 2021. "Myanmar Coup: China Blocks UN Condemnation as Protest Grows." *BBC News*, February 3, 2021. https://www.bbc.com/news/world-asia-55913947.

"China and Russia Veto US/UK-backed Security Council Draft Resolution on Myanmar." 2007. UN News. January 12. https://news.un.org/en/story/2007/01/205732.

Forced Migration of Rohingya: The Untold Experience. 2018. 1st ed. Ontario International Development Agency (OIDA). https://www.researchgate.net/publication/326912213_Forced_Migration_of_Rohingya_The_Untold_Experience.

"General Assembly, 23rd Session, Official Records, 3rd Committee, 1637th Meeting, Held on Thursday, 12 December 1968, New York." 1970. United Nations Digital Library System. https://digitallibrary.un.org/record/806622?ln=en.

Human Rights Council. 2014. "Report of the Detailed Findings of the Commission of Inquiry on Human Rights in the Democratic People's Republic of Korea." https://www.ohchr.org/en/hr-bodies/hrc/co-idprk/commission-inquiryon-h-rin-dprk

Human Rights Council. 2018. "Report of the Detailed Findings of the Independent International Fact-Finding Mission on Myanmar." https://www.ohchr.org/sites/default/files/Documents/HRBodies/HRCouncil/FFM-Myanmar/A_HRC_39_CRP.2.pdf.

Human Rights Council. 2023. "The Billion Dollar Death Trade: The International Arms Networks That Enable Human Rights Violations in Myanmar Conference Room Paper of the Special Rapporteur on the Situation of Human Rights in Myanmar." https://www.ohchr.org/sites/default/files/documents/countries/myanmar/crp-sr-myanmar-2023-05-17.pdf.

International Court of Justice. 1962. *Certain Expenses of the United Nations (Article 17, paragraph 2, of the Charter)*. Advisory Opinion. https://www.icj-cij.org/public/files/case-related/49/5259.pdf.

International Court of Justice. 2004. *Legal Consequences of the Construction of a Wall in the Occupied Palestinian Territory*. Report. https://www.icj-cij.org/files/case-related/131/131-20040709- ADV-01-00-EN.pdf.

International Court of Justice. 2019. *Application Instituting Proceedings and Request for Provisional Measures (The Gambia v. Myanmar)*. Application. https://www.icjcij.org/files/case-related/178/178-20191111-APP-01-00-EN.pdf.

Islam, Rizwanul. 2017. "Rohingya Crisis: Sanctions Must Target Myanmar Leadership." *NST Online*, October 3. https://www.nst.com.my/opinion/columnists/2017/10/286818/rohingya-crisis-sanctions-must-target-myanmar-leadership.

Islam, Rizwanul. 2020. "The Gambia V. Myanmar at the I.C.J.: Good Samaritans Testing State Responsibility for Atrocities on the Rohingya." *California Western International Law Journal* 51 (1): 77–131. https://scholarlycommons.law.cwsl.edu/cwilj/vol51/iss1/4/.

Islam, Moinul, and Jannatul Ferdous. 2021. "Rohingya Refugee Crisis: Toward a Sustainable Solution." *Journal of Governance, Security & Development* 1 (2): 1–22. https://doi.org/10.52823/ddhj7411.

Klein, E., and S. Schmahl. 2010. Article 10. In *The Charter of the United Nations: A Commentary, Volume I: Vol. I* (3rd ed., pp. 462–490). Oxford Law Pro. https://doi.org/10.1093/law/9780199639762.003.0022.

Martin, Viren Mascarenhas Brian Jacobi, Claire O'Connell, and Isabel San. 2019. "The Rohingyas' Plight: What Options Under International Law?" *The Diplomat*, January 16, 2019. https://thediplomat.com/2019/01/the-plight-of-the-rohingya-what-options-under-international-law/.

Motamedi, Maziar. 2023. "What's UN Resolution 377A, Can It Help in Efforts to Stop Israel-Gaza War?" *Al Jazeera*, December 11. https://www.aljazeera.com/news/2023/12/11/whats-un-resolution-377a-can-it-help-in-efforts-to-stop-israel-gaza-war.

"Myanmar: Security Council Meets Leaders Face-to-face." 2018. *UN News*. May 3. https://news.un.org/en/story/2018/04/1008582.

Nartey, Emmanuel K. 2022. "The Rohingya Crisis: A Critical Analysis of the United Nations Security Council and International Human Rights Law." *Athens Journal of Law* 8 (4): 449–74. https://doi.org/10.30958/ajl.8-4-6.

Öberg, Marko Divac. 2005. "The Legal Effects of Resolutions of the UN Security Council and General Assembly in the Jurisprudence of the ICJ." *European Journal of International Law* 16 (5): 879–906. https://doi.org/10.1093/ejil/chi151.

Richardson, Henry S. 2014. "Comment on Larry Johnson, 'Uniting for Peace.'" *AJIL Unbound* 108 (January): 135–40. https://doi.org/10.1017/s2398772300002026.

Secretary-General, United Nations. 1950. "Letter Dated 8 March 1950 From the Secretary-General to the President of the Security Council Transmitting a Memorandum on the Legal Aspects of the Problem of Representation in the United Nations." United Nations Digital Library System, March 9. https://digitallibrary.un.org/record/475227?ln=en.

"Situation of Human Rights of Rohingya Muslims and Other Minorities in Myanmar - Report of the Secretary-General (a/78/278) [EN/AR/RU/ZH] - Myanmar." 2023. ReliefWeb. August 31. https://reliefweb.int/report/myanmar/situation-human-rights-rohingya-muslims-and-other-minorities-myanmar-report-secretary-general-a78278-enarruzh.

Smith, Matthew. 2021. "How to Dodge the Chinese Veto on Myanmar." *Washington Post*, February 11. https://www.washingtonpost.com/opinions/2021/02/11/how-dodge-chinese-veto-myanmar/.

Sohn, Louis B. 1964. "Expulsion or Forced Withdrawal From an International Organization." *Harvard Law Review* 77 (8): 1381. https://doi.org/10.2307/1339157.

Stahn, Carsten. 2023. "From 'United for Peace' to 'United for Justice?': Reflections on the Power of the United Nations General Assembly to Create Criminal

Tribunals or Make Referrals to the ICC." *Case Western Reserve University School of Law Scholarly Commons* 55 (1). https://scholarlycommons.law.case.edu/jil/vol55/iss1/11.

The Charter of the United Nations 1945.

The Convention on the Prevention and Punishment of the Crime of Genocide 1948.

Tomuschat, Christian. 2008. "Uniting for Peace: General Assembly Resolution 377 (V)." Audiovisual Library of International Law. October 2008. https://legal.un.org/avl/ha/ufp/ufp.html.

"UN Commissions of Inquiry and Fact-finding Missions." 2014. House of Lords Library. June 14, 2014. https://lordslibrary.parliament.uk/un-commissions-of-inquiry-and-fact-finding-missions/.

United Nations General Assembly, 2017. "Situation of Human Rights in Myanmar." https://documents.un.org/doc/undoc/gen/n17/468/68/pdf/n1746868.pdf?token=1CCAusccelhPZcsFWo&fe=true.

United Nations. 1950. "'Uniting for Peace' UNGA Res 377 [V]." *United Nations.* https://www.un.org/en/sc/repertoire/otherdocs/GAres377A(v).pdf.

"Uniting for Peace Resolution (1950)." 2017. In *Oxford Public International Law.* https://opil.ouplaw.com/display/10.1093/law:epil/9780199231690/law-9780199231690-e568.

11

ROHINGYA REPATRIATION BEYOND THE COURTROOM

Geopolitics and the Limits of International Adjudication

Emraan Azad

Introduction

This chapter sets out its central argument at the outset: the voluntary, safe, and dignified return of the Rohingyas is primarily determined by the geopolitical interests of rival superpowers, overriding the impact of international legal fora such as the ICC and the ICJ. Thus, while international legal mechanisms are often cited as crucial for ensuring repatriation, their actual utility is minimal when compared to the decisive sway of political stakeholders. Notably, Rohingya repatriation is not presently an issue before the ICC but has been considered only in a limited way at the ICJ. Judicial developments reveal that international courts treat Rohingya repatriation as a peripheral matter, often yielding – knowingly or otherwise – to political actors who ultimately steer outcomes.

Still, many believe that the outcomes of international adjudication affect repatriation.[1] How and when this does so, however, remains uncertain, primarily due to various political equations. For the sake of argument, even if we concede that the ICJ could order repatriation and that Myanmar chose to comply, there are still challenges. Bangladesh, as the refugee host country, might disagree with Myanmar's plan, and the reverse could also occur. Theoretically speaking, moreover, could an order from the ICJ compel Bangladesh to agree to repatriation when it is not a party to the proceedings, not even as an intervener? To make it more complex, Article 94 of the UN Charter states: "(1) Each Member of the United Nations undertakes to comply with the decision of the International Court of Justice in any case to which it is a *party*" (emphasis added).

The chapter argues that the prospect of Rohingya repatriation does not rely on the outcome of ICJ or ICC cases. Legal initiatives adopted internationally

DOI: 10.4324/9781003771890-11

after the 2017 influx of the Rohingyas have made issues much more difficult, especially after Myanmar's 2021 military coup. This event triggered debates about repatriation at the national, regional, and global levels. A troubling political situation has also gripped Bangladesh since an authoritarian regime fell on August 5, 2024, after a mass uprising (Curtis 2025). Muhammad Yunus, appointed as Chief Advisor to Bangladesh's Interim Government after the regime collapsed, proposed seven actions. One of them includes "strengthening international justice mechanisms to pursue accountability for atrocities against the Rohingyas" (The Daily Star 2025). TThe Interim Government has not become a formal party in international cases. Even with recent talks among officials from Bangladesh, Myanmar, and "select" Rohingyas, ongoing international legal efforts likely help Myanmar delay the repatriation process. Drawing from real cases of atrocity crimes and how international courts handle them, the chapter argues that the fate of Rohingya repatriation is deeply tied to global politics – including the USA, China, India, and others.

This chapter has seven sections. After this introduction, the second section, "Unpacking the 'Genocide as Social Practice,'" explains Argentinean genocide scholar Daniel Feierstein's theory of "Genocide as Social Practice" and contextualizes it with what the Rohingyas have experienced over the years of a systematic process of "social reorganization" led by the Burmese state and non-state actors. Sections "Lessons from the Bosnian Refugee Crisis," "The Rohingya Issue at ICC," and "The Rohingya Issue at ICJ" show that, as with the Bosnian genocide cases in the 1990s, international courts have failed to ensure refugee return. The Rohingya case at ICC and ICJ will most likely yield the same result. Section "The Limits of International Law Problematizing the Crisis" illustrates how the inherent limits of international law make things worse, especially for politically fragile states like Myanmar and Bangladesh, which are caught in geopolitical rivalries among powerful nations and their allies. The chapter ends in the "Conclusion" by stating that implementation or non-implementation of international judicial decisions is not the main issue here. Instead, the problem lies in the international law edifice itself, which allows powerful states to choose compliance, shape limits, and decide which rules to follow or break. As a result, the outcomes of international adjudicatory mechanisms will have little effect on Rohingya repatriation unless the limits of international law are revamped with vigor and vitality, both in practice and in rhetoric. Any pressure created by these international justice institutions will be short-lived and insignificant, due to the shifting nature and considerable force of global politics.

Unpacking the "Genocide as Social Practice"

Daniel Feierstein, in *Genocide as Social Practice: Reorganizing Society under the Nazis and Argentina's Military Juntas*, presents genocide as a series of social changes. These changes involve predictable shifts in how people relate to one another and in what they value, though there are local differences (Feierstein 2014, 39). Simply put, genocide involves harmful social acts developed within a larger social process. Feierstein sees this "genocidal social practice" as a tool of power. It manages people as a group by aiming: (a) to destroy social relationships based on autonomy and cooperation by annihilating a significant part of the population (significant in terms of either numbers or practices), and (b) to use the terror of annihilation to create new models of identity and social relationships among the survivors (ibid, 14).

This idea of genocide as a technology of power takes its inspiration from the original concept of genocide offered by Raphael Lemkin,[2] who, by "genocide," would mean,

> one, the destruction of the national pattern of the oppressed group; the other, the imposition of the national pattern of the oppressor. This imposition, in turn, may be made upon the oppressed population [...] allowed to remain or upon the territory alone, after removal of the population and the colonization by the oppressor's own nationals.
>
> *(Lemkin 1944, 79)*

He further says "[the act of genocide] is directed against the national group as an entity, and the actions involved are directed against individuals, not in their individual capacity, but as members of the national group..." (ibid). In Lemkin's framing of genocide, terror and killing are not the ultimate goals of this technology of power. Instead, they are tools for something else. What is this something else? For Feierstein, it is a transformation or reorganization of social identity that imposes greater oppression on the oppressed. Destroying identity is meant to erase the identity of the oppressed and replace it with that of the oppressor. Feierstein explains that this process of using terror and killing to reshape identity involves three connected techniques (Feierstein 2023):

(a) Obscuring the image of victimhood: When the oppressor decides "who becomes a victim and when," it creates uncertainty, leaving people unsure if they will be persecuted. This uncertainty is the basis for the next two techniques.

(b) Betrayal to escape persecution: Group members, unsure if they are targeted, may try to survive by betraying others and showing the oppressor they are not part of the persecuted group. This behavior links directly to the third technique – generalization of distrust.

(c) Normalization of distrust: Genocide, as the technology of power, attempts to systematically normalize and inculcate a sense of distrust to break any bond, link, or connection among different people in the society. If the oppressor is able to create an atmosphere of distrust, it becomes difficult for the oppressed to form a counterhegemonic group. In such widespread social distrust, individuals lose faith in one another, and thus the three techniques, combined, extend beyond the acts of ordinary betrayal or persecution to consolidate power and sever the very fabric of society, redefining social structures to serve only the interests of those in control.

Feierstein further elaborates on these techniques by examining two historical cases: the reorganization of identities in Germany and across Nazi-occupied Europe from 1933 to 1945, and in Argentina during military rule from 1975 to 1983 (Feierstein 2014, 71–130 & 131–204). Now, let us consider how these techniques could apply to the Rohingyas.

To start with, the ambiguity in the definition of victims, we will find that different sections of people were persecuted throughout the Rohingya genocide. In popular literature, persecution is shown to have taken place against the Muslim Rohingyas. However, it would be useful to understand genocide as the technology of power if we could widen our view to include all the groups that were persecuted.

Persecution took place against religious priests/leaders and educators, political dissidents, union workers, students, Hindus, the elderly, and others who were autonomous or trying to create autonomy in their respective lives from the mainstream Buddhist community (Hoque et al. 2018, 35–44). Then, the persecuted included cultural groups. Of course, musicians, artists, and indigenous peoples were among them. There was also systematic violence against women based on sexual identity. In this process of annihilation, the oppressed were not believed to be fully human beings in the development of the Burmese society. The idea was that Burmese identity encompassed the territories the Buddhist Burmese could rule, so any people not considered part of that identity by the nationalist Burmese should be excluded from society. The authorities in power targeted the common element that persisted among these groups, namely the endeavor to construct autonomy or to develop an individual life. Military juntas were not alone in this project; surprisingly, Buddhist monks and the general public also participated in spreading the chauvinistic transformation of social identities.

This leads us to explore the second step of persecution, which involved a unification in the understanding of group identity. Anthropologically, the Rohingyas possess more than one identity: religious, ethnic, and cultural, and share a lot with the Bengalis from the southern part of Bengal (now belonging to Bangladesh) (Uddin 2020, 27–57). To many Burmese people, the Rohingyas are "illegal migrants" from Bengal and thus enemies to society (Zarni and Cowley 2014, 685). The perpetrators contemplated the "Rohingya-ness" as a singular thing, even though a Rohingya identity could be a fusion of religious and ethnic attributes. The construction of a singular Rohingya identity is problematic and could mean very different things. For example, the Rohingya-ness does not count the persons who have Rohingya origin only; it may even include someone who sympathizes with the Rohingya identity (Al Jazeera 2021). To the authorities, someone being a part of Rohingya-ness was a disruption to the Burmese identity. In this sense, anyone in Myanmar could be a part of Rohingya-ness, and thus, it is highly ambiguous and could possibly be arbitrarily applied.

In this backdrop, the Tatmadaw and radical Buddhists employed a cruel strategy, i.e., mongering terror within individuals to instigate various forms of betrayal. Terror aided the artificial cultivation of betrayal, which is generally not typical behavior. In perilous times, however, the instinct to survive made betrayal a potential norm for many Rohingyas in their mutual interactions. To the oppressor in Myanmar, the goal was to identify, through this paradigm of a general state of betrayal, the enemy who could be just trying to disrupt the Burmese social fabric.

Finally, recognizing the significant impact of trust on understanding any counterhegemonic configuration, the perpetrators in Myanmar generalized distrust as a technique to change the social fabric. Trust is a precondition for a reciprocal social bond among the oppressed, and this is why genocide as a technology of power attempted to destroy this element of trust in the Rohingya society.

Genocide as a social practice is quite effective at normalizing distrust and rupturing the core elements of the social fabric, creating a situation in which the fragmentation of the social fabric facilitates the reorganization of society toward greater oppression (Feierstein 2023). Quite understandably, Feierstein's treatment of genocide is different from what we accept as genocide as a "crime of the crimes" under international law, specifically in Article 2 of the UN Genocide Convention, 1948. However, an exploration of genocide as a social practice has been made here with a specific agenda to stress that the Rohingya genocide is a product of the politics of "social reorganization." Thus, despite whatever legal course is being launched globally to ensure justice for the Rohingyas, the pertinent discussion about their repatriation depends on politics rather than law. Of course, the Rohingya genocide has a legal take, but to comprehend the multilayered complexities of this intractable crisis, it is important to acknowledge that international judicial adjudication has very little to offer toward repatriation. It will become more apparent if one pays attention to what happened to the Bosnian refugees after the armed conflict broke out in former Yugoslavia (1992–1995) and the associated legal initiatives that took place at the ICJ and the ICTY.

Lessons from the Bosnian Refugee Crisis

The Bosnian war of 1992–95 was one of the brutal multi-ethnic conflicts in the former Yugoslav republics of Bosnia and Herzegovina, in which an estimated 100,000 people were killed, with 80% of the casualties being

Bosniaks/Bosnian Muslims. The Serbs persecuted Bosniak and Croatian civilians in areas under their control, which eventually resulted in an act of "ethnic cleansing" (Mirković 1996, 191–199). In July 1995, Bosnian Serb forces massacred as many as 8,000 Bosniak men and boys in the town of Srebrenica. This stands as the most enormous bloodbath in Europe since the Holocaust (Traynor 2010).

Amid the ongoing massacre, Bosnia, in 1993, filed a suit against Serbia in respect of a dispute concerning alleged violations of the UN Genocide Convention. The legal battle continued for a total of 14 years when, in 2007, the ICJ finally ruled that several crimes carried out against the Bosnian Muslims were not committed with the specific intent required by the legal definition of genocide, i.e., the intent to destroy the Bosnian Muslim group in whole or in part. However, the Court found that only the atrocities at Srebrenica amounted to a crime of genocide (ICJ 2007, 127). Mennecke and Tams show that even though the ICJ was, for the first time, called upon to decide on the substance of the Genocide Convention, it basically "displayed a cooperative approach to the ICTY as a separate international tribunal and avoided a ruling that could contribute to what is referred to as potential 'fragmentation of international law'" (Mennecke and Tams 2007, 73). To answer why the ICJ furnished substantial weight to the ICTY's jurisprudence and confirm what the ICTY concluded in its findings on Srebrenica and other crimes committed in Bosnia during the war, one could argue that the ICJ did so – perhaps to confer legitimacy to the ICTY, which was a creation of the UN Security Council in an unusual time with a definite mandate. In other words, it would have given an occasion for many to raise eyebrows with a lot of tough political questions regarding the legitimacy of the ICTY itself "if the ICJ had arrived at a different conclusion than the ICTY, for example, by not calling Srebrenica a genocide or by labeling the whole conflict in Bosnia as genocidal" (Mennecke and Tams 2007, 73–74).

Regarding the refugee crisis stemming from the conflict, it was revealed that around 1.4 million Bosnian refugees sought shelter in other former Yugoslav republics, and a total of around 650,000 reached European countries such as Germany, Austria, Croatia, and Sweden (Hageboutros 2016, 50). According to Valenta and Strabac, "[m]ore than two million people have had to leave their original homes, and more than one million people have left Bosnia-Herzegovina altogether as a result of the war in that country" (Valenta and Strabac 2013, 1).

Slightly touching upon the unique geopolitics of the Cold War in its final days in Europe, Hageboutros maintains that "[t]he Yugoslav wars, and especially the Bosnian conflict, forced European states confronted with the largest refugee crisis since World War II, to revise their asylum policies, specify their vague regulations on refugees, and attempt to develop a unified policy in response to the pressing issue" (Hageboutros 2016, 50). Therefore, in

Valenta's words, while Germany led the way by accepting the most refugees of any European country at 320,000, Austria received the second-highest number among non-Yugoslav European countries at 86,500 (Valenta 2011, 4). Again, the same Germany deprived the Bosnian refugees of accessing the labor market and education and instead required their instantaneous return from Germany when the war ended (Koser and Black 1999, 522–543; Valenta 2011, 11).

Although it is contended that a large number of refugees eventually returned to the country in the late 1990s, and that the majority were permanently resettled in several receiving countries in Europe, neither the ICJ nor the ICTY adjudication of the conflict contributed substantively to either return or resettlement. In what follows below, it is explained that international judicial bodies – both ICC and ICJ – have also not been able to bring any solution to the concern of Rohingya repatriation. Coupled with the constraints of international law, the geopolitics surrounding the matter has also made the future direction and sustainability of repatriation hugely difficult and uncertain.

The Rohingya Issue at ICC

On April 9, 2018, the Office of the Prosecutor (OTP) filed an application requesting the ICC to exercise jurisdiction under Article 12(2)(a) of the Rome Statute "over the alleged deportation of members of the Rohingya people from Myanmar to Bangladesh in the context of two waves of violence [of 2016 and 2017] in Rakhine" (ICC 2018, 31).

The Pre-Trial Chamber (PTC I), on September 6, 2018, delivered a positive decision finding that the ICC may exercise jurisdiction. The next day, the government of Myanmar issued a press release and strongly rejected the decision (ICC 2019b, 110). It denied all the allegations of deportation and vehemently stated that it "has not deported any individuals in the areas of concern and, in fact, has worked hard in collaboration with Bangladesh to repatriate those displaced from their homes" (ibid). In its version, Myanmar is both keen and capable enough "to investigate any crimes and violations of human rights in its own territory" (ICC 2019b). The press release referred to the launch of an Independent Commission of Inquiry (ICOE) to probe the allegations of human rights violations and other relevant matters about Rakhine. By dint of this, the government sought to underscore the importance of its initiatives "to bring about peace, stability and development in Rakhine State" vis-à-vis an international justice measure by the ICC (ICC 2019b). Unfortunately, the ICOE has not been proven effective at uncovering the truth and promoting reconciliation in Myanmar.

Next year, on July 4, the OTP made an application under Article 15(3) of the Rome Statute, requesting authorization from the PTC III, to begin "an investigation into the crimes within the Court's jurisdiction in which at least one element occurred on the territory of [Bangladesh], and which occurred within the context of two waves of violence in Rakhine State on the territory of [Myanmar]" (ICC 2019b, 5).

On November 14, 2019, the ICC Judges granted the OTP's request to commence the investigation (ICC 2019a). While issuing the authorization, the Court observed that the Rohingyas were forced to cross *en masse* the borders of Bangladesh owing to the coercive acts of the perpetrators, which took place in Myanmar. In this view, the crime against humanity of deportation was completed "when the victims left the area where they were lawfully present and fled to Bangladesh as a result of coercive acts and a coercive environment" (ICC 2019b, 24). Drawing on this, the Court concluded that the ICC has jurisdiction over Myanmar, although it is not a state party to the ICC, because part of the actus reus of the crime of deportation occurred in Bangladesh, a state party to the ICC. However, Myanmar rejected the ICC's decision, alleging the process was inconsistent with international law (Al Jazeera 2019).

Even though the OTP highlighted the importance of understanding the challenges in executing the repatriation and assessing potential criminal liabilities, the ICC's decision to authorize the investigation did not reflect the repatriation issue. In its submission on July 4, 2019, the OTP referred to the repeated failure of the repatriation process, mentioning that the Court may assess "the nature and cause of the obstacles to the timely return of the Rohingya displaced persons, and any related criminal liability" (ICC 2019b, 38–39 & 73–88).

Myanmar has been and remains unwilling to cooperate with the ICC, whose investigators have not yet secured permission to visit Rakhine. It allows Bangladesh government officials and Rohingyas to visit Rakhine to discuss possible repatriation of the Rohingyas, but not the ICC prosecutors to investigate the allegations of crimes. So far, the ICC Chief Prosecutor has visited Bangladesh twice and met with the Rohingyas. His staff members conducted eleven long-term missions to Bangladesh to interview witnesses and collect evidence. They organized 50+ meetings with civil society organizations to support investigations (ICC 2023). From the developments at the ICC, it is understandable that neither the Court nor the OTP will do anything about the return of the Rohingyas since, first, the issue is beyond their statutory mandates, and secondly, other UN agencies, namely UNHCR and IMO, and concerned states seem to have been working for the repatriation. The slow pace of the ICC proceedings is upsetting, and in recent years, the Court has been under pressure from powerful states, particularly the USA and Russia (ABC News 2025). Now, from the ICC, let us move to the ICJ to see what it has been doing regarding repatriation and whether there is any hope in the end.

The Rohingya Issue at ICJ

On November 11, 2019, The Gambia went to the ICJ instituting proceedings against Myanmar concerning alleged violations of the 1948 Genocide Convention. It requested that the Court issue a slew of provisional measures pending its determination of the case on the merits. One of the reliefs that The Gambia sought involved "the safe and dignified return of forcibly displaced Rohingya" (ICJ 2019d, 58) as a form of restitution.[3] However, section "E. Provisional Measures Requested" of the same application contained nothing about repatriation (ICJ 2019d, 66–67). In The Gambia's oral submission, the word "return" was pronounced twice with reference to ICJ's own *Qatar v. United Arab Emirates* case (2018), and "repatriation" appeared once as a passing footnote (ICJ 2019c, 58 & 47). The verbatim record also shows that none of the six provisional measures sought at the oral round addressed the repatriation matter (ibid, 66–72). On the contrary, uttering "repatriation" and "return" 28 and 17 times respectively, Myanmar ingeniously argued that it was already involved in discussion with Bangladesh with support from the UN organs to repatriate the Rohingyas, and provisional measures, if any ordered, would jeopardize its repatriation initiatives (ICJ 2019b). In their second round of oral observations, both The Gambia and Myanmar rebutted each other on the issue. Responding to The Gambia's request, the ICJ eventually adopted four provisional measures, without, however, saying anything about repatriation (ICJ 2020, 30–31).

On January 20, 2021, Myanmar raised four preliminary objections to the Court's jurisdiction and to the admissibility of The Gambia's application (ICJ 2021). All the objections were technical in nature and had nothing to do with the question of repatriation.

In its submission to Myanmar's objections, however, the Gambia raised the issues of reparations and repatriation, which the ICJ should have touched upon in the Preliminary Objections Judgment of July 22, 2022, but it did not. The Gambia wanted Myanmar: "[m]ust perform the obligations of reparation in the interest of the victims of genocidal acts who are members of the Rohingya group, including but not limited to allowing the safe and dignified return of forcibly displaced Rohingya and respect for their full citizenship and human rights and protection against discrimination, persecution, and other related acts, consistent with the obligation to prevent genocide under Article 1" (ICJ 2022, 11–13).

As shown above, both ICC and ICJ are now adjudicating the Rohingya situation. These fora would take a long time, of which we have no indication, to conclude whether Myanmar committed genocide, and if so, who to hold accountable. Already immersed in their institutional challenges (Sterio 2020, 468–475; Ogbodo 2012, 105–107), these world courts find it extremely difficult to navigate complex global politics while also fulfilling their routine mandates (Azad 2024). To understand this, coupled with the inherent limits of international law, in which the superpower-led politics often aggravate problems such as the Rohingya crisis, is now worth examining in the following section.

The Limits of International Law Problematizing the Crisis

A plethora of scholarship speaks volumes about how international law, being premised on the so-called state consent and sovereign equality, espouses the interests of a limited number of elites and imperial/dominant states. These states tend to selectively caricature interpretative tools to distance the concrete realities of politics from the abstract ideals of law and justice, which in turn often emerge as state practices to secure their interests (Henkin 1968, 7, 24, 33–34, 46; Goodman 2002, 540; Benvenisti 2008, 11).

Bolton elucidates this notion by arguing that international law does not exist as a system of norms founded within a system of fortifying limited authority – a "rule of law" – which rests on popular sovereignty. In Bolton's sense, international law has no such system – no Hartian "rules of recognition." Due to inherent structural problems, Bolton thinks international law has serious "legitimacy" and "compliance" crises, creating an imbalanced global relationship among the states. As it appears, Bolton accords more importance to moral and political questions than to legal questions regarding the legitimacy and/or compliance questions of international law. As to this issue, he supposes that international law has failed to acquire the "political consent" of the people and misses conceptual and institutional "enforcement, execution or compliance mechanisms" in both form and substance (Bolton 2000, 1–48).

Bolton's central thesis challenges the myth that international law is built on the principles of state consent and sovereign equality. Hence, international law does not reflect the preferences of all states as it cannot, and does not, bind the sovereign, independent state (ibid; also echoed in D'Amato 1984–1985, 1293–1314; Goldsmith and Posner 2005, 3–4, 7 & 14; Howse and Teitel 2010, 129). A similar, albeit somewhat radical, view is prevalent in Anderson's leftist thinking, who argues that "international law is neither truthfully international nor genuinely law" (Anderson 2023). The world's most powerful states formulate its contents, and as a discipline this lacks "sovereign authority capable of enforcing it on penalty of infraction" – in the absence of which, it "ceases to be law and becomes no more than opinion" (Anderson 2023).

Partially sympathizing with Anderson, Koskenniemi contends that his interpretation overlooks "the *legal infrastructure of global capitalism*" (Koskenniemi 2025, 18). To Koskenniemi,

> [t]his consists of the laws – public and private, domestic and international – that regulate practically all aspects of social life by distributing rights and duties, powers and vulnerabilities to groups across the world. The legal form of the sovereign nation-state and the concepts of contract and private property, along with their many permutations, have spread across the world over centuries of European imperial dominance. They are neither weak nor manipulable at will. On the contrary, they form a ubiquitous and immensely powerful aspect of the way we are all ruled.
>
> *(ibid)*

Chimni also echoes much of Koskenniemi's critique while considering international law as the instrument of making an "imperial global state." He opines that with the growing network of international institutions on economic, social, and political fronts, a "nascent global state" is being created whose "current task is to realize the interests of an emerging transnational capital and powerful states in the international system to the disadvantage of third world states and peoples." From a global south perspective, he finds international law to be an imperial project that perennially tends to Europeanize the legal order and operates in an undemocratic atmosphere of international relations (Chimni 2004, 1–37).

In line with this position, Anghie also maintains that "[t]he deep and enduring inequalities that afflict this planet might be attributed, simply, to inequalities in power: the strong dictate and the weak must comply" (Anghie 2005, 317). This has been an imperial legacy of the "civilizing mission" that persists in the postcolonial world we live in, and, sadly, "imperialism is a constant," to use Anghie's formulation, for the discipline of international law (Anghie 2005, 315).

Drawing a clue from this, Shahabuddin identifies international law as a core component of the ideology of the postcolonial state, which contributes to the marginalization of minorities. To illustrate, regarding the *uti possidetis* principle governing postcolonial boundaries, he believes that the minority crisis, like the Rohingya crisis, is deeply rooted in the very process of creating the postcolonial "national" state through the contrivance of international law. In this setup, he clarifies, the "national" represents the majoritarian who sits in the center, such as the military juntas in Myanmar, and the minorities, such as the Rohingyas, remain at the periphery. He criticizes the "liberal" ideas of equality and non-discrimination, which failed to protect the Rohingyas by acting as "the *modus operandi* of assimilation and the extinction of group identity." He condemns, among others, the postcolonial developmentalism model, which seeks to camouflage the embedded asymmetric power relations that continue to produce socio-economic fragility for the Rohingya-like minority groups (Shahabuddin 2021, 89–276).

With reference to how the great powers, such as the USA, China, India, and others, have approached the Rohingya crisis and its aftermath, Hein and Myers explain the asymmetric power relations of competing values and interests in the following words:

> Important US allies and partners in the Indo-Pacific, such as Australia, India, and Japan, have voiced their "concern" about the Burmese crisis but fear that excessive pressure would open the regime to greater Chinese influence. As a result, they have maintained or, in the case of India, expanded their economic and diplomatic ties to the junta and are unlikely to provide support to the Burmese resistance. [...] From the Chinese perspective, [on the other hand,] the outbreak of a civil war next door – China and Myanmar share a 1,300-mile border – was bad news for regional stability and for China's multibillion-dollar investments in Myanmar under the Belt and Road Initiative. China was and remains one of the Burmese military's leading arms suppliers, but it has never quite trusted the military's leadership, which it views as too unpredictable.
>
> *(Hein and Myers 2023)*

This scenario gives the impression that the whole Rohingya crisis is political in nature – undoubtedly. Nonetheless, it has a legal character as well, which is why the popular view holds that the crisis must be addressed by law and legal institutions. But the political milieu, as illustrated by Hein and Myers, in which "international law [evolves] does not pull states toward compliance contrary to their interests, and the possibilities for what international law can achieve are limited by the configurations of state interests and the distribution of state power" (Goldsmith and Posner 2005, 13). Plainly speaking, states – mostly the powerful ones – control the direction of international law for specific purposes and contexts. This has been the state of international law in which the Rohingya crisis unfolded, and we are still concerned. The geopolitics-driven international law has not only failed to protect the Rohingyas from persecution but also made their repatriation impossible, despite international justice efforts.

Conclusion

Drawing on Feierstein, this chapter has established that the destruction and displacement of the Rohingyas – the crux of the current refugee crisis – are direct products of "social reorganization" rooted in political power. As such, the prospects for voluntary, safe, and dignified Rohingya repatriation hinge on shifting geopolitical realities, not on international legal accountability mechanisms such as the ICC or the ICJ. This reinforces the core argument that international judicial adjudication, while morally significant, cannot meaningfully influence the future of Rohingya repatriation in the face of overriding global political interests.

For sure, the Rohingya genocide could be understood from a legal angle, but to grasp the manifold complexities of the crisis, it is crucial to be suspicious of the outcomes of the global courts about the return of the Rohingyas to Myanmar. To make it more straightforward, the chapter has returned to history and shows that the adjudication of the Bosnian genocide at international courts had no contribution to the effective repatriation of the Bosnian refugees in the 1990s and afterward. Thus, the quest for hope in the international adjudication system would not be very useful to the possibility of Rohingya repatriation.

Then, by identifying some of the inherent limits of international law, the chapter went on to assert that the international architecture itself further complicates the situation, as seen in the current case of Rohingya repatriation. The thrust of this argument is directed at the asymmetry of global power, in which the successes that less powerful states like Bangladesh can achieve in repatriation matters are no more than what the stronger party, in this case Myanmar, will allow. Any other outcome could only be achieved by a superpower, like the USA, China, or India, which has both a whopping economy and an inclination to use it to resolve the problem peacefully. Therefore, a sustainable solution seems to be a distant dream as long as Myanmar is on good terms with either superpower that enjoys veto power in the UN Security Council and holds competitive geopolitical allegiances/strengths vis-à-vis Bangladesh.

Lately, the ICC Chief Prosecutor has filed an application, now pending before Pre-Trial Chamber I, for a warrant of arrest against Myanmar's Acting President, Min Aung Hlaing. At the ICJ, a few states (e.g., Canada, Denmark, France, Germany, the Netherlands, the UK, and others) have been allowed to intervene in *The Gambia v. Myanmar* case. Such developments are encouraging and may also put pressure on Myanmar, but it is implausible to resolve the repatriation setback, as explained above.

In summary, the outcomes of international adjudicatory bodies – such as the ICC and the ICJ – will have little effect on the repatriation of the Rohingyas unless the fundamental limitations of international law are addressed. While these institutions offer moral value and may create temporary pressure, the realities of global politics ultimately prevail. Sincere progress on Rohingya repatriation requires acknowledging that international law, as currently practiced, enables powerful states to prioritize their interests and limit compliance. Until these structural issues are resolved, international adjudication will remain largely symbolic and ineffective in securing a sustainable solution for the Rohingya. Philippe Sands, one of the counsels in *The Gambia v. Myanmar*, aptly summarized this predicament at the ICJ: international law risks becoming "an unfortunate distraction" when states like Myanmar are given "the space and the freedom to act unfettered" (ICJ 2019a, 39). This underscores the chapter's central message: only a fundamental transformation of the international legal order, not the current adjudicatory outcomes, can create real hope for Rohingya repatriation.

Notes

1 Such anticipation has been succinctly elaborated upon in Islam 2021, 1–8. See also Islam and Muquim 2025, 155–182.
2 For a compelling account of how the crime of genocide originated and found its place in the large bodies of international law, see Sands 2016.
3 The Gambia also solicited the same relief in its written memorial on Myanmar's objections, see ICJ 2022, 13.

References

Al Jazeera. 2019. "Myanmar Rejects ICC Probe into Alleged Crimes Against Rohingya." October 15. https://www.aljazeera.com/news/2019/11/15/myanmar-rejects-icc-probe-into-alleged-crimes-against-rohingya.
Al Jazeera. 2021. "Myanmar's Pro-Rohingya Social Media Campaign Gathers Mass Support." June 14. https://www.aljazeera.com/news/2021/6/14/myanmars-pro-rohingya-social-media-campaign-shows-mass-support.
Anderson, Perry. 2023. "The Standard of Civilization." *New Left Review*, September-October (No. 143).
Anghie, Antony. 2005. *Imperialism, Sovereignty and the Making of International Law*. Cambridge: Cambridge University Press.
Azad, Emraan. 2024. "The Rohingya Crisis at the ICJ: Caught between Legal Technicalities and Limits of the Court." *CIL Dialogues: An International Law Blog*, October 18. https://cil.nus.edu.sg/blogs/the-rohingya-crisis-at-the-icj-caught-between-legal-technicalities-and-limits-of-the-court/.
Benvenisti, Eyal. 2008. "The Conception of International Law as a Legal System." *Tel Aviv University Law Faculty Papers* 83: 1–13.
Bolton, John. 2000. "Is There Really Law in International Affairs?." *Transnational Law and Contemporary Problems* 10: 1–48.
Chimni, B. S. 2004. "International Institutions Today: An Imperial Global State in the Making." *European Journal of International Law* 15(1): 1–37.
Curtis, John. 2025. "Bangladesh: The Fall of the Hasina Government and Recent Political Developments." *House of Commons Research Briefing No. 10096*, January 23. https://researchbriefings.files.parliament.uk/documents/CBP-10096/CBP-10096.pdf.
D'Amato, Anthony. 1984–1985. "Is International Law Really 'Law'?." *Northwestern University Law Review* 79: 1293–1314.
Feierstein, Daniel. 2014. *Genocide as Social Practice: Reorganizing Society Under the Nazis and Argentina's Military Juntas*. Translated by Douglas Andrew Town. London: Rutgers University Press.
Feierstein, Daniel. 2023. "Reorganizing Society Under the Nazis and Argentina's Military Juntas." *Lecture Delivered at the 12th Certificate Course on Genocide and Justice, Liberation War Museum*, August 25 (Recorded lecture file is with the author).
Goodman, Ryan. 2002. "Human Rights Treaties, Invalid Reservations and State Consent." *American Journal of International Law* 96(3): 531–560.

Goldsmith, Jack L., and Eric A. Posner. 2005. *The Limits of International Law*. Oxford: Oxford University Press.
Hageboutros, Joelle. 2016. "The Bosnian Refugee Crisis: A Comparative Study of German and Austrian Reactions and Responses." *Swarthmore International Relations Journal* 1(1): 50–60.
Hein, Ye Myo, and Lucas Myers. 2023. "Is Myanmar the Frontline of a New Cold War?: How America and China Are Reshaping the Burmese Civil War." *Foreign Affairs*, June 19.
Henkin, Louis. 1968. *How Nations Behave: Law and Foreign Policy*. New York: Praeger.
Hoque, Mofidul, et al., eds. 2018. *The Rohingya Genocide: Compilation and Analysis of Survivors' Testimonies*. Dhaka: Liberation War Museum.
Howse, Robert, and Ruti Teitel. 2010. "Beyond Compliance: Rethinking Why International Law Really Matters." *Global Policy* 1(2): 127–136.
ICC. 2018. *Prosecution's Request for Ruling on Jurisdiction in the Situation in the People's Republic of Bangladesh/Republic of the Union of Myanmar*. April 9. https://www.legal-tools.org/doc/4af756/pdf/.
ICC. 2019a. *Decision Pursuant to Article 15 of the Rome Statute on the Authorization of an Investigation into the Situation in the People's Republic of Bangladesh/Republic of the Union of Myanmar*. November 14. https://www.icc-cpi.int/sites/default/files/CourtRecords/CR2019_06955.PDF.
ICC. 2019b. *Request for Authorization of an Investigation Pursuant to Article 15 in the Situation in the People's Republic of Bangladesh/Republic of the Union of Myanmar*. July 4. https://www.icc-cpi.int/sites/default/files/CourtRecords/CR2019_03510.PDF.
ICC. 2023. "Statement: ICC Prosecutor Karim A. A. Khan KC Concludes Second Visit to Bangladesh." July 10. https://www.icc-cpi.int/news/icc-prosecutor-karim-khan-kc-concludes-second-visit-bangladesh-rohingya-must-not-be-forgotten.
ICJ. 2007. *Application of the Convention on the Prevention and Punishment of the Crime of Genocide (Bosnia and Herzegovina v. Serbia and Montenegro)* (Judgment). February 26. https://www.icj-cij.org/sites/default/files/case-related/91/091-20070226-JUD-01-00-EN.pdf.
ICJ. 2019a. *Verbatim Record 2019/20 of Public Sitting Held on Thursday, December 12, 2019, at 10 a.m., at the Peace Palace, President Yusuf Presiding, in the Case Concerning Application of the Convention on the Prevention and Punishment of the Crime of Genocide (The Gambia v. Myanmar)*. https://www.icj-cij.org/sites/default/files/case-related/178/178-20191212-ORA-01-00-BI.pdf.
ICJ. 2019b. *Verbatim Record 2019/19 of Public Sitting Held on Tuesday, December 10, 2019, at 10 a.m., at the Peace Palace, President Yusuf Presiding, in the Case Concerning Application of the Convention on the Prevention and Punishment of the Crime of Genocide (The Gambia v. Myanmar)*. https://www.icj-cij.org/sites/default/files/case-related/178/178-20191211-ORA-01-00-BI.pdf.
ICJ. 2019c. *Verbatim Record 2019/18 of Public Sitting Held on Tuesday, December 10, 2019, at 10 a.m., at the Peace Palace, President Yusuf Presiding, in the Case Concerning Application of the Convention on the Prevention and Punishment of the Crime of Genocide (The Gambia v. Myanmar)*. https://www.icj-cij.org/sites/default/files/case-related/178/178-20191210-ORA-01-00-BI.pdf.
ICJ. 2019d. *Application Instituting Proceedings and Request for the Indication of Provisional Measures (The Gambia v. Myanmar)*. November 11. https://www.icj-cij.org/sites/default/files/case-related/178/178-20191111-APP-01-00-EN.pdf.
ICJ. 2020. *Application of the Convention on the Prevention and Punishment of the Crime of Genocide (The Gambia v. Myanmar)* (Request for the Indication

of Provisional Measures Order). January 23. https://www.icj-cij.org/sites/default/files/case-related/178/178-20200123-ORD-01-00-EN.pdf.
ICJ. 2021. *Application of the Convention on the Prevention and Punishment of the Crime of Genocide (The Gambia v. Myanmar)* (Preliminary Objections of the Republic of Myanmar). January 20. https://www.icj-cij.org/sites/default/files/case-related/178/178-20210120-WRI-01-00-EN.pdf.
ICJ. 2022. *Application of the Convention on the Prevention and Punishment of the Crime of Genocide (The Gambia v. Myanmar)* (Preliminary Objections Judgment). July 22. https://www.icj-cij.org/public/files/case-related/178/178-20220722-JUD-01-00-EN.pdf.
Islam, Md. Rizwanul. 2021. "Ordering the Repatriation of the Rohingya." *Virginia Journal of International Law Online* 62: 1–8. https://static1.squarespace.com/static/5f0a3654a47d231c00ccd14f/t/64fe02261002d11ad726dad3/1694368294184/Vol_62_Islam.pdf.
Islam, Md. Rizwanul, and Naimul Muquim. 2025. "Repatriation of the Rohingya Through An ICJ Verdict: Utopia or an Equitable Remedy?." *Washington University Global Studies Law Review* 22: 155–182.
Koser, Khalid, and Richard Black. 1999. "Limits to Harmonisation: The Temporary Protection of Refugees in the European Union." *International Migration* 37(3): 522–543.
Koskenniemi, Martti. 2025. "The Laws that Rule Us: The Legal Infrastructure of Global Capitalism." *New Left Review*, July-August 2025 (No. 154).
Lemkin, Raphael. 1944. *Axis Rule in Occupied Europe: Laws of Occupation – Analysis of Government – Proposals for Redress.* Washington: Carnegie Endowment for International Peace.
Mennecke, Martin, and Christian J. Tams. 2007. "The Genocide Case Before the International Court of Justice." *Sicherheit und Frieden (S+F)/Security and Peace* 25(2): 71–76.
Mirković, Damir. 1996. "Ethnic Conflict and Genocide: Reflections on Ethnic Cleansing in the Former Yugoslavia." *The Annals of the American Academy of Political and Social Science (The Holocaust: Remembering for the Future)* 548: 191–199.
Ogbodo, S. Gozie. 2012. "An Overview of the Challenges Facing the International Court of Justice in the 21st Century." *Annual Survey of International & Comparative Law* 18(1): 93–113.
Quell, Molly. 2025. "ICC President Vows to Resist US and Russian Pressure Despite Sanctions and Threats." *ABC News*, December 1. https://abcnews.go.com/International/wireStory/icc-president-vows-resist-us-russian-pressure-despite-127994201.
Sands, Philippe. 2016. *East West Street: On the Origins of Genocide and Crimes Against Humanity.* London: Weidenfeld and Nicolson.
Shahabuddin, Mohammad, 2021. *Minorities and the Making of Postcolonial States in International* Law. Cambridge: Cambridge University Press.
Sterio, Milena. 2020. "The International Criminal Court: Current Challenges and Prospect of Future Success." *Case Western Reserve Journal of International Law* 52(1): 467–478.
The Daily Star. 2025. "Rohingya Crisis: Yunus Lays Out 7-Point Plan at UN Conference." October 1. https://www.thedailystar.net/rohingya-influx/news/rohingya-crisis-yunus-lays-out-7-point-plan-un-conference-3998731.
Traynor, Ian. 2010. "Srebrenica Genocide: Worst Massacre in Europe Since the Nazis." *The Guardian*, June 10. https://www.theguardian.com/law/2010/jun/10/hague-bosnian-serb-srebrenica-genocide1.

Uddin, Nasir. 2020. *The Rohingya: An Ethnography of Subhuman Life*. Oxford: Oxford University Press.
Valenta, Marko. 2011. *The Bosnian Diaspora: Integration in Transnational Communities*. Farnham: Ashgate.
Valenta, Marko, and Zan Strabac. 2013. "The Dynamics of Bosnian Refugee Migrations in the 1990s, Current Migration Trends and Future Prospects." *Refugee Survey Quarterly* 32(3): 1–22.
Zarni, Maung, and Alice Cowley. 2014. "The Slow-Burning Genocide of Myanmar's Rohingya." *Washington International Law Journal* 23(3): 683–754.

12

CITIZENSHIP LAW AND PRACTICE OF BANGLADESH

A Hurdle in the Way of Local Integration of the Rohingya Refugees

Nafiz Ahmed

Introduction

Much has already been said regarding the plight of the Rohingya refugees in Bangladesh. Other chapters of this book have given historical accounts of the Rohingya refugee crisis in Bangladesh. This chapter does not repeat what has already been said elsewhere in this book. Instead, it focuses on the possibility of a specific solution that has been suggested for the refugee crisis in Bangladesh, namely, local integration. By local integration, this chapter refers to the inclusion of the Rohingya refugees in the political, social, and economic fabric of the locality of their host country, which in this case is Bangladesh. This chapter argues that the Rohingya refugees must acquire the citizenship of Bangladesh to integrate into the locality of Bangladesh fully and to live with dignity. The chapter peruses the existing legal framework governing the acquisition of citizenship in Bangladesh to see if the Rohingya refugees may acquire Bangladeshi citizenship under the current framework. It shows that the Rohingya are not eligible to be citizens of Bangladesh by birth. It argues that under the current government policies, the refugees are not likely to acquire citizenship by naturalisation or marriage either. This chapter also demonstrates that there is very little scope for the judiciary to interfere in the matters of acquisition of citizenship by naturalisation. The chapter concludes by noting that if the Rohingya refugees are to be locally integrated into Bangladesh, the current legal framework governing citizenship has to be radically altered.

The Connection between Citizenship and a Dignified Life in Bangladesh

A single definition of citizenship has yet to achieve academic consensus. A somewhat theoretically appropriate definition of it was offered by Tilly,

DOI: 10.4324/9781003771890-12

who defined citizenship as a tie that "entails enforceable rights and obligations based on persons' categorical membership and agents' relation to the state." (Tilly, 1995) Tilly defines tie as "a continuing series of transactions [a bounded communication between one actor and another] to which participants attach shared understandings, memories, forecasts, rights and obligations." (Tilly, 1995) The Appellate Division of the Supreme Court of Bangladesh (AD) in *Government of Bangladesh v Mirza Shahab Ispahani*, defined citizenship as a "right which a State sees fit to confer upon certain individuals who are also its nationals." (Para 18) In the same case, the Court held that "citizens are those persons who have full political rights as distinguished from nationals who may not enjoy full political rights and are still downscaled in that country" (para 18). Thus, citizenship can be understood as a status or membership or agency that gives its holders certain rights by virtue of holding that status.

Indeed, in Bangladesh, certain rights can only be enjoyed by its citizens. The exclusive rights for Bangladeshi citizens are not only non-justiciable welfare rights. They are also justiciable civil and political rights. For instance, indispensable rights such as the right to equality, right to non-discrimination, right to hold public office, freedom of movement, freedom of assembly, freedom of association, freedom of speech, freedom of profession and trade, right to hold property, right to privacy, and rights that may derive from the aforementioned rights are exclusively granted to the citizens of Bangladesh. The Constitution, in its text, expressly mentions that these rights are exclusively granted to citizens of Bangladesh. For other fundamental rights, such as in Articles 32, 33, 35, and the right to life, the constitutional text avoids this exclusivity by using the term "person" instead of "citizen." Thus, to live a dignified life in Bangladesh, one needs to acquire citizenship. Although some may argue that local integration is possible without acquiring citizenship in Bangladesh,[1] one needs civil and political rights to live a life of dignity. Jeremy Waldron has offered an explanation of dignity by noting,

> Dignity is the status of a person predicated on the fact that she is recognised as having the ability to control and regulate her actions in accordance with her own apprehension of norms and reasons that apply to her; it assumes she is capable of giving and entitled to give an account of herself (and of the way in which she is regulating her actions and organising her life), an account that others are to pay attention to; and it means finally that she has the wherewithal to demand that her agency and her presence among us as a human being be taken.
>
> *(Waldron, 2012)*

While accepting Waldron's explanation of dignity, it can be said that if a person is not allowed to demand that her voice and presence are not treated with respect in her social and political life, she is deprived of her dignity as a human being. In Bangladesh, to live a life with dignity, one needs to at least enjoy civil and political rights like freedom of speech, association, trade, assembly, movement, and so on. A human being's status as a person with dignity sets her apart from non-human animals in the eyes of the law (Alam, 2023). Thus, to be truly integrated into Bangladesh, that is to say to have a life of dignity, the Rohingya need citizenship of Bangladesh.

Citizenship Laws in Bangladesh

The Constitution of Bangladesh states in Article 6 that "[t]he citizenship of Bangladesh shall be determined and regulated by law." Some of the laws governing the citizenship of Bangladesh were created after the emergence of Bangladesh's legal system,[2] while others were retained from the previous regimes by dint of Article 149.[3] The laws governing citizenship in Bangladesh are much less developed than some of their Western counterparts. Scholars have even gone as far as to call citizenship laws in Bangladesh "haphazard" (Paulsen, 2006). The issue of citizenship in Bangladesh is primarily governed by three pieces of legislation: the Citizenship Act 1951, the Bangladesh Citizenship (Temporary Provisions) Order 1972, and the Naturalization Act 1926. As this chapter discusses later, the laws governing the acquisition of citizenship in Bangladesh may often appear to contradict each other. To make sense of these contradicting laws, one must read the laws as one coherent body of laws. Some judgements of the Supreme Court of Bangladesh have also shed light on Bangladesh's citizenship laws.

In Bangladesh, one acquires citizenship at birth in two ways: *jus soli* (citizenship by birth) and *jus sanguinis* (citizenship by descent) (Hoque, 2016). *Jus soli* is a principle of citizenship law that encapsulates the concept that one acquires the citizenship of the soil on which she is born. *Jus sanguinis* encapsulates the idea that one inherits her parents' citizenship as a matter of blood right. If one does not acquire Bangladeshi citizenship at birth, she may acquire it by naturalisation (the Citizenship Act 1951, s. 9; The Naturalisation Act 1926, s. 3) or marriage (however, only if the applicant is a foreign woman married to a Bangladeshi man, not the other way around) (Citizenship Act 1951, s. 10). In the following parts, this chapter discusses the different methods the Rohingya refugees may use to acquire Bangladeshi citizenship and their chances of success. At the outset, it can be concluded that the Rohingya refugees are not entitled to receive citizenship by descent as they migrated to Bangladesh from Myanmar after the independence of Bangladesh and after the commencement of the three major pieces of legislation governing citizenship in Bangladesh. This chapter focuses on the laws governing citizenship by birth, naturalisation, and marriage to examine whether the Rohingya refugees can successfully acquire Bangladeshi citizenship and get locally integrated.

Citizenship by Birth

In its simplest form, the principle of *jus soli* stipulates that a person becomes a citizen of the country where she is born, even if neither of her parents is a citizen of that country. However, in modern-day practice, jus soli citizenship has become conditional (Hoque, 2016). The conditions include but are not limited to the residential status of the parents. Unlike in countries where jus soli is unconditionally and strictly followed, Bangladesh has never been a popular destination for "birth tourism" or "maternity tourism."[4] Thus, the understanding of the jus soli principle in Bangladesh differs from popular destinations of birth tourism. As discussed later in this part, although the text of the law recognises the jus soli principle, it is seldom (if ever) practiced (Hoque, 2016). The Citizenship Act 1951 and the Bangladesh Citizenship (Temporary Provisions) Order 1972 were both enacted primarily following two successful revolutions for independence. The 1951 Act was enacted after the partition of British India. British India was divided into two independent countries: India and Pakistan. Pre-1971 Pakistan comprised West Pakistan (the present-day Islamic Republic of Pakistan) and East Pakistan (the present-day People's Republic of Bangladesh). After the partition of British India, the region saw millions of people migrate from India to Pakistan and vice versa. The Citizenship Act 1951, which was originally the Pakistan Citizenship Act 1951, was enacted to determine who would be the citizens of Pakistan. Section 3 of the 1952 Act fleshed out the criteria for citizenship by birth for those born before the statute's commencement.[5] In 1971, through Bangladesh's War of Liberation, Bangladesh became an independent nation. To separate Bangladeshi citizens from Pakistani citizens, the 1972 Order was created. The AD explained the creation of the said Order by noting, "To meet the requirements of the new situation that emerged out of the independence of Bangladesh P.O. 149 of 1972 was brought into existence on 15 December 1972, one day before the commencement of the Constitution so that it might get the constitutional protection of an existing law." (*Bangladesh v. Golam Azam and Ors*) At Bangladesh's inception, citizenship by birth was provided for those who were born before Bangladesh's independence under section 2 of the Bangladesh Citizenship (Temporary Provisions) Order 1972. Since the Myanmar military's crackdown against the Rohingya and the following migration started in 1977, (Islam and Muquim, 2020) section 3 of the 1951 Act and section 2 of the 1972 Order are relevant to our discussion.

To understand whether the Rohingya born in Bangladesh are entitled to get Bangladeshi citizenship, we must peruse the laws governing citizenship by birth for those born after 26 March 1971 (Bangladesh's Independence Day). The citizenship by birth of those born in independent Bangladesh is dealt with by section 4 of the Citizenship Act 1951, which states,

> Every person born in Bangladesh after the commencement of this Act shall be a citizen of Bangladesh by birth:
>
> Provided that a person shall not be such a citizen by virtue of this section if at the time of his birth-
>
> (a) his father possesses such immunity from suit and legal process as is accorded to an envoy of an external sovereign power accredited in Bangladesh and is not a citizen of Bangladesh; or
>
> (b) his father is an enemy alien and the birth occurs in a place then under occupation by the enemy.

The above-quoted section deals with the citizenship by birth of those born in independent Bangladesh (those born after 26 March 1971). The only conditions to the jus soli principle provided in Section 4 of the 1951 Act are children of foreign diplomats, and enemies are not entitled to receive citizenship by birth. Thus, if we take the text of the law literally, Rohingyas born in the territory of independent Bangladesh ought to be granted citizenship by birth. However, as this chapter shows below, the current interpretation of this section differs from its ordinary meaning.

In addition to the conditions for citizenship by birth provided in the proviso to section 4 of the Citizenship Act 1951, additional conditions are provided in Article 2B of the 1972 Order. Article 2B of the Bangladesh Citizenship (Temporary Provisions) Order 1972 provides,

> (1) Notwithstanding anything contained in Article 2 or *in any other law for the time being in force*, a person shall not, except as provided in clause (2), qualify himself to be a citizen of Bangladesh if he-
>
> (i) *owes, affirms or acknowledges, expressly or by conduct, allegiance to a foreign state*, or
>
> (ii) is notified under the proviso to Article 2A:
>
> Provided that a citizen of Bangladesh shall not, merely by reason of being a citizen or acquiring citizenship of a state specified in or under clause (2), cease to be a citizen of Bangladesh.
>
> (2) The Government may grant citizenship of Bangladesh to any person who is a citizen of any state of Europe or North America or of any other state which the Government may, by notification in the official Gazette, specify in this behalf. [Emphasis added]

Thus, no law in force would grant citizenship to a person who owes, affirms, or acknowledges allegiance to a foreign state, be that expressly or by conduct, unless she falls within the exception noted in Article 2B (2) of the 1972 Order.

The Rohingya refugees do not identify themselves as Bangladeshi citizens. Repatriation, once suitable conditions are guaranteed, remains their primary demand (United Nations High Commissioner for Refugees, 2021).

Their demands include the guarantee of citizenship of Myanmar (Voice of America, 2023). The Rohingya demand that they are citizens of Myanmar by birth, and the Myanmar regime is wrongfully denying their citizenship. For instance, in a recent protest held in the Rohingya Camps in Cox's Bazar, one of the Rohingya leaders told Reuters, "[w]e are the citizens of Myanmar by birth. We want to go back home with all our rights, including citizenship, free movement, livelihood, safety, and security" (Voice of America, 2023). Since the Rohingya, both expressly and through their conduct, acknowledge allegiance to Myanmar, they cannot qualify themselves to be citizens of Bangladesh. Their disqualification stems from Article 2B of the 1972 Order, which disqualifies those who owe, affirm, or acknowledge allegiance to a foreign state (subject to the conditions mentioned above).

However, an adult Rohingya refugee, born in Bangladesh, does not owe affirm, or acknowledge allegiance to a foreign state, and may successfully claim to be a citizen of Bangladesh by birth. The citizenship status of such a refugee would have to be decided on a case-by-case basis. It would not be a leeway to affirming citizenship to all Rohingya refugees. It may create a scope for local integration of a few thousand Rohingya refugees at a future date. At the time of writing this chapter, the example remains completely hypothetical.

A similar distinction between those owing allegiance to a foreign state and those not doing the same had been made by the High Court Division of the Supreme Court of Bangladesh (HCD) in *Md. Sadaqat Khan (Fakku) and others v Chief Election Commissioner, Bangladesh Election Commission and others*. The case dealt with the citizenship status of the Urdu-speaking people living in ICRC camps in Bangladesh. The Urdu-speaking community in Bangladesh living in ICRC camps is popularly known as the "Biharis." They migrated from India to the then East Pakistan after the partition of British India. During the struggle for independence of Bangladesh, the Urdu-speaking people were against the creation of an independent Bangladesh (Muquim, 2023). After Bangladesh's independence, there were multiple efforts to repatriate members of the Bihari community, as many of them expressed the wish to go back to Pakistan. However, hundreds of thousands of Biharis were born in Bangladesh and never expressed their desire to move to Pakistan (Muquim, 2023). A large number of Biharis affirm their allegiance solely to Bangladesh. The *Sadaqat Khan* case arose after some of the Biharis living in the ICRC camps were denied the right to enrol as voters in Bangladesh (a right exclusively given to Bangladesh's citizens) (*Md. Sadaqat Khan*, paras 1–4). While determining the case, the Court noted,

The residents of the ICRC camps may be broadly divided into two categories:

(i) those who swore their allegiance to Pakistan and had in writing expressed their desire to take up resident in that country ; and

(ii) those who were of minor age at the time of liberation of Bangladesh and were not mature enough to express any preference as to their citizenship even if their parent had opted for Pakistan and those who were born in Bangladesh after 16th December 1972 (the year might be wrongly quoted in place of 1971) (*Md. Sadaqat Khan*, para 21).

The Court decided in *Sadaqat Khan* that those who identify themselves as "stranded Pakistanis" and owe, affirm, and acknowledge, expressly or impliedly, to Pakistan "may belong to a class and cease to be citizens of Bangladesh" (*Md. Sadaqat Khan*, para 36). The Court found that the election commission was not under any legal obligation to enlist as voters the group of Biharis who considered themselves to be Pakistanis. Thus, the Court applied the disqualification criteria provided in Article 2B. If the issue of citizenship of the Rohingya born in Bangladesh comes before the Court, the Court may apply the same principle to hold that since the Rohingya owe their allegiance to Myanmar, they are not entitled to be citizens of Bangladesh.

It is to be noted that the government of Bangladesh has the power to make an exception for the Rohingya community under Article 2B(2). However, it is doubtful that the government would make an exception for the Rohingya as the Bangladeshi government has been vocally opposed to local integration of Rohingya from the outset (Islam, 2023). Even after continuous pressure from international organisations (e.g., the World Bank) to integrate the Rohingya refugees into the host country, the government of Bangladesh has stood firmly to its position that repatriation of the Rohingya is its only goal (Porimol and Byron. 2021). This position remains the same after the recent change of government. Thus, it is highly unlikely that the government of Bangladesh will use its power to make an exception for Rohingya refugees under Article 2B(2). Therefore, any claim from the Rohingya refugees of Bangladeshi citizenship by birth is unlikely to succeed in the current framework.

Citizenship by Naturalisation

The Citizenship Act 1951 empowers the government of Bangladesh to grant citizenship to any person by naturalisation.[6] Naturalisation in Bangladesh is governed by the Naturalisation Act 1926 and the Naturalisation Rules 1961. Once an applicant is naturalised and takes the oath of allegiance, she is entitled to all the rights, privileges, and capacities and is subjected to all the obligations of a citizen born within Bangladesh (The Naturalisation Act 1926, s.7). The children of the naturalised citizens, mentioned in the naturalisation certificate, would enjoy the benefits of citizenship and carry the burdens of the same. Section 3 of the Naturalisation Act 1926 states,

> The Government may grant a certificate of naturalization to any person who makes an application in this behalf and satisfies the Government:
> (a) that he is not a minor; [21 years according to section 2(c)];
> (b) that he is neither a citizen of Bangladesh nor a subject of any state of which a citizen of Bangladesh is prevented by or under any law from becoming a subject by naturalization;
> (c) that he has resided in Bangladesh throughout the period of twelve months immediately preceding the date of the application, and has, during the seven years immediately preceding the said period of twelve months, resided in Bangladesh for a period amounting in the aggregate to not less than four years;
> (d) that he is of good character;
> (e) that he has an adequate knowledge of Bengali; and
> (f) that he intends, if the application is granted, to reside in Bangladesh or to enter or to continue in the service of the Republic in Bangladesh:
>
> Provided that nothing in clause (c) or clause (f) shall apply in the case of a woman who was a citizen of Bangladesh previously to her marriage to a person not citizen of Bangladesh and whose husband has died or whose marriage has been dissolved.

Most adult Rohingya refugees may satisfy the grounds of naturalisation provided in section 3 of the 1926 Act. However, naturalisation is not a right of the applicants. The Naturalisation Act 1926 grants the government absolute discretion to grant or refuse any application of naturalisation presented in the prescribed form (section 5). The Naturalisation Act 1926 even bars the filing of any appeal challenging the government's decision regarding a naturalisation application (section 5). Only the general principles of law that apply to all administrative, quasi-judicial, and judicial decision-making, such as the principles of natural justice,[7] may act as trappings to the government's discretionary power in deciding matters of naturalisation. As discussed in the previous section of this chapter, the government of Bangladesh has been abundantly clear that it does not want Rohingya refugees to integrate into Bangladesh. Consequently, it is highly unlikely that any application of naturalisation may be successful in the near future.

Apart from the obvious hurdle in the way of naturalisation of Rohingya refugees mentioned above, there are other challenges that a Rohingya refugee may face if she files an application for naturalisation in the current framework. Unlike countries that are popular destinations for migrants, Bangladesh does not have a separate robust administrative infrastructure for dealing with citizenship applications. To apply for citizenship by naturalisation, an applicant must file an application to the Immigration Wing of the Security Services Division of the Ministry of Home Affairs.[8] The Security

Services Division's website contains an application form for dual citizenship but does not contain an application form for stateless applicants. To apply for citizenship by naturalisation or permanent residence in Bangladesh, applicants need to provide information about their prior citizenship,[9] which the Rohingya refugees do not have. Therefore, before the Rohingya refugees can apply for Bangladeshi citizenship by naturalisation, the application procedure must be substantively revised.

Additionally, since the Immigration Wing of the Security Services Division is not used to handling hundreds of thousands of citizenship applications filed in close proximity, their internal structure must be changed, and their officials may need additional training. As noted before, an appeal against the decision of the government regarding a naturalisation application is barred by section 5 of the Naturalisation Act 1926. To ensure proper administration of justice, an appellate forum for applications of citizenship by naturalisation may be needed before allowing hundreds of thousands of naturalisation applications.

Citizenship by Marriage

As mentioned before, another way of acquiring citizenship in Bangladesh is by marriage. Section 10 of the Citizenship Act 1951 provides,

(1) Any woman who by reason of her marriage to a British subject before the first day of January, 1949, has acquired the status of a British subject shall, if her husband becomes a citizen of Bangladesh, be a citizen of Bangladesh.

(2) Subject to the provisions of sub-section (1) and sub-section (4) a woman who has been married to a citizen of Bangladesh or to a person who but for his death would have been a citizen of Bangladesh under sections 3, 4 or 5 shall be entitled, on making application therefore to the Government in the prescribed manner, and, if she is an alien, on obtaining a certificate of domicile and taking the oath of allegiance in the form set out in the Schedule to this Act, to be registered as a citizen of Bangladesh whether or not she has completed twenty-one years of her age and is of full capacity.

Therefore, the scope of obtaining citizenship by marriage is only limited to a woman whose husband is a citizen of Bangladesh. The process of obtaining Bangladeshi citizenship by marriage is not automatic. A woman seeking citizenship by marriage must apply for naturalisation after obtaining a certificate of domicile. The citizenship by marriage will be bestowed upon an applicant only after she takes an oath of allegiance. It is also a requirement for the applicant to be at least 21 years old and of full capacity. The law governing citizenship is transparently gender-biased as only a male Bangladeshi citizen can pass citizenship to his wife, but a female Bangladeshi citizen cannot pass citizenship to her spouse.

Acquiring citizenship by marriage is currently not an option for the Rohingya refugees. The Bangladesh government has prohibited the registration of marriages between Bangladeshi citizens and Rohingya refugees (Administrative Circular, 2017). The government of Bangladesh, through two circulars, prohibited the marriage registrars (kazi) from registering marriages between a Bangladeshi citizen and a refugee. After the issuance of the circulars, in *Babul Hossain v Bangladesh*, (Writ Petition No. 18163 of 2017) a case came before the HCD regarding a marriage between a Bangladeshi man and a refugee woman. The writ petition was filed by the father of Mr Shoaib Hossain Jewel, a Bangladeshi citizen who married a Rohingya refugee woman after they fell in love in a refugee camp in Cox's Bazar. Mr Jewel secretly brought his newly married wife outside of the refugee camps and went into hiding in fear of arrest. The writ petitioner filed the petition to seek protection of the HCD. However, the Court held that two offences took place prior to the filing of the petition. Firstly, Mr Jewel committed an offence by smuggling his wife out of the refugee camp. Secondly, the Court held that "the alleged marriage between Shoaib Hossain Jewel and the Myanmar national Rafiza is a blatant contravention of the notification... issued by the Law and Justice Division, Ministry of Law, Justice and Parliamentary Affairs." Consequently, the writ petition was dismissed with a cost of one hundred thousand BDT to be paid by the petitioner. Because of the government's restrictions on marriages between a Bangladeshi man and a Rohingya refugee woman, its unwillingness to grant citizenship by naturalisation to refugees, and the Apex Court's strict reading of the government circular, it is safe to conclude that citizenship by marriage is currently not an option for the Rohingya refugees.

After perusing the existing laws governing citizenship in Bangladesh, it may be concluded that the Rohingya refugees are not entitled to citizenship by birth. Their chances of acquiring citizenship by naturalisation or marriage depend wholly on government policy. If the government decides to change its stance against local integration of the Rohingya refugees in Bangladesh, only then the door of citizenship by naturalisation and marriage may open for the Rohingya refugees.

Scope of Interference by the Judiciary

Legitimate Expectation

In certain contexts, the doctrine of legitimate expectation may play a role in immigration and citizenship cases. The doctrine of legitimate expectation binds public authorities to their promises and past practices. The key questions that arise in a case in which the doctrine of legitimate expectation is invoked are "whether an expectation has arisen and, if so, how (if at all) it should be protected" (Elliot, 2019).

An example of the doctrine of legitimate expectation being invoked in an immigration case can be found in *A-G of Hong Kong v Ng Yuen Shiu*. In *Ng Yuen Shiu* the Privy Council decided an issue where the Hong Kong government announced that certain illegal immigrants would be interviewed individually before making a decision about deportation. Based on this announcement, the Privy Council quashed a deportation order where the immigrant was not interviewed. The Privy Council held that "when a public authority has promised to follow a certain procedure, it is in the interest of good administration that it should act fairly and should implement its promise so long as implementation does not interfere with its statutory duty."

The Supreme Court of Bangladesh also adopted the doctrine of legitimate expectation.[10] According to the AD, the doctrine of legitimate expectation stipulates that:

> [W]here a person is the victim of an unfavourable decision taken by a public authority, this may amount to an infringement of that person's legitimate expectation, where, for example, the decision contradicts an earlier promise or course of conduct on the part of the public authority concerned. *(para 18)*

A legitimate expectation does not necessarily create an enforceable right (*Food Corporation of India v. Kamdhenu*). However, if an authority fails to give due consideration to a legitimate expectation of a person while making a decision, such a decision may become arbitrary and violate the principle of non-arbitrariness. For an expectation to be legitimate, it must arise from a promise or representation of the government to take a certain action (*Kazi Mizanur Rahman* 18). If the government of Bangladesh made any promise to locally integrate the Rohingya refugees by granting them citizenship or implied the same through representation, the refugees may have had a legitimate expectation. However, since the government of Bangladesh has been careful and clear in maintaining its position against local integration, it is safe to say that no such legitimate expectation exists as of now.

Political Questions

Since the government of Bangladesh is maintaining a rigid stance against local integration, one may challenge the government's position before the Supreme Court of Bangladesh. The Rohingya refugees are not entitled to citizenship by birth, but one may pray before the Court to grant citizenship by naturalisation to Rohingya refugees. The Supreme Court of Bangladesh is bestowed with the power to perform judicial review of administrative and legislative actions by the Constitution of Bangladesh (Art. 102). It also has the power to issue any order to meet the ends of justice (art 104). However, any such challenge against the government's decision not to integrate the Rohingya refugees into Bangladesh is likely to fail if the Court sees the matter of citizenship by naturalisation as a political question. The doctrine of political questions, which the Supreme Court has accepted (*Special Reference No. 1 of 1995*), states that the judiciary cannot decide a case that is politically charged and typically falls within the scope of another branch's jurisdiction (*Baker v. Carr*).[11] As discussed above, the current legal framework grants the executive the absolute discretion to grant or reject applications for naturalisation. Therefore, if the Court uses the doctrine of political questions in the issue at hand, it may be unwilling to interfere as it entirely falls within the jurisdiction of another branch of the state.

Conclusion

As the chapter shows, if the Rohingya refugees were to fully integrate into the locality of Bangladesh and live a dignified life, they need to be citizens of Bangladesh. Under the existing laws, the Rohingya are not entitled to be citizens by birth or descent. Their only way of acquiring citizenship of Bangladesh may be through naturalisation. However, the government's actions at the time of writing this chapter indicate that an application for citizenship by naturalisation by a Rohingya refugee is unlikely to be successful. The jus soli principle may create a scope for integrating those refugees who were born in Bangladesh, have attained majority, and have not affirmed or acknowledged allegiance to a foreign state. However, it would not serve as an effective way to integrate all Rohingya refugees. If the government of Bangladesh decides to integrate the Rohingya refugees into its locality, it must change its legal framework governing matters of citizenship substantially. Otherwise, repatriation would remain the only option.

Notes

1 For instance, one author argues that while acquiring citizenship for local integration is ideal, the scope of constitutional protection for refugees may allow integration with acquiring citizenship. Alam, Jobair. 2023. 'Refugee Protection Under the Constitution of Bangladesh: The Rohingya Refugees in Context.' In *The Constitutional Law of Bangladesh Progression and Transformation at its 50th Anniversary,* edited by M Rafiqul Islam and Muhammad Ekramul Haque, 283, 287–96. Springer.

2 For more on the emergence of Bangladesh's legal system, see, Ahmed, Nafiz. 2023. 'Emergence of Bangladesh's Legal System: Revolutionary Legality and a New Rule of Recognition.' In *A History of the Constitution of Bangladesh:*

The Founding, Development and Way Ahead, edited by Ridwanul Hoque and Rokeya Chowdhury, 29–44. Routledge.

3 The Constitution of the People's Republic of Bangladesh, art. 149 states that "Subject to the provisions of this Constitution all existing laws shall continue to have effect but may be amended or repealed by law made under this Constitution."

4 Birth/maternity tourism can be understood as "the phenomenon of foreign women giving birth in a *jus soli* country in order to secure a favorable citizenship for their children." Harder, Lois. 2020. '"Maternity Tourism," Civic Integration and Jus Soli Citizenship in Canada.' *Revue Européenne Des Migrations Internationales* 36(4): 35.

5 Section 3 of the Citizenship Act 1951 states that,
At the commencement of this Act, every person shall be deemed to be a citizen of Bangladesh:
(a) who or any of whose parents or grandparents was born in the territory now included in Bangladesh and who after the fourteenth day of August, 1947, has not been permanently resident in any country outside Bangladesh; or
(b) who or any of whose parents or grandparents was born in the territories included in India on the thirty-first day of March, 1937, and who, except in the case of a person who was in the service of Bangladesh or of any Government or Administration in Bangladesh at the commencement of this Act, has or had his domicile within the meaning of Part II of the Succession Act, 1925, as in force at the commencement of this Act, in Bangladesh or in the territories now included in Bangladesh; or
(c) who is a person naturalised as a British subject in Bangladesh; and who, if before the date of the commencement of this Act he has acquired the citizenship of any foreign State, has before that date renounced the same by depositing a declaration in writing to that effect with an authority appointed or empowered to receive it; or
(d) who before the commencement of this Act migrated to the territories now included in Bangladesh from any territory in the Indo-Pakistan sub-continent outside those territories with the intention of residing permanently in those territories.

6 The Citizenship Act 1951, s. 9 states that, "[t]he Government may, upon an application made to it in that behalf by any person who has been granted a certificate of naturalisation under the Naturalisation Act, 1926, register that person as a citizen of Bangladesh by naturalisation."

7 The AD in *Abdul Latif Mirza v. Govt. of Bangladesh and* others, 31 DLR (AD) 1 (1979) held that

> It is now well settled that whenever any person or an authority is empowered by law to take an action or make a decision which may operate to the prejudice of another person, such person or authority is under an obligation to act judicially in taking such action or making such decision. That is to say, such person or authority is to take such an action or make such a decision on the basis of certain materials and observe the principle of natural justice unless otherwise provided by the enactment creating such a power. [43]

8 For more information on how to apply for citizenship by naturalisation in Bangladesh, visit the Security Services Department's website < https://ssd.gov.bd >.

9 For instance, see the form available on the Security Services Department's website < https://ssd.gov.bd/sites/default/files/files/ssd.portal.gov.bd/page/8f4042c5_9d53_4a43_81f0_27472f4fcef9/Dual_Citizenship_Form.pdf >.

10 See for example, *The Local Government and Engineering Department, People's Republic of Bangladesh v. Kazi Mizanur Rahman and Others* 32 BLD (AD) 177 (2012).

11 The definition of the doctrine of political question provided by the Supreme Court of the United States of America in *Baker v Carr* has been accepted by the Supreme Court of Bangladesh. See, for instance, *Special Reference No. 1 of 1995* 15 BLD (AD) 194 (1995).

References

Abdul Latif Mirza v. Govt. of Bangladesh and other, 31 DLR (AD) 1 (1979).

A-G of Hong Kong v Ng Yuen Shiu [1983] 2 AC 629.

Ahmed, Nafiz. 2023. "Emergence of Bangladesh's Legal System: Revolutionary Legality and a New Rule of Recognition." In *A History of the Constitution of Bangladesh: The Founding, Development and Way Ahead*, edited by Ridwanul Hoque and Rokeya Chowdhury, 29–44. Routledge.

Alam, Jobair. 2023. "Refugee Protection Under the Constitution of Bangladesh: The Rohingya Refugees in Context." In *The Constitutional Law of Bangladesh Progression and Transformation at its 50th Anniversary*, edited by M Rafiqul Islam and Muhammad Ekramul Haque, 283, 287–96. Springer.

Babul Hossain v Bangladesh, Writ Petition No. 18163 of 2017 https://thinklegalbangladesh.com/wp-content/uploads/2022/04/21-Final-High-court-Judgement.pdf

Baker v. Carr, 369 U.S. 186 (1962).

Bangladesh v. Golam Azam and Ors, 3 BLT (AD) 3 (1995).

Elliot, Mark. 2019. "Legitimate Expectation: Reliance, Process, Substance." *Cambridge Law Journal* 78(2): 260.

Food Corporation of India v. Kamdhenu Cattle Feed Industries Ltd, 1 SCC 71 (1993).

Government of Bangladesh v Mirza Shahab Ispahani, 8 BLD (AD) 41 (1988).

Harder, Lois. 2020. "'Maternity Tourism', Civic Integration and Jus Soli Citizenship in Canada." *Revue Européenne Des Migrations Internationales* 36(4): 35.

Hoque, Ridwanul. 2016. "Report on Citizenship Law: Bangladesh" (RSCAS/EUDO-CIT-CR 2016/14, 12. < https://cadmus.eui.eu/bitstream/handle/1814/44545/EudoCit_2016_14Bangladesh.pdf>

Islam, Rizwanul. 2023. "The Humane Yet Ambivalent Attitude Towards Persecuted People: A Potential Threat to Stability?" In *Integrated Approaches to Peace and Sustainability*, edited by Ayyoob Sharifi, Dahlia Simangan, and Shinji Kaneko, 103. Springer.

Islam, Rizwanul, and Naimul Muquim. 2020. "The Gambia v Myanmar at the I.C.J.: Good Samaritans Testing State Responsibility for Atrocities on the Rohingya." *California Western International Law Journal* 51(1): 78.

Md. Sadaqat Khan (Fakku) and others v Chief Election Commissioner, 28 BLD (HCD) 261 (2008).

Ministry of Law Justice and Parliamentary Affairs, Administrative Circular No. bichar-7/2n-75/2016–909 (25 October 2017).

Muquim, Naimul. 2023. "The Urdu-Speaking Community of Bangladesh: Forgotten Denizens or Putative Citizens?" *Emory International Law Review* 37(4): 691.

Palma, Porimol, and Rejaul Karim Byron. 2021. "Rohingyas in Bangladesh: No Question of Their Integration with Locals" *The Daily Star*, Dhaka, 31 July. < https://www.thedailystar.net/rohingya-crisis/news/rohingyas-bangladesh-no-question-their-integration-locals-2141006> Last accessed on 1 January 2024

Paulsen, Eric. 2006. "The Citizenship Status of the Urdu-Speakers/Biharis in Bangladesh." *Refugee Survey Quarterly* 25(3): 54.

"Rohingya Protest in Bangladesh, Demand Repatriation to Myanmar." 2023. Voice of America, 8 June. <https://www.voanews.com/a/rohingya-protest-in-bangladesh-demand-repatriation-to-myanmar/7128327.html> Last accessed on March 3, 2025.

Special Reference No. 1 of 1995, 15 BLD (AD) 194 (1995).

The Local Government and Engineering Department, People's Republic of Bangladesh v. Kazi Mizanur Rahman and Others, 32 BLD (AD) 177 (2012).

Tilly, Charles. 1995. "Citizenship, Identity and Social History." *International Review of Social History* 40 (Supp. 3): 1.

United Nations High Commissioner for Refugees. 2021. "The Displaced and Stateless of Myanmar in the Asia-Pacific Region" 2. < https://reporting.unhcr.org/sites/default/files/The%20Displaced%20and%20Stateless%20of%20Myanmar%20in%20the%20Asia-Pacific%20Region%20-%20January%202021.pdf> Last accessed on March 3, 2025.

Waldron, Jeremy. 2012. "How Law Protects Dignity." *Cambridge Law Journal* 71(1): 200.

13

INCLUSIVE REPATRIATION AND ROHINGYA WOMEN

A Critical Analysis

Ishrat Zakia Sultana

In the discussion of refugees, migration, statelessness, the last few decades of the 20th century and the first few decades of the 21st century have become remarkable. During this period, among the widely discussed refugee issues, the Rohingya crisis has drawn global attention. Originating in Myanmar, the crisis has severely affected millions of Rohingya men, women, and children who became stateless and also Bangladesh – that admitted the highest number of Rohingya after the persecution and genocide.

Undoubtedly, the Rohingya crisis is a highly complicated geopolitical issue and multiple factors have been responsible for making this problem unsolvable until now. For Bangladesh, repatriation is the only solution to the Rohingya crisis. This is also a demand of the Rohingya temporarily sheltered in Bangladesh. A series of dialogues and discussions have taken place on the solution to the Rohingya crisis, but how Rohingya men and women view repatriation and participate in the process of repatriation - has been outside of the discussions.

History shows that persecution, ethnic cleansing, and genocide – all are male-centric acts in terms of both decision and execution of all these inhuman acts. Similar to that, repatriation is also a male-centric act where the actors are male and voices of the male beneficiaries (although taken in a token form) are counted as the voices for all. According to UNHCR (2023), more than half of the stateless Rohingya in Bangladesh are women and girls. Is there any way to make the male-centric repatriation process into an inclusive process? Repatriation itself is an extremely complicated geopolitical issue. Hence, it is necessary to examine how women's rights, safety, and dignity during and after the repatriation have been considered.

DOI: 10.4324/9781003771890-13

Women become the first victims of abuse, oppression, and violence both in man-made war, conflict, and other forms of crisis and natural disasters. This has been noted in Rwanda, Bosnia Herzegovina, Palestine, Bangladesh, and other places where violence, conflict, and natural disasters took place. Much of the attention is given to women's physical victimization when it comes to the impacts of such man-made and natural disasters, not how the patriarchal structure excludes them from being part of solving the crisis. Some of the scholarly work focuses on the historical exclusion of the Rohingya (Ullah, 2011), security issues (Rahman, 2019), and living conditions of the Rohingya (Pittaway, 2008), women's sexual and reproductive health conditions of women (Jannat, Sifat, & Khisa, 2022), gender-based violence (Priddy, Berry, Doman, & Ahmed, 2022; Yousuf, Salam, Akter, & Salam, 2021 and others), etc. However, Rohingya women's representation and the inclusion of their concerns in a crucial issue like repatriation have always been unexamined.

In order to address this issue, the chapter shows how different endeavors of repatriation include and/or exclude the experiences of women, their trauma, abuses, and needs. It also shows how women perceive repatriation and what they expect to see upon returning to Myanmar.

The chapter is divided into the following sections: (a) research methods, (b) context of the Rohingya, (c) repatriation: global scenario and the case of the Rohingya, (d) Rohingya women, and (e) consequences of non-inclusive repatriation.

Methodology

The chapter draws on both the empirical and secondary sources of data. The empirical data were collected through field visits from 2014 to 2024. It mainly employed qualitative strategies. Semi-structured individual interviews and Focused Group Discussions (FGDs) were conducted with the Rohingya men and women eighteen years and above, national and international NGO workers, and policymakers. For secondary sources, the study relies on the existing literature as well as national and international media reports of the same timeframe. Participants were recruited through my personal network. The number of male respondents was higher than that of females.

The next section of this chapter focuses on the context of the Rohingya, which is important to understand the dynamics of repatriation, in what ways Rohingya women view repatriation, and how their voice is included and/or excluded in repatriation.

Context of the Rohingya Crisis

Bangladesh hosts the highest number of Rohingya who fled their own country, Myanmar. Historically, Myanmar – a land of diverse ethnic communities

– has never recognized the rights of all ethnic groups in its land. The Rohingya are excluded from Myanmar's officially recognized 135 ethnic groups. In fact, the exclusion of Rohingya in their own land was rooted in the past even before the independence of Myanmar. The British colonizers, historically, started the exclusion of the Rohingya. Clearly, colonization was a male-dominated patriarchal process – as well as a Western idea – where Rohingya women always simply became the witnesses and the victims of the consequences of the decisions taken by their male-dominated society. Neither the British colonizers in the past nor the Myanmar government at present looked at the importance of considering women's participation in the decision-making process.

It was all about demonstrating masculinity because "masculinity itself is both a colonial legacy, and an overtly western notion" (Prianti, 2019, p. 701). History shows that colonizers were men who, as noted by Connell (2005), were desperate "to conquer and silence others, who were perceived to lack masculine characteristics, such as female and colonized subjects" (Prianti, 2019, p. 701). As a result, instead of one's birthplace, the "British Empire in Burma created identities based on people's religions and ethnicities, as evident through the creation of the census in 1872" (Yusuf, 2014, p. 2). This is one of the many decisions that created a greater division between local Burmese and other ethnicities in Myanmar.

The first exodus of Rohingya to Bangladesh happened in 1796, and their descendants returned to Burma in 1885, after almost one hundred years of the exodus. It shows that the Rohingyas' connection to Bangladesh is longstanding, although Rohingyas hold a sense of belonging to Burma, not Bangladesh. On the one hand, as shown in Pittaway (2008), the Rohingya Muslims "were promised that if they supported the British, they would be given their own national area, but the British later reneged that promise" (p. 86). On the other, the religious predisposition and racism of the Burmese government have led to persecution, ethnic cleansing, and finally, genocide against the Rohingya Muslims in their own land (Sultana, 2019). Such discriminatory legacy was carried out by the Burmese military that registered all of its citizens prior to a national census in 1977 except the Rohingya (Pittaway, 2008). This event caused extreme violence, widespread killings, and rape; 200,000 stateless Rohingyas were pushed to Bangladesh by the military authority of Burma in 1978 (Loescher & Milner, 2008; Ullah, 2011). Because of consistent persecution in Burma, another major wave of 210,000 and 250,000 Burmese Rohingyas fled from Burma to neighboring Bangladesh between December 1991 and March 1992 (Un High Commisioner for Refugees, 2001).

After a series of unsuccessful negotiations between the government of Bangladesh and the UNHCR, as well as some forms of repatriation and refoulement (forcible return of refugees), 32,000 registered Rohingya have been housed in the two camps for years ("Bangladesh Plans to move Rohingya," 2015, n.p.) in Cox's Bazar district of Bangladesh, while the majority of them remained as "unregistered," managing temporary shelters in the nearby villages in Cox's Bazar. The latest exodus of the Rohingya happened in 2017. Altogether, according to the UN Resource Information Center (May 3, 2024), the number of Rohingya in Bangladesh has reached 1.1 million.

Their statelessness, lack of identity, and uncertainty with repatriation add multiple layers of vulnerability in the lives of Rohingya men and women differently.

Repatriation: Global Scenario and the Case of the Rohingya

According to the UNHCR's prescribed formula, there are three "durable solutions" (Crisp, 1984, p. 73). These are reintegration – assimilation of the refugees in the host countries, repatriation – return of refugees to their country of origin, and resettlement – sending the refugees to a third country. From the beginning of the Rohingya crisis, the government of Bangladesh has made its position clear on two matters regarding the Rohingya: the first, the Rohingya reside in Bangladesh temporarily and, the second, repatriation is the only solution to this crisis. Therefore, reintegration and resettlement were never on the priority list of Bangladesh.

Although Rohingya repatriation has turned into a complicated geopolitical issue, this is the "only solution" to the Rohingya crisis, according to Bangladesh, until the autocratic regime ends in 2024. As a host country, Bangladesh did not explore other viable solutions because of its firm position on repatriating the Rohingya. The interim government, however, has been looking for pragmatic alternative options such as creating a "safe zone guaranteed by UN" for displaced people in Rakhine (The Business Standard, October 14, 2024) while it did not discard the idea of repatriation. But what is the status of the repatriation of refugees across the world then?

Repatriation cases of refugees in African countries are perhaps good examples to use here. Although the success and failure of these repatriation cases are contested, they draw huge attention in the discussion of refugee repatriation. In Masuku and Nkala's (2018) word, "the refugee crisis in Africa is determined by the nature of the conflicts that have taken place" (p. 94) and "unresolved socio-economic and political insecurity" (p. 97), making refugee repatriation much harder than in other places. Ethiopian returnees from Djibouti in 1983, the 1989 Namibian repatriation exercise from Angola, the return migration to Somalia from Kenya in 1993–94, and the major Mozambican repatriation of 1994 are some of these repatriations that were widely criticized due to a failure to make these returns voluntary in the true sense.

Namibian returnees' case is often considered successful since all of them wanted to return to their homeland, but inadequate options for employment, limited support, and inhospitable attitude of the government raised questions about the sustainability of repatriation. On the other hand, none of the refugees "interviewed in March 1983 was willing to leave for Ethiopia, and some said would rather drown in the sea than return" (Crisp, 1984, p. 79). Conflicts, political and social complexities, and other factors were responsible for the unwillingness of the Ethiopian refugees. The return of the Somalian refugees from Kenya in 1993–1994 is often considered a successful example of repatriation to Somalia from Kenya in 1993 and 1994.

All the above examples show that repatriation is not an isolated issue. It involves multiple organizations, requires the consideration of different factors, and various initiatives in the post-repatriation period to make the returns of the refugees sustainable.

According to the UNHCR, its role is to assist "governmental and private efforts to promote voluntary repatriation or assimilation within new national communities" (Art. 8(c) of the UNHCR Statute). The article confirms that UNHCR's role is neither to initiate nor to work with the government on the repatriation issue but to provide support to the host country if an initiative for repatriation is undertaken. Therefore, expecting UNHCR – who is entrusted with the task of ensuring the protection of the refugees – and other development agencies – who have been engaged in providing services to the Rohingya in Bangladesh for a long time – cannot be considered a pragmatic idea. For instance, the UNHCR supported the initiatives taken for the repatriation of the Namibian refugees "to ensure that repatriation is voluntary; to take "appropriate action" to assist in the return of exiles within six weeks of adoption" (Mwase, 1990, p. 115).

Similarly, the international community has come forward with relief and sympathy for the Rohingya but not with the political and strategic support Bangladesh needed to make Myanmar agree to take the Rohingya back. Clearly, the investments of the US, China, Russia, Japan, Singapore, and other economically powerful countries in Myanmar are an important factor for these countries not to raise their voice on the Rohingya repatriation issue. That will surely affect both parties' economic interests.

Similar to other repatriation cases, rare or no participation of the refugees is noticed in the decision-making process of repatriation. But in the meetings and dialogues, it is the male representatives of government or other stakeholders who conduct the discussions, measure the challenges, and assess the possibilities of repatriation. Rohingya voice is almost mute here. The people who have gone through persecution, violence, ethnic cleansing, and genocide in their country of origin, their subjective understanding of returning home cannot be the same as that of the diplomats and political stakeholders. Therefore, the repatriation plan may not be durable in the end because of the absence of Rohingya voice.

Secondly, even though very few Rohingya men are included in some of the bilateral meetings and/or visits on repatriation, Rohingya women are not included. The patriarchal nature of various organizations involved in holding meetings and discussions for Rohingya repatriation rarely thinks about the inclusion of both male and female Rohingya in the repatriation initiative. It must be acknowledged that there may be similarities in practical gender needs for male and female, but strategic gender needs are different for male and female. Hence, excluding female Rohingya from the dialogues and meetings will lead to a biased and ineffective repatriation devoid of equality.

The following table – prepared on the basis of news and reports published in the top national media in Bangladesh in 2022 and 2023 – presents a summary of the meetings organized/visits made on the Rohingya repatriation issue. The participation of female Rohingya in these initiatives is quite insignificant.

S.No.	*Activities*	*Date*	*Actors/People Involved*	*No. of Male/ Female*	*Outcomes*
1	The Foreign Minister held a meeting with the US State Department's Assistant Secretary of State for Population, Refugees, and Immigration at the Foreign Service Academy on Bailey Road in the capital.	6–8 December 2022	The Minister of Foreign Affairs (Bangladesh) and the Assistant Secretary of State for Population, Refugees, and Migration	1 male and 1 female official	The US State Department's Assistant Secretary of State for Population, Refugees, and migration agreed to Rohingya repatriation.
2	Chinese Ambassador to Bangladesh talked about Rohingya Repatriation in a Handover Ceremony of Medical Supplies from Embassy of China in Bangladesh.	10 November 2023	The Chinese Ambassador and the Hospital Superintendent	Not mentioned	No outcome
3	A Rohingya delegation team visited Rakhine.	5 May 2023	20 Rohingya representatives and 7 Bangladeshi officials	17 male and 3 female Rohingya	The delegation team saw the environment is not favorable for repatriation.

(*Continued*)

S.No.	*Activities*	*Date*	*Actors/People Involved*	*No. of Male/ Female*	*Outcomes*
4	A Myanmar Delegation Team came to Cox Bazar to talk about repatriation.	31 October to 1 November 2023	36 people in the Myanmar Delegation	Not mentioned	The Delegation talked to 100 Rohingya families for repatriation and verified information of 180 Rohingya families.
5	The Director general-level talked about the repatriation of 3,000 Rohingyas in Nay Pyi Taw.	2–4 September 2023	Director General of the Myanmar Department of the Ministry of Foreign Affairs and Director General Political AUNGK	2 male officials	Two Myanmar Delegation teams came to Cox bazar to talk to the Rohingya.
6	China's special envoy for Asia discussed with Bangladesh government about the repatriation of 1,176 Rohingya.	30 July to 1 August 2023	China's Special Envoy for Asian Affairs, Foreign Minister of Bangladesh, Foreign Secretary of Bangladesh	3 male officials	They made a model village in Myanmar for Rohingya repatriation.
7	Prime minister of Bangladesh call on a farewell for Australian High Commissioner in Dhaka at her Ganabhaban in Dhaka.	24 December 2023	PM of Bangladesh, Australian High Commissioner, Prime Minister's Press Secretary, and Prime Minister's Principal Secretary of Bangladesh	6 male and 2 female officials	Australian High Commissioner committed to provide $235M for Rohingya Repatriation.

(Continued)

S.No.	Activities	Date	Actors/People Involved	No. of Male/ Female	Outcomes
8	Chinese Special Envoy for Asian Affairs came to Dhaka to talk with government official about Rohingya repatriation.	30–31 July 2023	Chinese Special Envoy for Asian Affairs, Foreign Minister, and Foreign Secretary of Bangladesh	3 male officials	Chinese Special Envoy for Asian Affairs visited Myanmar to discuss with the concerned authorities of repatriation.
9	The OIC and the European Union (EU) jointly gave a proposal to the United Nations about Rohingya repatriation.	15 November 2023	The Permanent Rep of Bangladesh to the UN and other 114 countries	Not mentioned	The United Nations accepted Rohingya Resolution.
10	A Pilot project is underway for Rohingya Repatriation.	May 2023 to Present	Bangladesh and Myanmar Military Government	Not mentioned	UN Expert suggests to suspend Pilot Project.
11	Second time a Myanmar Delegation team visited Teknaf.	1 November 2023	28 Myanmar Delegators	Not mentioned	The Myanmar Delegation team verified information of 60 Rohingya families.
12	Bangladcsh and Myanmar have discussed the repatriation of 3,000 Rohingya refugees.	September to December 2023	Bangladesh and Myanmar Officials	Not mentioned	No outcome

In fact, the above table reaffirms the uncertainty of repatriation, the lack of women's representation in the decision-making process of repatriation, and the very minimum representation of Rohingya women in it. Some of these meetings were part of a tripartite initiative mediated by China. Chinese Special Envoy for Asian Affairs Deng Xijun visited Dhaka twice in the middle of 2023. In 2023, the meetings and visits between Bangladesh and Myanmar raised expectations that repatriation would finally start even if it is on a very small scale. Even in December 2023, Dhaka and Naypyidaw were "in talks for the repatriation of 3,000 Rohingyas by December" 2023 (Molla, 2023). No repatriation began even at the end of 2024.

The data used in the above table are from December 2022 to December 2023. During this time, it is shown in the above table that only three women from the Rohingya community were involved in the preliminary initiatives related to the repatriation as opposed to seventeen men from their community. Such lower representation of Rohingya women confirms that Rohingya repatriation is a male-centric process. Regarding the Rohingya women's poor representation in repatriation initiatives, a Rohingya woman whom the author met in 2023 said,

> What the politicians do determines our fate. We are desperate to go back to our own country, but the situation there (in Myanmar) needs to be conducive. Otherwise, we Rohingya women will continue facing discrimination and violence even in our own land. No Rohingya woman wants that. I can't think of more. I just want to live an easy and peaceful life with my family.

Historically, conflict, killing, and genocide, etc. were instigated and carried out by men. The resolution of conflicts also came from men. Women were mainly in the roles of victims, passive witnesses of the events, and rarely active role players in a male-centric crisis to solve it. Viewing women in a process like repatriation has never been a norm. That is why it is usual to keep the Rohingya women outside the dialogues and meetings.

Rohingya Women

Culturally, and according to the findings of this study, Rohingya women are not very willing or confident to lead a team or work closely with men on decisions like repatriation. Because, since childhood, they were taught that these were "man's job". For Rohingya women and girls as well as the entire Rohingya community, marriage is the primary tool through which social and economic security can be ensured, as they are discouraged from working outside of the household (Inter Sector Coordiantion Group, 2017; Ripoll, 2018). As a result, education, skill development training, or access to technology or the internet are given less priority for Rohingya women both by themselves and by their male counterparts. However, a study with the Rohingya refugees in Nepal found that 77% of the male respondents owned cell phones compared to 37% of the female respondents out of the 51% of respondents who had internet access, and these Rohingya women held positive attitudes toward a woman in earning, accessing education, decision-making, and mobility (Keeni & Takashino, 2024).

On the one hand, there is an unwillingness of Rohingya women to gain access to education, information, technology, etc., and thus to be away from making decisions on issues like repatriation. On the other, the continuation of seeing men in the role of decision-makers has become a usual pattern, which affects the perception of both men and women in the society that men are more capable than women in handling this kind of "outside business". Both tendencies reflect the views of Talcott Parsons, Durkheim, and other sociologists of the early days. They believed that women were more suitable for domestic work than outside activities. These sociologists' views are manifested in the narrative of a Rohingya woman in Kutupalong camp: "I pass my day with cooking and worrying for our future. I heard about 'repatriation', but I think men of our community will manage it".

The Rohingya women, as part of their sociocultural norms, are taught to be submissive, passive, and dependent. They are not taught to be in the leading position but to be led by men. Moreover, after all the violence and lawlessness that the Rohingya women experienced during the genocide and ethnic cleansing, obviously, they may not have any strength left to raise their voices on repatriation. As a result, a male-centric approach has been employed in the entire process of repatriation that gives the impression that the Rohingya men's participation addresses the need for both men and women. Rohingya women, thus, are deprived of expressing their concerns and needs.

Their Subjective Perceptions, Unawareness, the Use of Religion

Many of today's Rohingya women do not know that there was Rohingya representation in the Burmese parliament even in the middle of the 20th century. Aye Nyunt, also known as Zurah Begum, was elected as one of the five Rohingya Muslim members of Parliament in the 1951 general election. Due to internal political changes, the spread of Buddhist nationalism, and strong trade and business ties with the global superpowers, Myanmar has become desperate to wipe out the Rohingya's existence in their land and has very skillfully conducted genocide against the Rohingya. As a result, today the Rohingya women's status as social and political beings is unrecognized. Such a lack of recognition not only creates barriers for them to achieve their rights but also shapes their subjective perception of themselves. The narratives of the Rohingya women depict that many of them consider themselves subordinate to men, as stated by one of my research participants at Kutupalong camp at Ukhia,

> We are women, we are bound to listen to what the male says. Because it is the husband in the family who has the absolute right to determine the right and wrong for the family. It's our destiny. What to do?

Rohingya women were oppressed and had very limited opportunities to gain knowledge, strengthen their skills, and take part in the decision-making process in the community and raise their voices on social issues during their lives in Myanmar. In Bangladesh, there is no reason to see any change in their situation. They pass down their subjective understanding regarding stereotypical gender roles from generation to generation. Such understanding is often influenced by their subjective religious faith, as demonstrated by Jannat, Sifat, and Khisa's (2023) study that the Rohingya women believe that "God will be angry if they use contraception while in physical relations with their husband" (p. 860). The young Rohingya girls receive this kind of message from the elderly females and follow them blindly. Such a situation allows early marriage, polygamy, and gender-based violence among the Rohingya community.

Since they use religion to justify their beliefs, at this point it is necessary to look at what religion talks about the status of women. The Quran refers to women and men as one another's "protectors" (Al Baqarah, 71) because the couples are "garments" for one another (At Tawbah, 187). The Rohingya women, from their early childhood, generally read the Quran as a holy book, but not as a source of guidance for them. As a result, they remain in the dark regarding the messages they should know and follow in their lives, and their society does not encourage them to do so.

The Intervention of Development Agencies

Some changes among the Rohingya female youth are noticeable in Bangladesh camps these days because of the intervention of the international development agencies that have undertaken several projects for skill development, improving literacy skills, and even income generation for the Rohingya females inside the camps. Also, initiatives of various NGOs help the Rohingya women gain confidence, overcome genocide-related trauma, and learn to raise their voices. Through arts, music, and handicrafts, the Rohingya women can express their current situation and future dreams. One of the young Rohingya women, after the accomplishment of a teamwork to draw a mural, shares her feelings,

> I never felt this kind of joy and sense of fulfillment. Since 2017, I have been haunted by trauma for losing some of my family members in Myanmar and I had thought that I pass my entire life crying. But art gave me strength to look back at myself and work for my own life. I can also be an example for others to overcome their sorrows and pains, and find meaning of life. I am now thinking of working as a community worker.

Social Construction of Gender Roles

Very few Rohingya women are able to take part in outside-home activities due to the social construction of gender roles in their community. Since Rohingya women are expected to be at home, many prefer not to get involved in these kinds of projects. Seeing Rohingya women sewing clothes at home for commercial purposes, however, is well accepted in their community. But most of the Rohingya women, after receiving skill development training, fail to utilize their skills and earn. One of the 38-year-old Rohingya women from a camp at Kutupalong showed her underutilized sewing machine in her room, saying that she did not know how to market her skill and get orders from the camp residents. She received tailoring training in the middle of 2021 and received just a few orders for dressmaking sporadically until 2023. In her words, "what's the point of a training if it does not help you to get orders and earn?"

Such evidence denotes that the support mechanism for the Rohingya's employment is heavily limited and it affects the lives of the Rohingya women negatively.

Stereotypical Structural Patterns

Although the "maternal mortality rate in Rohingya refugee camps in Bangladesh is significantly lower than in other refugee camps" (Jannat, Sifat, & Khisa, 2023, p. 861), Yousuf et al.'s (2021) study show that the Rohingya women have been facing a series of challenges such as gender-based violence, being abandoned by their husbands in the camps, early marriages, reproductive health issues that include teenage and unsafe pregnancies, and unsafe childbirth. Their material and social needs remain unfulfilled due to the former, and they fail to become self-aware enough to assess their beliefs due to the latter. Thus, not knowing the name of Zurah Begum – a female political leader of their own ethnic community – is not unusual.

Moreover, because of early marriage in the Rohingya community, female children lose their childhood and face unsafe and risky pregnancies. Intersectionality – being girl children, having no scope for education, being in poverty, being stateless and insecure, being in a patriarchal society, and being victims of community traditions – plays an important role in shaping the Rohingya girls' early marriages. In the words of a Rohingya mother of three young girl children, "being a mother of girl children is like you spend sleepless nights until you send them to in-law's house". When asked the reason, she said,

> Look, grown up girls are safer in their husband's house than in their parent's house. Girls are often bullied, assaulted, harassed in the camp. I'm very worried about my girls' safety. If something happens, how can I protect them? Nobody will marry them. What's the point of sending them to schools if they are assaulted before marriage? I heard a young girl was raped (by a Rohingya man) last week because she was pretty and was unmarried.

The above narrative refers to the concern of the Rohingya about the safety of their young daughters in the camp environment, which is one of the key reasons for early marriage among the Rohingya. However, it is also noticeable that education is not on the list of priorities for the girls as education fails to save the girls from assaults, according to the Rohingya mother. Therefore, they think that being stigmatized by their own community members for being assaulted can only be prevented through marriage. But what if the husband himself is abusive and/or fails to protect the wife? Or what if the husband marries another woman without the consent of the first wife? To respond, the mother said, "that's her (the wife's) fate". Polygamy among the Rohingya is common, but no known research shows the exact percentage or rate of polygamy among them. It is known as a bad act, yet their tradition is to accept what men do. Traditional patriarchal practices along with poverty and an unsafe camp environment encourage early marriages.

Bhasanchar-Ukhia: No Substantial Difference

My visit to Bhasanchar in 2023 reveals that Rohingya girls' access to only rudimentary education, women's access to limited healthcare, and no employment opportunities except for one garment factory make them feel detached from their relatives living in the Cox's Bazar camp. The relocation indeed provided them better housing compared to that of the Cox's Bazar camp, yet their longing to meet the known faces in Cox's Bazar, seeing children grow up without education, and fear of terrorists in the isolated camp of Bhasanchar make them feel further isolated, which affects their hope for repatriation. In one of the Rohingya women's words,

> I do not see any substantial difference between coming here (at Bhasanchar) and living in Cox's Bazar. I had some hope for repatriation. I felt like it was just the river (river Naf), if the situation would have been normal there (in Myanmar), I would have simply crossed the river to reach there and reunite with my extended family. But now, it feels like I am moving far way gradually from that hope.

The relocation decisions from Cox's Bazar to Bhasanchar never anticipated the feeling of isolation the Rohingya might have. Some of the female participants in Bhasanchar also informed that a good number of Rohingya women moved to Bhasanchar just because of their husbands' choice.

Gender-Based Violence

Apart from feeling isolated, Rohingya women are victims of gender-based violence in the camp. History shows that during the Rwandan genocide in 1994 and the war in Bosnia and Herzegovina from 1992 to 1995, GBV was considered a strategic tool to apply to the women (Priddy, Berry, Doman, &

Ahmed, 2022). This intersectionality – being women, being displaced, being in a conflicting situation – creates the scope of oppression against women. A similar situation applies to the Rohingya women. They are forced to endure GBV, which has been observed by Yousuf, Salam, Akter, and Salam's (2021) work as they found that the Rohingya women "are reported to be harassed while performing essential tasks, such as collecting water, using the latrine or feelings of 'shame' around using water, sanitation and hygiene (WASH) facilities" (p. 164). Some of these are practical gender needs, while others are strategic.

Rohingya women are victims of rape, trafficking, harmful traditional practices, forced early marriages, or domestic violence. In Bangladesh, GBV may not follow the same pattern as it did in "Myanmar's culture of violence against ethnic minority women" (Priddy, Berry, Doman, & Ahmed, 2022, p. 2), Rohingya women in Cox's Bazar are in fear of being raped by their own terrorist groups even inside their camp, are often trafficked by human traffickers, and are following some harmful traditional practices (such as early and forced marriage). Domestic violence is taken for granted by the Rohingya women and by their society. Their heightened sense of insecurity, along with subjective interpretation of religious guidance, makes them believe that it is okay to be beaten by their husband. Because if the husband abandons the wife, she has no place to go to seek justice.

Consequences of Non-inclusive Repatriation

Repatriation without considering the views of the Rohingya women may jeopardize their situation after their return to Myanmar, if they ever return. They may continue facing discrimination in education, health, employment, and other areas and may experience violence in domestic and social spheres. Hence, the repatriation process must listen to the expectations and thoughts of the Rohingya women to convert it into an inclusive repatriation. Without considering the importance of education, access to health, opportunities to develop their marketable skills and utilize these skills through their engagement in income-generating activities depending upon their interest, repatriation of the Rohingya will give birth to a new dimension of gender-based violence and frustrations among the Rohingya women, which will surely affect the Rohingya community. In order to facilitate the Rohingya women's access to services in their post-repatriation lives, the ongoing meetings and decisions regarding repatriation must consider both the practical and strategic gender needs of Rohingya women.

The six factors – their religious identity, gender, ethnic identity, level of education, poverty, and statelessness – affect the lives of the Rohingya women in Bangladesh. That is why the service providers and various stakeholders, including government bodies responsible for managing the Rohingya, need to include the women representatives from the Rohingya community in the discussions on repatriation.

Conclusion

The repatriation reality for the Rohingya refugee does not provide a promising picture. On the one hand, Myanmar showed no interest in it. On the other, Bangladesh's fragile diplomacy failed to create pressure on Myanmar to take their people back. As discussed in this chapter, globally, there are little or no successful instances of repatriation of the refugees that were voluntary, safe, and dignified.

Although repatriation of the Rohingya should take place between Bangladesh and Myanmar, the pressure, business ties, and political interest and relations between and among superpowers affect the decision and execution of repatriation significantly. Crisp (2019) suggests that "the repatriation process should become much more participatory and inclusive" (p. 22) so that the refugees – the subjects of repatriation – can exercise their agency and their representation is ensured. However, representation can be effective and equitable when both men and women are given a chance when the repatriation plan is shared with them and let them express their concerns and opinions. This may sound idealistic, but this can make Rohingya repatriation safe, voluntary, durable, and inclusive.

References

Bangladesh plans to move Rohingya refugees to island in the south. *The Guardian*. Retrieved from https://www.theguardian.com/world/2015/may/28/bangladesh-plans-to-move-rohingya-refugees-to-island-in-the-southConnell, R. W., & Messerschmidt, J. W. (2005).Hegemonic Masculinity: Rethinking the Concept: Rethinking the Concept. *Gender & Society*, *19*(6), 829-859.

Crisp, J. (1984, September). The politics of repatriation: Ethiopian refugees in Djibuti, 1977–83. *Review of African Political Economy*, *30*, 73–82.

Crisp, J. (2019, October). *Repatriation principles under pressure*. FMReview. Retrieved from https://www.fmreview.org/sites/default/files/FMRdownloads/en/return/crisp.pdf

Inter Sector Coordination Group. (December 17, 2017).ISCG Situation Report: Rohingya Refugee Crisis, Cox's Bazar. *Inter Sector Coordination Group*. Retrieved from https://reliefweb.int/report/bangladesh/iscg-situation-report-rohingya-refugee-crisis-cox-s-bazar-17-december-2017

Jannat, S., Sifat, R. I., & Khisa, M. (2023). Sexual and Reproductive Health Conditions of Women: Insights from Rohingya Refugee Women in Bangladesh. *Sexuality Research and Social Policy. 20* (1), 855–868

Keeni, M., & Takashino, N. (2024). Between tradition and change: Impact of displacement on gender norm perceptions among Rohingya refugees in Nepal. *Women's Studies International Forum, 103*. Retrieved from https://www.sciencedirect.com/science/article/pii/S0277539524000074?dgcid=rss_sd_all

Loescher, G., & Milner, J. (2008). Burmese refugees in South and Southeast Asia: A comparative regional analysis. In G. Loescher, J. Milner, E. Newman, & G. Toeller (Eds.), *Protracted refugee situations: Political, human rights and security implications* (pp. 305–355). United Nations University Press.
Maku, S., & Nkala, S. (2018). Patterns of the refugee cycle in Africa: A hazardous cycle with no end in sight? *Journal of African Union Studies*, 7(3), 89–105. Retrieved from https://www.jstor.org/stable/26890366
olla, M. A. M. (2023, September 6). Rohingya Repatriation: Likely to start in a few months | What are the challenges of repatriation of Rohingya? *The Daily Star.* Retrieved from https://www.thedailystar.net/rohingya-influx/news/rohingya-repatriation-likely-start-few-months-3411986
Mwase, Ngila R. L. 1990. 'Title:The repatriation, rehabilitation and resettlement of Namibian refugees at independence'. *The Community Development Journal: An International Journal for Community Workers, 25(2)*
Pittaway, E. (2008). The Rohingya refugees in Bangladesh: A failure of the international protection regime. In H. Adelman (Ed.), *Protracted displacement in Asia: No place to call home* (pp. 83–106). Ashgate Publishing Limited.
Prianti, D. D. (2019). The identity politics of masculinity as a colonial legacy. *Journal of Intercultural Studies*, *40*(6), 700–719. https://doi.org/10.1080/07256868.2019.1675612
Priddy, Grace, Zoe Doman, Emily Berry, and Saleh Ahmed. "Gender-Based Violence in a Complex Humanitarian Context: Unpacking the Human Sufferings among Stateless Rohingya Women." *Ethnicities* 22, no. 2 (2022): 215–232.
Rahman, A. (2019, November 11). Rohingya crisis – No solution is in sight. *South Asia Journal.* Retrieved from https://southasiajournal.net/rohingya-crisis-no-solution-is-in-sight/
Ripoll, S. (2018). *Social and cultural factors shaping health and nutrition, wellbeing and protection of the Rohingya within a Humanitarian Context.* Institute of Development Studies / UNICEF.
Sultana, I. Z. (2019). Rohingyas in Bangladesh: Owning Rohingya Identity in Disowning Spaces. *Doctoral Thesis.* York University.Retrieved from https://yorkspace.library.yorku.ca/server/api/core/bitstreams/31bda16f-bab6-4469-b26f-f8c54439bf42/content
Ullah, A. (2011). Rohingya refugees to Bangladesh: Historical exclusions and contemporary marginalization. *Journal of Immigrant & Refugee Studies*, *9*, 139–161.
UN High Commissioner for Refugees. (December 1, 2001).Inter-Parliamentary Union (IPU), *Refugee Protection: A Guide to International Refugee Law*, Retrieved from https://www.refworld.org/policy/legalguidance/unhcr/2001/31709
UNHCR, CARE, and ActionAid. (2020, September). An intersectional analysis of gender amongst Rohingya refugees and host communities in Cox's Bazar, Bangladesh. An Inter-Agency Research Report.
Yousuf, R., Salam, M. M., Akter, S., & Salam, A. (2021). Safety and security of sexual-reproductive health and gender-based violence among Rohingya refugee women in Bangladesh. *International Journal of Human and Health Sciences*, *5*(2), 163–170.
Yusuf. A. (July 3, 2014). Betrayed, denied, and abandoned.*The Daily Star.* Retrieved from https://www.thedailystar.net/betrayed-denied-and-abandoned-31430

14

THE QUEST FOR ROHINGYA REPATRIATION

What Happened and What's Next?

Ali Riaz

Introduction

In August 2017, when the Rohingyas from the Myanmar's Rakhine State began to flee in the face of 'genocide' (US Department of State 2022) perpetrated by the Myanmar Army (Tatmadaw) and took refuge in Bangladesh, the government of Bangladesh, after initial hesitation, opened the border and provided the shelter. Eight years have passed since. The number of refugees has swelled to 1.5 million from the initial 700,000 as more Rohingyas have crossed the border under continued persecution by the Myanmar military, governments in both Bangladesh and Myanmar have changed, the political landscape of the Rakhine State has significantly transformed with insurgent groups capturing a large swath of land, cases filed against Myanmar in the International Court of Justice (ICJ) and International Criminal Court (ICC) seem to have stalled, and international resolve to bring justice to the Rohingyas and repatriate the refugees has weakened despite new efforts in September 2025 with the UN organized high level international conference. These changes and developments have left the refugees in limbo; they continue to live in squalid conditions in the world's largest refugee camps, and desperation is setting in among them, especially among the youth. The likelihood of repatriation of the refugees seems to be fading.

The exodus, which was the third major since 1977 and unprecedented in terms of scale, scope, and rapidity, not only brought more than 700,000 persecuted people at the beginning but also revealed that the actions were well planned by the Myanmar regime and it continued in the subsequent years. Unlike the two previous occasions – in 1978–79 and 1991–92, there

DOI: 10.4324/9781003771890-14

is little indication that the refugees will return home. After the 2021 coup in Myanmar, the question of whether the refugees will ever be able to repatriate gained salience, and since 2023, a series of other global crises, for example, the war in Ukraine, atrocities in Gaza, as well as other developments have put the Rohingya refugee issue on the back burner. Since 2023, competing priorities and donor fatigue have contributed to the decline in aid (International Crisis Group 2023), and in 2025, the Joint Response Plan (JRP), a coordinated effort by over 100 partners, including UN agencies and NGOs, to support Rohingya refugees and their host communities in Bangladesh, has received only 35% of its total need. The renewed offensive of Ethnic Armed Groups (EAO) in various parts of Myanmar, especially in the northeast since October 2023, brought Myanmar back into the news cycle (Hein 2024) but it has also complicated the situation (ICG 2023).

It is against this background that the chapter explores the experiences of previous instances of repatriation of Rohingyas and compares them with the possibility of repatriation of the refugees who have arrived since 2017. It is worth recalling that besides three major exoduses, there were other instances when Rohingyas crossed the border to Bangladesh.

In this chapter, I argue that while the previous repatriation efforts were problematic on various counts, especially whether it was voluntary repatriation and whether these efforts had ignored the root causes, the issue of repatriation of the 2017 refugees has become highly complex for a host of reasons. These include the geostrategic interests of China and India, and domestic and regional political considerations of the Bangladesh government headed by Sheikh Hasina until August 2024. The Hasina regime was toppled in a popular uprising in July-August 2024. Nobel laureate Professor Muhammad Yunus has been heading an interim government since August 8, 2024, and is trying to pursue a more balanced foreign policy.

Persecution and expulsion of Rohingyas from Myanmar have a long history and are intrinsically tied to Myanmar's domestic politics, ethnic composition, and system of governance (Bulbel, Islam and Khan 2022; Uddin 2021; Ware and Laoutides 2018; Ibrahim 2006). However, this chapter only refers to the immediate socio-political-economic events pertinent to the repatriation issues of the Rohingyas in three episodes as a backdrop to each exodus.

Five sections follow the introduction. The first and second sections explore the extent of the refugee crisis in 1977–78 and 1991–92 respectively, the steps taken for repatriation and the roles various actors played. In the third section, the ongoing situation from the arrival of the Rohingyas in 2017 is examined. The fourth section discusses the causes of the current stalemate in the repatriation process. Some concluding remarks constitute the fifth section, which offers four possible paths forward.

The Influx and the Repatriation: 1978–1979

The first large-scale movement of Rohingyas began in April 1978 in the wake of a military operation by the Burmese military, reportedly against Muslim insurgents called Mujahideen. There have been past experiences of insurgencies by the Muslim community of Arakan since the 1940s against the government's discriminatory policies, but these insurgencies were tamed through security operations in 1951 and 1954. The government policy of designating the Rohingyas as 'illegal immigrants' in the 1963 census reignited an insurgency spearheaded by the Rohingya Patriotic Front (RPF) and Arakan Rohingya Islamic Front (ARIF). However, by the mid-1970s the activities ceased to exist due to the actions of the military regime of General Ne Win (Yager 1982, X).

The security operation launched in early 1978 by the military took a vicious turn by April as a reign of terror was unleashed under the more robust operation named Operation Nagamin. The goal of the operation was clear – to drive the 'foreigners' out of Burma 'back' to Bangladesh. The tactics used were brutal – burning villages and destroying mosques combined with killings, arrests, rape, and harassment of Rohingyas. The justification was to 'contain the secessionist move of the Arakanese Muslims' and 'the threat to the national security from the Arakan Community Party (ACP)' (Huq 1993, 133). But the entire operation evidently became an 'ethnic cleansing' (Coll 1992).

By July 1978, more than 200,000 Rohingyas took refuge in the camps in Bangladesh. The stream of refugees that crossed the borders overwhelmed the Bangladesh government as it was totally oblivious to what was occurring on the other side of the border. The exodus came as a surprise to the Bangladesh government (Huq 1993, 135), as it was under the impression that the military background of both General Ziaur Rahman and General Ne Win had created a rapport between them. Then President Ziaur Rahman visited Burma in July 1977, and he 'had been assured that the people genuinely settled for several generations would be treated fairly, even if they had no certificates' (Sarkar 2021).

On 9 July 1978, Bangladesh signed a bilateral agreement with the Myanmar regime, without any international supervision or third-party involvement. There was strong opposition from the refugees about a hasty agreement for their repatriation, especially because they were afraid of facing continued persecution upon return. But it became evident from the beginning that Bangladesh, which was ill-equipped to deal with the large-scale refugees, was more interested in sending the refugees back under any circumstances. According to then Foreign Minister Muhammad Shamsul Huq – 'The Government of Bangladesh, ... felt that the sooner the refugees could be repatriated to their respective homes in Burma, the better it would be for all concerned' (Huq 1993, 139). In so doing, the Bangladesh government neither consulted the refugees nor involved international actors.

The agreement categorized the refugees into three groups – those who hold National Registration Certificates (NRC) and their families (Category A), those who could provide any documents as evidence of their residency in Burma (Category B), and those who have no documents regarding their residency (Category C) (Huq 1993, 141). Two essential elements of any repatriation were missing from the agreement – safety of the refugees upon return and their voluntary consent. The UNHCR expressed concerns when it gathered from interviews of the refugees that they were unaware of the agreement and 'would only would do so [i.e., return] if they have no other alternative left, meaning that Bangladesh government compels them to leave the country' (Dock 2020). By Fall, it became evident that the GOB is poised to adopt any tactic, including using force 'if necessary' (Lindquist 1979). In this vein, the government began withholding food and other essential assistance, with no serious objections from the UNHCR and other international organizations (Lindquist 1979; Jeff 2018, 13). This led to the high number of deaths in the refugee camps, which eventually stood between 10,000 and 12,000 (Lindquist 1979; Huq 1993; Human Rights Watch 1996; Jeff 2018). UNHCR later raised concerns and put public pressure for increasing the food ration and succeeded in raising it to previous levels, but in September 1978, it had agreed to help the Bangladesh government in its repatriation program (Jeff 2018, 14). The UNHCR also worked with the Burmese government to facilitate the return of refugees as its representative visited the country several times. The refugees, faced with malnutrition, disease, and scarcity of food combined with several incidents of violence, had started to agree to repatriation. By the end of 1979, almost 95% of the refugees returned home (Crisp, 20184–). According to one account, a total of 187,250 refugees were repatriated (Abrar 1996).

The entire crisis raised questions about the bilateral agreement, treatment of the refugees by the Bangladesh government, the role of the UNHCR and volunteerism in repatriation, not to mention the implication of repatriation without addressing the cause of the crisis in the first place. As for the agreement, one positive interpretation was that the agreement recognized the Rohingyas as lawful residents when it said that Burma was willing to accept the return of the lawful residents and accepted almost all of them (Corr 2016). However, the agreement also stipulated that the repatriation is contingent on 'furnish[ing] evidence of their residence in Burma, such as addresses or any other particulars'. As such, many of those listed under Category C were left out of the process and stayed back in the refugee camps. The implementation of the agreement and repatriation of the Rohingyas clearly showed that the process was far from voluntary.

The political situation within Bangladesh and Burma had facilitated the process of repatriation as well. The refugee issue received very little attention in Bangladesh, and the policymaking process was skewed in the sense that President Ziaur Rahman and his cabinet had the exclusive power to decide the course, including the agreement (Huq 1993, 140). On the other hand, the Burmese government was looking for an opportunity to save face. While the crisis engendered international condemnation, no other country became engaged in the process of negotiation and repatriation.

The repatriation process ended by December 1979, described by Bangladesh and by the UNHCR as successful, but without any follow-up to what fates the returnees faced upon return. Although the UNHCR maintained its presence in Bangladesh, especially with the few refugee camps that housed those who were either declined to return or were not accepted by Burmese authorities, there was no palpable effort to address the cause that promoted such a large-scale exodus.

The Second Wave and a Familiar Result: 1991–1992

In late 1991 when Bangladesh began encountering a new wave of Rohingya refugees from Burma, which had officially named itself Myanmar, significant changes occurred within the country with implications for all citizens, but notably for Rohingyas. The first was the changes in the Citizenship Law 1982, the second was the power grab of the military after the popular uprising in 1988, the third was holding a relatively fair election in 1990 delivering victory to the opposition National League for Democracy (NLD) led by Aung San Suu Kyi which was annulled by the military. Bangladesh also had a noteworthy political change – the democratization process had started in early 1991 with a newly elected government led by Khaleda Zia of the Bangladesh Nationalist Party (BNP), widow of former President General Ziaur Rahman.

The Burma Citizenship Act of 1982 based citizenship on ethnicity and recognized 135 ethnic groups but excluded Rohingyas. The law granted citizenship to individuals residing in Burma who could trace their family residency prior to 1823. The law created three categories of citizenship: the first category applied to ethnic Burmans and members of the Kachin, Kayah, Karen, Mon, Arakan Buddhists, Shan, and any other ethnic group present in Myanmar prior to 1823 (though they did not include Rohingya Muslims, rendering them stateless), and granted them full citizenship. The second category granted partial 'associate' citizenship to the children of mixed marriages where one parent fell into the first category, as well as to individuals who had lived in Myanmar for five consecutive years, or to individuals who lived in Myanmar for eight out of the ten years prior to independence. Associate citizens could earn an income but could not serve in political office. The third category applied to the offspring of immigrants who arrived in Myanmar during the period of British colonial rule. In so far as the Rohingyas are concerned, the law made them stateless. The 1988 power grab of the military, as an aftermath of a popular uprising challenging the government, was followed by a brutal crackdown costing at least 10,000 lives (USBCIS 1988). The ruling military elites renamed the governing entity as the State Law and Order Restoration Council (SLORC) and changed the country's name to Myanmar in 1991.

It is against this background that Myanmar's new regime launched a new military operation in 1991 called 'Pyi Thaya' (Clean and Beautiful Nation). The official version was that the operation was targeting 'foreigners' and was a response to the increasing strength of the Rohingya Solidarity Organization (RSO), but analysts have suggested that the operation was intended to distract from the fallout of the popular uprising and victory of the NLD. The operation subjected Rohingyas to summary execution, rape, assault, and destruction of property, to name a few. Faced with this situation, between December 1991 and March 1992, at least 210,000 Rohingyas took shelter in Bangladesh. At the very early stage of the emerging crisis, Amnesty International confirmed that Rohingyas had been subjected to and continue to experience gross violations of human rights within Myanmar (Saha 2001, 39).

Although there were some border skirmishes between the two countries and news was coming out of the Arakan state that the military had started a large-scale operation, Bangladesh authorities were least prepared for a repeat of the 1978–79 refugee situation. The initial reaction of the government was muted while the UNHCR started to accommodate the refugees within the camps which were housing a small number of Rohingyas who didn't return during the 1979 repatriation process. Soon the number overwhelmed both the UNHCR and the Bangladesh government. Bangladesh, however, did not turn to the UNHCR, but instead adopted a strategy of bilateral diplomacy even before the large-scale refugee exodus began (Kamaluddin 1992, 24). Bangladesh's choice as the mediator was China as it had the most significant influence over the SLORC. But China showed no interest in playing a role, let alone pressure Myanmar to take back the refugees. Within a short period, the Bangladesh government turned to the international community and began to officially involve the UNHCR.

In April 1992, with the appointment of Ambassador Jan Eliasson, Under-Secretary General for Humanitarian Affairs as a representative of the Secretary General Boutros Boutros Ghali, the international community became directly involved in the repatriation issue. The effort came at the heel of calls for sanctions against Myanmar by Western countries which the ASEAN countries were resisting (Richardson 1992). Ambassador Eliasson's trip to Bangladesh and Myanmar resulted in a Memorandum of Understanding (MOU) between the two countries on 28 April 1992. Two aspects of the MOU are worth noting. First, the MOU stipulated that repatriation would be 'safe and voluntary'; second, unlike the 1978 agreement, Myanmar added two clauses – that those to be repatriated must be 'Myanmarese lawful citizens' and 'Myanmarese society members', and that Myanmar would not take back anyone without proper documents. Both clauses provided an advantage to Myanmar in selecting who it would accept. The latter one was highly problematic as Rohingyas didn't receive the Citizenship Security Card issued in 1989, and any other documents they had were either lost as they fled or were left in their homes. Nevertheless, the date set for the repatriation to begin on 15 May failed as most of the refugees declined to return.

Both parties initially rejected the idea of UNHCR's involvement in the process, especially because Myanmar was opposed to the involvement of the UNHCR. But the UNHCR did get involved, particularly in screening. Yet, the repatriation process stalled for various reasons including clashes between Bangladesh's security forces and refugees. With credible reports that Bangladesh had begun forcibly repatriating Rohingyas, the UNHCR decided to disassociate from any repatriation process in December 1992 (UN 1992). After Bangladesh halted the repatriation in early January 1993, the UNHCR reestablished its participation and the repatriation process resumed with UNHCR participation in February. The relationship was formalized in May through a Memorandum of Understanding (MOU) which stipulated:

> [Bangladesh and the UNHCR] shall cooperate with each other to ensure safe and voluntary repatriation of Myanmar refugees who opt to return under existing conditions ... on the basis of their (refugees) own judgement of the situation in their country ... The two sides shall cooperate with each other to prevent any attempt by any side to interfere with the exercise of freedom of option by the refugees.

The MOU also stipulated that UNHCR will 'undertake promotional activities to motivate refugees to return home'. In the following months, especially after signing an MOU with the Myanmar government in November 1993, the promotional activities gradually became active encouragement on the part of the UNHCR. However, with these steps in place, large-scale repatriation resumed in January 1994. Several rounds of violent incidents in the refugee camps, clashes between locals and the refugees, allegations that the Bangladesh government is coercing the refugees, the lengthy process of the Myanmar government to slow down the repatriation process, and the cyclone in May intermittently halted repatriation. Also, there were some differences between the Bangladesh government and the UNHCR on the interpretation of clauses of the MOU.

Despite these serious flaws and inadequate measures to protect the returnees, between April 1994 and December 1995, about 236,000 Rohingya refugees were repatriated (Amnesty International 2004), leaving about 21,500 in the camps (Grundy-Warr and Wong 1997, 86). Another account suggests the number of returnees as 190,000 of 210,000 (Saha 2001, 43). In the subsequent years, the Bangladesh government continued to appeal to Myanmar to take back the remainder of the refugees to no avail.

The repatriation process succeeded in sending most of the Rohingyas back to Myanmar but failed at various levels. The most important aspect is the failure to address the central issue – lack of citizenship of the Rohingyas. The forced displacement of the Rohingyas after taking away their citizenship made them a stateless community (Chickera 2018, 2021 Awan 2021). The agreements between Bangladesh and Myanmar and between Myanmar and UNHCR have not ensured the safety and security of the Rohingyas after their return. Besides, the process of repatriation raised questions about whether the UNHCR had remained true to its mandate of voluntary repatriation (Dock 2020). All of these continued to haunt not only the Rohingyas but Bangladesh, which faced the largest ever Rohingya refugee crisis in 2017.

2017 Exodus and an Uncertain Future

On 25 August 2017, a clandestine group named Arakan Rohingya Salvation Army (ARSA) launched coordinated attacks on about 30 security outposts in Northern Rakhine State, which was followed by the Myanmar Army's 'unlawful and grossly disproportionate campaign of violence marked by killings, rape and other sexual violence, torture, village burning, forced starvation tactics, constituting crimes against humanity under international law' (Amnesty International 2018). The attacks and the subsequent unleashing of a reign of terror came three days after an international commission named 'Advisory Commission on Rakhine State' headed by the former UN Secretary General Kofi Annan released its report (Kofi Annan Foundation 2017). The commission, appointed in 2016, was mandated to offer recommendations 'to surmount the political, socio-economic and humanitarian challenges that currently face Rakhine State' (Kofi Annan Foundation 2017).

The influx of the refugees and the scale of atrocities came as a surprise to many considering that unlike the previous two occasions – 1977 and 1992 – Myanmar was being ruled by an elected civilian government headed by Aung San Suu Kyi, a Nobel laureate for peace. Suu Kyi, a champion of democracy, came to power in 2015, which was seen by many as the beginning of the democratization process although the military retained veto power on major issues (for a critical profile of Suu Kyi, see Ellis-Petersen 2018). Instances of serious human rights violations, especially the persecution of Rohingyas, the legal measures denying citizenship to Rohingyas, and the attitude of the government toward the Rohingyas, all with deeply concerning indications, were ignored by the international community. In June 2012, an emergency was declared in Rakhine State in the wake of allegations that Muslim Rohingyas attacked Bamar Buddhists. What followed was a trial run of what was to come in 2017. Ethnic Rakhine villagers were bused in from outside Sittwe town and were given protections while they burned village after villages including Narzi – the largest Muslim neighborhood and economic hub in Sittwe. The rubble was bulldozed in the days that followed (Bauchner 2022).

More than 140,000 Rohingyas were then rounded up and put in secured segregated areas, essentially detention camps. President Thein Sein said, 'We will take care of our own ethnic nationalities, but Rohingyas who came to Burma illegally are not of our ethnic nationalities and we cannot accept them here'. The solution, he said, was to move them into United Nations-run camps or send them abroad (Radio Free Asia 2012). In the 2014 national census, the term Rohingya was replaced with Bengali, and the voters roll of 2015 elections didn't include the Rohingyas and other Internally Displaced Persons (IDPs) living in camps. The adoption of four laws related to the protection of race and religion in 2015 was targeted toward Muslims (Library of Congress 2015).

While the international community was turning a blind eye, warning bells were sounded by researchers that a genocide was in the making. An in-depth and detailed report published in 2015 by the International State Crime Initiative titled, 'Countdown to Annihilation: Genocide in Myanmar' insisted that the country reached the brink of a genocide (Green, MacManus and Venning 2015). Similar concern was expressed by other analysts (Nice and Wade 2016).

One of the surprising aspects was that the Bangladesh government remained oblivious to these developments, although it was facing periodic waves of refugees from Myanmar and two previous large-scale security operations in Rakhine State had resulted in thousands of people crossing the border.

There were other developments, political and social, within the country, which contributed to the making of the refugee crisis. These include the rise of MaBaTha (Association for the Protection of Race and Religion), which propagated a racist, xenophobic, and exclusionary nationalism. An extreme Buddhist movement under the aegis of the MaBaTha emerged after 2011 and was at the forefront of the 2012 attacks on Muslims (International Crisis Group 2017). The exclusionary nationalism of majority Bamar and ingrained Islamophobia, cultivated for decades, was mainstreamed. The populist streak within the NLD and its leader Aung San Suu Kyi led them to offer support to this growing sentiment. Besides, it was well-known that Suu Kyi had little sympathy for Rohingyas (Keane 2017), as she often parroted the military's line of argument and showed derision about Muslims (Fisher 2016).

Concurrent to these developments was the growing economic and strategic interests of China and India since 2011 in Rakhine State, which acted as a catalyst in the making of the genocide. Land grabbing, particularly by the military, was not new, but Rakhine State became prime land after planned investments from China and India began in the region. Since 2011, Myanmar has accelerated its drive for economic development, which reached a new height after the civilian government of Suu Kyi came to power in 2015. Investments from China, which has always been the principal backer of Myanmar, skyrocketed. India, on the other hand, started its own project called the Kaladan multi-modal project, costing about $500 million, which is designed to provide a sea-river-land link to its remote northeast through the Sittwe port by passing the vulnerable Siliguri Corridor. The primary objective of the Indian presence was to lessen China's influence on Myanmar and the region.

The complex interactions of these developments within Myanmar compounded the adverse situation for the Rohingyas, and when the military operation began, it became evident that the goal is to annihilate the community altogether. Rohingyas had no place to go but to cross the river Naf for safety. Then Prime Minister Sheikh Hasina, after some hesitation, embraced the refugees, saying that 'if we can feed 160 million, we can also feed others. We are ready to share our food. [...] We see people as human beings, so we are assisting them' (Nichols 2017). This move was evidently a humanitarian gesture as Bangladesh is not a signatory of the 1951 UN Refugee Convention and its Protocol 1967. The strategy paper adopted by the government in 2013 titled 'National Strategy on Myanmar Refugees and Undocumented Myanmar Nationals', known as 'The Rohingya Refugee Strategy', further highlighted the government's position of denying refugee status to fresh arrivals due to security concerns (Ashraf, 2021: 192). Since Myanmar's military crackdown on the Rohingyas in 2012, the Bangladesh government continued to follow the push back strategy and deny the Rohingyas entry into its territory (Rana and Riaz 2023). Ostensibly, the government could not foresee the possible number of refugees. Whether previous numbers, hovering around 250,000, had influenced the perception is an open question.

As the number of refugees grew and details of a planned execution of a genocide became evident from those who fled the country, western democratic nations issued strong condemnation and international organizations called for help. However, China – the longtime backer of the Myanmar military – took an ambiguous stand, and Russia sided with them. The regional power, often described as the world's largest democracy, India, extended its tacit support to Myanmar on the one hand while it assured Bangladesh, its closest ally in South Asia, that it would provide necessary help.

The Bangladesh government, including then Prime Minister Sheikh Hasina, promised to take robust actions to ensure that the Rohingyas can return to their homeland. In that vein, on 27 September 2017, a month after the crisis began, Sheikh Hasina made five-point recommendations at the

United Nations General Assembly (The Hindu 2017). These include immediately and permanently ending the violence and 'ethnic cleansing' unconditionally in Myanmar, the immediate dispatch of the UN Secretary-General's own investigative team to Myanmar, provision of security for all ordinary citizens without considering any race and 'religion', and to set up 'safe zones' under the direction of the United Nations inside Myanmar, assuring the take back of all Rohingya coercively evicted from Arakan to their homes in Myanmar, and execution of all suggestions by the Kofi Annan Commission Report.

However, departing from the stated position of involving international actors, on 23 November 2017, Bangladesh signed an 'arrangement on the return of displaced Myanmar persons sheltered in Bangladesh' (Aljazeera 2017). The agreement was almost verbatim of the 1992 agreement which neither addressed the citizenship issue nor spelled out an acceptable manner of verifications; instead, it had provided an advantage to Myanmar as it included the provision of repatriation of the 'lawful citizens'. UNHCR was not consulted by Bangladesh and Myanmar on the agreement (Westcott, Olarn and Wright 2017). It stipulated that Bangladesh would immediately seek assistance from UNHCR to carry out safe and voluntary returns, while Myanmar agreed only 'that the services of the UNHCR could be drawn upon as needed and at the appropriate time'. The agreement was not only contrary to the five points program Hasina placed in the UNGA, but a volte face of the Bangladesh government. Other serious inadequacies include the absence of freedom of movement of the repatriated refugees. The returnees' freedom of movement, according to the agreement, was subject to the 'conformity with existing laws and regulations', which were highly discriminatory to Rohingyas. The agreement was followed up with establishing a Joint Working Group in December 2017 and signing of a 'Physical Arrangement Agreement' in January 2018. On the other hand, UN agencies signed a Memorandum of Understanding (MOU) with the Myanmar government in June 2018 to facilitate the repatriation process (UN News 2018). These steps apparently set the stage for the repatriation process to start. But what was missing was the consent of the refugees; the agreements signed between the two countries and steps envisaged regarding repatriation had no input from the refugees.

The initial date of starting the process was set on January 23, 2018, which did not materialize. A second attempt was made by the Bangladesh government in November 2018, but it failed as refugees declined and it became known that the process was far from voluntary (International Crisis Group 2018). A similar attempt, reportedly coercing the refugees to return, was made in August 2019 with a similar fate. Although the failure of these efforts can be attributed to myriad factors, failing to provide citizenship to the refugees and ensuring their safety by the Myanmar government were crucial. Without these guarantees, refugees were least interested in moving back. China's involvement was formalized in September 2019 with the establishment of a 'tripartite joint working group'. Meanwhile, UNHCR and UNDP, and the Myanmar government signed a MOU in June 2018 (which was renewed in May 2020). By 2019, it became evident that the likelihood of repatriation was becoming dim as recognized by Steven Coliss of UNHCR in Bangladesh: 'the overt policy is return, while the objective reality is the return will be extremely difficult' (Solomon 2019). This growing pessimistic situation accelerated the government's plan to relocate 10% of the refugees to a remote island called Bhasan Char. The physical isolation of refugees from a larger number of their peers, restrictions on movements, and the island's vulnerability to natural disaster raised concerns and the UNHCR seriously objected to the plan. The government decided to move ahead without the involvement of the UNHCR and relocated about 29,000 Rohingyas. Afterwards, the UNHCR became involved in the process after securing some concessions from the government (Hossain and Janmyr 2022).

In 2020, all efforts to repatriate came to a halt due to the Covid-19 pandemic and the military coup in February 2021 deposing Aung San Suu Kyi-led civilian government stopped any substantive contacts between the two governments. After a long hiatus, Myanmar's new military regime resumed negotiations with Bangladesh in late 2022. The renewed interest of the military junta was not a result of a change of mind, but a strategic move to deflate the international pressure it was facing after the coup and the ongoing cases in the International Court of Justice (ICJ) and the International Criminal Court (ICC) for committing genocide against Rohingyas. The ICJ case, filed by Gambia in 2019, was undergoing the process at that time, despite Myanmar's objections, pursuant to the Genocide Convention (UN, n.d.). The ICC process was also in the investigation stage . In April 2023, China intensified its pressure to start a repatriation process at its earliest time, preferably no later than the end of the year. Subsequently, in March and April, Chinese officials visited Bangladesh and Myanmar and insisted on repatriation of a smaller number of refugees under a 'pilot project'. As noted by the United Nations,

> Under the pilot project, Rohingya refugees will not be allowed to return to their own villages, many of which were razed to the ground during the genocidal attacks of 2017. The refugees would pass through 'reception' and 'transit' centers in Maungdaw Township, after which they would be moved to a designated area of 15 newly constructed 'villages' – places they will not be allowed to leave freely.
>
> *(UN 2023)*

In May a group of refugees was sent to these 'model villages' as a part of the 'go-and-see' visit, which the refugees found to be inadequate. Analysts have described this as a 'farce' and insisted that a small-scale symbolic repatriation will be used by the Myanmar junta as a 'propaganda tool' (Hossain 2023).

On August 5, 2024, Bangladesh witnessed a dramatic shift in its domestic political landscape when Sheikh Hasina's autocratic regime crumbled in the wake of a 36-day popular uprising. Unprecedent atrocities were perpetrated by law enforcement agencies and regime loyalists during the upsurge, costing at least 1,400 lives according to a UN report (CNN 2025), and injured thousands and a new interim government took over on August 8, 2024.

Since the assumption of office, the interim government took various steps to revive the repatriation efforts. For example, it appointed a High Representative on the Rohingya issue (The Daily Star 2024), arranged a visit of UN Secretary General Antonio Guterres to the Rohingya Camps in March 2025 (Mishra 2025a), and floated an idea to provide a humanitarian corridor to support the Rohingyas inside Rakhine State, which created serious controversy and resistance from the Bangladesh Army (Mamun 2025). While these efforts succeeded in highlighting the ongoing plight of the refugees, little success has been achieved in this regard. In September 2025, Yunus issued a stark warning in his speech to the UN General Assembly that without international resolve to solve the issue, the situation will create desperation among the refugees. (Mishra 2025b). Yet the refugee camps continue to be what the UN Secretary General described as 'a stark reminder of the world's collective failure to find solutions' (Mishra 2025b).

What Helped to Create the Status Quo?

The experience of the past years and roles of various actors indicate few causes of the failure of any progress in repatriation.

The most important factor is the unwillingness of Myanmar to accept the refugees back. Both the civilian regime under Aung San Suu Kyi and the post-2001 military junta have clearly demonstrated that there is no intention of addressing the causes of grievances and reversing the course of persecuting the Rohingya community. The long-standing state policy of excluding Rohingyas from Myanmar society and state seems to be considered sacrosanct by the Myanmar elites. It is evident that without ensuring the inalienable rights of Rohingyas' citizenship, equality in human rights, and security, there is no possibility of a dignified return. Myanmar's position on these has hardened over time, thanks to the unqualified support of China, Russia, and India. These countries are acting as a shield in international fora against criticisms of Myanmar, let alone any punitive measures. The roles of China and Russia are due to the geopolitical tug-of-war between the United States and these countries on the one hand, with their economic interests on the other.

India's primary concern has been containing Chinese influence in the region, but also ensuring security in the restive northeastern region which has a narrow land connectivity with the remainder of the country. India wants a piece of the pie of economic benefits due to changes in the Arakan state. Most importantly, since the 2021 coup, India has emerged as the third largest supplier of weapons to Myanmar after China and Russia (Justice for Myanmar 2024) India's position on the Rohingya crisis was made clear at the very early stage of the current situation. Prime Minister Narendra Modi visited Myanmar on 5–7 September 2017, while hundreds and thousands of Rohingyas were fleeing the country. At a joint conference with then State Counselor Aung San Suu Kyi, Modi not only refrained from using Rohingya but offered unqualified support to the regime saying, 'We are partners in your concerns over the loss of lives of security forces and innocent people due to the extremist violence in Rakhine State' (The Wire 2017). Indian policy has been 'guided by a cold cost-benefit calculation concerning trade with Myanmar, maintaining its leverage vis-à-vis China, and safeguarding cooperation on counterinsurgency operations in its northeast' (Sahoo 2017).

Considering the situation, it is apt to say that Rohingyas have become a pawn in the great game (Fair 2018). While these three powers have aligned themselves with the Myanmar regime, the United States has not only become the largest donor for Rohingya refugees, both bilaterally to Bangladesh and to the multilateral bodies , but also has declared the actions of the Myanmar military as 'genocide' (BBC 2022) and imposed various kinds of sanctions (US Department of State 2024). Conflicting interests of global and regional powers can be summarized as in Table 14.1.

China's role warrants further elaboration. It became engaged with the Rohingya issue in September 2017 when it described those who were fleeing Myanmar as 'refugees' and offered to help Bangladesh face the crisis, but the Chinese official narrative soon changed the term to 'displaced people' (Mahmud and Rai 2023) Its official and explicit engagement began on 19 November 2017 when it offered itself as a mediator and recommended a 'three-phase solution'. It is understood to be behind the agreement signed between Bangladesh and Myanmar within a week. The proposed three-phase solution involved an immediate ceasefire to stop further displacement, dialogues between Bangladesh and Myanmar to be encouraged by the international community, and finding a long-term solution through addressing poverty as the root cause (Xinhua 2017). Between 2018 and 2020, China arranged at least three meetings between Bangladesh and Myanmar and established a tripartite framework in January 2021. China's involvement and interests in the crisis are far from humanitarian, let alone intended to alleviate the plight of the Rohingyas, but instead protects its geostrategic and economic interests as discussed before. The 2021 coup in Myanmar paused the effort, but it was resumed in early 2022 by the junta, and China

TABLE 14.1 Geo-Political/Economic Interests of Global and Regional Powers

Country	*Interests*
China	Long-standing relationship with Myanmar military; strategic interests in countering US/Western presence in the region; securing advantage in maritime security through limiting its dependence on South China Sea Lane for energy import; economic, especially in Arakan state involving Kyaukpyu port and pipeline; fear of Muslim ethnic community's regional influence due to Uighur situation.
Russia	Weapons trade – Myanmar imported 33% of its total $2 billion weapons purchase between 2011 and 2017; after the 2021 coup, until December 2022, Myanmar bought weapons of $1 billion, of which $406 million was from Russia; limiting US influence in the region, especially in Southeast Asia; fear of Muslim 'radicalism' due to Chechnya experience.
India	Strategic interest of countering Chinese influence in the region; securing border between Myanmar and four restive Northeast Indian states; develop shorter connectivity with Northeast states via sea and road bypassing the Siliguri Corridor (Chicken's Neck); business interests with the Kaladan Multi-modal project.
USA	Strategic interest of countering Chinese influence; opening of business opportunities; democratization of Myanmar. However, these long-standing policy has been practically discarded by the Trump in his second term starting January 2025.

once again became deeply involved and held a tripartite meeting in Kunming in April 2023.

One can ask what prompted the Hasina government to backtrack from its September 2017 position of involving the international community and accepting China's mediation and increasingly becoming reliant on China? One apparent factor is that China is the country's largest trading partner, and the Bangladesh government was unwilling to annoy China by relying on its competitor for solving a crisis which involves China's close friend. But there was a more important factor – Bangladesh's domestic political situation. Since 2009, when the AL led by Sheikh Hasina came to power, the relationship between the two countries began to warm up. Bangladesh began to experience serious erosion of democracy in 2011 and gradually turned into an electoral autocracy, especially after the 2014 election which was boycotted by the opposition (Riaz 2024a, 2019; Savoia and Asadullah 2019; Blair 2020; Hossain, 2020; Mostofa and Subedia 2021; BTI 2024). The regime's increasing turn to autocracy had brought it closer to China. As the ruling party embarked on economic growth and infrastructure developments as the justifications for abandoning democracy, China's deep pockets became a strong attraction as much as China's own interest in having a foothold next to India. These led to Bangladesh joining the Belt and Road Initiative (BRI) in 2016. As such, domestic political consideration, particularly the regime's ideological proclivity, had tilted the regime toward providing China a key role rather than relying on any other path.

The position was further solidified because of India's unwavering support to the Myanmar regimes – civilian and military. The India-Bangladesh relationship since 2009 had been described by both governments as 'a golden era'. India has remained the principal backer of the Hasina regime, as it served India's strategic, political, and economic agendas (Riaz, 2023). The extent of India's influence on Bangladesh's domestic politics has irked many within Bangladesh (Rahman 2023; Islam 2024). However, given the close political relationship with India, the Bangladesh government was unwilling to take an independent stance on the repatriation issue and seek international help in the repatriation process.

Conclusions: The Way Forward?

The preceding discussion has demonstrated that the repatriation process has apparently reached a dead end. The most preferred solution – safe, voluntary, and dignified return of the refugee – is contingent on creating an inclusive system of governance in Myanmar which ensures citizenship to Rohingyas with equal rights and is unlikely in short and medium terms. There is no political will within the Myanmar elites – civilian and military – to tread the path, nor is there an incentive for them to dismantle the apartheid system. The absence of both points to a continuation of the status quo.

It is also easily discernible from the comparison between earlier episodes and the present situation that, unlike the previous two occasions, global and regional powers, particularly China and India, have made the Rohingya refugees a pawn in the geopolitical game to expand their sphere of influence and prevent the United States' influence in the region. This great game was facilitated by Bangladesh's ruling party's autocratic disposition since August 2024 and its political dependence on India and China. The humanitarianism displayed in the early stage of the crisis among the Bangladeshis, especially among the local people, has dissipated. But the political considerations of the regime have put it in a bind. The opportunity the international attention offered to push for a durable solution has been squandered. The US position, especially under the Biden administration since January 2021, has been unambiguously supportive of the Rohingyas, but didn't succeed in shaping the events and facilitating the repatriation due to its lack of leverage on the Myanmar regime. Since Donald Trump assumed the presidency, especially his administration's policy of 'America First' has limited its presence on the global stage. In fact, the decision to dismantle US AID, international aid has declined remarkably, which has impacted severely on the humanitarian aid to Rohingyas.

There are four ways forward regarding the current refugee situation. The first is maintaining the status quo, or in other words, muddling through. This is increasingly becoming untenable, thanks to donor fatigue, a deteriorating security situation within the refugee camps, continued environmental degradation due to overcrowded camps, and increasing incidences of human trafficking, to name but a few. This option will prolong the plight of the refugees and create despair, contributing to the growth of a community with no future potential. However, beneficiaries of the situation, especially global and regional powers, would be pleased. Within this scenario, two governments, with the mediation of China, will continue to work, and occasional small-scale repatriation may take place, which will not create any serious dent in the crisis but provide some semblance of legitimacy to the Myanmar junta in the international arena.

The second option is to accept, albeit grudgingly, that Rohingyas will not be able to return to their homeland; therefore, be integrated into the Bangladeshi society as citizens. This option has several downsides including the challenge of their acceptance to society. Notwithstanding the social challenge, it will be a politically fraught issue; the incumbent will face serious backlash. Economically, there will be a twin blow – the loss of international funds that support the refugees and additional pressure on the job market and other social assistance Bangladeshi citizens receive from the government. Indeed, this may act as a pull factor and more Rohingya may cross the border. The upside of the option is to resolve the issue of refugees once and for all.

The third option is resettlement of the refugees to third countries. As Bangladesh is not a signatory to the 1951 Refugee Convention and the 1967 Protocol, it cannot ask for such help from the international community. However, the country did allow third-country resettlement until 2010 for refugees who came during the previous two large-scale exoduses. In 2022, as the government indicated that it is open to such a measure, the United States announced a resettlement program for vulnerable Rohingya refugees in collaboration (US Embassy in Bangladesh 2022) and began to resettle a small number of refugees in late 2023. While this is a welcome initiative, absent a large-scale resettlement program, it will not make any dramatic change. To do so, the Bangladesh government must sign the 1951 Convention and 1967 Protocol and make it one of the central planks of its renewed diplomatic initiative. The question remains how the backer of the status quo will take this step.

The fourth and final option is to bring about a significant change in Bangladesh's Myanmar policy and work with the insurgent groups, especially the Arakan Army (AA), as the latter is making significant progress in its operation against the junta since October 2023 (Riaz 2024b). The 'Three Brotherhood Alliance', a coalition of three ethnic armed organizations (EAOs) – the Myanmar National Democratic Alliance Army (MNDAA), the Ta'ang National Liberation Army (TNLA), and the Arakan Army (AA) – launched Operation 1027 against the military junta on October 27, 2023, in various parts of the country. The National Unity Government (NUG) – a government-in-exile which combines representatives elected in the 2020 election and ethnic minority leaders, has recognized the citizenship of Rohingyas and promised a safe, voluntary, and dignified repatriation of Rohingyas. The AA has tenuously accepted the NUG's position, and its political wing, United League of Arakan (ULA), has pledged to accommodate the Rohingyas in an independent state. However, unfortunately, as the AA has gained more ground and established control over a large part of Rakhine State, it has not made the lives of the Rohingyas better (ICG 2023; Avila 2025). Instead, it is reported that Rohingyas inside Myanmar are facing persecution from the regime where it has influence and from resistance groups where they have established their control.

References

Abrar, C.R. 1996. 'Repatriation of the Rohingya refugees.' Burma library. https://www.burmalibrary.org/docs21/Abrar-NM-Repatriation_of_Rohingya_refugees-en.pdf

Aljazeera. 2017. 'Myanmar, Bangladesh sign Rohingya return deal'. 23 November 2017. https://www.aljazeera.com/news/2017/11/23/myanmar-bangladesh-sign-rohingya-return-deal/

Amnesty International. 2004. 'Myanmar The Rohingya Minority: Fundamental Rights Denied'. Index Number: ASA 16/005/2004, https://www.amnesty.org/en/documents/asa16/005/2004/en/

Amnesty International. 2018. 'Myanmar: Attacks by the Arakan Rohingya Salvation Army on Hindus in northern Rakhine State'. Index number: ASA/ 16/8454/2018. 22 Mat 2018. https://www.amnesty.org/en/documents/asa16/8454/2018/en/

Ashraf, ASM Ali. 2021. 'Humanitarianism, national security, and the Rohingya refugee policy of Bangladesh.' *Strategic Analysis* 45(3): 184–206.

Avila. Drake. 2025. 'The Arakan Axis: Insurgency intensifies in Southwest Myanmar'. Stimson Center Issue Brief. 5 June. https://www.stimson.org/2025/the-arakan-axis-insurgency-intensifies-in-southwest-myanmar/

Awan, Shehmin. 2021. 'The Statelessness Problem Of The Rohingya Muslims'. *Washington University Global Studies Law Review* 19(1): 83–109. https://openscholarship.wustl.edu/law_globalstudies/vol19/iss1/7

Bauchner, Shayana. 2022. '"Nothing called freedom": A decade of detention for Rohingya in Myanmar's Rakhine state'. Human Rights Watch, 13 June 2022. https://www.hrw.org/content/382193

BBC. 2022. 'Myanmar Rohingya violence is genocide, US says'. 21 March 2022. https://www.bbc.com/news/world-asia-60820215

Blair, Harry. 2020. 'Bangladesh paradox.' *Journal of Democracy* 31(4): 138–50.

BTI (Bertelsmann Transformation Index), 2024. 'Bangladesh: Country dashboard'. https://bti-project.org/en/reports/country-dashboard/BGD

Bulbel, Kudrat, Nazmul Islam, and Sajid Khan, eds. 2022. *Rohingya Refugee Crisis in Myanmar: Ethnic Conflict and Resolution*. Singapore: Palgrave Macmillan.

Chickera, Amal. 2018. 'Statelessness and identity in the Rohingya refugee camps.' *Special Feature: Rohingya Refugees in Bangladesh: The Humanitarian Response, Humanitarian Exchange* 73: 7–10.

Chickera, Amal. 2021. 'Stateless and Persecuted: What Next for the Rohingya?.' Migration Policy Institute, Feature, 18 March 2021. https://www.migrationpolicy.org/article/stateless-persecuted-rohingya

CNN. 2025. 'UN rights office estimates up to 1,400 killed in crackdown on protests in Bangladesh'. CNN, 12 February. https://edition.cnn.com/2025/02/12/asia/un-rights-office-bangladesh-protests-crackdown-intl-latam

Coll, S. 1992. 'Fugitives from Burma fight for food.' *Washington Post* report in *Guardian Weekly*, 16 February.

Corr, Andres. 2016. 'Secret 1978 Document Indicates Burma Recognized Rohingya Legal Residence'. *Forbes,* 29 December. https://www.forbes.com/sites/anderscorr/2016/12/29/secret-1978-document-indicates-burma-recognized-rohingya-legal-residence/?sh=7a45d7475a79

Crisp, Jeff. 2018. Primitive people': the untold story of UNHCR's historical engagement with Rohingya refugees, 24 October 2018, https://odihpn.org/en/publication/primitive-people-the-untold-story-of-unhcrs-historical-engagement-with-rohingya-refugees/

Dock, Katie. 2020. 'Breaking a cycle of exodus: Past failures to protect Rohingya Refugees Should Shape Future Solutions'. Stimson Center. 21 June. https://www.stimson.org/2020/breaking-a-cycle-of-exodus/

Ellis-Petersen, Hannah. 2018. 'From peace icon to pariah: Aung San Suu Kyi's fall from grace'. *The Guardian,* 23 November. https://www.theguardian.com/world/2018/nov/23/aung-san-suu-kyi-fall-from-grace-myanmar

Fair, C Christine. 2018. 'Rohingya: Victims of a great game east'. *The Washington Quarterly* 41(3): 63–85.

Fisher, Max. 2016. '"No one told me I was going to be interviewed by a Muslim": Aung San Suu Kyi's Rohingya problem'. *Vox*, 28 March 2017. https://www.vox.com/2016/3/28/11306856/aung-san-suu-kyi-muslim-rohingya-bbc

Green et. al. 2015. 'Countdown to Annihliation: Genocide in Myanmar. International State Crime Initiative, Queen Mary, University of London.

Grundy-Warr, Carl, and Elaine Wong. 1997. 'Sanctuary under a plastic sheet: The unresolved problem of Rohingya refugees.' *Boundary and Security Bulletin*, International Boundaries Research Center, Durham University, Autumn, 79–91.

Hein, Ye Myo. 2024. 'Nine things to know about Myanmar's conflict three years on.' United States Institute of Peace (USIP). 30 April, 2024. https://www.usip.org/publications/2024/04/nine-things-know-about-myanmars-conflict-three-years

Hossain, Akhand Akhtar. 2020. 'Anatomy of creeping authoritarianism in Bangladesh: A historical analysis of some events that shaped the present state of Bangladesh's culture and politics.' *Asian Journal of Political Science* 28(1): 13–39.

Hossain, Tauhid. 2023. 'Rohingya repatriation, yet another farce'. Prothom Alo English, 5 September. https://en.prothomalo.com/opinion/61rp3byjz4

Hossain, Sanjeeb, and Maja Janmyr. 2022. 'Bhasan Char: Prison island or paradise? Are Rohingya refugees being denied their right to freedom of movement?' *Lacuna Magazine*. 12 May 2022. https://lacuna.org.uk/migration/bhasan-char-rohingya-refugees-right-to-freedom-of-movement/

Human Rights Watch. 1996. *Rohingya Muslims: Ending a Cycle of Exodus*, Vol. 8, No. 9(C). New York: HRW. September. https://www.hrw.org/legacy/summaries/s.burma969.html

Huq, Muhammad Shamsul. 1993. *Bangladesh in International Politics*. Dhaka: University Press Limited.

Ibrahim, Azeem. 2006. *The Rohingyas: Inside Myanmar's Hidden Genocide*. London: Hurst.

International Crisis Group (ICG). 2017. *Buddhism and State Power in Myanmar*. Brussels: ICG. 5 September. https://www.crisisgroup.org/asia/south-east-asia/myanmar/290-buddhism-and-state-power-myanmar

International Crisis Group (ICG). 2018. *Bangladesh-Myanmar: The Danger of Forced Rohingya Repatriation*. Brussels: ICG. 12 November. https://www.crisisgroup.org/asia/south-east-asia/myanmar/b153-bangladesh-myanmar-danger-forced-rohingya-repatriation

International Crisis Group (ICG). 2023. *Crisis Mounts for Rohingya Refugees in Bangladesh*. Brussels: ICG. 6 December. https://www.crisisgroup.org/asia/south-asia/bangladesh/355-crisis-mounts-rohingya-refugees-bangladesh

Islam, Arafatul. 2024. India's influence in Bangladesh: Support or meddling?' *DW*. 3 April 2024. https://www.dw.com/en/indias-influence-in-bangladesh-support-or-meddling/a-68432609

Jeff, Crisp. 2018, '"Primitive People': the untold story of UNHCR's historical engagement with Rohingya refugees.' *Special Feature: Rohingya Refugees in Bangladesh: The Humanitarian Response, Humanitarian Exchange*, 73.

Justice for Myanmar, 2024. 'India aiding and abetting Myanmar Junta atrocities through continued transfers of military equipment.' 27 March. https://www.justiceformyanmar.org/stories/india-aiding-and-abetting-myanmar-junta-atrocities-through-continued-transfers-of-military-equipment

Kamaluddin, S. 1992. 'The Rohingya exodus: Rangoon precipitates new problem for Dhaka'. *Far Eastern Economic Review* 155. 26 March.

Keane, Fergal. 2017. 'The Rohingya crisis: Why won't Aung San Suu Kyi act?' *BBC News*. 8 September. https://www.bbc.com/news/world-asia-41187517

Kofi Anan Foundation. 2017. 'Mediation and crisis resolution'. https://www.kofiannanfoundation.org/mediation-and-crisis-resolution/rakhine-final-report/

Library of Congress. 2015. 'Burma: Four "race and religion protection laws" Adopted'. 14 September. https://www.loc.gov/item/global-legal-monitor/2015-09-14/burma-four-race-and-religion-protection-laws-adopted/

Lindquist, Alan. 1979. 'Report on the 1978–79 Bangladesh refugee Relief operation'. June. https://www.networkmyanmar.org/ESW/Files/Lindquist-Report.pdf

Mahmud, Shahtaj, and Kriti Rai. 2023. 'China's role in conflict mediation: A case study of the Rohingya refugee crisis in Bangladesh'. In Xavier, C. & Jacob, J. T. (Eds.), *How China Engages South Asia: Themes, Partners and Tools*, 27–43. New Delhi: Centre for Social and Economic Progress. https://csep.org/rlagwwy

Mamun, Ezaz. 2025. 'The hidden stakes in the Rakhine corridor: Humanitarian aid or strategic incursion?' Dhaka Tribune. 18 May. https://www.dhakatribune.com/opinion/op-ed/381545/the-hidden-stakes-in-the-rakhine-corridor

Mishra, Vibhu. 2025a. 'In Bangladesh, UN chief vows to prevent Rohingya suffering as aid cuts loom'. *UN News*. 14 March. https://news.un.org/en/story/2025/03/1161121#:~:text=Guterres%20emphasised%20that%20his%20visit,Rohingya%20refugees%2C%E2%80%9D%20he%20said

Mishra, Bibhu. 2025b. 'After mass exodus, limbo: Rohingya refugees test international resolve'. *UN News*. 29 September. https://news.un.org/en/story/2025/09/1165984

Mostofa, Shafi, and D. B. Subedi. 2021. "Rise of competitive authoritarianism in Bangladesh'. *Politics and Religion* 14(3): 431–459.
Nice, Geofry, and Francis Wade. 2016. 'A genocide in the making'. *Foreign Policy.* 30 November. https://foreignpolicy.com/2016/11/30/a-genocide-in-the-making-burma-myanmar-rohingya/
Nichols, Michelle. 2017. 'Exclusive: Bangladesh PM says expects no help from Trump on refugees fleeing Myanmar'. *Reuters,* 18 September. https://www.reuters.com/article/us-myanmar-rohingyabangladesh-trump-exc/exclusive-bangladesh-pm-says-expects-no-help-from-trump-on-refugees-fleeing-myanmar-idUSKCN1BU07C
Radio Free Asia. 2012. 'Call to Put Rohingya in Refugee Camps'. 12 July. https://www.rfa.org/english/news/rohingya-07122012185242.html
Rahman, Zillur. 2023. 'Bangladesh-India relations: An increasingly complicated friendship'. *The Daily Star,* 12 December. https://www.thedailystar.net/opinion/geopolitical-insights/news/bangladesh-india-relations-increasingly-complicated-friendship-3492346
Rana, Sohel, and Ali Riaz. 2023. 'Securitization of the Rohingya refugees in Bangladesh.' *Journal of Asian and African Studies* 58(7): 1274–1290.
Riaz, Ali. 2019. *Voting in a Hybrid Regime: Explaining the 2018 Bangladesh Election.* Singapore: Palgrave MacMillan.
Riaz, Ali. 2023. 'Bangladesh election 2024: What role will India play?' *South Asia Source.* Atlantic Council, 15 June. https://www.atlanticcouncil.org/blogs/southasiasource/bangladesh-election-2024-what-role-will-india-play/
Riaz, Ali. 2024a. *Pathways of Autocratization: The Tumultuous Journey of Bangladeshi Politics.* London: Routledge.
Riaz, Ali. 2024b. 'Should Bangladesh recalibrate its Myanmar policy, especially toward the Arakan army?'. *The Diplomat,* 1 March. https://thediplomat.com/2024/03/should-bangladesh-recalibrate-its-myanmar-policy-especially-toward-the-arakan-army/
Richardson, Michael. 1992. 'ASEAN weighs moves against abuses in Burma.' *The New York Times,* 31 March. https://www.nytimes.com/1992/03/31/IHT-asean-weighs-moves-against-abuses-in-burma.html
Saha, K. C. 2001. 'Learning from Rohingya refugee repatriation to Myanmar'. *Refuge: Canada's Journal on Refugees* 19(3): 38–43.
Sahoo, Niranjan. 2017. 'India's Rohingya Realpolitik'. Carnegie Endowment for International Peace. 21 October. https://carnegieendowment.org/research/2017/10/indias-rohingya-realpolitik?lang=en
Sarkar, Prabir Kumar. 2021. 'OP-ED: Rohingya exodus in 1978: A history of systematic eviction". *Dhaka Tribune,* 31 August. https://www.dhakatribune.com/opinion/op-ed/256900/op-ed-rohingya-exodus-in-1978-a-history-of
Savoia, Antonio, and Niaz Asadullah. 2019. 'Bangladesh is booming, but slide towards authoritarianism could burst the bubble'. *The Conversation,* 28 February. https://theconversation.com/bangladesh-is-booming-but-slide-towards-authoritarianism-could-burst-the-bubble-112632
Solomon, Feiz. 2019. 'Rohingya muslims are stuck in Bangladesh's refugee camps'. *Time.* 23 May. https://time.com/longform/rohingya-muslims-exile-bangladesh/
The Daily Star. 2024. 'Khalilur Rahman appointed high representative on Rohingya issue'. 19 November. https://www.thedailystar.net/news/bangladesh/news/khalilur-rahman-appointed-high-representative-rohingya-issue-3756451
The Hindu. 2017. 'Hasina floats five-point peace plan'. 28 September. https://www.thehindu.com/news/international/hasina-floats-five-point-peace-plan/article61471142.ece

The Wire. 2017. 'In Suu Kyi meeting, Modi shares 'Concern' over extremist violence by Rohingya Outfit'. 6 September. https://thewire.in/174681/modi-aung-san-suu-kyi-myanmar-rohingya

Uddin, Nasir. 2021. *The Rohingya: An Ethnography of 'Subhuman' Life*. Oxford: Oxford University Press.

UN News. 2018. 'UN agencies and Myanmar ink agreement, setting stage for Rohingya return'. 6 June. https://news.un.org/en/story/2018/06/1011491

United Nations. 1992. 'Press release: Bangladesh urged to halt coerced returns'. REF/1006, 23 December.

United Nations. 2023. 'Bangladesh must suspend pilot project to return Rohingya refugees to Myanmar: UN expert'. 8 June. https://www.ohchr.org/en/press-releases/2023/06/bangladesh-must-suspend-pilot-project-return-rohingya-refugees-myanmar-un

United Nations. n.d. 'ICJ – The Gambia v Myanmar'. https://iimm.un.org/icj-the-gambia-v-myanmar/#:~:text=In%202022%2C%20the%20ICJ%20rejected,against%20a%20fellow%20signatory%20in

United States Bureau of Citizenship and Immigration Services (USBCIS). 1998. 'Burma [Myanmar]: State Law and Order Restoration Council (SLORC)/ State Peace and Development Council (SPDC)/ National League for Democracy (NLD)/ Burmese Dissidents,' 17 September, MYN98001.zny. https://www.refworld.org/docid/3df097254.html

US Department of State. 2022. 'Secretary Antony J. Blinken on the genocide and crimes against Humanity in Burma'. 21 March. https://www.state.gov/secretary-antony-j-blinken-at-the-united-states-holocaust-memorial-museum/

US Department of State. 2024. 'Burma Sanctions'. https://www.state.gov/burma-sanctions/

US Embassy in Bangladesh. 2022. 'Resettlement Initiative for Vulnerable Rohingya Refugees in Bangladesh'. https://bd.usembassy.gov/28983/

Ware, Anthony, and Costas Laoutides. 2018. *Myanmar's 'Rohingya' Conflict*. Oxford: Oxford University Press.

Westcott, Ben, Kocha Olarn and Rebecca Wring, 2017. 'Bangladesh-Myanmar agreement on Rohingya refugees revealed'. *CNN*. 28 September. https://www.cnn.com/2017/11/27/asia/rohingya-myanmar-bangladesh-agreement/index.html

Xinhua. 2017. 'China proposes three-phase solution to Rakhine issue in Myanmar: FM'. 20 November. http://www.xinhuanet.com/english/2017-11/20/c_136764392.htm

Yagar, Moshe. 1982. 'The muslims of Burma'. In Israeli Raphael (Ed.), *The Crescent in the East. Islam in Asia Minor,* 102–139. London: Curzon Press.

INDEX

For Product Safety Concerns and Information please contact our EU
representative GPSR@taylorandfrancis.com
Taylor & Francis Verlag GmbH, Kaufingerstraße 24, 80331 München, Germany

www.ingramcontent.com/pod-product-compliance
Ingram Content Group UK Ltd.
Pitfield, Milton Keynes, MK11 3LW, UK
UKHW020148200926
475702UK00016B/2605

* 9 7 8 1 0 4 1 2 9 9 1 3 4 *